JUDICIAL INDEPENDENCE UNDER THREAT

For over 100 years, the *Proceedings of the British Academy* series has provided a unique record of British scholarship in the humanities and social sciences. These themed volumes drive scholarship forward and are landmarks in their field. For more information about the series and guidance on submitting a proposal for publication, please visit www.thebritishacademy.ac.uk/proceedings

PROCEEDINGS OF THE BRITISH ACADEMY • 250

JUDICIAL INDEPENDENCE UNDER THREAT

Edited by
DIMITRIOS GIANNOULOPOULOS
AND YVONNE MCDERMOTT

Published for THE BRITISH ACADEMY
by OXFORD UNIVERSITY PRESS

Oxford University Press, Great Clarendon Street, Oxford OX2 6DP

© The British Academy 2022

Database right The British Academy (maker)

First edition published in 2022

British Library Cataloguing in Publication Data
Data available

Library of Congress Cataloguing in Publication Data
Data available

Typeset by Newgen Publishing UK
Printed in Great Britain by TJ Books Ltd, Padstow, Cornwall

ISBN Hardback 978-0-19-726703-5
ISBN Digital ebook (epub) 978-0-19-288470-1
ISSN 0068-1202

*To the late Brian Kerr, the Right Hon
the Lord Kerr of Tonaghmore*

Contents

List of Figures and Tables

Figures

Tables

Notes on Contributors

Daniel Aguirre is a Senior Lecturer in Law at Roehampton University, London. His research focuses on business and human rights in conflict situations. Previously, he worked as an international legal adviser for the International Commission of Jurists in Myanmar and for several other NGOs in Southeast Asia. He has lectured at Universities in the UK, Canada, Italy, Thailand and China.

Stina Bergman Blix is Professor of Sociology at Uppsala University, Sweden. She researches the role of emotions in professional work, rationality, law, theatre and qualitative methods. She is currently the principal investigator of an international comparative project (JUSTEMOTIONS) funded by the European Research Council investigating the emotive-cognitive process of judicial decision-making. Her work has been published in journals such as *Emotion Review, Qualitative Research* and *Symbolic Interaction*. Her latest co-authored book is *Professional Emotions in Court: A Sociological Perspective* (Routledge, 2018).

Moa Bladini is a Senior Lecturer at the Department of Law, Gothenburg University, Sweden. Her research fields are criminal law and criminal procedure law, often with interdisciplinary angles. Some of her previous research has focused on concepts such as truth and objectivity, legitimation and justice. She has developed her research around theoretical and methodological issues, recently using feminist legal studies and the sociology of emotions. She is currently working on two different themes: anti-gender hate speech online; and the sociology of emotions in legal decision-making in general, and in the application of rape laws in particular.

Martina Y. Feilzer is Professor of Criminology and Criminal Justice and Dean of the College of Arts and Humanities at Bangor University. Her research is on: public perceptions of criminal justice at local, national and European levels; the relationship between the media and public opinion of criminal justice; questions of legitimacy, trust in justice and penal policy; and comparative and historical criminal justice research. Martina is Co-Director of WISERD, the Wales Institute of Social and Economic Research and Data, at Bangor University, and Co-Director of the Welsh Centre for Crime and Social Justice.

Dimitrios Giannoulopoulos holds the Inaugural Chair in Law and is the Head of the Department of Law at Goldsmiths, University of London. He is an Academic Bencher of the Honourable Society of the Inner Temple and a Visiting Professor in Law at the Panteion University of Social and Political Sciences in Athens. He has published widely on custodial interrogation rights, improperly obtained evidence and the application of ECHR jurisprudence in the domestic criminal process. In recent years, he has developed a strong interest in the impact of Brexit on human rights, drawing on his cross-cultural research and public engagement work in the area, including as the founder and director of the 'Britain in Europe' think tank and 'Knowing Our Rights' project.

Dominic Grieve QC was Attorney General in the coalition government from 2010–2014. In June 2010, he was appointed a Privy Councillor. As Attorney General, Mr Grieve dealt with public law matters in the Supreme Court, European Court of Justice and before the European Court of Human Rights. He is most recently involved in work relating to unlawful detention and breaches of human rights by foreign states and advising on improving governance for a charity with international operations. Dominic is a Visiting Professor in Law, Politics and Human Rights at Goldsmiths, University of London, and a Bencher of the Middle Temple.

John D. Jackson is Professor of Comparative Criminal Law and Procedure at the School of Law, University of Nottingham, and a qualified barrister. He was previously Dean of the School of Law at University College Dublin from 2008–2011, and before that, he was Professor of Public Law at Queen's University Belfast from 1995–2008. He has held visiting professorships at Hastings College of the Law, University of California, and the Faculty of Law, University of New South Wales, and was a Fernand Braudel Senior Fellow at the European University Institute in 2007–2008. Since 2008, he has been a Parole Commissioner for Northern Ireland.

Schona Jolly QC is the Head of the Human Rights Practice Group at Cloisters Chambers, the former Chair of the UK's Bar Human Rights Committee and a Visiting Professor in Law at Goldsmiths, University of London. Over the past decade, Schona has been at the forefront of international human rights and rule of law work in countries around the world, including Central Asia, Egypt, Hong Kong, Turkey and across South Asia. Schona's work engages law and policy, and she has deep expertise in equality and discrimination law, with an international focus on minority rights.

Brian Kerr, The Right Hon the Lord Kerr of Tonaghmore, was a Justice of the Supreme Court of the United Kingdom from 2009–2020, the longest-serving justice on the Court. He served as Lord Chief Justice of Northern Ireland from 2004 to 2009 and was the last Lord of Appeal in Ordinary appointed before the creation of the Supreme Court. Undertaking his legal studies at Queen's University, Belfast, he was called to the Bar of Northern Ireland in 1970 and to the Bar of England and Wales at Gray's Inn in 1974.

Yvonne McDermott is a Professor of Law at Swansea University. From 2018 to 2021, she was Principal Investigator on the OSR4Rights project, a multi-disciplinary project that examines how open-source research has transformed the landscape of human rights fact-finding, funded by the ESRC. From 2022 to 2027, she will lead TRUE, a European Research Council Starting Grant-funded project that examines the impact of the rise of deepfakes on trust in user-generated evidence of human rights violations. She is Legal Adviser to the Global Legal Action Network (GLAN) and an Associate Academic Fellow of the Honourable Society of the Inner Temple.

Jan-Werner Müller is Roger Williams Straus Professor of Social Sciences and Professor of Politics at Princeton University. He studied at the Free University, Berlin, University College, London, St. Antony's College, Oxford, and Princeton University. From 1996 until 2003, he was a Fellow at All Souls College, Oxford, and from 2003 until 2005, he was Fellow in Modern European Thought at the European Studies Centre, St. Antony's College. Since 2005, he has been teaching in the Politics Department at Princeton University. Müller has been a visiting fellow at the Wissenschaftskolleg, Berlin, the Helsinki Collegium for Advanced Studies, the Institute for Human Sciences in Vienna, and a number of other institutes.

Raphaële Parizot is a full Professor of criminal law and criminal procedure at Paris Nanterre University, Vice President of the Association de Recherches Pénales Européennes, General Secretary of the *Revue de science criminelle et de droit pénal comparé*, and Co-Director of the Master of Criminal Law at Paris Nanterre University. She is a Doctor of Law from the University of Paris 1 Panthéon-Sorbonne and the University of Ferrara. Her Ph.D. thesis 'Criminal responsibility and organised crime: The symptomatic case of criminal conspiracy and money laundering in France and in Italy' was published in 2010.

Julian Petley is Honorary Professor of Film and Television at Brunel University. He is also a member of the editorial board of the *British Journalism Review* and of the advisory board of Index on Censorship. As a member of the National Council of the Campaign for Press and Broadcasting Freedom and a supporter of Hacked Off, he has made numerous submissions to official enquiries (including the Leveson Inquiry) and given evidence to parliamentary select committees. He is one of the principal editors of the *Journal of British Cinema and Television* and is actively involved in the Knowing Our Rights project, of which he was a co-founder.

His Honour Jeremy Roberts QC was called to the Bar in 1964 and practised in London and on the Midland and Oxford Circuit (later reconstituted as the Midland Circuit). He became a QC in 1982 and sat as a Recorder and Deputy High Court Judge before becoming one of the permanent judges at the Central Criminal Court in October 2000. On his retirement from that post in April 2011, he was appointed a member of the Press Complaints Commission. He has been a member of the Parole Board since 2010 and is a Master of the Bench at the Honourable Society of the Inner Temple.

Stephen Skinner is Professor of Comparative Legal History and Legal Theory at the University of Exeter and a founding member of Exeter Law School's Human Rights and Democracy Forum, which he convened from 2017–2021. His research is on the 'dark side' of law and democracy and covers two main areas: comparative legal history, focusing on the contextual background, substance and theory of criminal law under Fascism in Italy and liberal democracy in Great Britain during the 1920s–1940s; and the state's use of lethal and life-threatening force in the context of domestic policing and law enforcement.

David Alan Sklansky is Stanley Morrison Professor of Law at Stanford Law School and Faculty Co-Director of the Stanford Criminal Justice Center. He teaches and writes about criminal law, criminal procedure and evidence. His newest book is *A Pattern of Violence: How the Law Classifies Crimes and What It Means for Justice* (Harvard University Press 2021). Before joining the faculty of Stanford Law School in 2014, Sklansky taught at the University of California, Berkeley and UCLA. He won campus-wide teaching awards at both those institutions. Earlier, he practised labour law in Washington, DC, and served as an assistant United States attorney in Los Angeles.

John Thomas, The Right Hon the Lord Thomas of Cwmgiedd, was appointed as the Lord Chief Justice of England and Wales in 2013 and retired in October 2017. He was called to the Bar in 1969 and became a Queen's Counsel in 1984. He was appointed an Assistant Recorder in 1984, a Recorder in 1987 and a High Court judge in 1996. His other senior judicial leadership roles include Presiding Judge of the Wales and Chester circuit, Senior Presiding Judge for England and Wales, Vice President of the Queen's Bench Division and President of the Queen's Bench Division.

Acknowledgements

This collection started life as a British Academy conference, held at Carlton House Terrace in March 2018. We would like to thank the British Academy for supporting that conference and all the speakers, panel chairs and attendees who contributed to a lively and stimulating discussion. The Honourable Society of the Inner Temple, to which both the editors owe so much, personally and professionally, kindly sponsored a pre-conference dinner on that occasion. Special thanks are owed to Struan Campbell, Director of Education at the Inn.

We are enormously grateful to Portia Taylor, Production Editor at the British Academy, for her constant support and advice throughout this process. It is only thanks to Portia's patient guidance and understanding that this manuscript was finally completed, notwithstanding the global pandemic that led to several obstacles along the way. We would also like to extend our thanks to Helen Flitton, Project Manager at Newgen Publishing, for seeing this manuscript over the line.

We would like to take this opportunity to thank each of our authors for their outstanding contributions to this volume. It was a unique pleasure to work with them, and we are immensely grateful for the energy and intellectual rigour they have injected into this volume. We are very much looking forward to continuing to collaborate with them. The chapters in this volume were written between 2018 and 2020 and were updated in late 2021 to account for recent developments in this fast-moving area, wherever possible.

We were thrilled when the late Brian Kerr, the Right Hon the Lord Kerr of Tonaghmore, agreed to participate in our 2018 conference, and were touched by the modesty, openness and kindness he showed to us since then. We have very fond memories of being in his company during the pre-conference dinner. We had the enormous privilege to learn from him about episodes of his inspirational life in law and were humbled by the interest he showed in our work that night. With his characteristic warmth and charm, Lord Kerr provided a memorable and thought-provoking opening to the conference the following morning with his speech, beginning with the notorious line, 'Crisis? What Crisis?' Lord Kerr's erudite and illuminating talk forms the basis of the prologue to this volume, and it is our great honour to dedicate this volume to him. *Ar dheis Dé go raibh a anam dílis.*

Foreword

*THE RIGHT HON THE LORD KERR OF TONAGHMORE**

In the late 1970s, three words attributed to the Labour Prime Minister of the day, James Callaghan – or, as he was affectionately known, 'Sunny Jim' – were said to have caused the fall of the government. It was during a period that became known as the 'Winter of Discontent'. There had been a run on the pound in 1975 and again in 1976. Chancellor Denis Healey was forced to go, cap in hand, to the International Monetary Fund for a rescue loan. Inflation was running at 10%. The government sought to impose a cap on pay rises of 5%. Strikes abounded. Refuse collectors withdrew their labour. Petrol tanker drivers refused to make deliveries. The lasting images from the time are of rubbish in the streets and reports of bodies lying unburied in mortuaries.

The Prime Minister, Mr Callaghan, in the midst of this turmoil, went to an economic conference in Guadeloupe in the West Indies. He returned, looking relaxed and tanned. He was assailed at the airport by a horde of reporters demanding his comment on the emergency that gripped the country and was reported the following day as having said, 'Crisis, what crisis?'. It appears that in fact he did not utter those words at all. They were a confection by a *Sun* journalist, but they caught the mood of the nation and the government fell.[1]

There are many lessons to be learned from this story, not least the susceptibility of the general polity to influence from imaginative press reports, but that is not the focus of this essay. Two particular messages can be taken from that experience. First, that what qualifies as a genuine crisis is difficult to judge in contemporary experience. Second, that one man's crisis is another's challenging opportunity. There is, on reflection, perhaps a third lesson to be learned, and that is that our reaction to crises, perceived or real, is ultimately the true measure of the relative success of the discharge of our public duty and the contribution that we make to a properly functioning democracy.

This essay will begin by considering what we mean by crisis, keeping in mind that history is the only reliable judge of what that elusive concept may mean.

---

* Editors' note: Lord Kerr was one of the first contributors to this volume to submit his completed chapter to us, on 23 September 2019, on the eve of the UK Supreme Court delivering its historic prorogation judgment in *Cherry/Miller (No 2)* [2019] UKSC 41. The timing makes what he advocates in this chapter even more worthy of attention, namely that 'the judiciary should react with relative calmness and equanimity' even to criticisms of the judges and even their portrayal as 'enemies of the people' in the context of Brexit.

[1] Mr Callaghan had actually said 'I don't think other people in the world would share the view [that] there is mounting chaos.'

There are those who would suggest that the significant political uncertainty following the referendum on the United Kingdom's membership of the European Union constitutes a crisis. Whatever of that, it certainly presents a challenge for all the institutions of government, legislative, executive and judicial. It has shone a spotlight on the various roles that each of the organs of government has been and will be called on to perform. It has also given rise to occasions when the way in which the various institutions have been scrutinised – or even criticised – might partake of something approaching a censorious commentary. Even so, whilst this is perhaps an unduly sanguine view, this does not necessarily amount to a crisis in the true sense of the word.

If, however, we accept the premise that Brexit represents a crisis, and imagine that criticisms of the judges in the Divisional Court and their portrayal in a certain newspaper as 'enemies of the people' constitute a crisis of trust in the judiciary, how should the judiciary react?

This essay argues that the answer to that question is that the judiciary should react with relative calmness and equanimity. There are certain unalterable truths about the judiciary in this country that not even the most vituperative of commentators are likely to question. First, we are fortunate to live in a society where corruption and bribery are not features of our legal system. Economic and political interference with the exercise of judicial duties are not concerns here in the way that they are in many other jurisdictions. However, that does not mean that we should be complacent about the importance to be attached to judicial independence. Although it should be regarded as a given, its preservation is vital, and the contours of the exercise and assertion of our independence need constant reminder and, if necessary, renewal.

To put that in a more comprehensible way, what judges must remind themselves of is that their role can shift and change as the constitutional order alters, and as the understanding of their proper contribution and reaction to those changes develops.

There are, however, some fundamental features which are unchangeable and unchanging. It is axiomatic that judges must discharge their duty in a wholly independent, scrupulously impartial and conspicuously fair manner. The traditional template for the preservation of that independence is, of course, adherence to the fundamental constitutional principle of separation of powers. However, aspiration to adhere to that principle provides endless opportunity for lively debate and ongoing controversy. Of course, in early cases such as *McGonnell v UK*,[2] the answer was easily found. That was a case in which the principal judicial officer in Guernsey who had sat on the applicant's case was a senior member of all three branches of government: the judiciary, the legislature and the executive. The European Court of Human Rights was not unduly challenged in holding that the otherwise admirable versatility of this individual did not exactly chime with the notion of a true separation of powers. The discharge of his judicial role was not marked by the requisite

---

[2] (2000) 30 EHRR 289.

appearance of independence and impartiality, and the situation therefore breached the applicant's rights to a fair trial by an independent and impartial tribunal under Article 6 of the European Convention on Human Rights and Fundamental Freedoms.

More recent judicial debates in this area present rather subtler – or at least, more nuanced – problems. What role is there, if indeed a role remains, for deference by the judiciary to governmental decision? What is the influence that so-called institutional deference has in the review that judges conduct of legislation, both primary and subordinate? Whither intensity of review and anxious scrutiny?

Well, deference, at least in its conventional connotation, has received its quietus in a number of recent decisions in the Supreme Court. As Lord Sumption put it in *Lord Carlile of Berriew*:

> As a tool for assessing the practice by which the courts accord greater weight to the executive's judgment in some cases than in others, the whole concept of 'deference' has been subjected to powerful academic criticism At least part of the difficulty arises from the word, with its overtones of cringing abstention in the face of superior status. In some circumstances, 'deference' is no more than a recognition that a Court of review does not usurp the function of the decision-maker, even when Convention rights are engaged. Beyond that elementary principle, the assignment of weight to the decision-maker's judgment has nothing to do with deference in the ordinary sense of the term. It has two distinct sources. The first is the constitutional principle of the separation of powers. The second is no more than a pragmatic view about the evidential value of certain judgments of the executive, whose force will vary according to the subject matter.[3]

Beyond reservations about the appropriateness of the term 'deference', however, no general consensus has emerged about the role of the court in reviewing government decisions in the public law field. Over recent years there have been legal challenges to the 'bedroom tax', employment tribunal fees and restrictions on legal aid. A variety of approaches to the question of the level of judicial restraint to be exercised can be discerned in many of the judgments in those cases.

That diversity of view was perhaps best exemplified in the case of *Nicklinson*,[4] colloquially known as the 'assisted dying case'. Of the nine Supreme Court judges who sat on the case, two felt that the courts could and should declare the current law incompatible with the right to respect for private life under Article 8 of the ECHR. At the other end of the spectrum, two felt that the law in this area was a matter for Parliament alone and that the court should not consider making a declaration of incompatibility under any circumstances. The others fell somewhere in between.

There is a good deal of commentary about the impropriety of unelected judges second-guessing Parliament and the Executive in matters of social policy. This is

---

[3] *R (on the application of Lord Carlile of Berriew QC and others) (Appellants) v Secretary of State for the Home Department (Respondent)* [2014] UKSC 60, [22].
[4] *R (on the application of Nicklinson and another) (AP) (Appellants) v Ministry of Justice (Respondent)* [2014] UKSC 38.

not, however, what has happened, and nor is there any realistic prospect of this occurring. As explained in the *Nicklinson* case:

> An essential element of the structure of the Human Rights Act 1998 is the call which Parliament has made on the courts to review the legislation which it passes in order to tell it whether the provisions contained in that legislation comply with the Convention. By responding to that call and sending the message to Parliament that a particular provision is incompatible with the Convention, the courts do not usurp the role of Parliament, much less offend the separation of powers. A declaration of incompatibility is merely an expression of the court's conclusion as to whether, as enacted, a particular item of legislation cannot be considered compatible with a Convention right. In other words, the courts say to Parliament, 'This particular piece of legislation is incompatible, now it is for you to decide what to do about it.' And under the scheme of the Human Rights Act 1998 it is open to Parliament to decide to do nothing.
>
> What the courts do in making a declaration of incompatibility is to remit the issue to Parliament for a political decision, informed by the court's view of the law. The remission of the issue to Parliament does not involve the court's making a moral choice which is properly within the province of the democratically elected legislature.[5]

The essential point to make is that in reviewing legislation, the judiciary is doing no more than it has been asked – indeed, enjoined – by Parliament to do. The willingness of the democratic institution that is Parliament, prizing as it does its sovereignty, to allow its measures to be tested by the courts for their coherence with ECHR is a remarkable constitutional statement. It is an acknowledgement by Parliament that an external, apolitical and impartial agency should be able to consider the lawfulness of its actions. That decision of Parliament, with strong cross-party support in both Houses, to allow its legislative measures to be subject to scrutiny by independent courts is a historic constitutional landmark. It accorded to the courts an enlarged and vital role in reviewing actions of government. The discharge of that role is sometimes described as the realisation of a bipartite democracy.

The notion of bipartite democracy is, of course, not a new one. Its fundamental nature is recognised in the writings of Lord Steyn,[6] Ronald Dworkin and Lord Justice Laws.[7] Its essence is perhaps most neatly captured in a judgment of the former President of the Israeli Supreme Court, Aharon Barak:

> Democracy is not only majority rule. Democracy is also the rule of basic values and human rights as they have taken form in the constitution. Democracy is a delicate balance between majority rule and society's basic values, which rule the majority. [...] Take majority rule away from constitutional democracy, and you have struck at its very essence. Take the rule of basic values away from constitutional democracy, and you have struck at its very existence.[8]

---

[5] *Nicklinson*, [343]–[344].
[6] *Democracy Through Law* (2002) E.H.R.L.R. 723.
[7] *Law and Democracy* (1995) P.L. 72.
[8] *United Bank Ltd v Migdal Cooperative Village* 6821/92: 49(4) P.D. 221, 423.

It is likely that the important interplay between the vindication of basic values and majority rule will be a perennial feature of our constitutional democracy. It also seems that courts will remain the inevitable arbiter of those disputes.

Many commentators emphasise what may be described as the negative dimension to the way that our present system of judicial review functions. Some suggest that unelected judges wrongly arrogate to themselves power to review decisions which lie properly in the province of democratically elected ministers and members of the legislature.

It is not part of this essay to seek to deny the right of those who hold them to express those views. Nor, indeed, on this occasion, to seek to challenge them. The more fundamental point that is sometimes lost sight of in the discussion that surrounds this subject is that, if they are operating properly, all the institutions of the state, executive, legislative and judicial, share a common goal. They are, *au fond*, embarked on a joint endeavour to improve the lot of the society that it is a privilege to serve. For this reason, when debating how well (or otherwise) the doctrine of the separation of powers is operating, the fact that government decisions are, in appropriate circumstances, subject to independent verification, to a system of impartial proofing by a body of women and men of integrity, is not only an added guarantee of the soundness of decision-making, it is something which (if it is properly carried out) should be a source of reassurance rather than resentment on the part of the decision-makers themselves.

Introduction: The Judiciary Under Attack (and Why Safeguarding Judicial Independence Matters)

DIMITRIOS GIANNOULOPOULOS AND YVONNE MCDERMOTT

THIS VOLUME BRINGS together, elaborates upon and further advances scholarship that was, for the most part, initially presented at the British Academy conference on 'Challenges to Judicial Independence in Times of Crisis' that took place in March 2018 at the British Academy and that we had the unique pleasure to convene. The inspiration for the timely conversations that took place over two days at the home of the Academy in London, located only a short walk from the UK's leading political and legal institutions, including the Houses of Parliament, 10 Downing Street and the Supreme Court, came directly from observations about the progressively tense relationship between these institutions, exemplified by criticism of the judgment of the Divisional Court in the first *Miller* case.[1] The frustration directed by the press and politicians towards the judges who decided the case naturally set the tone for our exploration of an emerging crisis capable of undermining confidence in the UK's commitment to the separation of powers and the rule of law. In opening our conference, the former Lord Chief Justice, Lord Thomas, one of the Law Lords that had been personally targeted by the media, was quick to underline 'the need for constant vigilance to safeguard the independence of the judiciary'. He pointed out that the reaction to the *Miller* case included the 'notorious phrase "enemy of the people"' and 'other abuse', applied to his 'two senior colleagues and [him]self'.[2]

Brexit-driven criticism of the judiciary, and similarly disconcerting populist threats to judicial independence in other parts of the world, were at the forefront of thinking for many of the participants in the conference. Their contributions to this volume provide, in this way, a useful methodological tool, the function of which is

---

[1] *R (Miller) v Secretary of State for Exiting the European Union* [2016] EWHC 2768 (Admin).
[2] Lord Thomas, 'Epilogue: Judicial Independence: The Need for Constant Vigilance', in this volume.

twofold. They can shed light on how threats to judicial independence are perceived at the time they take effect, including by those personally and institutionally affected, enabling us to assess the immediate damage inflicted upon judicial independence. They simultaneously allow us to analyse these challenges as part of a longer continuum that can be separated from the political controversies of the time (of the conference), particularly those relating to the UK's exit from the European Union. These threats can be situated in their contemporary context against a wider legal and socio-political backdrop, and not just in relation to the United Kingdom.

Ultimately, this makes it possible for this volume to revisit one of the key temporal premises of the conference from which it derives, which explored challenges to judicial independence in what we perceived to be a 'time of crisis'. On this specific point of 'crisis', if any more proof was needed of the late Lord Kerr's insight and erudition, they took centre stage in his contribution to our conference.[3] Lord Kerr noted that even if Brexit had 'given rise to occasions when the way in which the various institutions have been scrutinised – or even criticised – might partake of something approaching a censorious commentary', this 'does not necessarily amount to a crisis in the true sense of the word', before pronouncing, with admirable stoicism, that 'the judiciary should react with relative calmness and equanimity'.[4] In other words, Lord Kerr's analysis enables us to abstract the locus of explanation from Brexit and crisis and to relocate it in a wider context with a focus on long-term solutions to threats to judicial independence. These may have violently manifested in recent years, particularly in view of populist politicians' frustration with constitutional checks and balances as an impediment to giving effect to far-reaching manifestos, but they have much deeper roots, laying bare the inherent tension between the executive and the judiciary. On the one hand, the executive seems intent on returning to antiquated ideas of sovereignty, seen as the sovereignty of the executive and, ultimately, of a Prime Minister armed with executive power that should go unchallenged.[5] On the other hand, the judiciary draws on a constitutional role that has fundamentally changed in recent decades to include far better capacity to hold the executive to account. By the time this manuscript entered its final stages of completion (December 2021), legislation had been proposed to give ministers the power to overrule judicial review decisions that they disagree with, and the latest proposals to replace the Human Rights Act with a British Bill of Rights, again addressing the government's misplaced perception that judges have been given too much power to the detriment of Parliament, had been proposed.[6]

---

[3] Lord Kerr, 'Foreword', in this volume.

[4] Lord Kerr, 'Foreword'.

[5] J. Petley and D. Giannoulopoulos, 'Attacks on Grieve and Bercow stem from flawed, feudal ideas of "sovereignty"', *openDemocracy*, 10 June 2019, online at: https://www.opendemocracy.net/en/opendemocracyuk/attacks-on-grieve-and-bercow-stem-from-flawed-feudal-ideas-of-sovereignty/ (last accessed 26 January 2022).

[6] S. Jolly, 'A human rights review needs care. Yet Raab is peddling propaganda', *Prospect magazine*, 16 December 2021, online at: https://www.prospectmagazine.co.uk/politics/a-human-rights-review-needs-care-yet-raab-is-peddling-propaganda (last accessed 26 January 2022). See also Better Human

It is against this backdrop that this volume seeks to address contemporary threats to judicial independence by situating them in their legal, philosophical, socio-political, comparative and historical contexts. To do so, the volume asks the fundamental question, normative and empirical, of why judicial independence matters, taking as a point of departure that judicial independence is a precondition for implementing the rule of law in the sense of securing equality of treatment under the law, independently of political influence or status, and achieving the promise of a transparent and liberal society where ruling by executive fiat does not substitute for democratic accountability and alignment with fundamental human rights. From this angle, it should trigger all sorts of alarms to see attacks upon judicial independence go hand in hand with equally coordinated efforts to dilute the rule of law, including, extraordinarily, in the UK, where the government introduced, and strongly defended in Parliament, legislation, the Internal Market Bill, that was going to 'authoris[e] direct and unequivocal breaches of a recently concluded bilateral treaty',[7] the Northern Ireland Protocol of the Withdrawal Agreement. 'Setting out explicitly to break international law in this way [was] without precedent', noted the House of Lords' Select Committee on the Constitution, adding that '[i]t jeopardise[d] international obligations the UK [had] recently ratified, undermine[d] domestic law and [was] contrary to the rule of law'.[8] The UK had adopted an 'extraordinary and retrograde position' that was 'both embarrassing and damaging', writes Jolly in this volume.[9] It was an 'entirely unprecedented moment in our modern political life in this country', which was 'massively damaging to our status us upholders of the international rules-based system we have helped create', commented Grieve in a recent public lecture, following the same line of thinking and expressing the same level of surprise and indignation that the vast majority of political, legal and academic experts in the UK expressed at the time.[10] When anti-European Convention on Human Rights polemic is added to the equation,[11] especially when its connections

---

Podcast, 'Why the Human Rights Act matters' (with K. Brimelow QC, D. Giannoulopoulos, F. Klug and A. Wagner), online at: https://podcasts.apple.com/gb/podcast/54-why-the-human-rights-act-matters/id1481010283?i=1000547085129. The podcast discusses why the Human Rights Act matters against the backdrop of renewed critiques by the government leading to the latest proposals for reviewing the Act and/or replacing it with a British Bill of Rights.

[7] House of Lords, Select Committee on the Constitution, 'United Kingdom Internal Market Bill', 16 October 2020, 162, online at: https://publications.parliament.uk/pa/ld5801/ldselect/ldconst/151/151.pdf (last accessed 26 January 2022).

[8] House of Lords, Select Committee on the Constitution, 'United Kingdom Internal Market Bill', p. 4.

[9] Schona Jolly QC, 'The Rule of Law across the World: A System in Crisis?', in this volume.

[10] D. Grieve, '"Taking back control": a recipe for chaos', Goldsmiths Law public lecture, 29 November 2021, online at: https://www.youtube.com/watch?v=STVM_abIXic (last accessed 26 January 2022).

[11] See, generally, D. Giannoulopoulos, 'Human rights laws protect us all. Now they are under threat', *Prospect magazine*, 19 March 2021, online at: https://www.prospectmagazine.co.uk/society-and-cult ure/save-human-rights-act-european-convention-government-review (last accessed 26 January 2022); D. Giannoulopoulos, 'The urgency of renewed UK commitment to human rights', *Prospect magazine*, 4 November 2020, online at: https://www.prospectmagazine.co.uk/politics/the-urgency-of-renewed-uk-commitment-to-human-rights (last accessed 26 January 2022); D. Giannoulopoulos, 'The Eurosceptic

with anti-juridicalism and perceived improper 'judicial power' are understood, we are left with a feeling of bewilderment about the state we are in with respect of the fundamental liberal democratic values of judicial independence and the rule of law, paradoxically in a country that has historically taken these to be a reflection of its national political identity.

It is sheer political opportunism that now threatens to undermine a national political identity in the UK of adherence to the rule of law, as was recently evidenced – in a different area, but with equal force – by the strong criticism that was directed by leading Conservative Party members at Bristol Crown Court jury's verdict in the 'Colston Four', the case of the four defendants who were charged with criminal damage in relation to the toppling of the statue of Edward Colston in Bristol in June 2020, whom the jury acquitted.[12] The Attorney General, Suella Braverman, commented on Twitter that '[t]rial by jury is an important guardian of liberty and must not be undermined. However, the decision in the Colston statue case is causing confusion.' She then added that she was 'carefully considering' whether to refer matters to the Court of Appeal (despite no apparent point of law having arisen that might require the Court of Appeal to clarify the law for future reference).[13] Other criticisms of the defendants' acquittal included that this had undermined the rule of law and it was setting a dangerous precedent, both counter-intuitive and – simply – factually incorrect statements. Crown Court judgments do not set precedents, and they are 'a sign of independent courts and a robust rule of law'[14] rather than the opposite; how could they be, when a jury returning a 'not guilty' verdict is purely performing its constitutional role, as it would be if it returned a 'guilty' one? It is the jury's entitlement, entrenched in the rule of law, to return any verdict they have reached; this 'is an example of the law in action, and not of a legal process

---

Right and (Our) Human Rights: the Threat to the Human Rights Act and the European Convention on Human Rights is Alive and Well', European Human Rights Law Review (2020), 225–242; D. Giannoulopoulos, 'What has the European Convention on Human Rights Ever Done for the UK?', *European Human Rights Law Review* (2019), 1–10; A. Wagner, 'After Brexit they will come for human rights – and this time the public debate must be won', *Prospect magazine*, 9 June 2019, online at: https://www.prospectmagazine.co.uk/politics/after-brexit-they-will-come-for-human-rights-and-this-time-the-public-debate-must-be-won (last accessed 26 January 2022).

[12] BBC News, 'Edward Colston statue: Four cleared of criminal damage', 5 January 2022, online at: https://www.bbc.co.uk/news/uk-england-bristol-59727161 (last accessed 13 January 2022). Edward Colston was 'a 17th-century shareholder in the Royal African Company when it shipped 84,000 Africans into slavery, including 12,000 children' who 'rose to become the equivalent of a modern chief executive' of the company that 'transported more Africans into slavery than any other company in the whole history of the slave trade in the north Atlantic'. D. Gayle, 'BLM protesters cleared over toppling of Edward Colston statue', *Guardian*, 5 January 2022, quoting historian David Olusoga, online at: https://www.theguardian.com/uk-news/2022/jan/05/four-cleared-of-toppling-edward-colston-statute (last accessed 13 January 2022).

[13] H. Siddique, 'Suella Braverman accused of politically driven meddling over Colston Four', *Guardian*, 7 January 2022, online at: https://www.theguardian.com/uk-news/2022/jan/07/suella-braverman-accused-of-politically-driven-meddling-over-colston-four (last accessed 13 January 2022).

[14] Siddique, 'Suella Braverman accused of politically driven meddling over Colston Four', *Guardian*, quoting Kirsty Brimelow QC, vice chair of the Criminal Bar Association.

undermined'.[15] The populists' narrative will disregard all this, however, and will take any opportunity given, be that by drawing on Euroscepticism (as with Brexit and the threats to withdraw from the European Court of Human Rights) or 'anti-wokeness' and the culture wars (as in the case of the Colston Four acquittals), indifferent to the damage inflicted upon the rule of law and public faith in the independence of the judiciary.

A populist narrative that enables the executive to adopt increasingly belligerent views on the need to respect the rule of law, be that in its domestic or international law dimensions, inevitably becomes of central importance to the analysis that contributors undertake in this volume, particularly as they set out to define the conditions more clearly for addressing present-day challenges to judicial independence. Attention is naturally drawn to *de jure* protections; legislation, more effective formal responses and constitutional 'checks and balances' are initially seen as pointing the way forward. At the same time, informal cultural factors also come to the fore as creative tools that can help secure judicial independence in practice. From that perspective, interesting questions arise concerning, for instance, what happens when domestic legal cultures clash with the need for reform, particularly where the pressures for reform are located in international law. Similarly, reflection is generated around the engagement of judges with politics and politicians, and with the public; how much is too much, and what happens, conversely, if the judiciary fails to acknowledge the political considerations that are intrinsically connected with the complex process of interpreting and applying the law?

This introductory chapter will begin to ask some of the questions raised above, with a view to sketching the wider normative and empirical parameters within which the contributions of our authors have taken shape and evolved. First, a few illustrations from a global vantage point of current threats to judicial independence will help showcase the gravity of the situation that judiciaries across the world are confronted with.

The judiciary under attack

Recent annual thematic reports by the UN Special Rapporteur on the independence of judges and lawyers to the General Assembly and Human Rights Council offer a useful introduction in the form of a sharp and painful realisation of unsettling practice on the ground that sometimes runs parallel, and gives effect, to a public narrative of anti-juridicalism that the executive aggressively promotes, but that sometimes, conversely, is also hidden from the public view, with the executive paying judicial independence lip service instead. To take a few examples, the

---

[15] D. A. Green, 'The Rule of Law and the Colston Four – and why a jury acquittal shows a legal system working and not being undermined', *The Law and Policy Blog*, 10 January 2022, online at: https://davidallengreen.com/2022/01/the-rule-of-law-and-the-colston-four-and-why-a-jury-acquittal-shows-a-legal-system-working-and-not-being-undermined/ (last accessed 13 January 2022).

2020 thematic report has documented 'the pattern of various forms of disguised sanctions imposed on judges to harass, punish or otherwise interfere with the legitimate exercise of a judge's professional activities'.[16] These are practices that develop underground whose 'aim is to induce a judge to dismiss the consideration of a case, to adjudicate a case in a particular way or to punish the judge for a decision taken in the exercise of the judicial function', with '[j]udges dealing with politically sensitive cases [being] particularly exposed to [them]'.[17] Disguised sanctions can be especially far-reaching, ranging from measures affecting security of tenure and conditions of service to attacks against the judiciary that may include threats and intimidation, collective dismissal and even arbitrary arrest and detention, as well as attacks on the prestige and authority of the judiciary. These are 'carried out by political parties, State institutions or non-State actors, such as powerful business enterprises', and 'may be addressed to the judiciary as a whole, depicting it as an inefficient, corrupt or unaccountable institution, or to particular categories of judges, for instance those dealing with politically sensitive cases'.[18] The Polish government's 'large-scale propaganda' against the judiciary is offered as an example of such attacks upon the prestige and authority of the judiciary.[19] But the list of countries from which examples of disguised sanctions are more generally drawn is wide-ranging and diverse, including countries such as Armenia, Georgia, Montenegro, North Macedonia, Sweden, Hungary, Kazakhstan, Latvia, Slovenia, Bolivia, Brazil, Ecuador, Guatemala, Moldova, Romania, Serbia, Slovakia, Switzerland, Uzbekistan, Hungary, Mongolia, Poland, Italy, the Russian Federation and Turkey.[20] It does not take long to see the spectre of illiberal democratic practice threatening judicial independence in this list, despite the assumed liberal democratic aspirations of the majority of the countries that feature there.

In a similar way, the Special Rapporteur's 2019 thematic report documents 'various forms of interference with the exercise of fundamental freedoms by judges and prosecutors',[21] including freedom of expression, freedom of association or concerning the judges' ability 'to make comments in defence of fundamental human rights and the rule of law'.[22] Such interference by the state takes the form

---

[16] United Nations General Assembly, 'Independence of judges and lawyers', Report of the Special Rapporteur on the independence of judges and lawyers, D. García-Sayán, A/75/112, 17 July 2020, p. 2, online at: https://documents-dds-ny.un.org/doc/UNDOC/GEN/N20/186/73/PDF/N2018673.pdf?Open Element (last accessed 26 January 2022).

[17] Report of the Special Rapporteur on the independence of judges and lawyers, García-Sayán, p. 2.

[18] Report of the Special Rapporteur on the independence of judges and lawyers, García-Sayán, [74].

[19] Report of the Special Rapporteur on the independence of judges and lawyers, García-Sayán, [74].

[20] Jolly's analysis on Turkey includes a reflection on trial observations that her colleagues at the Bar Human Rights Committee and she have undertaken in the country, which provide further evidence of an illegitimate sweep of the legal profession, civil society activists and human rights defenders that is taking place there. Schona Jolly QC, 'The Rule of Law across the World: A System in Crisis?', in this volume.

[21] United Nations General Assembly, 'Independence of judges and lawyers', Report of the Special Rapporteur on the independence of judges and lawyers, D. García-Sayán, A/HRC/41/48, 29 April 2019, p. 2, online at: https://documents-dds-ny.un.org/doc/UNDOC/GEN/G19/118/68/PDF/G1911868. pdf?OpenElement (last accessed 26 January 2022).

[22] Report of the Special Rapporteur on the independence of judges and lawyers, García-Sayán, [69].

of disciplinary sanctions that are imposed as 'an expedient to punish' judges or prosecutors for opinions they express or action they take in the exercise of their duties.[23] And in her 2016 report, the Special Rapporteur took particular care to highlight that a 'comprehensive legal framework and body of jurisprudence' on securing judicial independence did not provide protection in practice: 'the independence of judges, lawyers and prosecutors is still extremely vulnerable, is under attack or is merely non-existent, in many parts of the world', she stressed.[24]

The same degree of concern is expressed by the Council of Europe. In the 2021 annual report on the state of democracy, human rights and the rule of law across the continent, the Secretary General of the Council of Europe, Marija Pejčinović Burić, highlighted a 'clear and worrying degree of democratic backsliding' that predated the coronavirus pandemic but has been compounded by it. Threats to judicial independence form an important part of the analysis in the report that reveals 'a picture of democracy in distress'.[25] These threats range from the existence of 'legislation that allows and even facilitates undue influence or political interference over judicial appointments or the composition and functioning of judicial self-governing bodies' to measures that 'have aimed to weaken the security of judges' tenure or empower the executive authorities to discretionally replace court presidents',[26] and can be further illustrated by European Court of Human Rights jurisprudence.[27] The Commissioner for Human Rights at the Council of Europe, Dunja Mijatović, used similar language to describe the situation: 'we are now seeing increasing and worrying attempts by the executive and legislative to use their leverage to influence and instruct the judiciary and undermine judicial independence', he pointed out in September 2019, adding that 'governments and politicians [...] even resort to threats against judges'. He was drawing on examples from Hungary (where a number of legislative measures in the 2010s had created 'a risk of [...] politicisation' of the judiciary); Poland (where 'a publicly-financed campaign to discredit judges and negative statements by officials [...] has had a major impact on the functioning and independence of the country's justice system, including its constitutional court and council for the judiciary'); Romania (where he took note of a 'hastily conceived' reform of the judiciary and 'restrictions on magistrates' freedom of expression'); Turkey (where judicial independence had been 'seriously eroded during the state of emergency and its aftermath'); Italy

---

[23] Report of the Special Rapporteur on the independence of judges and lawyers, García-Sayán, [91].
[24] United Nations General Assembly, 'Independence of judges and lawyers', Report of the Special Rapporteur on the independence of judges and lawyers, M. Pinto, A/HRC/32/34, 5 April 2019, para 35, online at: https://documents-dds-ny.un.org/doc/UNDOC/GEN/G16/068/03/PDF/G1606803.pdf?Open Element (last accessed 26 January 2022).
[25] Council of Europe, Report by the Secretary General, 'State of Democracy, Human Rights and the Rule of Law', May 2021, p. 8, online at: https://www.coe.int/en/web/secretary-general/report-2021#page-0 (last accessed 26 January 2022).
[26] Council of Europe, Report by the Secretary General, 'State of Democracy, Human Rights and the Rule of Law', p. 16.
[27] *Guðmundur Andri Ástráðsson v Iceland*, Grand Chamber judgment, 1 December 2020 (Application No. 26374/18), [288]–[290].

(drawing attention to the Italian Minister of Interior who had 'verbally attacked three magistrates on social media over some decisions they rendered which he thought challenged the government's increasingly restrictive immigration policy'); and Serbia (where a judge of the Belgrade Appellate Court 'was subject to personal attacks and his professional qualifications and the quality of his work were brought into question', for expressing an opinion that a legislative proposal supported by the government – the introduction of life imprisonment without a possibility of conditional release for some of the gravest criminal offences – was incompatible with the case law of the European Court of Human Rights).

If we zoom in, from the Council of Europe to the European Union, further evidence is provided – in specific member states – of liberal democratic values in turmoil, with a deterioration of the rule of law and judicial independence front and centre. Nothing demonstrates this more starkly than Article 7 TEU procedures launched by the European Commission (on 20 December 2017) regarding Poland and the identical procedure initiated by the European Parliament (on 12 September 2018) regarding Hungary. The 'illiberal drift of this duo'[28] represents the next very serious challenge for the future of the EU. The *New York Times* bring this into sharp focus: '[w]hatever other disagreements EU members may harbor – and, as Britain's exit showed, these are many and deep – the concept of the Union as a community of democratic values has remained at its heart', it notes.[29] Put differently, the rule of law crisis in Poland and Hungary threatens the democratic foundations of the Union and, in doing that, it throws into doubt the Union itself; failure to effectively deal with this crisis now has the capacity to generate an illiberal wave that may prove impossible to stop later on. The decision of Poland's Constitutional Tribunal of 7 October 2021 that declared Articles 1, 2 and 19 of the Treaty on European Union to be partially unconstitutional,[30] and the immediate and stark response of the European Court of Justice, which has fined Poland €1 million per day for ignoring the ruling that was calling it to suspend the Supreme Court's disciplinary chamber,[31] demonstrate how serious a challenge to the rule of law the EU is facing in Poland (as it does in Hungary too), while also showing how determined its legal and political institutions now appear to be to tackle the rule of law crisis there. These developments provide a powerful illustration of the practical but also symbolic importance of judicial independence and the rule of law for liberal democracies. And so does the development by the

---

[28] Editorial, 'The EU puts its foot down on the rule of law – while the leaders of Poland and Hungary resist', *New York Times*, 22 November 2020, online at: https://www.nytimes.com/2020/11/22/opinion/eu-poland-hungary.html (last accessed 26 January 2022).

[29] Editorial, 'The EU puts its foot down on the rule of law', *New York Times*.

[30] See, e.g., J. Henley and J. Rankin, 'Polish court rules EU law incompatible with its constitution', *Guardian*, 7 October 2021, online at: https://www.theguardian.com/world/2021/oct/07/polish-court-rules-that-eu-laws-incompatible-with-its-constitution (last accessed 26 January 2022).

[31] CJEU, Press release No. 192/21, 27 October 2021, 'Order of the Vice President of the Court in Case C-240/21 R Commission v Poland', online at: https://curia.europa.eu/jcms/upload/docs/application/pdf/2021-10/cp210192en.pdf (last accessed 26 January 2022).

EU, in the past decade, of a number of instruments designed to enforce the rule of law, either by strengthening the promotion of these foundational values and prevention of attacks upon them (such as promoting structural reforms in member states or adopting an EU Justice Scoreboard that provides comparable data on the independence, quality and efficiency of national justice systems), or by directly responding to such attacks through infringement proceedings, a rule of law framework and, ultimately, the 'nuclear option' of Article 7 TEU, which sanctions serious breaches to the rule of law by suspending membership rights, including voting rights.[32]

The latest instrument that has come into force, a 'rule of law mechanism' that has been designed as a yearly cycle to promote the rule of law and that leads to the publication each year of a rule of law report, including member state-by-member state assessment in 27 country chapters, offers further evidence of the urgency of the situation in Poland and Hungary. The first Rule of Law Report, published in September 2020, highlights continuous concerns about judicial independence in Poland concerning changes to the retirement regime for Supreme Court judges and the procedure for appointing its First President, the independence and legitimacy of the Constitutional Tribunal, the composition of the National Council for the Judiciary mainly by politically appointed members, the risk that judges may be sanctioned because of the content of their decisions (including decisions to request preliminary rulings from the Court of Justice), new obligations for judges to disclose personal information such as their membership in associations as well as the fact that the Minister of Justice is at the same time the Prosecutor General.[33] The report paints a similarly disquieting picture about challenges to judicial independence in Hungary, such as the introduction of new special rules that have 'de facto increased the role of Parliament in judicial appointments' to the Supreme Court; the declaration as unlawful, by the Supreme Court, of an order for a preliminary reference to the European Court of Justice; or the creation of structural limitations that prevent the National Judicial Council from counterbalancing the powers of the President of the National Office for the Judiciary, who is elected by Parliament and entrusted with extensive powers relating to the administration of the court system. More worrying even is reference in the report to '[j]udges and lawyers [being] subject to negative narratives in the media', with government and pro-government media outlets attacking judicial decisions relating to human rights judgments such as 'those releasing convicts on parole, awarding compensation to

---

[32] European Commission, *Rule of Law Report 2020*, online at: https://ec.europa.eu/info/sites/default/files/rule_of_law_mechanism_factsheet_en.pdf (last accessed 26 January 2022).

[33] European Commission, *2020 Rule of Law Report*, Country Chapter on the rule of law situation in Poland, 30 September 2020, online at: https://eur-lex.europa.eu/legal-content/EN/TXT/?qid=160257 9986149&uri=CELEX%3A52020SC0320 (last accessed 26 January 2022). See also European Parliament, 'Rule of law in Poland: "overwhelming evidence" of breaches', 16 July 2020, online at: https://www.europarl.europa.eu/news/en/press-room/20200716IPR83505/rule-of-law-in-poland-over whelming-evidence-of-breaches (last accessed 26 January 2022).

Roma children segregated in schools and to inmates complaining about their detention conditions'.[34]

Narrowing the focus even further, from the EU back to the UK, it would naturally be interesting to correlate some of the attacks upon judges and courts that we have explored above – particularly where these relate to applications of international human rights – with similar concerns regarding judicial independence in the UK. The situation in Hungary or Poland differs substantially, of course, by the degree to which it undermines the foundations of judicial independence. At the same time, it is opportune to observe that we are not at all immune in the UK to ministers (and their ministries), MPs and even the Prime Minister targeting domestic courts or human rights lawyers simply for resorting to domestic human rights law and ECHR jurisprudence, for instance, to protect the rights of 'those who are unpopular, disenfranchised or otherwise politically powerless'.[35] Fresh in the memory of many readers will be the example of the Home Office, which, in August 2020, posted a promotional video on social media criticising 'activist lawyers' for frustrating the department's efforts to deport those who did not have the right to remain in the UK.[36] The Home Office eventually deleted the video, but the Home Secretary, Priti Patel, did not change course and in fact intensified her targeting of 'do-gooders' and 'lefty lawyers' in her speech to the annual Conservative Party conference in October of the same year.[37] The Home Secretary's stupefying assault on the rule of law and judicial independence was matched by the Prime Minister, Boris Johnson, who went so far as borrow Priti Patel's exact words when he told the same Conservative conference, two days later, that the criminal justice system was 'being hamstrung by lefty human rights lawyers, and other do-gooders'.[38]

---

[34] European Commission, *2020 Rule of Law Report*, Country Chapter on the rule of law situation in Hungary, 30 September 2020, online at: https://eur-lex.europa.eu/legal-content/EN/TXT/?qid=160258 2109481&uri=CELEX%3A52020SC0316 (last accessed 26 January 2022).

[35] N. Mavronicola, 'The unpopular (and) Article 3 ECHR', *Human Rights in Action*, 22 February 2021, online at: https://human-rights-in-action.blogspot.com/2021/02/the-unpopular-and-article-3-echr.html (last accessed 26 January 2022). See also Murray Hunt, who underlines the populist undertones of the treatment that UK politicians give to human rights judgments: 'In the UK today, decisions of the both the European Court of Human Rights and of UK courts under the Human Rights Act are frequently criticised, by both commentators in the media and elected politicians from across the political spectrum, for being profoundly "undemocratic". The examples are well known to everyone with an interest in human rights and are too numerous to catalogue […]'. M. Hunt, 'Introduction' in M. Hunt, H. J. Hooper and P. Yowell (eds), *Parliaments and Human Rights: Redressing the Democratic Deficit* (Oxford, Hart Publishing, 2015) 1, 5.

[36] J. Grierson and D. Taylor, 'Home Office wrong to refer to "activist lawyers", top official admits', *Guardian*, 27 August 2020, online at: https://www.theguardian.com/politics/2020/aug/27/home-office-wrong-to-refer-to-activist-lawyers-top-official-admits (last accessed 26 January 2022).

[37] M. Townsend, 'Top ministers urged Priti Patel to stop attacks on "activist lawyers"', *Guardian*, 18 October 2020, online at: https://www.theguardian.com/politics/2020/oct/18/top-ministers-urged-priti-patel-to-stop-attacks-on-activist-lawyers (last accessed 26 January 2022).

[38] O. Bowcott, 'Legal profession hits back at Johnson over "lefty lawyers" speech', *Guardian*, 6 October 2020, online at: https://www.theguardian.com/law/2020/oct/06/legal-profession-hits-back-at-boris-john son-over-lefty-lawyers-speech (last accessed 26 January 2022).

Equally noteworthy, on the other hand, were the quick reflexes shown by the legal profession. More than 800 legal professionals, including barristers, solicitors, legal academics and retired judges, immediately signed a letter inviting 'both the home secretary and the prime minister to behave honourably by apologising for their display of hostility, and to refrain from such attacks in the future'. The letter expressed deep concern at attacks 'on lawyers seeking to hold the government to the law'; such 'attacks endanger not only the personal safety of lawyers and others working for the justice system [...] they [also] undermine the rule of law which ministers and lawyers alike are duty bound to uphold', it concluded.[39] Eminent legal experts, such as the former director of public prosecutions, Lord McDonald QC, the former Supreme Court Justice, Lord Dyson, and the president of Magdalen College at the University of Oxford, Dinah Rose QC, added their voices of support to those that were being aired through the letter, castigating 'populist politicians' for resorting to 'ugly authoritarianism' and using the 'inflammatory language' of 'a demagogue', and even for 'whip[ping] up hatred against lawyers for simply doing their job'.[40]

Though it is no doubt astonishing that those at the highest echelons within the UK government would so openly and ferociously attack human rights lawyers and judges, it is arguably the executive's more dissimulated efforts to challenge judicial independence and the rule of law that we should be more worried about. These require of the legal profession, and society more broadly, not just quick reflexes, but the 'constant vigilance' that Lord Thomas advocates in this volume. They also confirm the vital importance of 'constant reminder and, if necessary, renewal' of judicial independence that Lord Kerr writes about in his prologue. A glance at plans for reform of human rights and administrative law in England and Wales that were underway at the time of writing brings to the fore hidden threats to judicial independence that can easily slip under the public's radar.[41] When the government announced its Independent Review of the Human Rights Act (HRA) in December 2020, it is likely that the wider public may have failed to notice that the Review marks a deviation from the pre-existing *direct* political aggression towards the ECHR to adopting a more nuanced narrative of compliance coupled with the need for change. As one of us pointed out elsewhere,[42] the Review stated in its call for evidence that it will be

---

[39] Letters, 'Ministers must end their attacks on lawyers', *Guardian*, 25 October 2020, online at: https://www.theguardian.com/law/2020/oct/25/ministers-must-end-their-attacks-on-lawyers (last accessed 26 January 2022).

[40] O. Bowcott, 'Lawyers call for apology from Johnson and Patel for endangering colleagues', *Guardian*, 25 October 2020, online at: https://www.theguardian.com/politics/2020/oct/25/lawyers-ask-johnson-and-patel-to-apologise-for-endangering-colleagues (last accessed 26 January 2022).

[41] Lord Kerr's prologue picks on these critiques of judicial review long before they eventually led to the government's current plans for reform, offering even more evidence of his insight and erudition. Lord Kerr, 'Foreword', in this volume.

[42] D. Giannoulopoulos, 'Human rights laws protect us all. Now they are under threat', *Prospect magazine*, 19 March 2021, online at: https://www.prospectmagazine.co.uk/society-and-culture/save-human-rights-act-european-convention-government-review (last accessed 26 January 2022). On the Independent Human Rights Act Review, see: https://www.gov.uk/guidance/independent-human-rights-act-review

proceed[ing] on the basis that the UK will remain a signatory to the Convention. But at the same time, it threw into question the UK's continued commitment to giving full effect to the rights and freedoms enshrined in the ECHR *domestically*, through the Human Rights Act.

It is equally revealing that the Review's

terms of reference were framed against a politically polarised backdrop, with allegations the Human Rights Act allows the judiciary to undermine the executive and questions over the relationship between domestic courts and the European Court of Human Rights.[43]

In the same vein, it is important to note that

[t]he Review of the HRA cannot be seen in isolation. Upon publication of the report of the Independent Review of *Administrative Law*, the Lord Chancellor, Robert Buckland, once again rehearsed in parliament the narrative that we must 'rebalance our system', but delivered it with an awkward paternalistic emphasis on the need – through reform of judicial review – to '*protect* the judiciary from unwanted political entanglements.' Protect the judiciary from themselves, in other words, by limiting their capacity to hold the government to account. It is what the HRA Review's terms of reference imply as well.[44]

Modern-day hostility against the judiciary in the UK has gone so far as recently to include a suggested change of name for the Supreme Court that would take into account – and counter – a perceived emerging 'sense of mission' for the Court. The proposal has come from the right-wing think tank Policy Exchange (its 'Judicial Power' branch), which is very closely connected to the Conservative Party, feeding ideas into it and shaping public policy.[45] The proposal takes issue with the Court allegedly seeing itself as having 'the role of constitutional court' and being a 'guardian of the constitution'. The Head of the Judicial Power Project, Richard Ekins, considers more specifically that 'this sense of mission is partly attributable to the title given to the Court as the Supreme Court' and would like to see 'the Court renamed as the "Upper Court of Appeal"'. This is discussed in a paper titled 'Reforming the Supreme Court' that contains two contributions, 'Should the UK Supreme Court be abolished' and 'Abolishing the Supreme Court: some questions and comments'.[46]

(last accessed 26 January 2022). On the Independent Review of Administrative Law see: https://www.gov.uk/government/groups/independent-review-of-administrative-law (last accessed 26 January 2022). See also D. Giannoulopoulos, 'Review of Human Rights Act asks the wrong questions', *Guardian*, 8 December 2020, online at: https://www.theguardian.com/law/2020/dec/08/review-of-human-rights-act-asks-the-wrong-questions (last accessed 26 January 2022).

[43] Giannoulopoulos, 'Human rights laws protect us all. Now they are under threat', *Prospect magazine*, 19 March 2021.

[44] Giannoulopoulos, 'Human rights laws protect us all. Now they are under threat', *Prospect magazine*.

[45] A. Beckett, 'What can they be thinking?', *Guardian*, 26 September 2008, online at: https://www.theguardian.com/politics/2008/sep/26/thinktanks.conservatives (last accessed 26 January 2022).

[46] D. Wyatt QC and R. Ekins, *Reforming the Supreme Court*, (London, Policy Exchange, 2020), online at: https://policyexchange.org.uk/wp-content/uploads/Reforming-the-Supreme-Court.pdf (last accessed 26 January 2022).

The above confirm the timeliness of this volume in relation to a picture of political discontent with the judiciary – and concrete actions that undermine its independence – in the UK and in the light of wider, damaging attacks upon judicial independence and the rule of law in Europe and globally. Some of the challenges discussed above are captured by contributions to this volume, which open up a range of perspectives, offering a kaleidoscopic view of a judiciary under attack (and the obvious and urgent need to defend it). These challenges include a populist vision of democracy that centres on defeating out-of-touch elites in the interests of the will of 'ordinary people', as emphasised by Sklansky, Skinner and Müller in their chapters. Feilzer, Petley and Roberts provide specific examples of how public opinion can be used to undermine institutions, with reference to sentencing, Brexit and parole decisions, respectively. As Feilzer and Grieve note, the upshot of this is that these 'moral panics' may distract from more serious threats, such as the chronic underfunding of the criminal justice system. Parizot and Jackson highlight how cherished fair trial guarantees – namely, the right to challenge the legality of one's detention and the right to a public trial – can be diluted or stripped away entirely in the context of anti-terror laws, while Jolly, Müller and Aguirre, draw from recent developments around the world (in Hong Kong, Turkey, Poland, Hungary, Myanmar among others) and domestically to highlight worrying attempts to stifle the judiciary's independence.

Defining judicial independence

Having enabled our contributors to draw on their individual interpretations of the 'polysemic' concept[47] of judicial independence, this volume brings to the surface a plurality of understandings concerning the diverse ways in which judicial independence, broadly conceived, manifests itself. Sklansky shows us that judicial independence in the United States is as much about prosecutors as it is about judges, for instance. Parizot then offers the contrasting view of France by exposing us to the controversies surrounding the question of whether public prosecutors should enjoy judicial independence, including in the light of diverging positions adopted by the Court of Justice of the European Union and the European Court of Human Rights.[48] Sklansky's normative analysis also brings us face-to-face with two visions of American democracy that shape our understanding of judicial independence.

---

[47] L. Heuschling, 'Why Should Judges Be Independent? Reflections on Coke, Montesquieu and the French Tradition of Judicial Dependance' in K. S. Ziegler, D. Baranger and A. W. Bradley (eds), *Constitutionalism and the Role of Parliaments* (Oxford, Hart Publishing, 2007) 199, 201.

[48] As John Bell notes, 'national histories and traditions colour the understanding of common values, such as judicial independence and democracy in the judicial process'. J. Bell, 'Judicial Cultures and Judicial Independence' in A. Dashwood, C. Hillion, J. Spencer and A. Ward, *The Cambridge Yearbook of European Legal Studies* (Oxford, Hart Publishing, 2002) 47. Judicial independence in the United States and France, and in the other legal systems examined in this volume, must therefore be analysed through the lens of the national histories and domestic legal tradition that have shaped their content.

The concept is perceived as a fundamental democratic safeguard for those adhering to pluralist theories of democracy, and as a side constraint on majoritarianism at best for those subscribing to populist theories instead. This can be contrasted with Grieve's view. The British former Attorney General starts by highlighting the normative foundations of judicial independence, pointing to the importance of the separation of powers for UK constitutional law. But he also draws attention to the need to understand judicial independence empirically. He explains that where judicial outcomes are 'adverse to [the politicians'] own opinion and that of sections of their electorate or the media to whom they look for approval and support', the ability of these politicians to defer to the judiciary in practice can 'erode quickly with the potential to create confrontation'.[49]

To better understand what judicial independence entails, we need to deconstruct the abstract notion into its various elements. We can point out that 'independence' is a 'rather strong notion' with a 'vigorously positive connotation' that centres on the idea of 'negat[ing] influence of some sort', and 'exemption from external control or support; freedom from subjection, or from the influence of others; individual liberty or thought of action'.[50] We can then proceed to distinguish between personal independence and institutional independence. If we concentrate on the conditions that are required so that individual judges will be empowered to negate external influence and control, and to exercise their individual liberty and thought of action when they assume responsibility for determining judicial outcomes, we can highlight the following elements as integral to the definition of judicial independence, in line with the United Nations' Basic Principles on the Independence of the Judiciary:[51] security of conditions of service including adequate remuneration, protected pensions, guaranteed tenure (until a mandatory retirement age or the expiry of the term of office) and the promotion

---

[49] Dominic Grieve QC, 'Judicial Independence Under Threat: What is the Matter With Our Politicians', in this volume.

[50] D. Zimmerman, *The Independence of International Courts: The Adherence of the International Judiciary to a Fundamental Value of Administration of Justice* (Oxford, Hart Publishing, 2014) 51–52. The Court of Justice of the European Union places strong emphasis on the idea of negating external influence or control within hierarchical institutional structures but also vis-à-vis external bodies and other sources. See the definition that it has adopted in *Associação Sindical dos Juízes Portugueses*, C-64/16, paragraph 44, and the case law it has drawn upon when doing so: 'The concept of independence presupposes, in particular, that the body concerned exercises its judicial functions wholly autonomously, without being subject to any hierarchical constraint or subordinated to any other body and without taking orders or instructions from any source whatsoever, and that it is thus protected against external interventions or pressure liable to impair the independent judgment of its members and to influence their decisions (see, to that effect, judgments of 19 September 2006, *Wilson*, C-506/04, EU:C:2006:587, paragraph 51, and of 16 February 2017, *Margarit Panicello*, C-503/15, EU:C:2017:126, paragraph 37 and the case-law cited).'

[51] United Nations, *Bangalore principles of judicial conduct 2002*, The Bangalore Draft Code of Judicial Conduct, 2001, adopted by the Judicial Group on Strengthening Judicial Integrity, as revised at the Round Table Meeting of Chief Justices held at the Peace Palace, The Hague, November 25–26, 2002, online at: https://www.unodc.org/pdf/crime/corruption/judicial_group/Bangalore_principles.pdf (last accessed 26 January 2022).

of judges based on objective factors such as ability, integrity and experience; the selection of judges based solely on appropriate training or qualifications in law; personal immunity from civil suits in the exercise of judicial functions; the expeditious and fair processing of a charge or complaint made against a judge; the determination of disciplinary or suspension proceedings in accordance with established standards of judicial conduct; and guaranteeing judges' freedom of expression and association.[52] A key parameter of judicial independence viewed from this angle relates to who is vested with the power to determine the above conditions. The question of who selects the judges – the government or fellow judges themselves – is of paramount importance in that respect, all the more so when it concerns those at the highest echelons of the judiciary, who assume responsibility for its leadership, the setting of institutional operating conditions as well as career progression (or lack thereof) in line with these conditions.[53]

It is equally critical that in addition to securing the independence of judges as individuals ('individual judicial independence'), we are, as a society, able to safeguard what current UK Supreme Court Justice, Lady Arden, calls 'institutional judicial independence'. This 'involves the notion that respect is given for the judiciary as an institution'.[54] The distinction between individual and judicial independence is not easily discernible as the two concepts are closely interlinked. Failure to provide security of service, for instance, will not only affect judges as individuals but also, inevitably, the integrity of the judiciary as an institution. Still, Lady Arden's specific reference to 'institutional judicial independence' is invaluable in that it

---

[52] 'Basic Principles on the Independence of the Judiciary, Adopted by the Seventh United Nations Congress on the Prevention of Crime and the Treatment of Offenders held at Milan from 26 August to 6 September 1985 and endorsed by General Assembly resolutions 40/32 of 29 November 1985 and 40/146 of 13 December 1985', online at: https://www.ohchr.org/en/professionalinterest/pages/indepe ndencejudiciary.aspx (last accessed 26 January 2022). See generally M. de S.-O.-l'E. Lasser, 'Judicial Appointments, Judicial Independence and the European High Courts' in T. Perišin and S. Rodin, *The Transformation or Reconstitution of Europe: The Critical Legal Studies Perspective on the Role of the Courts in the European Union* (Oxford, Hart Publishing, 2018) 121; B. Bricker, 'Party Polarization and its Consequences for Judicial Power and Judicial Independence' (2017) 10 *European Journal of Legal Studies* 161; E. Hong Ying Ngai, 'Judicial Independence in Hong Kong: a Gift Left Behind from the Colonial Times?' (2017) 26 *Nottingham Law Journal* 56; L. Heuschling, 'Why Should Judges Be Independent?', pp. 201–205; R. Stevens, '*The English Judges: Their Role in the Changing Constitution* (Oxford, Hart Publishing, 2002) 76.

[53] See generally F. Wittreck, 'German Judicial Self-Government – Institutions and Constraints' (2018) 19 *German Law Journal* 1931. As the former Justice at the UK Supreme Court, Lord Hughes, comments in this regard, '[i]t is a fundamental feature of the independence of judges not just that no one can tell me what to decide, nor even thinks to try, but also that I owed no one anything at all to my appointment. In our system, the appointment of judges is solely on legal merit. There is no government input into the choice'. A. Hughes, 'Making the rule of law a daily reality – from a lecture given by Master Anthony Hughes to the Singapore Academy of Law, on 12 September 2019', The Inner Temple Yearbook 2020–2021, p. 36, at p. 37, online at: https://www.innertemple.org.uk/membership-services-support/publicati ons/yearbook/ (last accessed 26 January 2022).

[54] The Rt Hon Lady Justice Arden DBE, 'Judicial Independence and Parliaments' in in K. S. Ziegler, D. Baranger and A. W. Bradley (eds), *Constitutionalism and the Role of Parliaments* (Oxford, Hart Publishing, 2007) 191.

places the onus on the executive – and relevant outside actors – to respect judicial independence, and on the judiciary to actively defend their independence vis-à-vis the executive and other external influences. 'If a reasonable, well-informed person would conclude that the judiciary had become allies of the executive branch, judicial independence was infringed', she explained.[55] The reverse is true as well. Where the executive branch attacks the judiciary simply for reaching particular outcomes that they disagree with, judicial independence is also infringed, shattering the public's confidence in the ability of courts to deliver justice. The executive must refrain from exercising influence upon the judiciary in all ways and forms, including through criticising, let alone penalising, it as an institution merely for applying the law.

Seen in this light, institutional judicial independence must also be understood as integral to the rule of law. Lord Judge makes the point graphically when he notes that judicial independence and the rule of law 'are as closely intertwined as a mutually dependent and loving couple after many years of marriage, where one simply cannot survive without the other'.[56] By acting as 'guardians of the rule of law', the judges enhance the accountability of the executive, notes Lord Judge, and he further develops the thesis with finesse by stressing that 'every exercise of political power must be accountable not only to the electorate at the ballot box, when elections take place, but also and at all times to the rule of law'.[57] In other words, the 'will of the people', expressed at the ballot box, does not supersede accountability via the rule of law. Court judgments rather 'fulfil the democratic will of the people as expressed in statutes passed by parliament', while judicial independence enables the 'democratic legitimation' of this process by offering the reassurance needed that external or improper influences play no role in determining the outcomes.[58] Or, as Lord Kerr puts it in this volume, 'in reviewing legislation, the judiciary are doing no more than it has been asked – indeed, enjoined – by Parliament to do'.[59]

We can sharpen the focus on the interplay between judicial independence and the rule of law by examining it against the backdrop of international human rights law, taking the example of the European Convention on Human Rights. As the President of the European Court of Human Rights, Judge Spano, observes:

> An efficient, impartial and independent judiciary is the cornerstone of a functioning system of democratic checks and balances. The judiciary's fundamental role in a democracy is to guarantee the very existence of the Rule of Law. In a democracy all persons and State authorities are bound by the law. Without the rule of law there can be no effective democracy. These are the constitutional cornerstones of the Convention system. They must not be destroyed or undermined [...] The principle of the rule of

---

[55] Arden, 'Judicial Independence and Parliaments' pp. 192–193.
[56] Lord Judge, *The Safest Shield: Lectures, Speeches and Essays* (Oxford, Hart Publishing, 2015) p. 273.
[57] Ibid,. p. 275.
[58] G. Sydow, 'Independence of the Judiciary in Germany' in *Constitutionalism and the Role of Parliaments*, K. S. Ziegler, D. Baranger and A. W. Bradley (eds) (Oxford, Hart Publishing, 2007) 225, 238.
[59] Lord Kerr, 'Foreword', in this volume.

law is an empty vessel without independent courts embedded within a democratic structure which protects and preserves fundamental rights… Without independent judges, the
Convention system cannot function.[60]

These accounts forge an important link between defining judicial independence and
understanding why it matters.

Why judicial independence matters

Judicial independence is integral to achieving the rule of law. The complex idea of
the rule of law can be reduced to very simple propositions that boil down to having a
law that determines relationships and dealings between individuals and a system that
ensures that this law is applied when a dispute arises.[61] In legal and political systems
determined by the rule of law

[y]ou need not only laws, but lawyers. You need practitioners who represent those in dispute. You need mediators and arbitrators. And you need judges. And all of these must be
independent and observe the highest standards […] [W]hat the rule of law requires is a
law dispassionately and independently applied'.[62]

Put differently, judicial independence matters as a *sine qua non* of the rule of law
and, ultimately, as a *sine qua non* of liberal democracy in view of the fact that '[t]he
rule of law is by international consensus central to what we regard as a democratic
state'.[63] Take judicial independence out of the equation and we immediately undermine the foundations of the legal system, and put liberal democracy at risk, at our
own peril.[64] As Stephen Skinner observes in this volume, the 'apparent crisis of
liberal democracy and the separation of powers [is] also a crisis of the rule of law',
and it 'can pave the way for an authoritarianism that will most probably entrench
itself further if unopposed and could lead to something more extreme'.[65]

Following this line of argument, while pausing for a moment to reflect on how
the rule of law also encompasses affording adequate protection to fundamental
human rights,[66] we are quickly led to observe that judicial independence is an
equally important precondition for securing human rights. Judicial independence,

---

[60] R. Spano, 'Independence of Justice and Rule of Law', Strasbourg, 9 November 2020, online at: https://
rm.coe.int/speech-by-mr-spanos-president-echr-conf-ministers-justice-09-november-/1680a04f3b (last
accessed 26 January 2022).
[61] Hughes, 'Making the rule of law a daily reality', p. 36.
[62] Hughes, 'Making the rule of law a daily reality', p. 36.
[63] Hughes, 'Making the rule of law a daily reality', p. 36.
[64] As the former president of the European Court of Human Rights, Linos Alexandre-Sicilianos, noted
in *Baka v Hungary*, 'the rule of law is hardly imaginable without an obligation on the State to offer
safeguards for the protection of judicial independence'. *Baka v Hungary*, Application No. 20261/12, 23
June 2016, concurring opinion of Judge Linos Alexandre-Sicilianos, para. 15.
[65] S. Skinner, 'Identifying Dangers to Democracy: Fascism, the Rule of Law and the Relevance of
History'.
[66] T. Bingham, *The Rule of Law* (London, Penguin Books, 2010) 66.

human rights and the rule of law are inexorably linked in states aspiring to make real the promise of 'justice for all' that underpins our liberal democratic values.[67] This can also be translated in a demand, within the separation of powers, that the executive empathises with the constitutional and institutional responsibilities that the rule of law and human rights generate for courts and judges, who may therefore 'have to take a different line from that of any parliament'.[68] The maintenance of the rule of law and enforcement of human rights (against the wishes of the executive or Parliament if need be) is the courts' 'primary function', and only 'courts usually have authority to pronounce finally and authoritatively on the meaning and effect of [human] rights'.[69] Since '[t]heir independence from the political arena [is what] gives them [this special authority]',[70] attacks on judicial independence can undermine their ability to pronounce finally and authoritatively on human rights. This demand on the executive can be made with even greater urgency when we consider the need to protect the fundamental rights of minorities, of the unpopular, the rights of those that great parliamentary majorities and the 'strongman' politics of our populist times will frequently 'other' and dismiss. An independent judiciary, freed from the executive's pressure and critique, may be their only hope, 'the best solution',[71] even if there will still always be substantial obstacles to overcome in the path to achieving equality before the law, especially if we understand law – from the viewpoint of critical legal studies – as an inherently conservative force, developing within societies that are often conditioned to oppose reform in the pursuit of social justice.

Judicial independence can therefore be seen as an important enabler for effecting human rights protection, but it is also a fundamental human right itself. It is an integral part of Article 6 of the European Convention on Human Rights, for instance, as the Court's very comprehensive jurisprudence in this area clearly illustrates.[72] In interpreting Article 6, 'the Court has repeatedly insisted, for more than thirty years, that a court must be independent both of the parties and of the executive', drawing

---

[67] As the Commissioner for Human Rights at the Council of Europe, Dunja Mijatović, has put it, 'European citizens should hold their governments to account when these take measures that undermine the rule of law, democracy and human rights. When the rule of law [l'État de droit] and the independence of judges become fragile, it is also human rights that are put in danger'. D. Mijatović, 'L'indépendance des juges et de la justice menacée', 3 September 2019, online at: https://www.coe.int/en/web/commissioner/blog/-/asset_publisher/xZ32OPEoxOkq/content/the-independence-of-judges-and-the-judiciary-under-threat?_101_INSTANCE_xZ32OPEoxOkq_languageId=fr_FR (last accessed 26 January 2022).

[68] D. Feldman, 'Democracy, Law, and Human Rights: Politics as Challenge and Opportunity' in M. Hunt, H. J. Hooper and P. Yowell (eds), *Parliaments and Human Rights: Redressing the Democratic Deficit* (Oxford, Hart Publishing, 2015) 95, p. 111.

[69] Feldman, 'Democracy, Law, and Human Rights: Politics as Challenge and Opportunity' p. 111.

[70] Feldman, 'Democracy, Law, and Human Rights: Politics as Challenge and Opportunity' p. 111.

[71] A. Barak, *The Judge in a Democracy* (Princeton University Press, 2006). See also Alan Paterson who elaborates on Barak's point about the judiciary as the 'best solution'. A. Paterson, *Final Judgment: The Last Law Lords and the Supreme Court* (Oxford, Hart Publishing, 2013) 307.

[72] D. Zimmerman, *The Independence of International Courts: The Adherence of the International Judiciary to a Fundamental Value of Administration of Justice* (Oxford, Hart Publishing, 2014) 425.

on elements of personal judicial independence (relating to appointment and term of office, for instance), but also on 'the existence of guarantees against outside pressures' as well as the need to guarantee the 'appearance of independence'.[73] To move from the Council of Europe across to the EU, judicial independence – conceived as a fundamental human right – occupies an equally central position in the EU Charter of Fundamental Rights. Article 47 of the Charter, which guarantees the right to 'an independent and impartial tribunal', has, in recent years, had a seismic effect in enabling human rights protections to shield European citizens – though not always successfully – against systemic attacks on the rule of law.[74]

The importance of these considerations is amplified when examined against the current socio-political context, domestically and internationally. To take the UK as a key illustration of developments at the domestic level, it is instructive to note again that there has 'been a sea change in the role of the judges' in recent decades, and that this has gone hand in hand with a (reverse) gradual loss of influence suffered by other actors (including local government, the civil service, the unions, academia, the Church and the armed forces)[75]. As the judicial role – or so-called judicial power – increases, so does the need to guarantee the judiciary's independence; there is simply much more that is at stake, including the state of human rights, with the judiciary having become gatekeepers for their protection. It is, of course, often objected that giving the executive greater control should be the direct effect of the judiciary's accumulation of wider power. This would perhaps be a convincing argument if the concern about 'judicial power' was followed by a consideration of alternative constitutional 'checks and balances' and other mechanisms for ensuring that the executive can be held to account, including potentially reviving some of the older protections mentioned above. But this is clearly not the case, as evidenced by the fact that attacks on judicial independence run parallel to attacks on the legitimacy of other constitutional safeguards, administrative law or human rights (and human rights actors) as acceptable limitations on executive power.

On the international plane, it is likewise doubtless true that there is an urgent need to protect judicial independence. In the context of dealing with the Covid pandemic, we have seen the proliferation of 'derogations, restrictions and suspensions of fundamental rights, including changes to the distribution of functions and powers among different organs of the state'.[76] These have placed the judiciary 'at

---

[73] *Baka v Hungary*, Application No. 20261/12, 23 June 2016, concurring opinion of Judge Linos Alexandre-Sicilianos, para. 2.
[74] For example, the right to 'an independent and impartial tribunal' has, in recent years, become the litmus test in the jurisprudence of the Court of Justice of the European Union in relation to determining the compatibility of European Arrest Warrant proceedings with fundamental human rights and the rule of law. See, notably, *Aranyosi and Căldăraru v Generalstaatsanwaltschaft Bremen*, joined cases C-404/15 and C-659/15 PPU, 5 April 2016 (Grand Chamber); Justice for Minister and Equality (LM), C-216-18 PPU, 25 July 2018 (Grand Chamber).
[75] R. Stevens, '*The English Judges: Their Role in the Changing Constitution* (Oxford, Hart Publishing, 2002), p. 139.
[76] Council of Europe, Report by the Secretary General, 'State of Democracy, Human Rights and the Rule of Law', May 2021, p. 15.

the forefront of the efforts to fight against the pandemic, while preserving the fundamental freedoms and protecting the most disadvantaged members of society'.[77] In the pessimistic scenario that this global pandemic is seen as a harbinger of what may come, in relation to the climate crisis or future global pandemics, for instance, both in terms of future threats and potential authoritarian – or pseudo-democratic – responses to them, it becomes even more important to equip our judiciaries with the liberal democratic tools required to deal with such crisis. Here we can look back (to historic examples where we have dealt with exigent circumstances and the law of exception) to look forward; John Jackson's analysis of how the UK negotiated the challenging terrain of guaranteeing judicial independence while fighting terrorist violence for over 50 years allows us to do so.[78]

Věra Jourová is right to remind us that 'we were naive in the past' to think that 'the rule of law principle is there forever; that it will work without any problems; that it is automatic, some kind of Perpetuum mobile; that fundamental rights will be always respected everywhere; that the protection of minorities will be in place everywhere'.[79] They are not, and we must enable the judiciary to protect them.

Conditions for addressing contemporary challenges to judicial independence

With a forward-looking lens, the identification and analysis of challenges to judicial independence needs to follow through to a reflection on the conditions that can help us effectively address contemporary challenges to judicial independence. '[F]ormal, legal or *de jure* [protections of judicial] independence', to speak like Judge Robert Spano,[80] constitute the obvious starting point. The first observation that can be made from this angle concerns an apparent intensification of the efforts that the international community has undertaken in recent decades to prevent attacks upon judicial independence. These rely on a variety of formal tools, including formal legal obligations such as those stemming from international human rights conventions and transnational law (and the international court jurisprudence that gives them effect), but also tools that are provided by soft-law instruments as well as political commitments generated in the context of international action plans

---

[77] Council of Europe, Report by the Secretary General, 'State of Democracy, Human Rights and the Rule of Law', p. 15.

[78] J. Jackson, 'Judicial Independence and Countering Terrorism in the UK', in this volume.

[79] S. Zsiros, 'European Commission widens its horizons in crackdown on corruption and abuse of law' (interview with Věra Jourová, Vice President of the European Commission for Values and Transparency), *Euronews*, 2 October 2020, online at: https://www.euronews.com/2020/10/02/european-commission-widens-its-horizons-in-crackdown-on-corruption-and-abuse-of-law (last accessed 26 January 2022).

[80] R. Spano, 'Independence of Justice and Rule of Law', Strasbourg, 9 November 2020, online at: https://rm.coe.int/speech-by-mr-spanos-president-echr-conf-ministers-justice-09-november-/1680a04f3b (last accessed 26 January 2022).

and dialogue taking place in intergovernmental committees.[81] Then there are less formal instruments that may nonetheless provide quasi-legal or *de jure* protection; the example from the United States of conventions ('unwritten rules of political behaviour') acting as 'a super-protection for judicial independence, a protection that works over and above legal rules' offers a good illustration.[82]

Possible solutions to threats to judicial independence must be conceptualised even more broadly and creatively if we are to avoid the perpetual risk of empty rhetoric, or worse, the practice of using law to give initiatives that undermine the judiciary's independence a veneer of constitutionality and compliance with human rights. Ensuring that healthy budgets and appropriate working conditions are put in place, including adequate remuneration and realistic workloads for our judges, can function as an equally, if not more, effective guarantee than legal and constitutional protections, for instance.[83] To have a chance at achieving more than incremental change and making true the normative promise of judicial independence, we need to adopt a holistic approach that will require the different branches in the separation of powers to look into the mirror and confront the institutional dilemmas they may be faced with. The process will inevitably have to start with thinking more deeply about who threatens judicial independence and why, and what conditions may be further aggravating these threats (or reducing their force instead).

In that regard, it is naturally interesting to correlate threats to judicial independence with political theories that attempt to explain why political actors would ever willingly accept restrictions on their own power by ceding control of particular

[81] Council of Europe, Report by the Secretary General, 'State of Democracy, Human Rights and the Rule of Law', May 2021, p. 15, online at: https://www.coe.int/en/web/secretary-general/report-2021#page-0 (last accessed 26 January 2022). The Report takes the examples of the ECHR, Recommendation CM/Rec(2010)12 of the Committee of Ministers 'Judges: independence, efficiency and responsibilities' and the Council of Europe Plan of Action on Strengthening Judicial Independence and Impartiality (Sofia Action Plan).

[82] T. L. Grove, 'The Origins (and Fragility) of Judicial Independence' (2018) 71 *Vanderbilt Law Review* 465, 539–540.

[83] G. Gee, R. Hazell, K. Malleson and P. O'Brien, *The Politics of Judicial Independence in the United Kingdom's Changing Constitution* (Cambridge, Cambridge University Press, 2015). See also the decision of the Court of Justice of the European Union in *Associação Sindical dos Juízes Portugueses*, C-64/16, para 44, where the Court stressed that 'the receipt by [members of the judiciary] of a level of remuneration commensurate with the importance of the functions they carry out constitutes a guarantee essential to judicial independence'. It is of particular interest that the case concerned the temporary reduction in the amount of remuneration paid to members of the judiciary (in specific courts), in the context of the Portuguese State's budgetary policy guidelines that had been adopted as part of the austerity effort dictated by the need to reduce Portugal's excessive budget deficit. The Court concluded that the salary-reduction measures at issue could not be considered to impair judicial independence, as they were 'in the nature of general measures seeking a contribution from all members of the national public administration' and were temporary in nature. Its decision nonetheless has important ramifications for addressing 'remuneration' as an essential practical guarantee of judicial independence. See also L. Pech and D. Kochenov, 'Respect for the Rule of Law in the Case Law of the European Court of Justice: A Casebook Overview of Key Judgments since the Portuguese Judges Case', online at: https://papers.ssrn.com/sol3/papers.cfm?abstract_id=3850308 (last accessed 26 January 2022).

areas of activity to courts in the first place. Explanations of potential benefits to politicians include 'having independent courts solve politically difficult or sensitive policy issues' or relying on courts as effective mechanisms for enforcing the incomplete political bargains – between opposing parties – that are reflected in legislation, particularly when this engages with controversial issues.[84] In other words, independent courts allow politicians to share or even shift responsibility to the judiciary for decision-making in specific matters. To stay with this point, we can reframe the wider issue as one where the political establishment simply tolerates judicial power to the extent that it anticipates being able to draw practical advantages from doing so. 'Insurance' or 'electoral market' political theories are of particular interest in this respect. According to these theories, the extent to which political parties might be open to accepting a strong and independent judiciary depends on their ability to predict their political future; the more confident they are that they will dominate future elections, the more starkly opposed to judicial independence – and the restrictions that stem from it upon their power – they are likely to become. The reverse will happen where there is great polarisation in the political system, making political parties turn their attention to strengthening 'minoritarian institutions and rules – notably, judicial review and judicial independence-enhancing rules – that will help them to maintain a check on government when they are out of power'.[85] This may help explain why the rise of authoritarian regimes or populist politicians and parties, coupled with attacks on constitutional checks and balances that may help cement them in power, goes hand in hand with attacks on judicial independence, particularly in the context of illiberal democracies that weaponise majoritarian interests, while portraying judicial interpretations that protect the rights of minorities as 'woke' and 'elitist', and as defiant of the 'will of the people'. Jan-Werner Müller's chapter in this volume offers many examples that concentrate on right-wing populists and validate the hypothesis that 'attacks on judicial independence are indeed part of the logic of populism itself'.[86]

Liberal democracy is not immune to such crude political calculations, of course, as the political scientist Will Davies demonstrates, taking Brexit and Trump as case studies. He argues that 2016 was a rupture with the idea that some frameworks and institutions, such as 'the rule of law' or 'respect for the integrity of democratic processes', could continue to be seen as sitting outside politics, providing some

---

[84] B. Bricker, 'Party Polarization and Its Consequences for Judicial Power and Judicial Independence' (2017) 10 *European Journal of Legal Studies* 161, and reference there to the following: J. Rogers, 'Information and Judicial Review: A Signaling Game of Legislative-Judicial Interaction' (2001) 45 *American Journal of Political Science* 84; M. Graber, 'The Non-Majoritarian Difficulty' (1993) 7 *Studies in American Political Development* 35; W. Landes and R. Posner, 'The Independent Judiciary in an Interest-Group Perspective' (1975) 18 *Journal of Law & Economics* 875.

[85] B. Bricker, 'Party Polarization and Its Consequences for Judicial Power and Judicial Independence' (2017) 10 *European Journal of Legal Studies* 161, 162–163.

[86] Jan-Werner Müller, '"Enemies of the People": Populism's Threat to Independent Judiciaries' and Stephen Skinner, 'Identifying Dangers to Democracy: Fascism, the Rule of Law and the Relevance of History', both in this volume.

'rules of the game within which disagreements and disputes take place'.[87] Rather it was now obvious that 'there was huge political capital to be gained' from 'directly confronting and challenging' and from 'publicly belittling or even trivialising' key legal and political institutions 'whose authority depends on the idea that they are, maybe not beyond rebuke, but somehow external to the field of battle of politics'.[88]

It is from within the political framework of liberal democracy that we can also ask whether the concerns of the executive over increasing 'judicial power' could somehow be assuaged by affording parliaments a more substantial role. The argument has particular appeal when developed in connection with critiques of human rights that concentrate on the democratic deficit of the courts that put them in action and give them effect. The proposed solution is to find ways to empower politicians to play a more active role in the parliamentary processes that shape these rights, to ensure politicians 'take ownership of human rights norms and begin to feel that they have a meaningful role to play in discussing and debating what those norms require law and policy to look like'; this can help fill the democratic deficit gap.[89]

Similar questions can be asked about the role other democratic institutions – and the body politic more broadly – can play in safeguarding judicial independence. There is little that can be achieved solely through legislative reform unless it is followed by a shift in cultural attitudes towards the judiciary. So, our media has to change; it has caused significant damage upon the judiciary in recent years. But change is clearly not around the corner, nor do we seem to have a realistic plan about how to bring it about. As Julian Petley meticulously demonstrates in this volume, focusing on the example of the UK, 'the majority of the national press is far more likely to endorse [the government's] fetishization of executive power than it is to answer [calls] to protect the independence of the judiciary'.[90]

And the public can no longer stay silent, observe from the sidelines; judicial independence is integral to the rule of law and *our* human rights, and we must actively protect it. But how far can we go in attempting to do so? Jan-Werner Müller's chapter goes so far as to examine the hypothesis of '[m]echanical tit-for-tat retaliation' to populist action undermining the judiciary, but only to explain that this 'should be resisted in favour of what can be called democracy-preserving or even democracy-enhancing reciprocity: measures the other side won't like, but that can be justified with genuine democratic principles'.[91] Müller's chapter equally usefully points out how judges and legal officials forced to retire, or in other ways struck out of courts and democratic institutions by the populists, can assist with efforts to protect or restore judicial independence such as by forming 'parallel,

[87] RSA, *How did we get here? With William Davies*, 24 September 2020, online at: https://www.facebook.com/rsaeventsofficial/videos/vb.1243843545637571/353700195984314/?type=3&theater (last accessed 26 January 2022).
[88] RSA, *How did we get here? With William Davies*, 24 September 2020.
[89] Hunt, 'Introduction', p. 12.
[90] Julian Petley, '"Enemies of the People": Article 50, the Press and Anti-Juridicalism', in this volume.
[91] Jan-Werner Müller, '"Enemies of the People": Populism's Threat to Independent Judiciaries', in this volume.

independent institution[s]' that will educate the public and generate a 'bottom-up construction to oppose the power of argument to the arbitrariness of power'.

The judiciary must also proactively seek to transform itself. Becoming more representative of the people it has the fundamental mission to protect should become a key priority.[92] As Feilzer's chapter notes in relation to the UK, progress in this area 'is painfully slow in reaching the most senior levels of the judicial system', while, from a reverse angle, 'there is growing disproportionality in the ethnic make-up of the youth custodial population and the wider prison population across the whole criminal justice system'.[93] The need for the judiciary to modernise and transform itself could not be more urgent at the time of the Black Lives Matter movement and the wider struggle for equality and racial justice.

Finding the courage to show its 'human, passionate' nature, which demystifies the classic narrative of the dispassionate judge, could be another priority for the judiciary. By admitting to 'the subtle emotional processes and emotion management that guide the logical application of abstract principles as well as the everyday interaction of legal proceedings', the judiciary can future-proof; it will be enabled to distance itself from the 'populist portrayal of judges as detached from the reality of everyday life and to the idea of AI replacing judges in legal decision-making', as Moa Bladini and Stina Bergman Blix show in our volume.[94] In his wide-reaching keynote speech in our conference, and epilogue in this volume, the former Lord Chief Justice, Lord Thomas, similarly stressed that we need dialogue and openness from the part of the judiciary to enhance the public's understanding of judicial independence. He then went on to elaborate on the nine areas we need to concentrate on to achieve this: efficiency, governance, modernisation, court administration, judicial appointments, public accountability, communications, community engagement and international engagement.[95]

We have come to conclude this chapter by highlighting only some of the conditions that are required for addressing challenges to judicial independence, both future and contemporary, having thus set the scene for the thought-provoking contributions that follow.

---

[92] L. Thomas QC, 'What does it mean to be anti-racist in a profession full of privileged people', Inner Temple's Reader's lecture, 15 February 2021, online at: https://www.innertemple.org.uk/education/education-resources/readers-lecture-series/what-does-it-mean-to-be-anti-racist-in-a-profession-full-of-privileged-people/ (last accessed 26 January 2022).

[93] Martina Y. Feilzer, 'Understanding Judicial Independence in the Age of Outrage', in this volume.

[94] Moa Bladini and Stina Bergman Blix, 'The Judge Under Pressure: Fostering Objectivity by Abandoning the Myth of Dispassion', in this volume.

[95] Lord Thomas, 'Epilogue: Judicial Independence: The Need for Constant Vigilance', in this volume.

Part I

Identifying and Understanding Threats to Judicial Independence

1

'Enemies of the People': Populism's Threat to Independent Judiciaries

JAN-WERNER MÜLLER

Anything can happen ... If we do not protect democracy, democracy will not protect us.
Aharon Barak

Is POPULISM PER se connected to what the editors call 'anti-juridicalism'?[1] Some recent pronouncements by actors widely considered right-wing populists could certainly make one think so: János Lázár, one of Hungarian Prime Minister Viktor Orbán's right-hand men, speaks of a 'majoritarian democracy ... where there is no need for democratic brakes and counterweights'; Polish Justice Minister Zbigniew Ziobro justifies his decapitation of the Polish judiciary by saying that Poland is 'a democracy ... not a court-ocracy'; and former Austrian Interior Minister Herbert Kickl stipulates that 'law has to follow politics' (not to speak of Donald Trump's claim that a judge would not give him a 'fair shake' because of his Mexican ancestors).[2]

I shall suggest that attacks on judicial independence are indeed part of the logic of populism itself, as I understand that term.[3] Populists claim that only they represent the people, with the consequence that whatever is (or can be construed as)

---

[1] D. Giannoulopoulos and Y. McDermott, 'Introduction', in this volume.
[2] Quotations from W. Freeman, 'Colonization, Duplication, Evasion: The Institutional Strategies of Autocratic Legalism' (paper on file with author); BBC News, 'Poland MPs Back Controversial Judiciary Bill, 15 July 2017, online at: https://www.bbc.com/news/world-europe-40617406; Z. Byron Wolf, 'Trump's attacks on Judge Curiel are still jarring to read', 28 February 2018, online at: https://www.cnn.com/2018/02/27/politics/judge-curiel-trump-border-wall/index.html (last accessed 26 January 2022).
[3] This chapter is mainly about the consequences of populism, not its causes. A critique of populism does not amount to saying that citizens never have legitimate reasons to vote for parties that can be described as populist; it also does not follow from the fact that populist leaders are antipluralists with clear authoritarian tendencies that all those how vote for them are necessarily committed antipluralists. I underline what should be an obvious point in response to a widespread claim that liberal democrats can merely engage in empty 'moralizing' when confronted with the supposed 'populist wave'.

Proceedings of the British Academy, **250**, 27–44, © The British Academy 2022.

criticism from non-elected, independent institutions gets dismissed as illegitimate (this applies to free media as much as the judiciary). However, this should not lead us to expect that populists in power will necessarily create situations characterised by total legal chaos, or even just officially dispense with constitutional courts and a nominal commitment to the independence of judges. There is, I argue, a particular populist art of governance that we still underestimate at our own cost; that art includes various ways of faking constitutionalism – which is to say: a façade of judicial institutions co-exists with populists in fact maximising opportunities to exercise arbitrary power in the name of a homogeneous, virtuous people.

At the same time, populists' attacks on judges should not make us fall into the trap of simply asserting judicial independence as if it were a self-evident (or even self-executing) ideal. Judicial independence is a contested normative concept;[4] genuine tensions arise between imperatives of independence and accountability. Especially in light of a worrying trend by – in the broadest sense – liberals to sing the praises of technocracy and 'gatekeeping' (as in: keeping the great unwashed out of politics), it is important to respond to attacks on judicial independence in a way that does not close off room for democratic contestation. Put differently, one should not deny that there is plenty of space for reasonable disagreement, and outright political conflict, about what 'independence' should mean in practice:[5] judicial autonomy is not the same as judicial supremacy, and much of the critique of judicial power put forward in recent years by defenders of 'political constitutionalism' can be debated *without* critics of judicial review having to become in any meaningful sense 'populists'.[6]

What is populism anyway?

Populism, one often hears, is about being critical with elites or feeling angry towards the establishment. If that is indeed the case, then it seems only too obvious why judges would be the target of populists – for they are, of course, part of a society's elite, no matter how often they assert that 'a judge is always part of the people'.[7] But is 'criticism of elites' really all there is to populism? I submit that not everyone who criticises elites is automatically a populist. After all, any decent civics textbook would instruct us to be vigilant with the powerful; keeping a close eye on elites can in fact plausibly be seen as a sign of good democratic engagement by citizens.

---

[4] It is also a 'solution concept'. See J. Waldron, 'Is the Rule of Law an Essentially Contested Concept (In Florida)?', *Law and Philosophy*, 21 (2002), 137–64.
[5] See also G. Helmke and F. Rosenbluth, 'Regimes and the Rule of Law: Judicial Independence in Comparative Perspective', *Annual Review of Political Science*, 12 (2009), 345–66.
[6] R. Bellamy, *Political Constitutionalism* (Cambridge, Cambridge University Press, 2009), and J. Waldon, 'The Core of the Case Against Judicial Review', *Yale Law Journal*, 115 (2006), 1346–1406.
[7] A. Barak, 'A Judge on Judging: The Role of a Supreme Court in a Democracy', *Harvard Law Review*, 116 (2002), 19–162, 57.

Of course, when in opposition, populists criticise governments (and other political parties). But, crucially, they also claim something else: they assert that *they, and they alone*, represent what populists often call 'the real people' or 'the silent majority'. That might not sound so bad – an assertion about a particular representative relationship is not the same as, for instance, racism, fanatical hatred of the European Union, or a fundamental opposition to the rule of law enforced by independent judges. And yet this claiming of a monopoly – as we shall see, it is always a distinctly moral monopoly – of representing the real people has two highly detrimental consequences for democracy: first, populists denounce all other contenders for power as fundamentally illegitimate. At stake is never just a disagreement about policy or even values – which is, of course, completely normal (and, ideally, productive) in a democracy. Rather, populists immediately personalise and moralise political conflict: the others, they insist, are simply 'corrupt' and 'crooked'. These rotten characters allegedly do not work for 'the people' at all, but only for themselves (i.e., the establishment), or multinational corporations, or the EU, or some other entity disconnected from the real people. In this respect, Donald Trump's rhetoric during the 2015–2016 presidential campaign – or, for that matter, the 2020 one – were extreme cases, but his rhetoric was not really an exception. All populists, in one way or another, engage in the kind of talk we heard from Trump about Hillary Clinton and, later on, the Biden family.

Less obvious is a second consequence: populists insinuate that all citizens who do not share their ultimately symbolic construction of 'the people' and hence, logically, do not support the populists should have their status as belonging to the proper people put into doubt. Think of Nigel Farage claiming, during the night of the fateful referendum, that Brexit had been a 'victory for real people'. He implied that the 48% of British citizens who voted to stay in the EU might not be quite real – which is to say: not part of the real British people at all (or, perhaps, in the case of Farage, specifically the English people). Or think of Trump announcing at a campaign rally in May 2016: 'The most important thing is the unification of the people – because the other people don't mean anything'; or think of a Trump sycophant like Ohio representative Jim Jordan tweeting 'Americans love America. They don't want their neighbourhoods turning into San Francisco.'

Simply put: the populist decides who the real people are; and whoever does not want to be unified on the populist's terms is completely and utterly excluded – even if they happen to have a British or an American passport. Populists try to reduce all political conflict to questions of belonging. Those who disagree with them are not merely wrong (as any politician would say about their opponent); rather, they are 'unAmerican' (a term Trump kept deploying), or they are said to have 'treason in their genes' (according to Polish strongman Jarosław Kaczyński).

The crucial indicator of populism, then, is not some vague 'anti-establishment sentiment'. Criticisms of elites (including judges) may or may not be justified, but they do not automatically pose a threat to democracy; in fact, sometimes the opposite might be the case. Rather, what matters – and what is dangerous for democracy and the rule of law – is populists' anti-pluralism. They always exclude others at two levels: at the level of party politics, they present themselves as the only legitimate representatives of the people; hence, all others are at least morally excluded. And, less obviously, at the level of the people themselves, those who do not share the populists' symbolic construction of the 'real people' (and, as a consequence, do not support the populists politically) are also shut out. In sum: populism invariably involves a claim to a moral monopoly of representing the supposedly real people – and it inevitably results in what one might call a form of exclusionary identity politics.[8]

Note that I have not identified populism with any particular policy position. Today, it is often assumed that being 'anti-immigration', speaking even in favour of trade restrictions, or being profoundly anti-EU are all best described as 'populist'. I do not think we are helping our capacity for political judgment – which, after all, consists not least in making proper distinctions – if we run all these disparate phenomena together. We have much more precise concepts available to capture them: nativism, for instance, protectionism, or various degrees of Euroscepticism. Of course, there can be an elective affinity, such as between right-wing populism and the demand to close borders (after all, the pure ethnos in whose name populists speak needs to be protected and preserved) – but, in principle, policy positions and a particular representative claim about the people are two different things.[9]

Populism is also not the same as nationalism. Nationalists attribute moral significance to nationality – understood, for the most part, as a shared culture – as such. A nationalist does not have to be a populist, which is to say: they do not have to claim that they and they alone represent the people understood as a particular nation. Of course, it is not an accident that virtually all right-wing populists in our era are also nationalists: they need to provide concrete content to the notion of 'the people' in whose name they claim uniquely to be speaking. The nation is the most obvious (which is not to say: natural) way of doing so. But there are also populists who are not nationalists (or at least not primarily nationalists): think of Hugo Chávez and his successor Nicolás Maduro (clearly, there came a point during Chávez's reign when legitimate disagreement was no longer possible; those opposed to the project of 'socialism for the twenty-first century' were simply declared traitors or in some other way morally unacceptable).

Let me clear up what I consider one further widespread misunderstanding of populism (one that also has far-reaching consequences for how we think about the rule of law): conventional wisdom has it that all populists want to bring politics closer to the people or necessarily clamour for direct democracy.[10] They certainly do say that they are the only ones who care for the 'people's will'. But they are

---

[8] Which is not to say that all identity politics has to be exclusionary, let alone populist. I address the issue in my book *Fear and Freedom: For Another Liberalism* (forthcoming).

[9] For the fruitful theoretical notion of a representative claim, see M. Saward, 'The Representative Claim', *Contemporary Political Theory* 5 (2006), 297–318.

[10] It is important to disentangle direct democracy and populism not least because concerns about the latter have led to a problematic revalidation of professionals and gatekeepers on the part of liberals.

hardly interested in an open-ended, genuinely bottom-up process where citizens debate policy issues and then eventually reach their own conclusions. Rather, what populists take to be the people's 'real will' is derived from what they stipulate to be the real people – and, as explained above, for the populists, not all citizens will automatically be part of that real people. In other words, the right policy choice tends to be deduced from the symbolic construction of the real people; while a figure like Trump claims 'I am your voice', the fact is that nobody else has even really spoken or been consulted; the 'people's will' is a purely theoretical proposition.

I underline this point because the critique of populism has often included direct democracy and referenda in particular in the phenomenon of populism itself. But that is too hasty. A referendum has a very specific meaning for populists: the role of voters is just to check the right box and confirm what the populist leaders have always already been saying about the real people. These leaders do not value participation as such, they certainly do not in principle oppose the political principle of representation. Rather, they think that as long as they are not in power, we have the wrong – that is to say, corrupt and treacherous   representatives; once they are in government, criticism of representative democracy as such usually ceases. It is not an accident that nowhere have populists in power actually implemented institutional innovations that could meaningfully be described as forms of direct democracy.[11]

Note one other implication of the conceptual sketch suggested at the beginning of this chapter: populists can do significant damage to a democratic political culture even if they never enter government. After all, populist parties that do not do so well at the polls have to face an obvious contradiction: how can it be the case that the populists are the people's only morally legitimate representatives and yet fail to gain overwhelming majorities at the ballot box? Populists do not all opt for what might seem the easiest way out of this contradiction – but plenty do when they in effect suggest that one should think less of a silent majority and more of a *silenced* majority. By definition, if the majority could express itself, the populists would always already be in power – but someone or something must have prevented the majority from making its voice heard. Put differently: populists more or less subtly suggest that they did not really lose an election at all but that corrupt elites (possibly including judicial elites) were manipulating the process behind the scenes. Think again of Trump: when he left it open whether he would accept an election victory by Hillary Clinton, he effectively called into question the integrity of the US election system. Plenty of supporters understood well enough what he

---

See for instance J. Rauch and B. Wittes, 'More professionalism, less populism', online at: https://www.brookings.edu/wp-content/uploads/2017/05/more-professionalism-less-populism.pdf (last accessed 26 January 2022) and I. Shapiro and F. M. Rosenbluth, *Responsible Parties: Saving Democracy From Itself* (New Haven, Yale University Press, 2018). What this rather overlooks is that populists and authoritarians are hardly ever brought to power by 'the masses'; rather, it is elites who decide to end democracy. See N. Bermeo, *Ordinary People in Extraordinary Times: The Citizenry and the Breakdown of Democracy* (Princeton, Princeton University Press, 2003).

[11] I discount the highly manipulated, and manipulative, 'national consultations' organised periodically by the Hungarian government.

really meant: according to one survey, 70% of his followers thought that if Clinton became President, the outcome must have been 'rigged'. In 2020, Trump repeated the trick: he could not possibly lose the election; hence he falsely alleged widespread fraud.

To be sure, anyone can criticise the US election system – in fact, there is clearly plenty to criticise (campaign finance is only the most obvious pathology). And, once again, such criticisms can be a sign of good democratic engagement. What is not compatible with democracy is the populists' claim, which comes down to saying: 'Because we did not win, our system must be bad and corrupted.' In this manner, populists systematically promote conspiracy theories and undermine the trust of citizens in their institutions – and thereby damage a given political culture. And that can be true even if they never get anywhere close to the actual levers of power.

I do not suggest that all populists will necessarily resort to this strategy to explain away their failures. At the very least, though, they will be tempted to make a distinction between the *morally* and the *empirically* correct outcome of an election (think of Hungarian far-right populist Victor Orbán claiming, after losing the 2002 Hungarian elections, that 'the nation cannot be in opposition'; or remember Andrés Manuel López Obrador, arguing, after his failed bid for the Mexican presidency in 2006, that 'the victory of the right is morally impossible' and declaring himself the only 'legitimate president of Mexico').[12] In this manner, populists keep invoking an amorphous 'real people' who would have made a different political choice. For instance, the losing candidate in the 2016 presidential elections in Austria, far-right populist Norbert Hofer, claimed about the winner, the Green politician Alexander Van der Bellen, that the latter had been 'counted correctly, but not elected' (*gezählt, aber nicht gewählt*); in other words, he insinuated that his opponent had indeed received more votes – but that nevertheless he had not really been chosen (as if a real choice could somehow happen by acclamation or some other process not involving the secret ballot). As the German constitutional lawyer Christoph Möllers has put it, there is a difference between *counting* majorities and *feeling* majorities.[13] In many situations, populists will play off sentiments against numbers – not recognising that in the end, numbers, and the process of correctly counting, are all we have in a democracy. De facto, they employ a conceptual opposition proposed by Carl Schmitt in the 1920s: on the one hand, the merely 'statistical' (and mechanical, and supposedly liberal and bourgeois) counting of votes; on the other hand, an almost mystical articulation of the real people's genuine will, through acclamation or some other prima facie non-institutionalised means. As Schmitt put it:

> The unanimous opinion of one hundred million private persons is neither the will
> of the people nor public opinion. The will of the people can be expressed just as

[12] K. Bruhn, '"To hell with your corrupt institutions!": AMLO and populism in Mexico', C. Mudde and C. R. Kaltwasser (eds.), *Populism in Europe and the Americas: Threat or Corrective for democracy?* (New York, Cambridge University Press, 2012), 88–112.
[13] Personal communication.

well and perhaps better through acclamation, through something taken for granted, an obvious and unchallenged presence, than through the statistical apparatus that has been constructed with such meticulousness in the last fifty years. The stronger the power of democratic feeling, the more certain is the awareness that democracy is something other than a registration system for secret ballots. Compared to a democracy that is direct, not only in the technical sense but also in a vital sense, parliament appears an artificial machinery, produced by liberal reasoning, while dictatorial and Caesaristic methods not only can produce the acclamation of the people but can also be a direct expression of democratic substance and power.[14]

As said above, I do not mean to suggest that populists always play off the people's will against existing institutions. But they do have a permanent incentive to do so, which has led to the common perception that populism is per se somehow 'anti-institutional' or even 'anti-law' (or, variations on the same theme, anti-procedural or at least anti-positivist). Is this view plausible? To answer this question, we need to get a clearer sense of what populists generally do when in power.

The populist art of governance

There is a widespread sense – especially among liberals in the broadest meaning of that term – that populists almost by definition cannot govern. This is sometimes based on the notion that populists are all anti-elitists and that when they are in power, they themselves will have become the elite; ergo, they cannot persist with an anti-elite stance (you cannot criticise yourself in government) and hence cease to be populists. But it is also frequently asserted that all the policy ideas of populists are horrendously simplistic and that populists are, in essence, demagogues who seduce citizens with false promises. Once in office, none of the irresponsible promises can be kept (no walls will actually be built, no hugely favourable deals with the EU will be concluded). Populists will then lose electoral support – or they will 'moderate' and 'govern responsibly', and will, in effect, cease being populists. The consequence of all these scenarios in the liberal imagination is clear enough: sooner or later, the problem of populism solves itself; populism is not a sustainable proposition when it comes to actual governing.

This is a comforting view. It is also demonstrably false. For one thing, while populist parties necessarily protest against elites, this does not mean that populism in government will become self-contradictory. All failures of populists in

---

[14] C. Schmitt, *The Crisis of Parliamentary Democracy*, trans. E. Kennedy (Cambridge, MA, The MIT Press, 1988), pp. 16–17. Conversely, an opponent of Schmitt such as Hans Kelsen would insist that the will of Parliament is not the popular will, but that the popular will is in fact impossible to discern: all we can verify are election outcomes, and everything else, according to Kelsen, (in particular an organic unity of the people from which some interest above parties could be inferred) amounts to a 'metapolitical illusion' See H. Kelsen, *Vom Wesen und Wert der Demokratie* (1929, Aalen, Scientia, 1981), p. 22. Kelsen also concluded that modern democracy inevitably had to be party democracy. I have benefitted from discussions with Carlo Invernizzi on this point.

government can still be blamed on elites acting behind the scenes, whether at home or abroad (here, again, we find the not so accidental connection between populism and conspiracy theories). Many populist victors continue to behave like victims; majorities act like mistreated minorities. Hugo Chávez, for instance, would always point to the dark machinations of the opposition – that is to say, the officially deposed 'oligarchy' – and to the US trying to sabotage his 21st-century socialism. Turkish president Erdoğan would present himself as a plucky underdog; he'd forever be the street fighter from Istanbul's tough neighbourhood Kasımpaşa, bravely confronting the old, Kemalist establishment of the Turkish republic – long after he had begun to try to concentrate all political, economic and, not least, cultural power in his own hands.

More important still: we have in our era a number of glaring examples that show that not only can populists govern, they can in fact govern specifically as populists, which is to say: as actors who on a fundamental level do not accept the legitimacy of an opposition. What does that mean in practice?

Most obviously, populists will counter criticisms by independent, non-elected institutions with the claim that they have been chosen by the people – and uniquely represent them. This is by no means new: Napoleon III already threw the charge 'who elected you?' at the press and described it as an 'illegitimate rival of the public authorities' (Trump obviously went a step further when he regularly maligned the media as 'the enemy of the American people').[15] Less obvious – and in some respects novel – are other techniques that characterise the populist art of governance.

To start with, populists try to colonise or 'occupy' the state. Think of Hungary and Poland as recent examples. One of the first changes Orbán and his party Fidesz sought after coming to power in 2010 was a transformation of the civil service law so as to enable them to place loyalists in what should have been non-partisan bureaucratic positions. Both Fidesz and Jarosław Kaczyński's Law and Justice party (PiS) also immediately moved against the independence of courts. Strategies varied: they packed them, they cut back their powers, they purposefully overloaded them and they constructed entirely new parallel institutions effectively to replace existing courts.[16]

A frequent justification was that the courts ignored the genuine will of the people and that government by judges was as such illegitimate (Kaczyński diagnosed the problem of 'legal impossibilism'). Not every justification had to involve a full-frontal attack on the role of the judiciary in a democracy as such: ingenuous exercises were undertaken in selective comparative constitutionalism to prove that what populist governments were doing by way of 'reform' only

---

[15] P. Rosanvallon, *Good Government: Democracy beyond Elections*, trans. M. DeBevoise (Cambridge, MA, Harvard University Press, 2018), p. 112.
[16] For the Polish case, see the excellent volume by W. Sadurski, *Poland's Constitutional Breakdown* (New York, Oxford University Press, 2019).

emulated institutional arrangements in liberal democracies generally considered above suspicion.[17] And, sometimes, things got personal without looking somehow 'anti-institutional': populists levelled the accusation that a large number of jurists were simply leftovers from a previous, non-democratic era (in both Poland and Hungary, leaders claimed that the transition in 1989 had been incomplete and that their blatantly authoritarian moves were bringing about real democracy).[18] Whoever criticised any of these measures has been vilified as doing the bidding of the old elites or as being an outright traitor.

At the same time, populists are careful not to beak any procedural rules, if they can at all avoid it.[19] Where they have large enough majorities, they will reshape existing institutions in a nominally legal manner and insist that procedural correctness, so to speak, demonstrates that they still adhere to the rule of law. Hungary's new constitution – passed without any support from parties other than Fidesz and without a referendum – is a prime example. Where populists lack the necessary number of deputies to change the constitution, they are more likely also to violate procedural rules, as happened with PiS' attack on the Constitutional Tribunal, or engage in 'statutory anti-constitutionalism', which is to say: statutory amendments outside the regular constitution-changing process such that what should be the judicial guardian of the constitution is de facto disabled.[20]

Such a strategy to consolidate or even perpetuate power is not exclusive to populists, of course. What is special about populists is that they can undertake such state colonisation openly. Why, populists can ask indignantly, should the people not take possession of their state through their only rightful representatives? Why should those who obstruct the genuine popular will in the name of civil service neutrality or judicial independence not be purged?

Note how this strategy also implicitly reduces both civil servants and judges to the role of claiming to 'speak for the people'. 'The people' are of course understood

---

[17] As the Venice Commission asserted in response to such exercises: 'In constitutional law, perhaps even more than in other legal fields, it is necessary to take into account not only the face value of a provision, but also to examine its constitutional context. The mere fact that a provision also exists in the constitution of another country does not mean that it also "fits" into any other constitution. Each constitution is the result of balancing various powers. If a power is given to one state body, other powers need to be able to effectively control the exercise of this power. The more power an institution has, the tighter control mechanisms need to be constructed. Comparative constitutional law cannot be reduced to identifying the existence of a provision the constitution of another country to justify its democratic credentials in the constitution of one's own country. Each constitution is a complex array of checks and balances and each provision needs to be examined in view of its merits for the balance of powers as a whole'. See http://www.venice.coe.int/Newsletter/NEWSLETTER_2013_03/1_HUN_EN.html (last accessed 26 January 2022).

[18] Media authorities were also captured; the signal went out that journalists should not report in ways that violate the interests of the nation (which were of course equated with the interests of the governing party)

[19] K. L. Scheppele, 'Autocratic Legalism', *University of Chicago Law Review*, 85 (2018), 545–583.

[20] M. Ziólkowski, 'Statutory Anti-Constitutionalism', *Washington International Law Journal*, 28 (2019), 487–526.

as the current majority (or even de facto a numerical minority, as in the US and Poland, where the majority of voters opted against right-wing populist leaders); once that move has been accepted, civil servants and judges must automatically be perceived as illegitimate (whereas that move can be blocked if we deny that these actors claim to speak for the people in the first place; or assert that judges speak for the people who authorised the constitution,[21] or even that they in fact protect the legal architecture of majoritarian democracy, in particular through upholding rights constitutive of democracy as such – such as free speech, free assembly and other crucial aspects of the law of democratic elections).[22]

Populists also engage in the exchange of material and immaterial favours for mass support – in short: 'mass clientelism'. Again, such conduct is not exclusive to populists: many parties reward their clientele for turning up at the voting booths, though few would go so far as Austrian arch-populist Jörg Haider, who literally handed out hundred-euro bills to 'his people' on the streets in his Austrian state of Carinthia. What – once more – makes populists distinctive is that they can engage in such practices openly and with moral justifications: after all, for them, only some people are really *the* people and hence deserving of the support by what is rightfully their state. Without this thought, it is hard to understand how Erdoğan could have politically survived all the revelations about his regime's corruption that had started to come out in 2013.

Populist-authoritarian regimes today do not comprehensively mobilise societies in the name of grand ideological projects – that is one of the obvious differences with fascism. True, they hold up ideals of the 'real Turk', the 'real Hungarian', etc. In that sense, they do advance larger cultural projects (and the education systems and culture industries in Turkey and Hungary, for instance, have been profoundly reshaped in accordance with such collective self-representations). But these more or less coercive attempts at permanently establishing a particular form of cultural hegemony have gone hand in hand with much more mundane practices of self-enrichment, which are at least partly explained by the fact that the absence of any countervailing powers makes capturing state institutions for economic gain an irresistible proposition.

Lack of constraints makes self-dealing with a veneer of legality possible – and then in turn reinforces the need to capture the legal apparatus to avoid punishment in the future. If everything came down to ideology, populists would not have to fear losing power so much – after all, they nominally subscribe to democratic values. Crucial is the fact that populist leaders, at least in some cases, have created extended 'political families', which, mafia-style, pledge absolute loyalty in exchange for ample material reward and, crucially, protection into the indefinite

---

[21] As Barak puts it, 'the choice is not between the wishes of the people and the wishes of the judge. The choice is between two levels of the wishes of the people'. See 'A Judge on Judging', 51.

[22] See in particular the work of Richard Pildes and Stephen Gardbaum, 'Comparative Political Process Theory' (forthcoming).

future.[23] As a Hungarian observer points out, 'the main benefit of controlling a modern bureaucratic state is not the power to prosecute the innocent, it is the power to protect the guilty'.[24]

Ideology can function here partly as a reliable indicator of political-familial submission; less obviously, going along with provocations and outrageous norm-breaking by the leader becomes a litmus test for those whom one reasonably suspects of actually still believing in proper democratic standards. Norm-breaking can thus also become a way to compromise members of the political family – and their conformity in turn establishes reliability and trust (a perennial problem for the original form of the mafia).

Another less obvious aspect of such new 'mafia states' appears to be the following (I say 'appears' because what I present here is what I take to be a plaus-ible hypothesis, not a claim with a firm empirical basis at this point): as Ernst Fraenkel famously demonstrated, the Nazi state was not characterised by complete chaos and lawlessness; there were plenty of areas of life where 'arbitrary domin-ation' would have seemed an absurd description, given that so much proceeded in normal, predictable ways: marriages were concluded and annulled, business contracts were written and enforced, etc.[25] Alongside these large areas of legal nor-mality, however, there was always the threat of the 'prerogative state', which could act in completely unpredictable and of course unaccountable ways. Fraenkel coined the term 'dual state' to capture this configuration of legal normality alongside naked exercises of power.

What if today we are again faced with 'double states' – except that the realm of politics, broadly speaking, in many respects remains one of normality (plus some legal-looking manipulations), whereas one's fate in the economy is subject to arbi-trary decisions? Or perhaps not so arbitrary – for if it is indeed the case that loy-alty to the extended political family becomes crucial for any kind of economic success, then punishments are foreseeable. At the same time, these practices are not so easily detectable by outside critics, for they can always be disguised as having been dictated by economic or financial necessity.[26]

There is one further element of populist statecraft that is important to understand. Populists in power do everything they can to repress – but also in particular, mor-ally and symbolically, to delegitimate – civil society protest. Again, harassing civil society is not a practice exclusive to populists. But for them, opposition from within civil society creates a particular symbolic challenge: it potentially undermines their claim to exclusive moral representation; by definition, if the populists uniquely represent the people, people cannot be out there demonstrating against them. Hence

---

[23] By far the best analysis is provided in B. Magyar, *Post-Communist Mafia State: The Case of Hungary* (Budapest, CEU Press, 2016).

[24] Quoted in D. Frum, *Trumpocracy* (New York, Harper Collins, 2018), 53.

[25] E. Fraenkel, *The Dual State: A Contribution to the Theory of Dictatorship*, trans. E. A. Shils (New York, Oxford University Press, 2017).

[26] I am indebted to Kim Lane Scheppele for this point.

it becomes crucial to argue (and supposedly 'prove') that civil society is not civil society at all, and that what can seem like popular opposition on the streets has nothing to do with the real people. This explains why Putin, Orbán and PiS in Poland have gone out of their way to try to discredit NGOs as being controlled by outside powers (thus also the legal measure to force them to declare themselves 'foreign agents'). This also makes it so significant that, rather than pushing back against criticism, Trump simply tweeted that the millions who marched against his 'Muslim travel ban' were simply 'paid-up activists' (he repeated the charge against critics of Brett Kavanaugh, but, for good measure, also declared them to be 'evil').

If nothing else, populists have used protest to prolong and deepen the culture wars on which all populists thrive: they point to a minority of protesters that is allegedly not part of the real people – in fact, the protestors are actively betraying the homeland, according to the populists – and reassure their own supporters that they are the real, righteous people. The lesson here is of course not that citizens should refrain from going out on the streets to protest; it is only that one has to be aware of how swift and sophisticated populists are when it comes to incorporating protest into their own narratives to justify their exclusionary identity politics.

In a sense, populists try to make the unified people in whose name they had been speaking all along a reality on the ground: by silencing or discrediting those who refuse Putin and Orbán's representative claim (and, sometimes, by giving them every incentive to exit the country and thereby separate themselves from the pure people: 500,000 Hungarians have left in recent years). Thus, a PiS government or Fidesz government will not only create a PiS state or a Fidesz state – it will also seek to bring into existence a PiS people and a Fidesz people. In other words, populists create the homogeneous people in whose name they had been speaking all along: populism becomes something like a self-fulfilling prophecy.

Jurists can play an important role in these projects; as said above, it is simply not true that populists are per se opposed to institutions or that their preferred mode of doing politics is somehow lawless. They simply deploy a notion of the people such that they themselves ought not to be constrained by independent judges. Having said that: judges are undoubtedly part of an elite, and there have also been instances when 'anti-elite'-sentiments conventionally associated with populism have been mobilised – especially in contexts where charges of a liberal juristocracy can have some prima facie plausibility.[27]

It is important to understand that, at least sometimes, there is a more particular animus against liberal professions at work – a sense that has not been created by populists *ex nihilo*, but which was prepared by, for shorthand, neoliberalism. What I mean specifically is the suspicion that professionals – be they academics, doctors, lawyers or even journalists – run a kind of closed shop through requiring specialised education and training. Once inside their self-created system, they can relax; unlike

---

[27] R. Hirschl, *Towards Juristocracy: The Origins of the New Constitutionalism* (Cambridge, MA, Harvard University Press, 2007).

those engaged in business, who are mercilessly exposed to the punishments meted out by objective market mechanisms, they can get away with a lax attitude towards their own products. Margaret Thatcher evidently assumed that most professors, other than in the hard sciences, were just wasting taxpayers' money by sitting around drinking tea and spouting leftist nonsense. The turn toward simulating markets inside universities and the National Health Service – through a relentless 'audit culture' which would have given central planners in the Soviet Union the pleasure of instant recognition – was to make professionals compete, work properly and, above all, become accountable to society at large, i.e., taxpayers. The latter were assumed to think that the whole game of professionalism was probably always rigged, that 'liberal elites' simply reproduce themselves in a world where in fact there are no real standards.

When Donald Trump revealed his cabinet appointments, some observers pointed with glee to what they thought was an obvious contradiction: how could a supposed populist surround himself with corporate bosses and Wall Street figures with a combined worth of 4.3 billion dollars – all epitomising the elite, after all? What such critics failed to see was precisely that these exceptional human beings weren't professionals: their success (and 'hard work') could be measured objectively, in dollars; they were obviously competent and capable of implementing the real people's will – unlike professionals who would always end up distorting it, while lecturing everyone on how they simply knew better because, after all, they had more education.[28]

Right-wing authoritarian populists are not simply 'anti-elite'; they target particular elites – including jurists and journalists who are accused of being unfair and unbalanced. With Trump, this was always obvious; but there are more subtle ways of denying that professionals are anything special: during the pandemic, Boris Johnson, shifting to a more and more presidential style of press conference, insisted on first taking a question from 'Michelle in Cornwall', making it plain that any citizen would be as capable as journalists to ask the important questions (the question Michelle, a hotel owner, ended up asking was 'Please can we ask how tourism within the UK will be managed in the coming weeks?')

Populist constitutions?

To the extent that there is a meaningful debate about populism and constitutionalism and the rule of law, it suffers from several unfortunate characteristics: first, the discussion becomes conflated with the normative controversy about the merits of majoritarianism (and, conversely, judicial review); second, there is no clear, or even just discernible, distinction between popular constitutionalism, on the one

---

[28] See also J. C. Williams, *White Working Class: Overcoming Class Cluelessness in America* (Cambridge, MA, Harvard Business Review, 2017).

hand, and populist constitutionalism, on the other (or, to invoke a somewhat related conceptual opposition: political constitutionalism versus judicial review);[29] and third, and most important: 'populism' becomes a vague placeholder for 'civic participation' or 'social mobilization' (and, conversely, weakening of the power of judges and other elites). Quite apart from the vagueness of the concepts used (or perhaps related to this vagueness), there is the fact that debates about populism and constitutionalism – especially in the US – quickly turn emotional: accusations of elitism and 'demophobia' start to fly, and theorists are suspected of having bad 'attitudes toward the political energy of ordinary people' or accused of promoting ochlocracy (or at least juristocracy).[30]

Populists, as hopefully has become clear in this chapter, are not generally 'against institutions' as such (in fact, there is no 'politics without institutions' available anyway). They are 'against institutions' that, in their view, fail to produce the morally (as opposed to empirically) correct political outcomes deduced from their symbolic construction of the 'real people'. This happens when they are in opposition; populists in power will be fine with institutions – which is to say: *their* institutions.

As mentioned earlier, those populists who have enough power will probably seek to establish a new populist constitution – both in the sense of a new socio-political settlement and a new set of rules for the political game. It is tempting to think that with the latter they will seek a system that allows for the expression of an unconstrained popular will or somehow reinforce the direct, institutionally unmediated relationship between a leader and the proper people.

I've already suggested that things are not so simple: the claim for an unconstrained popular will is plausible for populists when they are in opposition – after all, they want to play an authentic expression of the people off against the actual results of an existing political system. In such circumstances, it is also plausible for them to say that the vox populi is one – and that checks and balances, divisions of power, etc., cannot allow the singular will of the virtuous and homogeneous people to emerge clearly.

But when in power, populists will in all likelihood be much less sceptical about constitutions as a means of creating constraints on what they interpret to be the popular will – except that the popular will has first to be ascertained by populists, then constitutionalised, and then constrained constitutionally. Or, picking up a distinction elaborated by Martin Loughlin: positive constitutionalism is followed by negative constitutionalism.[31] Populists will seek to perpetuate what they regard as the proper image of the morally pure people (the proper constitutional identity, if you will) and then constitutionalise policies that they find to conform to that image

---

[29] The main reference point for debates about popular constitutionalism in the US remains L. Kramer, *The People Themselves* (New York, Oxford University Press, 2004).

[30] R. D. Parker, '"Here the People Rule": A Constitutional Populist Manifesto', *Valparaiso University Law Review*, 27 (1993), 531–84; here 532.

[31] M. Loughlin, 'The Constitutional Imagination', *Modern Law Review*, 78 (2015), 1–25.

of the people.[32] A populist constitution will not necessarily privilege popular participation, nor will it necessarily 'constitutionalize the charisma' of a popular leader in the way Bruce Ackerman has suggested.[33]

Apart from these features – which are explained yet again by the underlying moral claims of populism – there is a more mundane goal that constitutions might achieve for populists: they can help to keep populists in power. Of course, one might say that even this goal still has a moral dimension related to the underlying populist imagination: as the only legitimate representatives of the people, populists should perpetually be in office. If the perpetuation of power becomes the aim, then there's also the possibility that populists treat the constitution as a mere façade while operating quite differently behind the façade.[34]

A recent example of 'populist constitution-making' is the constitution – officially named 'Fundamental Law' – of Hungary, which came into effect at the beginning of 2012. The constitution had been preceded by a non-binding 'national consultation' to which, according to the government, about 920,000 citizens responded.[35] The outcomes of that consultation could be freely interpreted by the constitution-makers so as to fit their general conception that the 2010 parliamentary elections had resulted in a 'revolution at the voting booths' because the winning party had received a two-thirds majority in Parliament. This 'revolution' had supposedly yielded an imperative mandate to establish what the government termed a new 'national system of cooperation' – and to write a new constitution. The preamble of the document, or 'National Avowal', ended up constitutionalising a very particular image of the Hungarian people as nationalists committed to survival in a hostile world, as good Christians, and as an ethnic group that can be clearly distinguished from minorities living with the proper Hungarians. In some of the institutional provisions – especially in the Amendments and the Transitional Provisions (which de facto had constitutional status) – the perpetuation of populists in power was clearly the goal.[36] Age limitations and qualifications for judges were introduced so as to remove professionals not in line with the governing populist party (discriminatory constitutionalism, one might say); the competences and structure of the constitutional court (the crucial check on government power before the introduction of the 'Fundamental Law') were re-engineered; and the terms of office-holders chosen by the governing party were made unusually long (nine years in many cases), with a view, it seems, to constrain future governments in line with a supposed popular

---

[32] G. J. Jacobsohn, *Constitutional Identity* (Cambridge, MA, Harvard University Press, 2010).

[33] B. Ackerman, *Revolutionary Constitutions: Charismatic Leadership and the Rule of Law* (Cambridge, MA, Harvard University Press, 2019).

[34] For the notion of a façade constitution, see G. Sartori, 'Constitutionalism: a preliminary discussion', *American Political Science Review*, 56 (1962), 853–864.

[35] R. Uitz, 'Can you tell when an illiberal democracy is in the making? An appeal to comparative constitutional scholarship from Hungary', *International Journal of Constitutional Law*, 13 (2015), 279–300, p. 286.

[36] Uitz, 'Can you tell when an illiberal democracy is in the making?, p. 286. Uitz also underlines what she calls the 'constitutional parochialism' of the Fundamental Law.

will. As Uitz has put it, the constitution-drafters displayed 'open political discretion in selecting veto players for the new constitutional regime'.[37]

We can safely say that once populist constitution-making is complete, political pluralism will be severely limited. Courts and judges will then fulfil roles that have been generally identified for nominally independent judiciaries in authoritarian regimes: they help to legitimate the regime (especially if in politically non-sensitive areas they rule against the ruling party), they assist in maintaining social control and they maintain a favourable climate for foreign investment (especially if the mafia state can successfully be separated from the parts of the economy that are open to outside companies).[38]

Concluding and further thoughts

It is not an accident that populists attack independent judiciaries. Populists claim that they and they alone represent what they often call 'the real people' or 'the silent majority'. This claim to a moral monopoly of representation leads them to contest the legitimacy of not only other political parties, but also of non-elected institutions like the media and courts. Of course, there can be situations where the latter really are corrupt or blocking large-scale social and political change for the sake of preserving the power of existing elites. But this is rather different, to put it mildly, from contemporary onslaughts on the rule of law, where constitutional courts have been effectively destroyed for the simple reason that they happened to be independent. Hence it is also important not to think that populists merely criticise judicial supremacy – a view with which plenty of theorists of democracy might be sympathetic;[39] it is also not that they merely mobilise public opinion against particular decisions (something that happened spectacularly after the German Constitutional Court's 1995 crucifix decision)[40] – rather, it is independence as such that is the problem for populists, and advocates of political constitutionalism should be seduced into thinking that populists are really their allies.

A widespread view holds that populism is a form of mass politics that does not tolerate constraints or even institutions per se. This idea (often combined with clichés from 19th-century mass psychology) is highly misleading. Populists are perfectly capable of creating their own legal institutions, even if, in many cases, their point is precisely *not* to constrain the populists but to put in place veto players for future

---

[37] Uitz, 'Can you tell when an illiberal democracy is in the making?, p. 292.

[38] T. Moustafa and T. Ginsburg, 'Introduction: The Function of Courts in Authoritarian Politics', T. Moustafa and T. Ginsburg (eds.), *Rule by Law: The Politics of Courts in Authoritarian Regimes* (Cambridge, Cambridge University Press, 2008), 1–22.

[39] See, for instance, Ryan Doerfler and Samuel Moyn, 'Democratizing the Supreme Court' (forthcoming) for a powerful argument in favour of 'disempowering' the Court, as opposed to simply expanding or reshuffling personnel.

[40] For a revealing account from a judge's point of view: D. Grimm, *Advocate of the Constitution* (Oxford, Oxford University Press, 2020).

governments. Hence it is also a mistake to associate populism with direct democracy or empowerment of ordinary citizens as such; quite the opposite: in states like Hungary, the government has tried to shrink the space for popular self-determination by writing many highly contestable policy decisions into the constitution.

One last thought in answer to the question of how jurists, and professionals more generally, might want to respond to populist attacks. As Aharon Barak has emphasised, judges are also always educators; and they can explain why the protection of fundamental rights is not some luxury benefiting liberal elites but something that actually is of most importance to the most vulnerable members of society.[41] They can also explain why 'telephone justice' will in all likelihood also turn out to be a disaster for supporters of a regime – for they will always be at the arbitrary will of whoever is more powerful.[42] And they can try to take the lead in speaking out about the corruption we see so often in populist regimes, more particularly.

When institutions like a constitutional court have been captured by ruling populists, retired judges can form a parallel, independent institution. They may take on the same cases as the hijacked judiciary and issue judgments that demonstrate what a truly autonomous body would have decided. This has been attempted in Poland, where the Constitutional Tribunal had been captured by the ruling party.[43] Here, a kind of dual state is not an imposition from above but a bottom-up construction to oppose the power of argument to the arbitrariness of power.[44]

Note, though, how all such pedagogical efforts (or even outright critique of populists) depend on a halfway intact public sphere; citizens need to be able to hear and read what still-independent judges want to say. That assumption of sufficient openness and media pluralism precisely cannot be taken for granted in populist regimes. Systematic attacks on judges might also sow distrust in the judiciary as a whole, and, as Stephen Breyer once said, 'the judicial system…floats on a sea of public opinion'.[45] That sea can turn very rough.

Which leads to a very last thought: if political play is not merely rough, but plainly unfair, the question is whether fire ought to be fought with fire: game theorists tell us that we can re-establish proper rule-following by answering every tat with a tit – except that responding to unfairness with unfairness might lead to a downward spiral of norms violations; fighting fire with fire could burn down the house as a whole.

It's crucial to realise that not all norm violations in dealing with political conflict are the same. Not every invention of an insulting nickname on Twitter must

---

[41] Barak, 'A Judge on Judging', 38.

[42] 'Judicial Independence: Remarks by Justice Breyer', Georgetown Law Journal, 95 (2007), 903–7.

[43] With thanks to Tomasz Konçewicz.

[44] Obviously, there is a grey area here: not all cases have one correct decision; and in any case, not all judgments by courts in non-democracies are issued on order from the rulers (the fact that packed courts in Moscow and Budapest sometimes act like independent institutions only serves to confuse outside observers and makes it harder to discern that on the cases that really matter to Putin and Orbán, they tend to fall in line).

[45] 'Judicial Independence: Remarks by Justice Breyer', 903.

be answered with the same childishness; the best answer to suppression of our voters is not somehow keeping out partisans of the other side. Mechanical tit-for-tat retaliation – even if sometimes emotionally satisfying – should be resisted in favour of what can be called democracy-preserving or even democracy-enhancing reciprocity:[46] measures the other side won't like, but that can be justified with genuine democratic principles.[47] In the US context, think of giving statehood to DC and Puerto Rico (in whose case the injustice of 'no taxation without representation' should make sense to all American citizens).

The question is of course whether conduct that might appear to mirror that of populists – court-packing being the obvious example, or disempowering a court more generally – can ever be permissible. The answer is highly context-dependent; but it's also not just a matter of the balance of political forces. Those intent on countering populists and engaging in what might appear as norm-breaking have to be able to tie their measures back to basic democratic principles of freedom and equality; more particularly, they must succeed in making the case for judicial independence (again, not supremacy) as part of democracy as such, and then con-vincingly show that they are restoring the independence of the judiciary, not just reappropriating it for partisan purposes.

The good news is that many citizens see the point. When the Law and Justice party tried to take over the Polish Constitutional Tribunal (and then the Supreme Court), citizens came out and projected the words 'Our Court' on the judges' building; they not only listened to Chopin piano pieces but sang the constitution (with 55 people intoning different articles) in addition to the national anthem.[48] In India, the preamble was read at protest gatherings against Modi's discriminatory citizenship laws, and the recordings were shared on Twitter, YouTube and TikTok.

The bad news is that neither 'TikToking' nor 'the constitution' has achieved much at the time of writing....[49]

---

[46] Andreas Schedler, 'Democratic Reciprocity', *Journal of Political Philosophy* (forthcoming).

[47] Schedler, 'Democratic Reciprocity'.

[48] The artist Maria Górnicka made people sing the constitution onstage; the performance featured 55 people from different parts of the political spectrum. S. Baer, 'The Rule of – and Not by Any – Law. On Constitutionalism', *Current Legal Problems*, 71 (2018): 337–38.

[49] A. Getachew, 'Living Constitutions', online at: https://www.dissentmagazine.org/article/living-consti tutions. See also A. Clinton and M. Versteeg, 'Courts' Limited Ability to Protect Constitutional Rights', *University of Chicago Law Review*, 85 (2018), 293–336.

2

The Rule of Law Across the World: A System in Crisis?

SCHONA JOLLY QC

IT WAS TRULY an extraordinary month (September 2020) in which I found myself writing this chapter on the rule of law. As then Chair of the Bar Human Rights Committee of England and Wales (BHRC), my work frequently involved countries with poor records on the rule of law. As international human rights lawyers, our work is to encourage, persuade or take steps seeking to require governments to abide by their obligations to uphold international law. A state's commitment to international law is a commitment towards achieving a more peaceful, secure world order in which individual human rights and freedoms can be better realised. As the daily needs of citizens in an increasingly interdependent world – as regards the environment, trade, regulation of multinational bodies and industries, and public health – the national order cannot exist in a vacuum. The international legal order provides the framework within which requirements of accountability, certainty and transparency between states are governed. Some of these commitments are rooted in trade and commerce, while others lie in treaties created in the post-war consensus that sought a 'never again' promise to our collective humanity.

Liberal democracies often seek to demonstrate the moral and legal chasm between themselves and their authoritarian counterparts by highlighting the failure of those who refuse to abide by international law. In the turbulent year that was 2020, as China has sought to impose its will on Hong Kong while batting away serious and credible allegations of the most egregious human rights abuses in Xinjiang, or as the standoff in Belarus stripped people of their fundamental rights in broad daylight, many democratic nations have sought to make those governments accountable by requiring them to uphold international law. Where diplomacy has failed, sanctions have been imposed for the violation of human rights obligations in international treaties.[1] This becomes particularly important where avenues of

---

[1] On 29 September 2020, the UK imposed landmark sanctions on Alexander Lukashenko, his son and senior figures in the Belarusian government under the UK's new human rights sanctions regime. The

Proceedings of the British Academy, **250**, 45–64, © The British Academy 2022.

legal challenge before international courts are heavily restricted or unavailable.[2] Cynically, China itself has sought to retaliate with the language of international law when seeking to denounce those states who have challenged its authoritarian policies and clampdown in Hong Kong. Although China's claims are simply wrong, its decision to retort in this way is a revealing glimpse into a reverse acknowledgement of the moral authority behind international law, as part of the rule of law, even among seemingly the most arduous opponents.

It is into these troubled waters that extraordinary events in the United Kingdom took place in September 2020 (the time of writing). A government minister has stood up in the Houses of Parliament and stated that Britain intends to violate international law apparently in a 'very specific and limited way'[3] with respect to an international Brexit treaty with the EU. This has then been underlined through the production (and voting through) of the Internal Market Bill amidst risible attempts to defend acknowledged violations of international law by Cabinet ministers, the Attorney General, the Scottish Advocate General (until he resigned) and the Lord Chancellor himself. On its Third Reading, not one member of Britain's Conservative Party actually voted against a bill that represents a naked power grab, even as it breached the rule of law, from both a domestic[4] and an international perspective. It has generated a predictably strong reaction,[5] a formal legal response from the European Commission and, at the time of writing, uncertainty about the outcome of this storm.[6]

Britain historically has played a very significant role in the founding and development of rule of law principles. In Tom Bingham's seminal work on the rule of law, his eighth and final principle as to the foundation for the rule of law is that it requires compliance by the state with its obligations in international law as in national law. This was wryly noted in a letter from the House of Lords Constitution Committee[7]

---

sanctions 'have been imposed as part of a coordinated international approach with Canada, in a bid to uphold democratic values and put pressure on those responsible for repression.' See Press Release, 'Belarus: UK sanctions 8 members of regime, including Alexander Lukashenko', 29 September 2020, online at: https://www.gov.uk/government/news/belarus-uk-sanctions-eight-members-of-regime-includ ing-alexander-lukashenko (last accessed 26 January 2022).

[2] The Bar Human Rights Committee of England and Wales called for the UK to apply sanctions in respect of Xinjiang under the Global Human Rights sanctions programme in July 2020. At the time of writing, however, the FCDO has not yet implemented any such action.

[3] BBC News, 'Northern Ireland Secretary admits new bill will "break international law"', 8 September 2020, online at: https://www.bbc.co.uk/news/uk-politics-54073836 (last accessed 26 January 2022).

[4] R. Cormacain, 'The United Kingdom Internal Market Bill and Breach of Domestic Law', *UK Const. L. Blog*, 23 September 2020.

[5] M. Savage and T. Helm, 'Top Lawyers slam Suella Braverman for wrecking UK's reputation', *Guardian*, 12 September 2020, online at: https://www.theguardian.com/politics/2020/sep/12/top-lawy ers-slam-suella-braverman-for-wrecking-uks-reputation (last accessed 26 January 2022).

[6] Editors' note: a joint statement by the co-chairs of the EU-UK Joint Committee on 8 December 2020 confirmed that there had been agreement on all outstanding issues relating to implementation of the Withdrawal Agreement. This included an agreement by the UK to withdraw the controversial rule of law provisions (clauses 44, 45 and 47) in the Internal Market Bill. See Joint statement by the co-chairs of the EU-UK Joint Committee, 8 December 2020, online at: https://ec.europa.eu/commission/presscor ner/detail/en/STATEMENT_20_2346 (last accessed 26 January 2022).

[7] Online at: https://committees.parliament.uk/publications/2514/documents/24959/default/ (last accessed 26 January 2022).

to the Lord Chancellor in the throes of this crisis. Indeed, that also is the position pursuant to the Ministerial Code, as confirmed by the Court of Appeal in 2018.[8] Yet, remarkably, Attorney General Suella Braverman has stated that the Ministerial Code is not enforceable.[9] At the time of writing, the flagrant dismissal of international law remained government policy.

This extraordinary and retrograde position was both embarrassing and damaging. The damage extended beyond its own reputation, consequence and authority. Regardless of whether the Johnson government ultimately proceeded with or achieved its mission, enormous damage has been done to Britain's ability to criticise other states for their failure or refusals to be bound by international law. It also punctured the authority of the rule of law itself, creating a moral vacuum both at home and abroad, opening the door to authoritarian states to wave airily back at criticism in the face of egregious violations of fundamental rights. It is to some of those egregious violations that I turn in this short consideration of how a weakened rule of law impacts fundamental rights in practice.

As populist governance has exploded across liberal democracies in recent years, so too has the unrelenting attack against the institutions required to ensure adherence to the rule of law. Political crisis, whether real or confected, can be exploited as cover for slippage in accountability while blurring the separation of powers. Institutions that provide checks and balances or that guard this separation of powers may be treated by a power-hungry executive as inconvenient roadblocks to be removed. Legislatures may be weakened or bypassed;[10] media organisations blacklisted, taken over or removed;[11] and civil society may be forced out from meaningful activity through, for example, rules restricting funds or the permeation of a climate of hostility and fear.[12] As all or any of these attempts are made, the role of the judiciary becomes acutely heightened. A truly independent and impartial judiciary underpins the rule of law and may pose a significant challenge for an executive determined to grab power. The courts, through an independent legal profession and judiciary, often represent the last chance for citizens who are otherwise disempowered,

---

[8] *R (Gulf Centre for Human Rights) v Prime Minister, Chancellor of the Duchy* [2018] EWCA Civ 1855.

[9] A. G. Braverman was asked questions about the Ministerial Code at the Bar Council AGM on Saturday 12 September 2020, as reported in Savage and Helm, 'Top Lawyers slam Suella Braverman for wrecking UK's reputation'.

[10] See, for example, the UK government attempt to prorogue Parliament: *R (on the application of Miller) (Appellant) v The Prime Minister (Respondent) Cherry and others (Respondents) v Advocate General for Scotland (Appellant) (Scotland)* [2019] UKSC 41.

[11] See, for example, the almost complete takeover of much of Hungary's independent media landscape. In July 2020, the editor in chief of Hungary's most widely read news site was fired, with many of its journalists quitting in response: B. Novak and M. Santora, 'Hungary's Independent Press Takes Another Blow and Reporters Quit', *New York Times*, 24 July 2020, online at: https://www.nytimes.com/2020/07/24/world/europe/hungary-poland-media-freedom-index.html (last accessed 26 January 2022).

[12] See, for example, India's targeting actions towards NGOs by targeting those in receipt of foreign aid, including well known human rights layers Indira Jaising and Anand Grover, as well as organisations such as Amnesty International whose funds have been frozen after years of threats and harassment: R. Khosla, 'By kicking Amnesty out, India is betraying its founding ideals', *Guardian*, 1 October 2020, online at: https://www.theguardian.com/commentisfree/2020/oct/01/amnesty-india-tarnish-reputation (last accessed 26 January 2022).

disadvantaged or defeated by the might and resources of the state. This remains true in democracies and authoritarian regimes alike. An attack on independent courts can never be, in that populist adage, in the name of the people. For it represents an attack on the people themselves. The result is, not infrequently, that those in power seek to undermine both the lawyers and the judicial institutions themselves.[13]

Such has been the picture, in varying degrees, from Hungary to Poland, from Trump's America to Bolsonaro's Brazil, and from India to the Philippines. Neither has Britain been immune from these challenges. The World Justice Project Rule of Law Index 2020[14] examines the state of the rule of law in 128 countries and jurisdictions by scores and rankings based on eight factors.[15] It defines the rule of law by four overarching principles, namely Constraints on Government Powers, Absence of Corruption, Open Government and Fundamental Rights. It adds Order and Security, Regulatory Enforcement, Civil Justice and Criminal Justice as additional critical tools to assess the fuller picture pertaining to the rule of law. In 2020, the United Kingdom sat at 13 in the global rankings, Hong Kong SAR ranked at 16, Hungary and India took up mid-ranking positions at 60 and 69, respectively, China sits at number 88, while floundering towards the bottom was Turkey at 107.[16]

Other eminent writers have explored the details and history of what the rule of law, as an oft-repeated yet tricky-to-pin-down concept, actually entails. In this short essay, I want to explore practically how the law itself can be weaponised as a means to weaken the rule of law, and the damaging consequences of a judiciary that lacks independence.

Weaponising the law

'For my friends anything. For my enemies, the law.'

Hungary

'Hungary today can no longer be regarded as a democracy but belongs to the growing group of hybrid regimes, sitting in the "grey zone" between democracies

---

[13] S. Jolly, 'Why the *Daily Mail* is wrong about the judiciary', *The Lawyer*, 4 November 2016, on the 'Enemies of the People' Brexit scandal, online at: https://www.thelawyer.com/daily-mail-wrong-judiciary-2/(last accessed 26 January 2022); see also Lord Thomas' comments with regard to the UK Home Office comments on 'Activist lawyers': J. Rees, 'Asylum seekers: Human rights lawyers "not political"', *BBC News*, 2 October 2020, online at: https://www.bbc.co.uk/news/uk-wales-54356083 (last accessed 26 January 2022).

[14] World Justice Project, *Rule of Law Index 2020*, online at: https://worldjusticeproject.org/sites/default/files/documents/WJP-ROLI-2020-Online_0.pdf (last accessed 26 January 2022).

[15] One obvious difficulty with these rankings is that they are not able to respond quickly to swift deteriorations as they happen on the ground.

[16] Turkey scores as follows in the global rankings: Constraints on Government Powers 124/128, Absence of Corruption 60/128, Open Government 97/128 and Fundamental Rights 124/128.

and pure autocracies.' So said Freedom House in its critical analysis of the state of the rule of law in Hungary in 2020.[17]

The year 2020 alone demonstrated how the law can be usurped by a powerful executive to override checks and balances, particularly under cover of crisis. The introduction of legislation in Hungary granting sweeping and disproportionate emergency powers as part of the response to the Covid-19 pandemic, and that effectively permitted Prime Minister Victor Orbán to rule by decree, caused alarm.[18] The measures included prison sentences for anyone deemed to be 'spreading mis-information' about Covid-19, which created fear among journalists since it was inevitably capable of hindering the accurate, independent reporting that is essential in such a crisis. Following the end of emergency measures, an omnibus bill permitted many of the emergency measures to be made permanent, including unrelated measures ending legal recognition for transgender people. Moreover, a special authorisation act was passed that allowed Orbán to continue to pass decrees in more limited circumstances. Such action came on the back of a decade in which the Fidesz Party, led by Orbán, enacted a series of reforms that have targeted the institutions providing critical checks and balances of his government, including in relation to the independence of the judiciary,[19] civil society,[20] universities and the media. Opposition parties and voices critical of the government (often referred to as 'Soros agents') have been targeted and restricted. The country, sitting within the EU, is now considered only to be 'partly free' by Freedom Home in its 2020 analysis.[21] Alongside Poland, Hungary is clearly the subject of EU concern about the independence of the judiciary, both through long-running Article 7 procedures and through its 2020 Rule of Law report,[22] but it remains to be seen how strenuously the regional body is prepared to tackle the acute rule of law crisis in its midst.[23] In an almost classic example of seeking to weaponise the law to weaken the rule of law, Hungary and Poland announced jointly an intention to set up a separate institute to assess the rule of law in EU member states.

---

[17] Freedom House, *Nations in Transit 2020: Hungary*, online at: https://freedomhouse.org/country/hungary/nations-transit/2020 (last accessed 26 January 2022).

[18] Bar Human Rights Committee of England and Wales, letter to Viktor Orbán, 1 April 2020, online at: https://www.barhumanrights.org.uk/wp-content/uploads/2020/04/BC-BHRC-Letter-to-PM-Orban-re-emergency-powers-legislation_1-April-2020.pdf (last accessed 26 January 2022).

[19] FIDH, 'Judicial Independence (Still) Under Threat in Hungary', December 2019, online at: https://www.fidh.org/IMG/pdf/hungary_admin_court_system_brief_latest_version.docx.pdf (last accessed 26 January 2022).

[20] CJEU Article 7(1) TEU proceedings against Hungary, *Commission v Hungary (Transparency of associations)* (C-78/18).

[21] Freedom House, *Nations in Transit 2020: Hungary*.

[22] European Commission, *2020 Rule of Law Report*, 30 September 2020, online at: https://ec.europa.eu/info/publications/2020-rule-law-report-communication-and-country-chapters_en (last accessed 26 January 2022).

[23] L. Pech, K. L. Scheppele and W. Sadurski, 'Before It's Too Late: Open Letter to the President of the European Commission regarding the Rule of Law Breakdown in Poland', *VerfBlog*, 28 September 2020, online at: https://verfassungsblog.de/before-its-too-late/ (last accessed 26 January 2022).

Hong Kong

Hong Kong, designated a Special Administrative Region, has been run by a distinct set of laws and rules following the Sino-British Joint Declaration, when Britain handed over sovereignty in 1997. As part of the 'one country, two systems' policy, the Hong Kong Basic Law guarantees until 1947 freedoms that are not available to those in mainland China. The Basic Law expressly preserves the International Covenant on Civil and Political Rights (ICCPR) as applicable to the Hong Kong Special Administrative Region. It assures Hong Kong citizens of rights such as freedom of speech and of the press, and freedom of association, of assembly, of procession and of demonstration.

The rule of law has been a strong contributor to Hong Kong's economic prosperity and stability. But as Beijing's intentions and ambitions have become more daring and urgent, that same strength of law is being corrupted through its use as a political tool by Beijing in support of its aim to achieve 'territorial integrity'. Some lawyers and academics openly refer to Beijing's strategy as 'lawfare'[24] or 'abusive legalism', such that the authorities in Hong Kong and Beijing use, and abuse, the legal system as a tool to achieve their political goals.

A new National Security Law came into force on 1 July 2020 in Hong Kong that dramatically undermined the 'one country, two systems' arrangement. Imposed by Beijing without any meaningful consultation[25] and published just an hour before it came into force, the law was a textbook example of that so-called lawfare. While the language of human rights was paid lip service through the opening sections, the absence of detail in this vague and sweeping law told another story.

The national security law marked the culmination of a year in which the authorities had provoked a crisis, dramatically mishandled its response and then sought to impose order by a unilateral assertion of authority. In 2019, mass protests had been triggered by the government's proposed bill to permit extradition to mainland China. The Hong Kong government claimed that this was a necessary measure in response to a high-profile case in which a Hong Kong citizen escaped from Taiwan after allegedly murdering his pregnant girlfriend while on holiday in Taipei. Although he eventually confessed, Hong Kong was unable to prosecute him for the murder domestically because it had taken place in another jurisdiction. The proposed extradition law went far beyond what was required to 'plug loopholes in Hong Kong's overall cooperation mechanism in criminal and juridical assistance matters'.[26] The proposals created widespread alarm that judicial independence and

---

[24] See, for example, A. Dapiran, *City on Fire: The Fight for Hong Kong* (London, Scribe UK, 2020).

[25] The Hong Kong Bar Association noted the failure to meaningfully consult, adding that that the 'decanting of a mainland law affecting individual rights and obligations into the laws of Hong Kong without it passing through the Legislative Council is a constitutional novelty.'

[26] The Government of the Hong Kong Special Administrative Region, 'LCQ3: Fugitive Offenders and Mutual Legal Assistance in Criminal Matters Legislation (Amendment) Bill 2019', online at: https://www.info.gov.hk/gia/general/201905/22/P2019052200565.htm (last accessed 26 January 2022).

fundamental and fair trial rights would be compromised, and that they would be used to silence the growing democracy movement in opposition. Alongside other legal organisations, BHRC produced a detailed paper[27] concluding that the proposed amendments failed to adequately protect human rights and would 'fundamentally imperil the operation of the rule of law' because 'insofar as the proposals would introduce any human rights examination at all, they are vested in Hong Kong's Chief Executive whom, in view of her function and the nature of her appointment, would lack or appear to lack the necessary impartiality and independence to adjudicate such issues.'

The consequences of that extradition bill, and the protests that followed, have been severe. Although the administration eventually did withdraw the bill, many in Hong Kong by then had begun their own push for genuine democracy, angered by the official and police response to the protests and the intransigent response to their legitimate concerns about their fundamental rights. Although over the year of widespread protest, a minority, often extremely young, did resort to violence, police brutality was widely reported and filmed.[28] Meanwhile, the scale and power of Hong Kong's pro-democracy movement, which was registered in landslide wins during local elections, clearly alarmed Beijing.[29]

This, then, is a brief background to the imposition of the new so-called National Security Law in Hong Kong. I have described this elsewhere as an 'alarming legal and ideological takeover'.[30] Its stated aim included safeguarding the 'sovereignty, unification and territorial integrity of the People's Republic of China.' Its provisions were very broadly drafted, capturing potentially an extremely wide category of persons and which could catch almost any act of dissent. Sweeping provisions on extraterritoriality meant that this could extend theoretically to

[27] Bar Human Rights Committee et al, *Joint observations on the human rights implications of the Fugitive Offenders and Mutual Legal Assistance in Criminal Matters Legislation (Amendment) Bill 2019*, 14 June 2019, online at: http://www.barhumanrights.org.uk/wp-content/uploads/2019/06/FINAL-Joint-observations-on-the-human-rights-implications-of-the-Fugitive-Offenders-and-Mutual-Legal-Assistance-in-Criminal-Matters-Legislation-3.pdf (last accessed 26 January 2022); see also letter of Hong Kong Bar Association, 12 June 2019, to Carrie Lam, which also called for the Bill to be withdrawn.
[28] Bar Human Rights Committee of England and Wales, 'BHRC raises serious concern over reports of police brutality in Hong Kong', 13 September 2019, online at: https://www.barhumanrights.org.uk/bhrc-raises-serious-concern-over-reports-of-police-brutality-in-hong-kong/ (last accessed 26 January 2022); K. Leung, 'Hong Kong protests: police used disproportionate force and made poor decisions, says British expert who resigned from IPCC review', *South China Morning Post*, 23 May 2020, online at: https://www.scmp.com/news/hong-kong/politics/article/3085775/hong-kong-protests-police-used-disproportionate-force-and (last accessed 26 January 2022).
[29] T. Cheung, 'Hong Kong elections: pan-democrats celebrating landslide win vow to keep up pressure on city's beleaguered leader to address protesters' demands', *South China Morning Post*, 25 November 2019, online at: https://www.scmp.com/news/hong-kong/politics/article/3039306/hong-kong-elections-pan-democrats-celebrating-landslide-win (last accessed 26 January 2022).
[30] S. Jolly, 'Why Hong Kong's new national security law is a coup dressed up in statute', *Prospect magazine*, 11 July 2020, online at: https://www.prospectmagazine.co.uk/magazine/why-hong-kongs-new-national-security-law-is-a-coup-dressed-up-in-statute-carrie-lam-human-rights (last accessed 26 January 2022).

anywhere in the world. Fair trials were threatened. The law contained a warning not to make any statement or behave in a manner endangering national security that could have, or be interpreted to have, a chilling effect on the independence of the judiciary. 'National security', as in so many power grabs by democratic and authoritarian governments alike, was loosely defined to cover very wide-ranging conduct. One of the most chilling aspects of the law, provoking the same dark fears that arose out of the extradition bill itself, was that it permitted trials to take place on the mainland or permitted mainland prosecutors or courts to be used in murkily defined circumstances. The law contained the provision for secret trials and barely coded warnings aimed at defence lawyers. These are a sample of the provocations towards the fundamental rights Hong Kongers have enjoyed until now. The new law so significantly jeopardised the rule of law and fundamental rights that UN Special Rapporteurs took unprecedented action in issuing a joint call for decisive measures to protect fundamental freedoms in China, which included a call for the law to be withdrawn.[31]

There is good reason to fear that Hong Kong has moved quickly towards a ban on any political speech. The law has been invoked in political protests. Democracy movements have disbanded. Schools have been required to review their libraries, removing any books that 'possibly violate' the new law. The Office of the United Nations High Commissioner for Human Rights has expressed alarm at the arrests of protestors following the introduction of the law. The examples abound. Moreover, as the months have passed, the reality and consequences of the law were becoming clear and sinister. Chief Executive Carrie Lam and Education Secretary Kevin Yeung have stated that there is no separation of powers between the executive, legislature and judiciary, which unsurprisingly the Hong Kong Bar Association have described as 'unfounded and inconsistent with the unambiguous provisions of the Basic Law prescribing and delineating the functions of the three branches of government'.[32] The Hong Kong and Macau Affairs Office has reportedly stated that 'some people in Hong Kong are "trying to confuse the public" by advocating the concept of a separation of powers adding that their intention was to expand the power of the legislature and the judiciary, undermine the authority of the Chief Executive, reject Beijing's comprehensive jurisdiction over the SAR, and turn Hong Kong into an independent political entity'.[33] This position was not a far cry from suggesting secession, which is a crime under the national security law. Clearly, the consequences of the law were alarming.

---

[31] United Nations Office of the High Commissioner for Human Rights, *UN experts call for decisive measures to protect fundamental freedoms in China*, Geneva, 26 June 2020, online at: https://www. ohchr.org/EN/NewsEvents/Pages/DisplayNews.aspx?NewsID=26006&LangID=E (last accessed 26 January 2022).

[32] Statement of the Hong Kong Bar Association (HKBA) about the Separation of Powers Principle, 2 September 2020, online at: https://www.hkba.org/sites/default/files/20200902%20-%20HKBA%20st atement%20on%20separation%20of%20powers%20%28E%29.pdf (last accessed 26 January 2022).

[33] RTHK, 'Separation of powers talk aimed at HK independence', 7 September 2020, online at: https:// news.rthk.hk/rthk/en/component/k2/1548359-20200907.htm (last accessed 26 January 2022).

A breakdown in the rule of law impacts widely. Business dealings in a country where there is a lack of due process and legal certainty inevitably impacts business stability.[34] There are real data privacy and safeguarding of information concerns that arise from the law as well. Its passage was followed swiftly by Implementing Regulations that granted alarmingly wide police powers. These covered search, seize and freezing of assets, and such sweeping authority over the flow of information online that many of the tech giants have suspended their cooperation with the Hong Kong authorities on data processing. Ultimately, the vague and expansive wording in the law potentially left employees, clients and users all exposed.

One interesting feature woven into the new law was what might be described as a conspiracy theory. Beijing's convenient explanation for the 2019 protests was that they reflected the interfering foreign hand. It is interesting to reflect how there is a pattern of conspiracy in similar incursions around the world where authoritarian leaders seek to present their measures as a response to the interfering hand often of a foreigner (or sometimes, as in the case of Turkey's Erdoğan, 'the parallel state'). Hong Kong's new security law, then, contained an entire section on 'colluding' with 'external elements', including the crime of 'seriously disrupting the formulation and implementation of laws or policies' by the central or Hong Kong government, as well as engaging in other undefined 'hostile activities' against Beijing or Hong Kong's government. It included 'provoking by unlawful means hatred among Hong Kong residents towards the Central People's Government or the Government of the region.' The fear of the alleged 'meddling' foreign hand extended beyond states to NGOs and civil society who support the cause of democracy. New structures were empowered to 'take necessary measures to strengthen the management of and services for organs of foreign countries and international organisations'. This represented a chilling threat towards the free press[35] and appeared designed to isolate anyone working towards democracy in Hong Kong.

In a previous article, I described 'the dangerous haze of this law' as 'an invitation to capricious rule. Dark shadows have been cast over dissent, freedom of expression and the pro-democracy movement itself. The consequences are as yet unclear, and lawyers will want to fight for the city's embedded rule of law and freedoms, but the terrain looks tough ahead'.[36]

Britain has strongly spoken out against these measures, and in a welcome recognition of the dangers inherent by these steps, it has offered up to 3 million

---

[34] See the example of HSBC, caught in the crossfire of the National Security Law: K. Makortoff, 'How HSBC got caught in a geopolitical storm over Hong Kong security law', *Guardian*, 30 September 2020, online at: https://www.theguardian.com/world/2020/sep/30/how-hsbc-got-caught-in-a-geopolitical-storm-over-hong-kong-security-law (last accessed 26 January 2022).

[35] T. Grundy, 'Hong Kong press freedom assured if media give 100% guarantee they will not commit security offences, says Lam', *Hong Kong Free Press*, 7 July 2020, online at: https://hongkongfp.com/2020/07/07/hong-kong-press-freedom-assured-if-media-give-100-guarantee-they-will-not-commit-security-offences-says-lam/ (last accessed 26 January 2022).

[36] Jolly, 'Why Hong Kong's new national security law is a coup dressed up in statute'.

Hong Kong residents the opportunity to apply for citizenship. It is therefore ironic, at least, that the selfsame alleged justification of 'territorial integrity' that China invoked has been seized by Prime Minister Johnson and members of his government as an excuse for violating international law during these extraordinary times in the United Kingdom. The moral hazard created by crossing a constitutional line is not only that it becomes easier to slip away from previously unthinkable boundaries, but that it becomes a precedent that others can cite back to justify their own dishonourable or unlawful actions.

An independent judiciary

Article 14 of the ICCPR provides that 'everyone shall be entitled to a fair and public hearing by a competent, independent and impartial tribunal established by law'.

An independent and impartial judiciary is an essential feature of the rule of law. Laws are interpreted and applied by judges whose courtrooms may be the last line of defence against an unscrupulous, almighty executive. So, the tenure, discipline, suspension and removal of judges forms an important part of maintaining the independence of the judiciary.[37] The hollowing out of the judiciary is a common factor in many countries with weak rule of law. The extension of political tentacles into the judiciary may result in 'packed' courts, ensuring judgments favourable for the executive, but even where the impact is not so blatant, it may infect the quality and impartiality of decision-making among sitting judges.

Poland

Europe has not been adrift from this phenomenon. A trend of backsliding in the rule of law among some EU member states has been growing and heightened during the Covid crisis. Poland has faced a wholesale political attack on its judicial independence since 2015, when a series of crises relating to its judiciary and courts were provoked through the newly elected Law and Justice Party (PiS). Initially, the issues centred on removing Constitutional Court judges who had been appointed through the previous Parliament.[38] This was followed by a set of sham 'reforms' in 2017 proposed by PiS and then voted through by its parliamentary majority. These empowered the Minister of Justice to remove all current Supreme Court judges, retire them and then designate those judges of the Supreme Court who would remain in active service. A critical component of that new court would be to adjudicate on disciplinary proceedings against judges.

---

[37] See, further, The United Nations *Basic Principles on the Independence of the Judiciary* (1985); The International Bar Association's *Minimum Standards of Judicial Independence* (1982).
[38] See, for example, Venice Commission (2016), *Poland – Opinion on the act of the Constitutional Tribunal*, 108th plenary session, CDL-AD (2016) 026-e, Venice.

The country became the first EU member state to be subject to the EU Commission's Rule of Law Framework in January 2016,[39] initially over the issues relating to the Constitutional Tribunal. It then became subject to Article 7(1) TEU proceedings in 2017. The so-called judicial reforms were provisionally suspended twice in two separate interim orders by the Court of Justice of the European Union (CJEU) in 2018. On 8 April 2020, the CJEU[40] specified[41] that Poland must immediately suspend the application of the national provisions on the powers of the Disciplinary Chamber of the Supreme Court with regard to disciplinary cases concerning judges. Despite this being fundamental to the preservation of the rule of law, the independence of the judiciary and a function of its Treaty obligations, Poland's Disciplinary Chamber[42] failed to comply,[43] claiming that the CJEU ruling violated Polish sovereignty.

In addition, a recent spate of cases concerning the independent judiciary and the removal of judges have been communicated to the European Court of Human Rights.[44] A Dutch court has now ruled that Polish courts[45] are no longer independent from its executive and legislative branches and accordingly will no longer extradite suspects to Poland under the European Arrest Warrant.[46] The rule of law crisis continues unimpeded in Poland and there are, as yet, no sufficient signs that this serious crisis in the midst of the EU is being properly or sufficiently tackled.[47]

---

[39] L. Pech, 'Systemic Threat to the Rule of Law in Poland: What should the Commission do next?', *VerfBlog,* 31 October 2016, online at: https://verfassungsblog.de/systemic-threat-to-the-rule-of-law-in-poland-what-should-the-commission-do-next/ (last accessed 26 January 2022).

[40] *European Commission v Poland*, Case C-619/18 R, Grand Chamber, 17 December 2018.

[41] Pursuant to Article 19(1) TEU, which provides that 'Member States shall provide remedies sufficient to ensure effective legal protection in the fields covered by Union law.'

[42] 'The Disciplinary Chamber, whose establishment in 2017 has been severely criticised by the EU Commission and the Venice Commission on rule of law grounds, has been found not to constitute a court, within the meaning of both EU and Polish law, by the Labour and Social Security Chamber of the Supreme Court, by application of the European Court of Justice ruling of 19 November 2019 in Joined cases C-585/18, C624/18 and C-625/18. Notwithstanding these judgments, Polish authorities have encouraged the Disciplinary Chamber to continue to operate. As observed by the European Commission on 14 January 2020, this open disregard for the rule of law creates "a risk of irreparable damage for Polish judges" while also "increasing the chilling effect on the Polish judiciary': See further BHRC and Bar Council, Letter to Polish President of 19 March 2020.

[43] L. Pech and P. Wachowiec, '1095 Days Later: From Bad to Worse Regarding the Rule of Law in Poland (Part I)', *VerfBlog,* 13 January 2019, online at: https://verfassungsblog.de/1095-days-later-from-bad-to-worse-regarding-the-rule-of-law-in-poland-part-i/ (last accessed 26 January 2022).

[44] *Grzęda v Poland* (application no 43572/18); *Xero Flor w Polsce Sp. Z o.o. v Poland* (application No. 4907/18); *Broda and Bojara v Poland* (applications no 26691/18 and 27367/18); *Żurek v Poland* (application no 39650/18); *Sobczyńska and Others v Poland* (applications no 62765/14, 62769/14, 62772/14, 11708/18); *Reczkowicz and Others v Poland* (applications no 43447/19, 49868/19, 57511/19).

[45] Similar concerns have been raised in both Spanish and German courts: see E. Schaart and Z. Wanat, 'Dutch court: Polish judiciary no longer independent', *Politico,* 31 July 2020, online at: https://www.politico.eu/article/dutch-court-polish-judiciary-no-longer-independent/ (last accessed 26 January 2022).

[46] *Rechtbank Amsterdam*, Parketnummer 13/751021-20, 31 July 2020, online at: https://uitspraken.rechtspraak.nl/inziendocument?id=ECLI:NL:RBAMS:2020:3776 (last accessed 26 January 2022).

[47] Pech, Scheppele and Sadurski, 'Before It's Too Late: Open Letter to the President of the European Commission regarding the Rule of Law Breakdown in Poland'.

Where the judiciary is corrupted in this way, whether overtly or through an environment of fear, lawyers themselves become the last line of defence and therefore are often vulnerable to unfair attack by unscrupulous governments, or even arbitrary arrest and detention, which has been a cause for serious concern in, for example, both Egypt[48] and Turkey over recent years. What is reflected through these attacks on lawyers – including cases of arbitrary detention, enforced disappearance and charging lawyers under overly broad definitions of terrorism – is the systematic attack on judicial proceedings themselves, which are politicised by the state and then become an inherent part of an inside pattern of destruction of the rule of law itself. Having worked personally and extensively on human rights issues in both countries, there are lamentable similarities of authoritarian descent in which the law itself is held hostage and fundamental human rights become the major casualty.

Turkey

The rule of law in Turkey, and in particular the independence of the judiciary, was already significantly compromised before the attempted coup of 15 July 2016 and the subsequent two-year state of emergency imposed. A political corruption scandal in late 2013, in which allegations led directly to (then) Prime Minister Recep Tayyip Erdoğan's Cabinet and family, had resulted in a public falling-out between Erdoğan and influential Muslim preacher Fethullah Gülen, with whom the government had previously been on excellent terms.[49] The impact of this political crisis on the rule of law was described as a 'turf battle to control state institutions, [in which] the line between legal and illegal ha[d] become dangerously blurred.'[50] Following a visit to Turkey in December 2015, the International Commission of Jurists concluded:

> The problem of undue influence by the executive or other political interests on the Turkish judiciary, while complex, deep-seated, and persisting over many decades, has recently reached new levels of gravity. Since 2014, legislative and practical measures further eroding the already compromised independence of judges, prosecutors and

[48] See, for example, *Targeting the last line of Defence: Egypt's attacks against lawyers* (International Commission of Jurists and the Tahrir Institute for Middle East Policy, September 2020); D. Risley, 'Former President Morsi's Attacks on the Judiciary, and Judicial Backlash', *Egypt Justice*, 10 June 2015).

[49] H. Gurhanli, 'Political crisis and the question of rule of law in Turkey', *OpenDemocracy*, 15 January 2014, online at: https://www.opendemocracy.net/en/political-crisis-and-question-of-rule-of-law-in-turkey/ (last accessed 26 January 2022); see also, H. Barkey, 'Gul may be winner in Turkey's "mother of all battles"', *AL-Monitor*, 18 December 2013, online at: https://www.al-monitor.com/pulse/originals/2013/12/gul-winner-edrogan-battle-gulen-turkey.html (last accessed 26 January 2022).

[50] E. Peker and J. Parkinson, 'Turkish Corruption Probe Turns Into Turf Battle', *Wall Street Journal*, 8 January 2014, online at: https://www.wsj.com/articles/turkish-corruption-probe-turns-into-turf-battle-1389215758?tesla=y (last accessed 26 January 2022).

lawyers have made the rule of law increasingly fragile and unreliable…key institutions of the justice system – the judiciary, prosecution and legal profession – face serious threats to their integrity and ability to carry out their functions fairly and effectively. The judiciary, weakened by increasing government control, now appears ill-equipped to provide a check on excessive executive power through proper judicial review of its laws and actions. There are indications that these developments are already having serious consequences in allowing violations of human rights to go unaddressed by the justice system.[51]

The corruption allegations led to the public denouncing of a 'parallel state', said to be controlled by Gülen and his movement. The state of emergency declared after the attempted coup led to dramatic changes in the legal framework, and a 2017 referendum, brought forward by Erdoğan's ruling AKP party under the severe restrictions of the emergency, shifted power to a more powerful presidential system. Democratic checks and balances have been very substantially eroded, such that the Venice Commission considered that Turkey risked degeneration into 'an authoritarian presidential system'.[52]

By 2019, the position had worsened dramatically. Dunja Mijatović, the Council of Europe Commissioner for Human Rights, set out her concerns about the independence of the Turkish judiciary, which had been 'seriously eroded during the state of emergency and in its aftermath', including by way of constitutional changes regarding the Council of Judges and Prosecutors and the suspension of ordinary safeguards and procedures for the dismissal, recruitment and appointment of judges and prosecutors during the two-year state of emergency.[53] She stated that:

> the existing tendency of the Turkish judiciary to put the protection of the state above that of human rights was significantly reinforced, and the criminal process appears to often be reduced to a mere formality, especially in terrorism-related cases. In countless other cases, the judiciary is literally bypassed even for measures seriously affecting individuals' core human rights, such as certain travel restrictions or the right to practise as a lawyer.[54]

In the years following the attempted coup, my BHRC colleagues and I have carried out many trial observations in Turkey. There have been waves of dismissals in

[51] International Commission of Jurists, *Turkey: The Judicial System in Peril. A Briefing Paper* (Geneva, 2016), p. 22.

[52] *Turkey – Opinion on the amendments to the Constitution adopted by the Grand National Assembly on 21 January 2017 and to be submitted to a National Referendum on 16 April 2017*, adopted by the Venice Commission at its 110th Plenary Session (Venice, 10–11 March 2017).

[53] D. Mijatović, 'The independence of judges and the judiciary under threat', 3 September 2019, online at: https://www.coe.int/en/web/commissioner/-/the-independence-of-judges-and-the-judiciary-under-threat (last accessed 26 January 2022).

[54] D. Mijatović, 'Turkey needs to put an end to arbitrariness in the judiciary and to protect human rights defenders', 8 July 2019, online at: https://www.coe.int/en/web/commissioner/-/turkey-needs-to-put-an-end-to-arbitrariness-in-the-judiciary-and-to-protect-human-rights-defenders (last accessed 26 January 2022).

public office,[55] including judges,[56] prosecutors, academics and civil society,[57] as well as an unrelenting crackdown on any opposition, who may be those perceived to support or those portrayed as members of the Fethullahist Terrorist Organization (FETÖ). In reality, this was an illegitimate sweep of journalists,[58] the legal profession,[59] civil society activists and human rights defenders. Many of these individuals appear to have been targeted on the basis of their work, which prosecutors have sought to portray as terrorism in the course of implausible conspiracy theory contrived as indictments. We have worked closely with legal colleagues, NGOs and civil society in Turkey to seek to understand the expanding scale of the corruption of the legal system. The Constitution of Turkey[60] solemnly promises that 'no individual or body empowered to exercise this sovereignty in the name of the nation shall deviate from the liberal democracy indicated in the Constitution and the legal system instituted according to its requirements…' Notwithstanding this, and Articles 2 and 138 of the Constitution, which uphold the principles of the rule of law and an independent judiciary, the damage wrought on Turkey's purported liberal democracy by a highly politicised and increasingly inexperienced judiciary (as new judges are appointed to replace those purged) has gravely impacted on fundamental rights in Turkey, including fair trial rights; it has permitted the persecution of many individuals deemed by the government to constitute opposition, through arbitrary arrest, punitive use of pre-trial detention and conviction.

[55] US Country Reports on Human Rights Practices 2019, Turkey: 'Since the 2016 coup attempt, authorities have dismissed or suspended more than 45,000 police and military personnel and more than 130,000 civil servants, dismissed one-third of the judiciary, arrested or imprisoned more than 80,000 citizens, and closed more than 1,500 nongovernmental organizations (NGOs) on terrorism-related grounds, primarily for alleged ties to the movement of cleric Fethullah Gulen, whom the government accuses of masterminding the coup attempt, and designated by the government as the leader of the "Fethullah Terrorist Organization" (FETO)'.

[56] At least 3,673 judges and prosecutors were dismissed in the aftermath of the failed coup: *Joint submission to the Universal Periodic Review of Turkey* by ARTICLE 19, P24, PEN International, English PEN, Reporters Sans Frontiers (RSF), International Press Institute (IPI), Freemuse, European Centre for Press and Media Freedom (ECPMF), IFEX and Norsk PEN, for consideration at the 35th Session of the Working Group in January 2020 July 2019.

[57] See, for example, Taner Kılıç, Honorary Chair of Amnesty International Turkey, who was arrested in June 2017 and spent more than 14 months in pre-trial detention; see also leading civil society figure Osman Kavala, professor Yiit Aksakolu and 14 other prominent human rights defenders including journalists Can Dündar and Çidem Toker who were indicted on charges of 'attempting to overthrow the government' or 'preventing the government from doing its duty'.

[58] See, for example, the trials of Ahmet Altan (former editor of *Taraf* newspaper and writer), Nazlı Ilıcak (journalist for *Özgür Düşünce*), and Mehmet Altan (economics professor) were convicted of 'attempting to overthrow the constitutional order' (Article 309(1)) for their alleged involvement in the coup attempt.

[59] Human Rights Watch, *Lawyers on Trial: Abusive Prosecutions and Erosion of Fair Trial Rights in Turkey*, 10 April 2019, online at: https://www.hrw.org/report/2019/04/10/lawyers-trial/abusive-prosecutions-and-erosion-fair-trial-rights-turkey (last accessed 26 January 2022).

[60] Turkish Constitution, translation online at: https://global.tbmm.gov.tr/docs/constitution_en.pdf (last accessed 26 January 2022).

Executive influence over the judiciary,[61] throughout the structure and integrity of the justice system, is significant and flagrant.[62] There has been a 'wholesale dismantling of the independent judiciary'[63] by which judges have been purged, replaced with those who are perceived to support government. Punitive or retributory measures towards judges who are perceived to act against the executive are common.[64] It is not uncommon for President Erdoğan himself to comment on a matter which is *sub judice* (for example, in connection with the Gezi Park trial where Erdoğan stated, 'We will stand up against those who try to shoot this nation from inside').[65] This manifests in a climate of fear[66] that impacts not only the judges,[67] but prosecutors and lawyers, and ultimately both civil society and the broader society at large.

We have conducted detailed trial monitoring in cases of journalists and human rights defenders, and the European Court of Human Rights has also given judgment in some of those cases. Fair trial rights are now openly curtailed, and the dispensation of justice can be entirely arbitrary. Indictments are fatally flawed, often a series of conspiracies barely strung together and without the basics of supportive evidence.[68] Prosecutors are visibly disinterested, sitting together with judges and

---

[61] Following the constitutional amendments adopted in Turkey in 2017, four members of the Council of Judges and Prosecutors were appointed directly by the President of Turkey and seven members elected by Parliament 'without a procedure guaranteeing the involvement of all political parties and interests'. Both the Commissioner for Human Rights and the Venice Commission held that it did not offer adequate safeguards for the independence of the judiciary, increasing the risk of decisions and appointments being subject to political influence.

[62] Joint submission to the Universal Periodic Review of Turkey.

[63] Joint submission to the Universal Periodic Review of Turkey.

[64] See, for example, the Turkish Council of Judges and Prosecutors (CJP) investigation into the three judges of the Istanbul 30th Heavy Penal Court who, on 18 February 2020, acquitted the defendants in the 'Gezi Par trial due to a lack of evidence.

[65] A. Shaw, 'Erdogan responds to detention of leading cultural activist Osman Kavala', *The Art Newspaper*, 24 October 2017, online at: https://www.theartnewspaper.com/news/Erdoğan-responds-to-detention-of-leading-cultural-activist (last accessed 26 January 2022).

[66] In his closing statement, Ahmet Turan Alkan stated the following to the Court: 'It is no longer law but political powers which guide law. Anyone, prosecutors, judges, soldiers are all afraid of the ruling party. A public sector now afraid of each other. Government is using these arrests as a stick to beat with. You [judges] know better than me...In custodial prison, up on the 7th floor, I came across a previous judge, someone who once worked as a judge. He told me that he had been a judge on the 7th floor [in court], but now he was on the minus 7th floor in custodial prison. It is abnormal that judges or prosecutors fear suspension or arrest, or feel tense before issuing a ruling. They should stand straight, dominant, even though the political arena changes. Nobody has the right to politicise the judiciary. This is your problem.'

[67] International Commission of Jurists, 'Turkey: ICJ and IBAHRI urge Turkey's Council of Judges and Prosecutors to cease probe into Gezi Park trial judges', 28 February 2020, online at: https://www.icj.org/turkey-icj-and-ibahri-urge-turkeys-council-of-judges-and-prosecutors-to-cease-probe-into-gezi-park-trial-judges/ (last accessed 26 January 2022).

[68] *Joint submission to the Universal Periodic Review of Turkey* above, in which it is noted that as many as 50,000 people were arbitrarily detained with the use or download of the encrypted *Bylock* app given as evidence, and many thousands more dismissed or subject to disciplinary procedures on the same grounds.

appearing as one side. The production of evidence is often either late, embarrassingly cherry-picked or non-existent, with assumptions and inferences being drawn where none are logically available. Examples include legitimate comment pieces in traditional[69] or social media, or television appearances in which 'subliminal messages' have been alleged to be transmitted to viewers or readers.[70] We have seen the legitimate professional work of both lawyers and journalists, as well as civil society activists and human rights defenders, abused and illegitimately portrayed in indictments as so-called evidence of their involvement in terrorism. No matter how imaginary the quality of the evidence, defendants may remain in pre-trial detention for years; their bail applications are routinely refused without adequate reasons. Judges chop and change, or are chopped and changed, so that there is a total breakdown in consistency as drawn-out trials progress. The public and family members or the press are often removed at whim on the pretext that the courtrooms are too small. Despite all those substantive and procedural failings, defendants are convicted on the basis of the weakest or even non-existent evidence.

The appellate route remains defiantly littered with unexplained barriers, such as the refusal to implement decisions of higher Turkish courts[71] or the European Court of Human Rights.[72] Increasingly, we have seen that where eventually a defendant is acquitted, he has been rearrested or re-charged on spurious grounds to ensure he remains in detention. For example, on 18 February 2020, Osman Kavala and his eight co-defendants were acquitted on charges of 'attempting to overthrow the government by force and violence' in the Gezi Park trial. Kavala, however, was not released, and his detention was re-ordered on one of the initial grounds for his detention again. It is notable that President Erdoğan had criticised the acquittal publicly before he was detained again. A court then ordered his detention on another charge some weeks later, but relying on the same evidence and pursuant to the first investigation file relating to the coup attempt. Kavala appealed to the Constitutional

---

[69] See, for example, the *Cumhuriyet* trial: On 26 April 2018, 17 staff and board members of the opposition newspaper *Cumhuriyet* were convicted of 'assisting a terrorist organisation whilst not being a member' under Article 220(6) of the Criminal Code. The only evidence introduced in the proceedings was their professional body of work.

[70] See, for example, '*Şahin Alpay & others v Turkey*: Zaman Newspaper: Journalists on trial', *BHRC Interim Report*, June 2018, online at: http://www.barhumanrights.org.uk/wp-content/uploads/2018/07/Zaman-TRIAL-OBSERVATION-INTERIM-REPORT-FINAL-1-1.pdf (last accessed 26 January 2022).

[71] The UN Working Group on Arbitrary Detention found the detention of 10 of the *Cumhuriyet* journalists to be arbitrary in a decision of 26 July 2017, but their decision was not implemented. On 3 May 2019, the Turkish Constitutional Court found a violation of Kadri Gürsel's rights to liberty, security and freedom of expression by his extended pre-trial detention but not in five other identical cases of his former colleagues.

[72] Rulings of the Turkish Constitutional Court and the European Court of Human Rights, effectively ordering the release of Mehmet Altan and Şahin Alpay were ignored by the lower courts. On July 2018, Mehmet Altan was released pending the outcome of his appeal against his conviction and sentence. On 2 October 2018, an appellate court upheld the verdict of 'aggravated life sentence' for Ahmet and Mehmet Altan. On 5 July 2019, the Supreme Court of Appeals overruled the life sentence in the case of Ahmet Altan, Mehmet Altan and Nazlı Ilıcak, and a new trial commenced in October 2019. Ahmet Altan remains in detention, while Mehmet Altan was released under judicial control measures.

Court on the basis that there was not sufficient evidence to justify his continuing arrest and detention, and that authorities had not implemented the ECHR judgment of December 2019. On 29 September 2020, Turkey's Constitutional Court then postponed its review of Kavala's appeal, submitted in May purporting to rely on an impending new 'espionage' indictment against him, which was submitted by Istanbul prosecutors mere hours later. Notwithstanding a call from the Council for Europe for Kavala's release, at the time of writing, he remained incarcerated. It was nothing short of a declaration by Turkey that the international order now holds little sway over a politicised prosecution and judicial system that will not afford accountability, justice or redress.

It gets worse. Under cover of the crisis provoked by the coronavirus, the Turkish government has made inroads also on dismantling the independent bar through watering down the independent bar associations that seek to hold government to account on fundamental human rights,[73] and further, by arresting scores of lawyers.[74] As freedom of expression has come under sustained attack, a new sweeping social media law has been introduced that would force social media platforms to comply with any government demands to block or remove content. As with Hong Kong, the means of expression among an already tightly controlled population was being threatened through force of the law. The impact this was likely to have on groups and individuals who have continued to fight for their own rights and Turkey's liberal democracy in the public space would be a significant increase in censorship and arrest. Another avenue of accountability became closed down, and there was a real risk that social media platforms themselves, however much they might seek to challenge the decisions, would become used as an instrument of Turkish repression.

Turkey's judiciary is now being both punished and weaponised. The executive appears to have no qualms about using the judiciary as a means to obstruct and remove the opposition it perceives in civil society, institutions, journalists, lawyers and even social media platforms. The impact of this systematic attack on the judiciary is a grave breakdown in the rule of law with far-reaching consequences for Turkey's democracy. Meanwhile, as the list of Turkish cases before the European Court of Human Rights spirals, the power of the Court to control the drastic decline in Turkey's rule of law appears increasingly fragile.

As Zafer Yılmaz argues, 'the strategic legalism and accompanying multi-layered emergency have provided smooth paths for consolidating Erdoğan's presidential regime and containing any mobilization for democracy by combining subtle strategies

---

[73] The bar associations were not consulted, and 78 of 80 signed a statement opposing the plan. See Human Rights Watch, 'The Reform of Bar Associations in Turkey: Questions and Answers', 7 July 2020, online at: https://www.hrw.org/news/2020/07/07/reform-bar-associations-turkey-questions-and-answers (last accessed 26 January 2022).

[74] Human Rights Watch, 'Turkey: Lawyers Arrested in Terror Probe', 16 September 2020, online at: https://www.hrw.org/news/2020/09/16/turkey-lawyers-arrested-terror-probe (last accessed 26 January 2022).

of judicial repression, colonization of state institutions, proliferation of liminal judicial venues, and finally, introduction of twilight zones into the legal system.'[75]

India

The judiciary shall decide matters before them impartially, on the basis of facts and in accordance with the law, without any restrictions, improper influences, inducements, pressures, threats or interferences, direct or indirect, from any quarter or for any reason.
– Principle 2, UN Basic Principles on the Independence of the Judiciary

Improper influence, or the appearance of improper influence or pressure from the executive over the courts, may take place by different means in different political systems. Whether or not this represents a direct interference by the executive with the judiciary, the appearance of such bias itself can be deeply damaging to the rule of law. That the law must apply equally to all is a basic principle of the rule of law.

Further from the spotlight of the world's media, India's Supreme Court has become the object of credible and serious criticism for becoming a 'facilitator' for government.[76] For several years, the Court has been mired in challenges to its institutional credibility.[77] For all the progressive judgments it has passed, there are many worrying examples of dangerous judicial deference to the government, which has undermined perceptions of its ability to hold government accountable as a separate institution of power. This has appeared especially acute since the Bharatiya Janata Party (BJP) won national elections in May 2019, returning Prime Minister Modi for a second term. Arguably the clearest instance lies in the Supreme Court's handling of the situation provoked by government pursuit of the revocation of the special constitutional status of Jammu and Kashmir, which resulted in the division of the state into two separate federally governed territories. In Kashmir, this was accompanied by additional military deployments, strict curfews and a state-wide internet shutdown. Moreover, thousands of people were imprisoned in 'preventative' detention, including high ranking legal professionals, journalists and elected leaders.[78] The communications blackout in Jammu and Kashmir seriously affected regular life, the proper flow of information, as well as the routine functions of the courts. As BHRC stated at the time, 'in circumstances in which grave and widespread human rights violations are being alleged, disabling the justice system substantially compounds the crisis.'

---

[75] Z. Yılmaz, 'Erdoğan's presidential regime and strategic legalism: Turkish democracy in the twilight zone', *Southeast European and Black Sea Studies* (2020) 20(2), 265–287.
[76] G. Bhatia, 'A Constitutionalism Without the Court', *Indian Constitutional Law and Philosophy blog*, 1 August 2020, online at: https://indconlawphil.wordpress.com/2020/08/01/iclp-turns-7-a-constituti onalism-without-the-court/ (last accessed 26 January 2022).
[77] S. Biswas, 'The Crisis facing India's Supreme Court', *BBC News*, 17 November 2017, online at: https://www.bbc.co.uk/news/world-asia-india-41994842 (last accessed 26 January 2022).
[78] BHRC and Bar Council letter to PM Modi of 21 November 2019.

The Indian Supreme Court's response to the crisis not only failed in its role as the ultimate arbiter of fundamental rights, but gave a free pass to the government through a combination of invented ad hoc order, delay and obfuscation. Those petitions that sought to challenge the lockdown were adjourned repeatedly. Worse, habeas corpus petitions were met with the extraordinary suggestion that the petitioners themselves could go to Kashmir to 'meet' those individuals who were detained, instead of the government being required to justify and/or produce them. As delays and extensions continued, so the violation of fundamental rights continued unabated by serious intervention by the Supreme Court. Some five months later, the Court handed down judgment that set out the standards of judicial review applicable, without actually applying them to the government's actions.[79] Eventually, a further five months on, the government was requested by the Court to decide upon the validity of its own actions, yet again refusing to actually consider the merits of the petition on the internet lockdown.[80] As the one-year anniversary of those internet restrictions passed, serious question marks arose over not only the content of those judgments (or non-judgments), but the manner of the evasion and the 'executive enablement' they have provided.[81]

As Justice Jackson, a former United States Supreme Court Justice, observed in 1949: '...there is no more effective practical guarantee against arbitrary and unreasonable government than to require that the principles of law which officials would impose upon a minority must be imposed generally. Conversely, nothing opens the door to arbitrary action so effectively as to allow those officials to pick and choose only a few to whom they will apply legislation and thus to escape the political retribution that might be visited upon them if larger numbers were affected. Courts can take no better measure to assure that laws will be just than to require that laws be equal in operation.'[82]

Conclusion

This short essay seeks to convey the multiple prongs of attack taking place on the rule of law at both domestic and international levels in the last year alone. While some such attacks are openly authoritarian, other attacks are hidden behind the law itself, proclaiming that they form part and parcel of a normal legal regime, or that they constitute reforms intended to improve the institutions they are in fact damaging or destroying. In this way, the law may be weaponised against those who

[79] G. Bhatia, 'The Devil's in the (future) Detail: The Supreme Court's Internet shut-down Judgment', Indian Constitutional Law and Philosophy blog, 10 January 2020.
[80] M. Naniwadekar, 'The Supreme Court's 4G Internet Order: Evasion by Abnegation', The Quint, 11 May 2020, online at: https://www.thequint.com/voices/opinion/the-supreme-courts-4g-internet-order-evasion-by-abnegation (last accessed 26 January 2022).
[81] Bhatia, 'A Constitutionalism Without the Court'.
[82] *Railway Express Agency Inc. v New York* 336 US 106, 112–3 (1949).

most rely on its fair dispensation. Where democratically elected governments seek to dismantle the law from within, this may be, as Kim Lane Scheppele terms it, 'autocratic legalism'.[83] In Scheppele's words, such leaders 'use their democratic mandates to launch legal reforms that remove the checks on executive power, limit the challenges to their rule, and undermine the crucial accountability institutions of a democratic state. Because these autocrats push their illiberal measures with electoral backing and use constitutional or legal methods to accomplish their aims, they can hide their autocratic designs in the pluralism of legitimate legal forms.'[84]

---

[83] K. L. Scheppele, 'Autocratic Legalism', Univ Chicago Law Rev (2018) 85(5) 545–583.
[84] Scheppele, 'Autocratic Legalism', at 547–548.

3

Judicial Independence Under Threat:
What Is the Matter With Our Politicians?

DOMINIC GRIEVE QC

THIS VOLUME IS a reflection of the concern that judicial independence is under threat and, as Lord Thomas writes, requires 'constant vigilance' to preserve. As a former MP who has argued both in support of judicial independence at times when it has come under attack, but also in favour of the current legal structures that underpin the judiciary's role in upholding human rights and the rule of law, including the Human Rights Act and the UK's adherence to the ECHR, I have had many opportunities over the years to engage with parliamentary colleagues on these matters. In this essay, I propose, at the risk of being seen as devil's advocate, to start by examining why some politicians and their linked circle of supporters, including policymakers and journalists, have become irritated by and critical of judicial power. An understanding of this is important if we are to find a way forward that minimises the political risk to judicial independence that this irritation and criticism might pose.

It would, I think, be rather hard to find any politician or, indeed, member of the public who did not believe in the principle of judicial independence as an abstract concept. The UK judiciary is rightly held in high esteem for its lack of corruption and its independence from the other branches of government. Nevertheless, that does not mean that its decisions are universally applauded. Parliament may be the law-making body, but the application of the law is the preserve of the courts. As judges know and have to accept, the decisions they make are open for comment and criticism. While criticism ought to be tempered by an awareness of the need to show respect for the separation of powers, the reality is that politicians will find it hard to do this if a judicial decision appears averse to their own opinion and that of sections of their electorate or the media to whom they look for approval and support. This is likely to be more so in an age when politicians come under growing pressure from social media to comment and take sides on myriad controversial topics.

An example of this can be seen in the history of what have come to be known as super-injunctions. These have been used very sparingly by the courts as interim

Proceedings of the British Academy, **250**, 65–73, © The British Academy 2022.

measures to restrain the publishing of information that is said to be confidential and private and to prohibit the publication of the existence of the order as otherwise its purpose might be undermined. It has always been recognised that they are exceptional. Unsurprisingly, however, the orders have also been objected to by sections of the press and the public as they have prevented the reporting of the names of litigants and the background of cases. In 2011, this led to John Hemming MP using parliamentary privilege to circumvent an anonymised privacy injunction. It happened two years after the *Trafigura* case, which had raised the incorrect belief that the courts were trying to gag Parliament in breach of the Bill of Rights of 1688 and an intervention from Lord Judge asserting that this was not the case. In 2011, the senior judiciary responded promptly by setting up an inquiry by Lord Neuberger to report on the use of such injunctions and its publication largely brought the controversy to an end. But the episode is illustrative of the problem that can arise if judicial decisions are seen as flawed or objectionable by parliamentarians. The separation of powers and the mutual deference that should be shown by one to the other can erode quickly with the potential to create confrontation.

But more fundamental than this example has been the evident frustration at a political level that the legal framework that has been created by and for the United Kingdom makes it difficult for governments to govern in what is seen by government to be the widest public interest. This centres in particular on a belief that there is an overemphasis on individual rights at the expense of the rights of the majority whose views are therefore being ignored, thus undermining democratic legitimacy.

There is, of course, an irony in this. This is not, with a few exceptions, the stand-alone creation of the judiciary through its judgments. Rather, it is the result of decisions of successive governments since the end of the Second World War to accept the constraints of international legal obligations on how a government should behave towards those subject to its authority, some of which have then been incorporated into domestic law and become directly enforceable through the courts. This was both predictable and predicted. When the UK signed up to the ECHR, the 10 key rights originally protected under the Convention were, with the exception of Article 8 on privacy and family life, a classic exposition of the 'liberties' that successive generations of British politicians and the British public have claimed as our shared and exceptional inheritance. The rights fit with a romanticised national narrative traceable back through the Bill of Rights of 1688, Habeas Corpus to Magna Carta. Yet for all that, when the Convention was being promoted in the late 1940s, adherence to it was controversial. There was anxiety that the UK would find itself fettered by an international legal obligation that was to be interpreted as a last resort by an international tribunal. The Labour Lord Chancellor, Lord Jowitt, feared that 'the real vice of the document ... consists in its lack of precision ...'.[1] Contemporary FCO advice to Ministers warned against signing a 'blank cheque'. It read 'to allow governments to become the object of

---

[1] Lord Jowitt, memo to the Cabinet Office for a Cabinet meeting CAB/130/64, October 1950.

such potentially vague charges by individuals is to invite Communists, crooks and cranks of every type to bring actions'.[2]

Nearly 70 years on, it is remarkable and significant how these themes keep on repeating themselves. In 2015, the 800th anniversary of the Magna Carta, the then Prime Minister, David Cameron, lauded both the Charter and the principles underpinning the Convention. Only the year before, the Conservative Party published a position paper that asserted that 'Both the recent practice of the Court (ECtHR) and the domestic legislation passed by Labour (the HRA) has damaged the credibility of rights at home'.[3] The European Court was accused of subverting the intentions of the Convention's draftsmen by developing its jurisprudence outside the scope of its remit. There was talk of a programme of fundamental change, with the repeal of the HRA and its replacement by a new British Bill of Rights that could 'clarify' rights, particularly under Articles 3 and 8, to prevent their alleged abuse in respect of deportation by changing the tests to be applied. The Convention rights were to be confined to 'cases that involve criminal law and the liberty of the individual and other serious matters',[4] with Parliament setting a threshold below which no Convention right would be enforceable. It also sought to break the link between the jurisprudence of Strasbourg and our own so that no account need be taken of that court's rulings. The UK was to demand a special status where European Court judgments were merely advisory or, if this could not be achieved, leave the Convention. That would leave us with a domestic Bill of Rights with all areas of irritation removed and subject to parliamentary supremacy in respect of primary legislation. This then featured in the Conservative manifesto of 2015. It has lurked around ever since, particularly in the criticisms of right-leaning think tanks such as Policy Exchange, which is conducting a review into this in its Judicial Power Project. At the time of writing, the utterances of the Prime Minister's chief adviser, Dominic Cummings, on the need to leave the ECHR were revealing of a continuing focus on this subject.

The origins of this irritation can be traced to decisions of the European Court that go back a long way. But while early adverse decisions of the Court seem to have been tolerated, even if not welcomed by some politicians – an example being the judgment of *Campbell and Cosans v UK*,[5] which effectively started the end of corporal punishment in schools – it was the early 1990s that saw a significant change in government attitude to the European Court. Michael Howard, as Home Secretary, complained that the decision of the court in *Chahal v UK*,[6] to prevent the deportation of a Sikh terrorist to India on the grounds of the risk of torture and despite the assurances he had secured, usurped a decision that ought

[2] FCO, draft memo FO/371/78936, July 1949.
[3] Conservative Party, 'Protecting Human Rights in the UK' (October 2014), p. 3, online at: https://adam1cor.files.wordpress.com/2014/10/protecting-human-rights-in-the-uk-copy1.pdf (last accessed 26 January 2022).
[4] Conservative Party, 'Protecting Human Rights in the UK', p. 6.
[5] *Campbell and Cosans v UK* [1982] 4 EHHR 293.
[6] *Chahal v UK* [1996] 23 EHHR 413.

to have been left to the executive. David Cameron was his special adviser at the time. Concerns about strong governance being weakened and the Convention being abused to assert the rights of the 'undeserving' at the expense of the law-abiding have, then and since, coloured the Conservative Party's attitude to the enactment of the HRA.

But criticisms have not come exclusively from Conservatives. A strident and hostile attitude exists in some sections of the press, and even Labour and the SNP have at times shown a reluctance to support the European Court and the Convention on issues that might not be electorally popular. The silence by both these parties on a political response to the European Court judgment in *Hirst v UK*[7] on prisoner voting is illuminating in this respect. Indeed, the Labour government, which enacted the Human Rights Act in 1998 as a reasoned response to the need for individuals to be able to assert Convention rights domestically, seemed to lose its enthusiasm for the consequences fairly quickly under the threat of terrorism post 9/11. This initiated a period of marked deterioration in relations between the government and the judiciary, starting with the passage of the Anti-Terrorism Crime and Security Act 2001. Part IV of this provided for the indefinite detention of foreign nationals designated as terrorism suspects and thus required derogation from Article 5(1) (f) of the ECHR. The consequent litigation, resulting from the derogation from Article 5 and the judgment of the House of Lords in *A and others v Secretary of State for the Home Department*,[8] in which it declared the legislation to be discriminatory and made a declaration of incompatibility for breach of Article 14, set the scene for estrangement. The then Home Secretary wanted a meeting with senior judges to ascertain what might be acceptable to them and was understandably rebuffed as this would prejudice judicial impartiality in any subsequent case. And inevitably, some of the consequences were political. Backbenchers in Parliament were emboldened to reject the government's alternatives of 90- and 42-day pre-charge detention, and the government saw its security policy come under sustained criticism. Worse still for the Labour government, the gradual emergence of evidence of UK involvement in allegations of serious human rights breaches by the US and the litigation that ensued led to a breakdown of trust in the propriety and integrity of the government in relation to the litigation it faced. The decision of the Court of Appeal in *Binyam Mohammed v Foreign Secretary*[9] to order the disclosure of documents containing information that had been provided by the US under the 'Control Principle' (previously upheld in our courts), which guaranteed their confidentiality, marked the nadir of mutual incomprehension. The basis of the decision was that the material was already available to the public from US litigation and disclosure was required in the interests of justice. The government saw it, not unreasonably, as a potentially disastrous blow to our standing as a reliable partner

---

[7] *Hirst v UK* (No. 2) (2006) 42 EHRR 41.
[8] *A and others v Secretary of State for the Home Department* [2004] UKHL 56.
[9] *Binyam Mohammed v Secretary of State for Foreign Affairs* [2010] EWCA Civ 65.

of the US, which was vital to maintaining our own national security and protecting British citizens from terrorism.

This tension may, in some respects, be beneficial. Gone is any suggestion that the judiciary are just Lions under the Throne, placed there to sometimes growl at but broadly support the executive in its work. As commented on elsewhere, the decisions of the Supreme Court in *R (Miller) v Secretary of State for Exiting the European Union*[10] on the legal requirements for triggering of Article 50 and *R (Miller) v the Prime Minister* and *Cherry and others v Advocate General for Scotland* on Prorogation[11] all show a robust willingness to interpret our written and unwritten constitutional rules and conventions in a manner that suggests that threats to judicial independence are having little practical impact and we should perhaps be worrying more about the chronic underfunding of our justice system as the greater threat. Furthermore, for all the angry denunciations of the judiciary, these decisions can be seen as standing up squarely for the sovereignty of Parliament against executive fiat, even if some MPs seemed unable to see this because it did not fit with their short-term political goals.

But tension may also produce unnecessary problems on both sides. At the root of some parliamentary and government fears is the belief that, in a constitutional system that is increasingly rights-based, the judiciary might try to ignore or overrule parliamentary sovereignty altogether. This may appear to lawyers far-fetched, but there are a few straws in the wind that can be used to support such an analysis of the judicial direction of travel. In *Jackson v the Attorney General*, Lord Steyne suggested that 'in exceptional circumstances involving an attempt to abolish judicial review or the ordinary role of the courts, the Appellate Committee of the House of Lords or a new Supreme Court may have to consider whether this is a constitutional fundamental which even a sovereign Parliament acting at the behest of a complaisant House of Commons cannot abolish.'[12]

Such a doomsday scenario has always looked rather hypothetical because no Act of Parliament has come close to such a total violation of principle. Nevertheless, in the case of *Evans v The Attorney General*,[13] the Supreme Court certainly put a shot across Parliament's bow. It was my duty, as the matter related to a previous Labour administration, to have to decide whether or not to exercise the right of executive veto provided for in clear terms in the Freedom of Information Act, to overrule a decision of the Upper Tier Tribunal that the Prince of Wales' correspondence with ministers should be disclosed. I decided to exercise the veto as my own conclusions, on review of the issues and the balance of public interest, differed significantly from those of the Tribunal.

---

[10] *R (Miller) v Secretary of State for Exiting the European Union* [2017] UKSC 5.
[11] *R (Miller) v the Prime Minister* and *Cherry and others v Advocate General for Scotland* [2019] UKSC 41.
[12] *Jackson v the Attorney General* [2005] UKHL 56 [102].
[13] *Evans v The Attorney General* [2015] UKSC 21.

The Supreme Court struck that decision down, not on the basis that it was unreasonable, but because it considered that Parliament could not have intended to give a minister the power to overrule a court and that in the absence of the statute spelling out the power in terms that were in its opinion crystal clear, it would interpret the statute to confine the ministerial discretion within boundaries so narrow that it effectively made that part of the Act unworkable for the future. The judgment exposed sharp differences of view within the court, with a minority satisfied that the statute provided the discretionary power I had exercised on what was not a matter of law but public policy. But it is clear that a majority of the Court were deeply concerned at what they saw as a power improperly given by Parliament to ministers to overrule a court judgment contrary to the theoretical principles of the rule of law. They then engaged in some highly creative statutory interpretation to find a way of negating it while trying to avoid a stark constitutional collision.

The oddity of the issue in that case is that the history of the Freedom of Information Act shows that no such collision was intended by the executive or Parliament. The original intention had been for the Upper Tier Tribunal's decision to be merely advisory for ministers. It was only during the passage of the legislation that the government agreed to increase the powers of the Tribunal to be determinative with a judicially reviewable executive override. The intentions of both Parliament and government on this were indeed, in my view, crystal clear, but the Supreme Court judgment chose to ignore them. The truth is that the legislative proposal had not been thought through properly. Using a Superior Court of Record in this way in either the original or the amended form was unsatisfactory. But whether that justified the Supreme Court decision is debatable.

Finally, in these examples of what alarms politicians, I would also cite the obiter dicta of Lord Kerr in *R (SG and others (previously JS and others)) v Secretary of State for Work and Pensions*[14] concerning the lawfulness of the benefit cap. One of the arguments advanced was that the government had failed to take account of the best interests of the child as required by Article 3(1) of the United Nations Convention on the Rights of the Child. This treaty is not incorporated into our law but is an international treaty obligation. With no international tribunal to interpret or enforce, however, its content is essentially aspirational, although there is well-settled law that where a legislative provision is ambiguous, there is a presumption that Parliament intended to legislate in a manner that does not involve the breach of an international treaty.

Lord Kerr, in his dissenting judgment, went much further than this. He suggested that such a treaty obligation should be directly enforceable in domestic law on the basis that as the UK had chosen to subscribe to its standards by

---

[14] *R (SG and others (previously JS and others)) v Secretary of State for Work and Pensions* [2015] UKSC 16.

entering into the treaty, it should be held to account in the domestic courts for its actual compliance.

This may appear logical, but if it were to form the basis of a future judgment of the Supreme Court, it would also be revolutionary in our dualist system. The truth is that many of these international treaties would never have been signed or at least drafted in the form they are in if domestic judicial enforcement had been the expectation and intention. It is not hard to see why politicians might view such an outcome as damaging to their ability to govern. And in circumstances where more of domestic life becomes affected by international affairs, that view fuels a fear that the judiciary might take over government unless checked.

Despite this, however, the evidence is not clear that we are at risk of an imminent confrontation and consequent undermining of judicial independence, even if some commentators enjoy predicting it. Politicians, tending to use words loosely, are often surprised at how their strong expressions in the heat of debate about judges' decisions are taken more seriously by judges than is warranted by their real opinions. Today's burning issue is soon replaced by a different one in the world of politics and public opinion. Judges tend to measure their words much more carefully because they matter much more.

Some of the issues touched on in this essay already seem rather faded. David Cameron's intentions towards the HRA, set out in the Conservative Party paper, only appeared deep within his 2015 manifesto. This may, in part, be because the paper received a very poor reception for its serious factual errors and consequential defects in argument. But more importantly, private opinion polling for the Conservatives at the time showed that a desire for a Bill of Rights and repealing the HRA was not in the top 10 priorities of the electorate and was only supported by 16% of those polled. Since the Brighton Declaration of 2012, there has been a continuing diminution in the number of UK cases before the European Court, and the prisoner voting stand-off has been resolved without the need of primary legislation and without any domestic political fallout at all. Complaints about judicial activism in the field of human rights have diminished. Scrapping the HRA may still draw applause at a Conservative Party conference, but it seems to have little resonance elsewhere.

It is also noteworthy that the latest Conservative manifesto of 2019 seems to focus on more recent events. Written in the aftermath of the *Miller* cases, it focused on 'the relationship between Parliament, government and the courts, the functioning of the Royal Prerogative; the role of the House of Lords; and access to justice for ordinary people.' It then refers to the need for our security services to be able to defend us and appears to link this to updating 'the HRA and administrative law to ensure that there is a proper balance between the rights of individuals, our vital national security and effective government.' It goes on: 'We will ensure that judicial review is available to protect the rights of the individuals (sic) against an overbearing state, while ensuring that this is not abused to conduct politics by another means or to create needless delays.' It then promises a 'Constitution,

Democracy and Rights Commission' set up within a year to look in depth at all these issues and come up with proposals 'to restore trust in our institutions and in how our democracy operates'.[15]

Much was made at the time of the implied threat to judicial review contained in the text. But in the six months since, this seems to be losing its topicality as the *Miller* cases arose from such exceptional circumstances. The security services are not to my knowledge demanding any changes to the HRA. No commission has yet been appointed. At present, the threat to judicial discretion has come in the clauses of the Overseas Operations (Service Personnel and Veterans Bill). This proposes removing judicial discretion by providing an absolute six-year limitation period on tort and human rights claims both against the state and individuals arising out of military operations abroad. It also proposes a discriminatory system of criminal justice for alleged offences committed abroad in a military setting, in that UK service personnel will be protected from such prosecutions after five years save in exceptional circumstances and states that the government will consider derogation from the HRA for such operations if this is needed. It is not at all clear how this will work or resolve any underlying issues, and the proposals appear poorly thought through and badly drafted; ironically, a perfect recipe for legal challenges. They have already been denounced by a retired Chief of the General Staff as contrary to all the principles for which the armed forces stand. I will be interested to see if it is taken further in its current form.

All this makes me rather more optimistic than some that threats to judicial independence, which arise from the frustrations of politicians when limits are at various times placed upon them by judges upholding the rule of law and international legal obligations, will probably not lead to further conflict and crisis. But that does not remove the need for better dialogue with politicians and an effort at mutual understanding of both the role of the judiciary and the reality and benefits of participating in and helping shape an international rules-based system, which

---

[15] By the time this manuscript entered its final stages of completion (December 2021), the promise to set up a 'Constitution, Democracy and Rights Commission' had been superseded, first by a consultation on judicial review reform (and the government introducing the Judicial Review and Courts Bill, which in the end proved 'quite modest' in regard of the reforms that it aimed to bring forward (compared to what the government was initially considering), even if the government, via the justice secretary, then intimated that it was considering making changes to the law that would include creating (highly controversial) powers to 'correct' judicial decisions that ministers considered to be 'incorrect'. See, generally, J. Rozenberg, 'Reviewing judicial review: how far will Raab go?', A Lawyer Writes blog, 17 October 2021, online at: https://rozenberg.substack.com/p/reviewing-judicial-review-d6d (last accessed 26 January 2022); M. Elliott, 'Undermining the rule of law? A comment on the Justice Secretary's Daily Telegraph interview, Public Law for Everyone, online at: https://www.youtube.com/watch?v=MfOWpnmo8Rw&t=21s (last accessed 26 January 2022). Equally importantly, the government announced a consultation on the Human Rights Act reflecting its 'commit[ment] to updating the Human Rights Act 1998' and 'replac[ing] it with a Bill of Rights, in order to restore a proper balance between the rights of individuals, personal responsibility and the wider public interest'. See Ministry of Justice, 'Human Rights Act Reform: A Modern Bill of Rights', online at: https://www.gov.uk/government/consultations/human-rights-act-reform-a-modern-bill-of-rights (last accessed 26 January 2022).

inevitably has to be interpreted by our judiciary and international tribunals if it is to work as intended.

Sixty years ago, the House of Commons was full (some argue too full) of practising lawyers who were familiar with the role of the judiciary and were, where needed, defenders of the legal system even if not necessarily in agreement with an individual decision. The special role of the Lord Chancellor as the most senior member of the judiciary, embedded in the heart of government, was key in this respect. Today, and despite the solemn oath that goes with the office, this duty has at times been treated as optional where it has clashed with the political views and ambitions of the office holder. There are also signs of greater pressure on law officers to put upholding the rule of law second to the political and transactional needs of government. As this undermines the trust of the judiciary in a government's standards of behaviour, it makes any dialogue between the two much more difficult.

The willingness of senior members of the judiciary to appear before parliamentary committees has in contrast been helpful to an understanding of the judiciary's role and its concerns as to how justice can be delivered within the budget that is being provided – a growing crisis issue on which many MPs still remain unsighted (although there are recent indications that the government may provide more funds). But this still leaves, in my experience, a gap of understanding as to how our system of law operates. The suggestions of Lord Thomas, in his own essay, on improvements to communication between the judiciary and other organs of the state are I am sure the right way forward. I agree with him that they can be done without compromising judicial independence, even if they are undoubtedly going to be an extra burden. The opportunity to do this now is good, as the ending of the UK's membership of the EU has removed what was, for some, the greatest irritant in respect of judicial power and a principal source of criticism of judicial decisions. It may even be the case that the 'Commission on the Constitution, Democracy and Rights' could play a constructive role in this as well if it is not set up as a blind simply to justify and reinforce a particular policy direction. If it is not a serious project, then the history of such previous initiatives suggests its conclusions will soon be lost in another level of political noise that leads nowhere.

4

Understanding Judicial Independence in the Age of Outrage

MARTINA Y. FEILZER

THIS CHAPTER DISCUSSES whether judicial independence is under threat in England and Wales from public demands for the judiciary to more closely follow public opinion on questions of sentencing and other issues of criminal justice relevance, such as prisoner voting rights and considerations of human rights protections. It examines whether political claims of an increasingly anti-democratic judiciary reflect public views or are an attempt to undermine judicial independence as a tool of accountability and scrutiny of governmental decision-making. A number of authors in this volume call for vigilance against threats to judicial independence. The origin and nature of such threats matter. If there is indeed a loss of public faith in the independence and legitimacy of the judiciary, this would be a grave threat; however, if the threat originates from more narrow political interests exploiting superficial readings of the public mood, the threat can be countered with more confidence. This chapter aims to illuminate some of the dimensions of public opinion, public trust in, and the legitimacy of, the judiciary.

The chapter starts by setting out the social context in which debates on judicial independence take place. It introduces some of the dimensions of public opinion of the judiciary and reflects upon the difficulty of recognising a need for judicial reform while defending the fundamental principles of judicial independence.

Judicial independence in the 'age of outrage'

In 2017, Haidt entitled a lecture on liberal democracy at the Manhattan Institute as the 'Age of Outrage' and captured features of a fast-moving world driven by a 24-hour news cycle and social media platforms reducing the events of the world of politics, natural disasters, mass casualty events and crimes to short snappy headlines ready for angry commentary and calls for immediate action. He spoke of increasing

Proceedings of the British Academy, **250**, 74–87, © The British Academy 2022.

political polarisation in the US since 1990 and the role of a changing media landscape in generating a sense of 'drowning in outrage stories'.[1] This new world is exploited by a new guard of populist politicians fuelling and even generating public anger, abdicating responsibility for policy decisions to others, and who appear to be entirely resistant to accountability for their actions and words.

Additionally, there is evidence of significant threats to judicial independence in a number of younger democracies. In Hungary, the Orbán government introduced legislative changes in 2018 to limit the independence of the judiciary by binding judicial decisions to the political purpose of legislation and setting up a new administrative court system headed by a political appointee.[2] This was the latest in a slow erosion of organisational independence of the judiciary observed since 2012.[3] The Orbán government is further accused of undermining and discrediting individual judges as well as attacking the freedom of the press and threatening civil society.[4] Similar warnings have been sounded in Poland, and in late April 2020, the European Commission launched an infringement procedure on Poland in relation to new legislation alleged to undermine the independence of the judiciary.[5]

The European Commission recognises the importance of a well-functioning judiciary as a foundation to the rule of law and publishes the EU Justice Scoreboard, which is now in its seventh edition.[6] It divides considerations of the judicial system into three sections: efficiency of justice systems, quality of justice systems and independence. The UK was ranked ninth out of the (then) 28 EU member states in terms of perceived independence of courts and judges among the public. The scoreboard provides evidence that the concerns about judicial independence in Hungary are shared by a majority of the Hungarian public, with just over 40% of respondents perceiving judicial independence to be 'good' or 'very good'. Figures were similar in Poland, with just under 40% of respondents perceiving judicial independence to be 'good' or 'very good'.[7]

---

[1] J. Haidt, *The Age of Outrage. What the current political climate is doing to our country and our universities*, Wriston Lecture for the Manhattan Institute, 15 November 2017, online at: https://www.city-journal.org/html/age-outrage-15608.html (last accessed 14 May 2021).

[2] OSCE, 'Independence of the Judiciary under attack in Hungary: Statement by Hungarian Helsinki Committee', 12 September 2018, online at: https://www.osce.org/files/f/documents/b/e/393824_0.pdf (last accessed 26 January 2022).

[3] Amnesty International, *Fearing the Unknown. How rising control is undermining judicial independence in Hungary* (Amnesty, 2020), online at: https://www.amnesty.eu/wp-content/uploads/2020/04/FINAL_Fearing-the-Unknown_report_Amnesty-Hungary_E1.pdf (last accessed 14 May 2021).

[4] Amnesty International, *Fearing the Unknown*.

[5] European Commission, 'Rule of Law: European Commission launches infringement procedure to safeguard the independence of judges in Poland', 29 April 2020, online at: https://ec.europa.eu/commission/presscorner/detail/en/ip_20_772 (last accessed 14 May 2021).

[6] European Commission, *The 2019 EU Justice Scoreboard* (Luxembourg: Publications Office of the European Union, 2019), online at: https://ec.europa.eu/info/sites/info/files/justice_scoreboard_2019_en.pdf (last accessed 26 January 2022).

[7] European Commission, *The 2019 EU Justice Scoreboard*, p. 44.

Political scientists raise concerns about the stability of democracy in the 21st century,[8] and in this context and the examples set out above, media and political attacks against the judiciary take on a threatening tone and raise the question of the sanctity of judicial independence in established democracies such as England and Wales. Thus, it is important to establish whether there is public support to the attacks or whether they are purely politically motivated aiming to undermine 'a central institution of accountability' for those in power[9] and should be called out as such.

In England and Wales, the rhetorical attacks against the judiciary centre on three main claims: that judges are out of touch with ordinary people and act on behalf of elites who do not share ordinary people's experiences of crime, and that they act against majority views and public opinion.[10] Such attacks are played out in newspaper headlines of judges as 'Enemies of the People' and public anger at soft sentences imposed by judges and magistrates.[11] While there is some concern about the particular salience of these attacks, in the context of criticism of sentencing decisions, such attacks are not as novel and unprecedented as is sometimes claimed. In fact, the narrative of an 'out of touch' judiciary thought to be too lenient when sentencing offenders goes back decades, if not longer. In his seminal work, Pearson commented on the recurring master-narratives that sentencers could not keep up with rises in crime due to being too soft on crime: 'The police and magistrates have had their hands tied by the interference of sentimentalists and do-gooders.'[12] Pearson recorded repeated mentions of the role of soft justice and judicial leniency in parliamentary debates and media coverage going back hundreds of years, concluding that 'the pre-occupation with [growing] lawlessness belongs more properly to a remarkably stable tradition.'[13]

This stable tradition of criticising the judiciary for leniency in sentencing has continued in England and Wales and is supported by survey evidence since at least the 1960s. Banks et al. report on survey research in 1966 in which 'over 90% [of respondents], thought that [...] (ii) inadequate severity of court sentences were important factors, more than 70%, thinking they were very important.'[14]

---

[8] M. D. Bonner, M. Kempa, M. R. Kubal and G. Seri, 'Introduction: Police Abuse in Contemporary Democracies' in M. D. Bonner et al (eds.), *Police Abuse in Contemporary Democracies* (London: Palgrave Macmillan, 2018), p. 10.

[9] Bonner et al., 'Introduction', p. 16.

[10] For a recent summary, see S. Grimmelikhuijsen and K. van den Bos, 'Specifying the information effect: reference points and procedural justifications affect legal attitudes in four survey experiments' *Journal of Experimental Criminology*, 18 (2020), online first 30 January 2020, 2.

[11] Headline in the *Daily Mail*, 4 November 2016. Similar headlines signalling public outrage at sentencing decisions appear frequently in a range of different papers – e.g., *The Sun* 'Outrage of soft justice' or its campaign to name and shame judges considered unduly lenient 'Judges on trial', 12 June 2006; 'Child pornography ruling angers critics', *Guardian*, 26 January 2007, among others.

[12] G. Pearson, *Hooligan – A History of Respectable Fears* (Basingstoke, Macmillan, 1983), p. 3.

[13] Pearson, *Hooligan*, p. 212.

[14] C. Banks, E. Maloney and H. D. Willcock, 'Public attitudes to crime and the penal system', *British Journal of Criminology*, 15(3) (1975), 228–240.

Between the late 1980s and 2011, the British Crime Survey/Crime Survey for England and Wales asked respondents to indicate their thoughts on the question 'Are the courts too harsh, too lenient or about right?' Around three-quarters of respondents felt that sentences were too lenient, and that proportion remained consistently high throughout that period (from a high of 79% in 1989 to a low of 74% in 2010/11; see Figure 4.1).

The question on leniency was dropped from the Crime Survey in England and Wales, but in 2019, new research commissioned by the Sentencing Council on Public Knowledge of, and Confidence in, the Criminal Justice System and Sentencing used the leniency question and found that 70% of respondents felt sentencing was too lenient.[15] These attitudinal trends are relatively stable (see Figure 4.1), despite significant and, at times, dramatic changes to sentencing practices in England and Wales over the past 40 years. These changes include the introduction of sentencing guidelines, the introduction and abolition of Indeterminate Sentences Imprisonment, increases in the lengths of average sentences of imprisonment, a reduction of the use of community sentences and many more. Public attitudes seem remarkably impervious to actual changes in sentencing practices and patterns, which raises important questions about how these could be influenced.

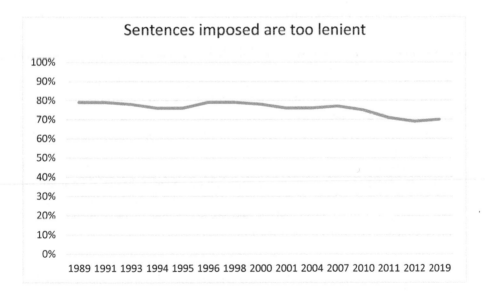

Figure 4.1 Are sentences imposed by the courts …?

Source: British Crime Survey/Crime Survey for England and Wales; Marsh 2019, 24

[15] N. Marsh, E. McKay, C. Pelly and S. Cereda, *Public Knowledge of and confidence in the criminal justice system and sentencing* (London: Sentencing Council, 2019), online at: https://www.sentencing council.org.uk/wp-content/uploads/Public-Knowledge-of-and-Confidence-in-the-Criminal-Justice-Sys tem-and-Sentencing.pdf (last accessed 26 January 2022), p. 24.

Legitimacy and public trust in judges

To what extent do media and political criticisms of the judiciary represent public opinion on questions of judicial independence and judicial legitimacy? Is such public opinion 'primarily a communication from the citizens to their government',[16] with the expectation that the communication requires government action to ensure that the judiciary follow public opinion more closely? Or are such attacks exploiting public narratives that are only superficially held and do not reflect actual or deep-seated doubts over the appropriate role and independence of the judicial system?

Attacking the judiciary as an institution and individual judges as anti-democratic on behalf of a dissatisfied public raises significant questions about the legitimacy of the judiciary. Beetham has set out different aspects or conditions of legitimacy. The first condition of legitimacy is legal validity, the extent to which the institutional arrangements conform to established law and are implemented and exercised within the law.[17] This condition is always in danger of being reduced to pure proceduralism if this assumption excludes considerations of the normative validity of the legal framework according to moral and political principles. A further condition of legitimacy is the belief in legitimacy or perceived legitimacy, following Weber.[18] In the criminal justice context, and in relation to the various institutions that contribute to the process, including the police, the judiciary, prisons and probation, perceived legitimacy has been further split into several components; internal legitimacy, felt by those subjected to criminal justice actions such as police stops or court sentencing and thought to impact on individual levels of compliance; external legitimacy, felt by the audience not directly affected by punishment (i.e., the general public);[19] and self-legitimacy, the confidence of their own authority of those working in the criminal justice system (e.g., police officers and judges) as well as their sense that they occupy a special position in society.[20]

Public opinion is part of external legitimacy and a vital component of societal belief in the judiciary's legitimacy. As highlighted above, it brings with it all the problems of measurement as well as the artificial need to 'divorce people's beliefs about legitimacy from their grounds or reasons for holding them', which lie in the actual characteristics of a regime.[21] The independence of the judiciary is regarded as

---

[16] H. Speier, 'Historical Development of Public Opinion.' *American Journal of Sociology* 55 (1950), 376–388 at 376.

[17] D. Beetham, 'Towards a Social-scientific Concept of Legitimacy' in *The Legitimation of Power. Issues in Political Theory* (London, Palgrave, 1991) p. 4.

[18] Beetham, 'Towards a Social-scientific Concept of Legitimacy', p. 6.

[19] A. E. Bottoms, 'Theoretical Reflections on the Evaluation of a Penal Policy Initiative' in L. Zedner and A. Ashworth (eds) *The Criminological Foundations of Penal Policy* (Oxford, Oxford University Press, 2003), pp. 107–196.

[20] B. Bradford and P. Quinton, 'Self-legitimacy, police culture and support for democratic policing in an English Constabulary', *British Journal of Criminology* 54 (2014), 1023–1046, at 1032.

[21] Beetham, 'Towards a Social-scientific Concept of Legitimacy', p. 10.

a cornerstone of democratic political systems, and indeed it is the 'master narrative of judicial work in sentencing'.[22] Many countries claim the independence of their judiciary, but of course, how such judicial independence is implemented varies, from the US' elected judicial figures[23] to lay sentencers, from executive models of judicial administration to judicial self-management.[24] Judicial independence is driven by impartiality, the judge as a neutral, unbiased figure passing judgement solely on the details of a case and the law 'without fear or favour, affection or ill will', and insularity, the independence of the judiciary from the executive and legislative branches of government.[25] To some extent, these two factors distinguish between the independence of judiciary as institution and individual judges,[26] and highlight that the concept of judicial independence has numerous aspects and relies on a range of conventions. While a definitive definition of what constitutes an independent judiciary is difficult to find,[27] these aspects include the separation of powers, an independent judicial appointments system, fiscal independence, judicial accountability, judicial powers over sentencing and the protection from politicians commenting on judicial decisions, among others.

There is some dispute and a degree of inherent contradiction on whether independence simply means freedom from interference or complete insulation from politics and the public and its views. For a judge's 'decision is always spoken in the name of the law, which appears to us as the will of the sovereign people.'[28] In that regard, judges 'exercise a great power on behalf of the people through the state [...].'[29] Of course, the principle of judicial independence and its normative and legal validity is in no doubt. The right to trial by an impartial and independent tribunal is protected as a fundamental international human right by Article 6(1) of the European Convention on Human Rights and Article 10 of the Universal Declaration of Human Rights, and is a core principle of democratic states. Importantly, it protects the principle of accountability of those in power in government, which is 'fundamental to the rule of law'.[30] Civil society can only provide 'social accountability' by 'shaming wrongdoers, demanding answers for the wrongdoing and activating institutional mechanisms of accountability' when it has access to independent judicial institutions, including courts and other oversight

---

[22] F. Jamieson, 'Judicial Independence: the master narrative in sentencing practice', *Criminology and Criminal Justice*, 21 (2019), 133–150, published online first 9 April 2019, p. 14.

[23] Hanssen reviews the five different procedures by which US judges are appointed: F. A. Hanssen, 'Is There a Politically Optimal Level of Judicial Independence?', *American Economic Review*, 94 (2004), 712–729.

[24] B. C. Smith, 'Models of judicial administration and the independence of the judiciary: A comparison of Romanian self-management and the Czech executive model', *Public Administration and Development*, 28 (2008), 85–93.

[25] Smith 'Models of judicial administration', 86.

[26] Jamieson, 'Judicial Independence', 4.

[27] Jamieson, 'Judicial Independence', 3–4.

[28] Jamieson, 'Judicial Independence', 8.

[29] Jamieson, 'Judicial Independence', 8.

[30] Bonner et al., 'Introduction', p. 18.

commissions.[31] Thus, threatening the independence of the judiciary threatens the ability of civil society to hold those in power to account and becomes a fundamental threat to democracy.

External legitimacy and judicial independence

The evidence presented above suggests that a significant proportion of the public considers the sentences imposed in the courts of England and Wales as too lenient, and this appears to resonate strongly with the media and political attacks against the judiciary. However, extensive research over the past 20 years from a number of different jurisdictions has provided evidence that attitudes to sentencing respond to the provision of information. Support for the 'cognitive deficit model'[32] and using information-based approaches to influencing public opinion comes from three different sources: the role of education in appearing to influence opinion in survey research, methodological advances in measuring public opinion, and experimental research.[33] The role of respondents' level of education in influencing public attitudes towards sentencing and the judiciary is contested – while higher levels of education are associated with better levels of knowledge of the criminal justice system and certain attitudes towards criminal justice such as less punitivity, these associations are not strong.[34]

Survey research designed to elicit specific attitudes about sentences, rather than global ones, demonstrates that the public is in fact not as punitive as it is made out to be.[35] This research locates sentences within the specifics of individual cases through vignettes and finds that the public's sentences are much closer to actual judicial practice than expected, closing what has been called the 'punitiveness gap'.[36] Additionally, providing a reference point for members of the public in expressing attitudes for sentencing either by providing sentencing data on comparative cases or indicating that a sentence is 'high' or 'low' for comparable cases, means that by anchoring respondents' attitudes to real-life examples and data, a

---

[31] Bonner et al., 'Introduction', p. 19.

[32] I. Loader, 'Playing with Fire? Democracy and the Emotions of Crime and Punishment', in S. Karstedt, I. Loader and H. Strang (eds), *Emotions and Crime* (Oxford, Hart Publishing, 2011), pp. 347–362, at 348–351.

[33] S. Maruna and A. King, 'Public Opinion and Community Penalties', in A. Bottoms, S. Rex and G. Robinson (eds.), *Alternatives to Prison: Options for an Insecure Society* (Cullompton, Willan, 2004), pp. 83–112 at p. 98; S. Maruna and A. King, 'Once a Criminal, Always a Criminal? "Redeemability" and the Psychology of Punitive Public Attitudes', *European Journal on Criminal Policy and Research* 15 (2009), 7–24, at 18.

[34] For a discussion, see M. Hough, B. Bradford, J. Jackson and J. V. Roberts, *Attitudes to sentencing and trust in justice: exploring trends from the crime survey for England and Wales* (London, Ministry of Justice, 2013), pp. 15–27.

[35] See, e.g., M. Hough, 'People Talking about Punishment', *The Howard Journal of Criminal Justice* 35 (1996), 191–214.

[36] I.e., the difference between judicial sentencing practice and public expressions of appropriate sentencing: J. W. de Keijser, P. J. van Koppen and H. Elffers, 'Bridging the Gap Between Judges and the Public? A Multi-Method Study', *Journal of Experimental Criminology* 3 (2007): 131–161, at 132;

more accurate assessment is possible.[37] This suggests that the cognitive deficit model may reflect methodological problems in survey research that uses global questions that are insufficiently sensitive to respondents' attitudes and are simply inaccurate as indicators of public views of sentencing.[38]

In light of the questions on how far global survey measures accurately assess public attitudes to sentencing, political and media claims to represent the public's dissatisfaction in this regard become harder to believe. Nevertheless, while Jamieson suggests that most research on public attitudes to sentencing has avoided the debate in how far judges should be expected to be responsive to public opinion on sentencing,[39] the idea of responsiveness is linked to wider debates of the legitimacy of the judiciary, which I will set out in the next section. Additionally, the need for responsiveness in contrast with judicial independence is a concern that occupies judges' minds, as illustrated in this quote by a judge in Jamieson:

> I suppose it's to know that you are, in a sense, unimpeachable in terms of what you do, provided you don't misbehave. Then ... you should try to make something of your independence, and not be unduly influenced by what is thought to be the public mood which, as I say, is a very doubtful concept indeed.[40]

Jamieson suggests that judges' sense of self-legitimacy is tied strongly to the notion of judicial independence, in the sense of individual judges transcending subjective views and remaining 'above the battle'. Thus, any attacks on judicial independence, real and imagined, go to the core of judges' own sense of authority and the role they play in society.

The above analysis shows that on one side, we have the assessment of judicial sentencing practices, which is malleable and responds to an information effect,[41] and on the other side, the question of the normative role and position of the judiciary and individual judges. The focus has been on attitudes based on questions of correspondence between sentencing practices and public attitudes as the 'punitiveness gap' was seen as a threat to trust in the judiciary.[42] Nevertheless, some studies have focused on understanding what the public regard as important features of the judiciary.

Hough, 'People Talking about Punishment', 191–192; M. Hough and D. Moxon, 'Dealing with Offenders: Popular Opinion and the Views of Victims', *The Howard Journal of Criminal Justice* 24 (1985), 160–175, at 171.

[37] Grimmelikhuijsen and van den Bos, 'Specifying the information effect', 13.

[38] For a more detailed discussion of the impact of methodology, see J. V. Roberts, M. Feilzer and M. Hough, 'Measuring Public Attitudes to Criminal Justice', in D. Gadd, S. Karstedt and S. Messner (eds), *The Sage Handbook of Criminological Research Methods* (London, Sage, 2011), pp. 282–296 and M. Y. Feilzer, 'A Review of Public Knowledge of Sentencing Practices' in J. V. Roberts (ed.), *Exploring Sentencing in England and Wales* (London, Palgrave, 2015) pp. 61–75.

[39] Jamieson, 'Judicial Independence', 2.

[40] Jamieson, 'Judicial Independence', 7.

[41] Grimmelikhuijsen and van den Bos, 'Specifying the information effect'.

[42] I.e., the difference between judicial sentencing practice and public expressions of appropriate sentencing: De Keijser et al., 'Bridging the Gap Between Judges and the Public?', 132; Hough, 'People Talking about Punishment', 191–192; Hough and Moxon, 'Dealing with Offenders', 171.

Elffers and de Keijser reported on Dutch research on the public's view on whether judges should be more responsive to public opinion based on the assumption that judicial responsiveness to public attitudes contributes to public belief in legitimacy while threatening judicial independence. It became clear that there was a mismatch, a gap, between what judges assumed the public wanted and the views expressed by respondents.[43] Overall, Dutch respondents did not want to see a 'responsive' judge and valued the independence of the judiciary. The most important trait of a judge was to be 'just', ranked among the five most important traits by 92% of respondents and by 42% as the most important trait. In second place of importance, impartiality was ranked among the five most important traits of a judge by 82% of respondents (and by 22% as the most important trait – the second-highest rating), and independence by 71% of respondents (and by 14% as the most important trait – the third-highest rating). Only 33% of respondents felt that judges should be aware of public opinion, and 3% regarded this as the most important trait of a judge.[44] Further survey research in the Netherlands suggested 'a large majority of the public (71%) want judges to focus on specifics of the case instead of public opinion'.[45]

In England and Wales, measures of public trust in the judiciary are expressed through regular surveys such as Ipsos Mori's Veracity Index.[46] The latest results of that Index suggest that trust in judges to tell the truth is stable and healthy – see Figure 4.2. This contrasts strongly with trust expressed in the professions most prominently involved in criticising the judiciary, journalists and politicians.[47] Grimmelikhuijsen and van den Bos further support the evidence of a divergence between survey findings in relation to public opinion on sentencing levels and expressions of trust in judges.[48]

The European Social Survey in 2010 assessed a number of different components of public trust in the courts, including the trust in procedural fairness and competence. These were expressed through questions on how often respondents felt that courts make fair and impartial decisions and how often they make mistakes and let guilty people go free. The discussion of fair and impartial decision-making relates to questions of procedural justice, the extent to which any interaction with

[43] H. Elffers and J. de Keijser, 'Different Perspectives, Different Gaps: Does the general public demand a more responsive judge?' In H. Kury (ed.) *Fear of Crime – punitivity: New developments in theory and research* (Brockum, Universitätsverlag Brockmeyer, 2008), pp. 425–446.

[44] Elffers and de Keijser, 'Different Perspectives, Different Gaps', p. 466.

[45] J. W. De Keijser, 'Penal theory and popular opinion. The deficiencies of direct engagement', in J. Ryberg, Jesper and J. V. Roberts (eds.), *Popular punishment. On the normative significance of public opinion* (Oxford, Oxford University Press, 2014) pp. 101–118.

[46] Ipsos Mori, *Ipsos/Mori Veracity Index 2019*, online at: https://www.ipsos.com/sites/default/files/ct/news/documents/2019-11/trust-in-professions-veracity-index-2019-slides.pdf (last accessed 14 May 2021). Ipsos Mori conducts the survey annually with a representative sample of British adults.

[47] Ipsos Mori Veracity Index 2019; Ipsos Mori, Ipsos MORI Veracity Index 2018, online at: https://www.ipsos.com/sites/default/files/ct/news/documents/2018-11/veracity_index_2018_v1_161118_public.pdf (last accessed 14 May 2021); Ipsos Mori, Trust in professions: Long term trends, online at: https://www.ipsos.com/ipsos-mori/en-uk/trust-professions-long-term-trends (last accessed 14 May 2021).

[48] Grimmelikhuijsen and van den Bos, 'Specifying the information effect', 4.

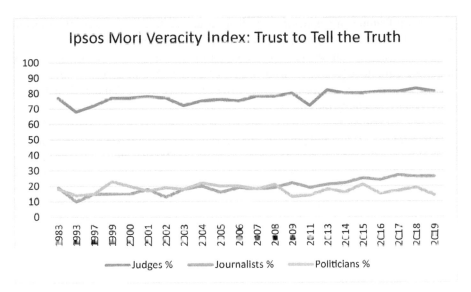

Figure 4.2 Ipsos Mori Veracity Index, selected professions, 1983–2019
Source: Ipsos/Mori Veracity Index 2017, 2018, 2019

representatives of the criminal justice system is considered fair, and how individuals are treated in that interaction.[49] Proponents of procedural justice theory regard the process and the interaction as more important than the outcome of criminal justice processes and procedurally just treatment centres around opportunity to participate in the interaction (voice), neutrality, treatment with respect, and trust in the authorities.[50] Grimmelikhuijsen and van den Bos, in their experimental research, found that providing respondents with procedural cues, i.e., explaining the procedures followed by judges to arrive at their sentence, had a significant effect on the assessment of a particular sentence and increases trust in judges.[51]

In terms of the ESS, respondents from the United Kingdom expressed relatively high levels of trust in the courts' impartiality (scoring above 6 points on a scale of 1–8) but also medium to high levels of support for the suggestions that courts often make mistakes and let guilty people go free (scoring 5 points on a scale of 1–8).[52] The British Social Attitudes Survey run annually asked questions about the health of British democracy and aimed to assess the expectations and evaluations of democracy. Budd and Fitzgerald found that 'people attach importance to essential

---

[49] T. R. Tyler, 'Public Trust and Confidence in Legal Authorities: What do majority and minority group members want from the law and legal institutions?' *Behavioural Sciences and the Law,* 19 (2001), 215–235, at 216.
[50] Tyler, 'Public Trust and Confidence in Legal Authorities', 231.
[51] Grimmelikhuijsen and van den Bos, 'Specifying the information effect', 12–13.
[52] European Social Survey, 2010, p. 9.

procedural features of democracy' and that 'equal treatment by the courts (scoring 8.9 out of a scale of 1–10) and legal constraints on government authority (8.6)' were regarded as highly important.[53] Indeed, equal treatment by the courts was seen as the most important feature of democracy just ahead of 'free and fair elections'.[54] Nearly one in five respondents (18%), however, perceived a democratic deficit in the equal treatment by the courts.[55]

The concern about equal treatment by the courts is particularly strong among ethnic minority groups and points to the need to look beyond headline statistics on trust in judges or attitudes to sentencing when considering the legitimacy of the courts. In 2017, a Centre for Justice Innovation report[56] highlights the trust deficit among minority ethnic groups in relation to the perception of equal treatment in the courts, and there is established evidence of differential treatment of minority ethnic people in the criminal justice system in England and Wales.[57]

While such concerns are not highlighted by politicians and the media to the same extent as some of the broader public narratives highlighted above, they are potentially more damaging in undermining the legitimacy of the rule of law among certain demographic groups. This is illustrated very strongly by the Black Lives Matter protests that took place across the globe in the summer of 2020.

Understanding external legitimacy

In this chapter, I have set out some empirical evidence in relation to aspects of the legitimacy of the judiciary with a particular focus on external legitimacy. Research suggests that at one level, there is a punitiveness gap between the public and the judiciary that raises concerns about the external legitimacy of judicial decision-making, particularly sentencing. On the other hand, there is significant evidence that the public support the principles of judicial independence, trust judicial processes, and see the judiciary as a key institution in ensuring that the government are held to account.

---

[53] S. Budd and R. Fitzgerald, 'Democracy: Critical consensus? Britain's expectations and evaluations of democracy', in A. Park, C. Bryson and J. Curtice (eds.), *British Social Attitudes: The 31st Report* (London, NatCen Social Research, 2014), online at: www.bsa-31.natcen.ac.uk (last accessed 14 May 2021).

[54] Budd and Fitzgerald, 'Democracy: Critical consensus?', p. 1.

[55] Budd and Fitzgerald, 'Democracy: Critical consensus?', p. 13.

[56] P. Bowen, *Building Trust. How our courts can improve the criminal court experience for Black, Asian and Minority Ethnic defendants* (Centre for Justice Innovation, 2017), online at: https://justiceinnovat ion.org/sites/default/files/media/documents/2019-03/building-trust.pdf (last accessed 14 May 2021).

[57] R. Hood, *Race and Sentencing: A study in the Crown Court* (Oxford, Clarendon Press, 1992); S. Shute, R. Hood and F. Seemungal, *A Fair Hearing: Ethnic Minorities in the Criminal Courts* (Devon, Willan Publishing, 2005); D. Lammy, *The Lammy Review: An Independent Review into the Treatment of, and Outcomes for, Black, Asian and Minority Ethnic Individuals in the Criminal Justice System* (London, Lammy Review, 2017), online at: https://assets.publishing.service.gov.uk/government/uploads/system/ uploads/attachment_data/file/643001/lammy-review-final-report.pdf (last accessed 14 May 2021).

Experimental research has highlighted methodological shortcomings that create certain public views. For example, when individuals respond to questions about the appropriateness of the sentences imposed by the courts, without additional information, they will lack a reference point and will need to 'find one'. Thus, they might either consider this question in the context of high-profile cases covered in the media or fall back on public narratives on sentencing as an easily accessible reference point. Public narratives draw on cultural texts and assumptions and are used explicitly in public discourses – political and media discourses – and are invoked as anchoring or reference points for communication with a purpose – to make a point or a claim.[58]

Similarly, public trust in judges seems remarkably stable on some measures but does respond to experimental interventions and procedural cues. Grimmelikhuijsen and van den Bos have further extended research on the information effect and found that procedural cues and the provision of reference points have the greatest impact in terms of moderating sentencing attitudes and, significantly, trust in judges. In contrast, other indicators of external legitimacy exploring the public's normative views on questions of judicial traits and judicial independence suggest considerable support for the principle of judicial independence and the primary role of the courts as a venue for fair and impartial decision-making. The extent to which these attitudes respond to information or other experimental interventions has not been explored to the same extent.

Understanding public trust in the judicial system and public attitudes to its various aspects is fundamental to assessing the validity of calls for reform or attacks against certain features of the judicial system. This, however, is only possible with a thorough grasp of the methodological characteristics and shortcomings of various research methods. It is clear that simple narratives of a punitive public perceiving sentencing to be too lenient and judges to be out of touch can take hold and trigger reforms despite a lack of support for those narratives or the reform approaches from the available research evidence.

Outrage, complacency and the need for change

The focus in the analysis above was to set out whether media and political criticisms of the judiciary should be seen as reflecting a lack of trust in the judicial system and democratic calls for limits on judicial independence at an institutional and individual level. It has become clear that readings of public opinion on these matters

---

[58] M. Bamberg, 'Considering counter-narratives', in M. Bamberg and M. Andrews (eds.), *Considering counter-narratives: narrating, resisting, making sense* (Amsterdam/ Philadelphia, John Benjamins Publishing, 2004), pp. 351–371 at p. 358. For a more detailed discussion of public narratives on crime and criminal justice, see M. Y. Feilzer, 'Public Narratives of Crime and Criminal Justice: Connecting "small" and "big" stories to make public narratives visible', in M. Althoff et al (eds), *Conflicting Narratives of Crime and Punishment* (London, Palgrave Macmillan, 2020), pp. 63–84.

are multidimensional and highly complex, and thus any one-dimensional interpretation of this complexity is bound to fall victim to oversimplification. However, none of the evidence reviewed suggests that the judiciary is under pressure from the public to abandon the principles of judicial independence, and the political and media attacks claiming to represent public views appear to be serving a different purpose.[59] For those defending judicial independence, it is vital to know the purpose and nature of such attacks, and rather than engendering complacency, the judiciary should be wary in its responses and willingness to engage with remedies to appease perceived public will.

On the other hand, the judiciary should not be immune from all calls for reform and modernisation. There should be some recognition of areas ripe for reform and their impact on the legitimacy of the judiciary. The judiciary has been criticised for a lack of representativeness of the general population in terms of age, gender, ethnicity and class. This issue has been recognised, and while some progress has been made in diversifying the judiciary, it is painfully slow in reaching the most senior levels of the judicial system, as acknowledged only in 2019 by the Lord Chief Justice and in particular in addressing the question of social diversity.[60]

A second major concern relates to the question of differential sentencing practices and their impact on minority communities as well as certain socioeconomic groups. Growing disproportionality in the ethnic make-up of the youth custodial population and the wider prison population support Lammy's conclusion that reforms are needed across the whole criminal justice system, including the courts, to address the over-representation of certain groups. A number of studies[61] have provided evidence that differential sentencing practices and systemic biases make a contribution to the over-representation, and a concerted recognition of, and effort to, examine this issue by the judiciary would be a positive step forward.

On more practical terms, a decade of under-resourcing the judicial system has led to an insufficiently agile and modern court infrastructure. Covid-19 has had a dramatic impact in speeding up the move to 'virtual' court hearings, but the system is creaking under the backlog of court cases and the impact on victims, defendants and professionals in the system. The under-resourcing has also had an impact on access to justice, and denying the public access to the justice system will

---

[59] The UK government's decision to establish an independent panel to look at judicial review is based on frustration at 'political' decisions made by the judiciary. The panel is charged with considering 'whether the right balance is struck between the rights of citizens' to challenge executive decisions and the need for effective and efficient governance': Ministry of Justice Press Release, 'Government launches independent panel to look at judicial review', 31 July 2020 online at: https://www.gov.uk/government/news/government-launches-independent-panel-to-look-at-judicial-review (last accessed 26 January 2022).

[60] Lord Chief Justice of England and Wales, The Right Hon Lord Burnett of Maldon, 'A changing judiciary in a Modern Age', Treasurer's Lecture 2019, online at: https://www.judiciary.uk/wp-content/uploads/2019/02/19022018-MT-Treasurers-Lecture-FINAL-FOR-PUBLISHING.pdf (last accessed 26 January 2022).

[61] Hood, *Race and Sentencing*; Shute et al. *A Fair Hearing*.

have a detrimental impact on levels of trust.[62] There is a danger that by rejecting manufactured calls pitching the public and the judiciary against each other, other more valid reform calls go unheeded.

In conclusion, the evidence presented here suggests that the fundamental principle of judicial independence appears to be safe from public calls for change and can be staunchly defended against political and media attacks. In fact, in many respects, the focus on concerns about public views of the judiciary serves as a distraction from some fundamental threats to the functioning of the judicial system, threats to trust in justice, and valid and overdue calls for reform. It is vital that the judiciary, as all democratic institutions, remains open-minded to considered calls for reform and change, recognising constructive criticisms of its shortcomings.

---

[62] OECD, *Trust and Public Policy: How Better Governance Can Help Rebuild Public Trust* (Paris, OECD Publishing, 2017) pp. 141–149.

5

'Enemies of the People': Article 50, the Press and Anti-Juridicalism

JULIAN PETLEY

ON 3 NOVEMBER 2016, the High Court of England and Wales ruled that the government could not use prerogative powers in order to trigger Article 50 of the Lisbon Treaty and so begin the UK's exit from the European Union. Instead, the government would need to secure Parliament's consent to do so.[1] The following day, significant sections of the national press launched vituperative front-page attacks on the judges concerned: the Lord Chief Justice, Lord Thomas of Cwmgiedd; the newly appointed Master of the Rolls, Sir Terence Etherton; and Lord Justice Sales, the Lord Justice of Appeal. The *Mail*'s now-notorious headline was 'Enemies of the People', with the strapline 'Fury over "out of touch" judges who defied 17.4m Brexit voters and could trigger constitutional crisis'; the *Telegraph* heralded the battle of 'The Judges Versus the People'; and the *Express* trumpeted that 'We Must Get Out of the EU', with the strapline 'Three judges yesterday blocked Brexit. Now your country really does need you ...'. *The Sun* focused primarily on those who brought the case, demanding 'Who Do EU Think You Are?', with the strap 'Loaded foreign elite defy will of Brit voters', accompanied by a photo of a laughing Gina Miller, who, together with Deir Tozetti Dos Santos, had brought the Article 50 case.

It is worth stressing that all of the above were presented as news stories, and front-page ones at that, even though, starting with their headlines, they are deeply imbued with the newspapers' own editorial positions, which are particularly evident in their emotive language but which also clearly shape their selection of interviewees and use of images. It is therefore extremely hard to square them with Clause 1(4) of the Editors Code of Practice that sets out the rules that publications regulated by the Independent Press Standards Organisation (IPSO) have agreed to

---

[1] *R (Miller) v Secretary of State for Exiting the European Union* [2016] EWHC 2768 (Admin) (3 November 2016).

Proceedings of the British Academy, **250**, 88–109, © The British Academy 2022.

follow. This states: 'The Press, while free to editorialise and campaign, must distinguish clearly between comment, conjecture and fact'.[2]

Within days of the judgment, Brexit-supporting politicians were demanding the home addresses of the judges so that people could protest on their doorsteps, there were warnings of rioting in the streets if the 'will of the people' was thwarted, and UKIP leader Nigel Farage announced plans for a mass demonstration the day before the judgment was appealed at the Supreme Court. Obviously, the blame for all this cannot be laid solely at the door of the Brexit press, but such were the inflammatory tones in which these papers 'reported' the judgment, tones that became even more raucous when the stories instantaneously triggered a veritable tsunami on social media, that it is extremely difficult to conceive of these stories as having no agency whatsoever.

Newspaper influence

In recent years, it has become commonplace to argue that what appears in the national press in the UK has much less impact on people's views than it once did. This is for two reasons. First, because national press circulation has fallen dramatically.[3] Second, because most people now receive much of their news from elsewhere – either online and/or the broadcast media.[4] But while the first claim is undoubtedly true, the second needs to be qualified because (a) much of the UK national press has a very considerable online presence (*MailOnline* being the key example); (b) many stories on social media have their origins in British tabloid newspapers, which quite deliberately design stories to act as clickbait; and (c) there is growing evidence[5] that the overwhelmingly right-wing bias of most of the English national press is beginning to skew the news agenda of the public service broadcasters, and particularly the BBC, in spite of their statutory duty to present news and current affairs programmes with due impartiality.

However, arguments about newspapers' supposed lack of influence on their readers ignore the equally important question of the relationship between national newspapers and governments in Britain. This is, given the quite remarkably close relationship between the majority of national titles and Conservative governments,

[2] IPSO, *Editors' Code of Practice*, available online at: https://www.ipso.co.uk/editors-code-of-practice/ (last accessed 26 January 2022).
[3] F. Mayhew, 'UK national newspaper sales slump by two-thirds in 20 years amid digital disruption', *Press Gazette*, 26 February 2020, online at: https://www.pressgazette.co.uk/uk-national-newspaper-sales-slump-by-two-thirds-in-20-years-amid-digital-disruption/ (last accessed 26 January 2022).
[4] Ofcom, News Consumption in the UK: 2019, online at: https://www.ofcom.org.uk/__data/assets/pdf_file/0027/157914/uk-news-consumption-2019-report.pdf (last accessed 26 January 2022).
[5] For example, S. Cushion, A. Kilby, R. Thomas, M. Morani and R. Sambrook, 'Newspapers, Impartiality and Television News', *Journalism Studies*, 19 (2018), 162–181. J. Petley, 'Pressure Points: The BBC and the Extreme Centre', in G. Williams (ed.), *It's the Media, Stupid! The Media, the 2019 Election and the Aftermath* (Pontefract, Campaign for Press and Broadcasting Freedom/North, 2020), pp. 102–113.

a relationship that is perfectly obvious at election times but that clearly manifests itself on occasions such as the one examined in this article. This relationship is entirely symbiotic and circular: Conservative newspapers habitually represent Conservative politicians and their policies, particularly those emanating from the right-wing of the party, in a highly favourable light.[6] Widespread positive press coverage is then taken by the Conservatives, whether in government or opposition, to represent 'public opinion', thus giving their policies a veneer of democratic legitimacy that they may not actually merit in numerical terms. By the same token, dissident voices, either within or outside Parliament, are either marginalised, misrepresented, demonised or quite simply ignored altogether.[7] Thus, even though decreasing numbers of people actually read Britain's national newspapers, it is vital to understand the political and ideological tenor of what routinely appears within their pages, given the key role that these papers play in the political process. *Bien pensant* liberals who would not dream of looking inside the *Mail*, *Sun*, *Express* and *Telegraph* really cannot afford to ignore their contents, and I have therefore quoted from them liberally in the course of this article. It is also important to appreciate not simply the contents of these articles but also their tone and their sheer quantity.

Populism and anti-juridicalism

In this chapter, I analyse the stories about the Article 50 judgment that appeared in the *Mail*, *Express* and *Telegraph* in its immediate aftermath as disturbing expressions of distinctly anti-juridical sentiment. Such sentiment is in fact a key aspect of the now much-discussed phenomenon of populism, but it is curious that this particular feature has not received as much attention as might have been expected, given that it involves a subject as serious as the delegitimisation of the rule of law.

There is currently a great deal of debate over what actually constitutes populism that cannot detain us here. However, as Cas Mudde and Cristóbal Rovira Kaltwasser note, there is general agreement that:

> All forms of populism include some kind of appeal to 'the people' and a denunciation of 'the elite'. Accordingly, it is not overly contentious to state that populism always involves a critique of the establishment and an adulation of the common people.[8]

A classic example of populist sentiment would be Nigel Farage's speech when the result of the Brexit referendum was announced on 24 June 2016, in which he claimed that it was a victory for 'the real people, for the ordinary people, for the

---

[6] R. Greenslade, *Press Gang: How Newspapers Make Profits from Propaganda* (London, Macmillan, 2003).

[7] J. Curran, I. Gaber and J. Petley, *Culture Wars: The Media and the British Left*, 2nd edn (London, Routledge, 2019).

[8] C. Mudde and C. R. Kaltwasser, *Populism: A Very Short Introduction* (Oxford, Oxford University Press, 2017), p. 5.

decent people' and boasted that 'we have fought against the multinationals, we have fought against the big merchant banks, we have fought against big politics, we have fought against lies, corruption and deceit.'[9]

Anti-juridicalism can be understood as a form of specifically penal populism and frequently finds expression in claims that the courts are 'out of touch' and far too 'soft' on criminals, claims that are a particular speciality of much of the national press in Britain.[10] The villains of the piece here are not only liberal judges but remote government officials, fat cat lawyers and ivory tower academics – in other words, the denizens of what in right-wing circles is habitually dismissed as the 'criminal justice establishment'. This is what home secretary Michael Howard had in his sights when he told the Conservative Party conference in October 1996:

> Prison works. It ensures that we are protected from murderers, muggers and rapists – and it makes many who are tempted to commit crime think twice ... This may mean that more people will go to prison. I do not flinch from that. We shall no longer judge the success of our system of justice by a fall in our prison population.

In this scheme of things, there is a vast gulf between the 'will of the people' – in particular what 'the people' expect of the criminal justice system – and the policies and practices of those working in it, especially in the courts, who are denounced as the epitome of the 'liberal elite', excoriation of which has loomed so large in English politics in the past few years. Penal populism has little or no time for the complexities of due process, the rights of the accused or the possibilities of rehabilitation, and is bitterly opposed to what it regards as the establishment's 'behind closed doors, we-know-best methods of administering justice, and their inability to empathize with, or attend to, the anxieties of the public and experience of victims'.[11] As John Pratt puts it:

> Penal populism attempts to reclaim the penal system for what it sees as the oppressed majority and harness it to their aspirations rather than those of the establishment, or those of liberal social movements that pull in the opposite direction to which it wants to travel. When rights are referred to in penal populist discourse, it is usually the rights of the public at large to safety and security, and the withdrawal of rights from those very groups (immigrants, asylum seekers, criminals, prisoners) on whose behalf other social movements are campaigning for.[12]

---

[9] Z. Williams, 'Nigel Farage's victory speech was a triumph of poor taste and ugliness', *Guardian*, 24 June 2016, online at: https://www.theguardian.com/commentisfree/2016/jun/24/nigel-farage-ugliness-bullet-fired (last accessed 26 January 2022).

[10] For a highly detailed discussion of the role played by the press in the formation of criminal justice policy, see M. Dean, *Democracy under Attack: How the Media Distort Policy and Politics* (Bristol, The Policy Press, 2012) pp. 107–210, and Martina Y. Feilzer, 'Understanding Judicial Independence in the Age of Outrage', in this volume.

[11] I. Loader and R. Sparks, 'Penal Populism and Epistemic Crime Control', in A. Liebling, S. Maruna and L. McAra (eds), *The Oxford Handbook of Criminology*, 6th edn, (Oxford, Oxford University Press, 2017), p. 103.

[12] J. Pratt, *Penal Populism* (London, Routledge, 2007), p. 2.

It is thus entirely unsurprising that those newspapers that attacked the judiciary in the matter of Article 50 were precisely the same ones that had already established a long and deeply dishonourable track record of attacking the European Convention on Human Rights and the Human Rights Act 1998 since they regarded both of these as serving only to intensify the courts' already over-liberal inclinations. These papers' treatment of human rights ever since the Human Rights Bill was introduced in 1997 constitutes a veritable compendium of stories heavily infused with anti-juridical sentiments, and their assaults on the High Court in November 2016 were thus able to draw very effectively on a vast and polluted reservoir of populist *ressentiment* that they had assiduously been filling for over 20 years.[13]

'Enemies of democracy'

The *Express* was the only national newspaper to have supported UKIP in the 2015 general election, and its political editor, Patrick O'Flynn, had been elected in 2014 as UKIP's member of the European Parliament for the East of England, serving as its economic spokesman until May 2015. On 4 November 2016, his paper proclaimed that the Article 50 decision represented 'a crisis as grave as any our country has faced since the dark days when Churchill vowed we would fight them on the beaches', and lamented that 3 November was 'the day democracy died'. In full populist flow, the paper went on to complain that:

> Ordinary people clearly do not trust MPs of any party to make this momentous decision on their behalf, which is why on June 23 there was a popular revolt against the elitists who deem we are too stupid to know what's best for us. Now, with no hint of irony, some of the highest legal minds in the land decide to hand back to that Westminster cabal the very power the people believe they should not be trusted with.

It continued:

> Nor have the courts ever expressed concern about UK powers being handed to the EU – only when the flow is about to be reversed does the judiciary step in. Where were the self-styled champions of British sovereignty when the Mother of Parliaments was being forcibly sterilised by the European Communities Act and then politically raped by the treaties of Maastricht, Dublin and Lisbon?[14]

The *Mail*'s coverage[15] on 4 November employed one of its favourite weapons in its unceasing war on those with whom it disagrees: thumbnail sketches of their careers,

---

[13] J. Petley, 'Podsnappery: Or Why British Newspapers Support Fagging', *Ethical Space*, 3 (2006), pp. 42–50; D. Mead, '"You Couldn't Make It Up": Some Narratives of the Media's Coverage of Human Rights', in K. S. Ziegler, E. Wicks and L. Hudson (eds), *The UK and European Human Rights: A Strained Relationship?* (Oxford, Hart Publishing, 2015), pp. 453–472.

[14] 'After judges' Brexit block now your country really needs you: We MUST get out of the EU', *Express*, 4 November 2016, online at: https://www.express.co.uk/comment/expresscomment/728602/Brexit-jud ges-block-leave-EU-referendum-High-Court (last accessed 26 January 2022).

[15] J. Slack, 'Enemies of the people: Fury over "out of touch" judges who have "declared war on democ-racy" by defying 17.4m Brexit voters and who could trigger constitutional crisis', *Daily Mail*, 3 November

consisting largely of selected details absolutely guaranteed to raise the hackles of readers to whose views, famously, it is so minutely attuned. Such sketches appear to be purely descriptive but are in fact loaded with connotations that typical *Mail* readers would find highly disagreeable. Nothing is to be gained by reproducing all the smears and innuendos here, but a small sample will suffice to demonstrate the journalistic tactics being employed. Thus, Lord Thomas is described as 'a committed Europhile'. The paper also reveals that 'in 2013, he rebuked Sir Paul Coleridge for "bringing the judiciary into disrepute" after speaking out in favour of traditional marriage and describing the devastating impact of family break-up on children', the 'traditional family' being a cornerstone of *Mail* ideology. Sir Terence Etherton is labelled as 'the first openly gay judge to be made a Lord Justice of Appeal' and 'the epitome of a modern judge', who 'served for two years as chairman of the Law Commission – the government's legal reform body – where he was credited with suggesting "enlightened" ways of updating laws' (note the revealing use of scare quotes here). Finally, Lord Justice Sales is damned by his association with *Mail* arch-enemy Tony Blair: it is pointed out that he came from the same chambers (11 KBW) that 'defended the Blair government in a 2005 court challenge over the decision not to hold a public inquiry into the Iraq war' and 'charged taxpayers £3.3 million in six years during his tenure as Mr Blair's First Treasury Counsel'.

That day's edition of the *Mail* also contains a column by Richard Littlejohn headed 'We Can't Let Brexit be Derailed',[16] which claims that:

> What we're seeing now is an attempted coup designed to overthrow the will of the British people. Yesterday's decision by three unelected judges to side with the sore losers who want to scupper Britain's departure from the European Union is a constitutional outrage. It is a victory for vested interests and the enemies of democracy.

Much of the article is taken up with attacking Remainer MPs and those who brought the High Court action, but it is hard to avoid the conclusion that, in true anti-juridical fashion, the judges are firmly included among the 'enemies of democracy'. An article in the same issue by Dominic Raab headed 'Wrecking Tactics Will Only Backfire'[17] is taken up largely with an attack on 'an unholy alliance of City fund managers, Lib Dem peers and die-hard Remain campaigners' rather than on the judges, although it does strike a distinctly anti-juridical note in accusing the latter of indulging in 'ivory-tower reasoning'.

2016, online at: https://www.dailymail.co.uk/news/article-3903436/Enemies-people-Fury-touch-judges-defied-17-4m-Brexit-voters-trigger-constitutional-crisis.html (last accessed 26 January 2022).

[16] R. Littlejohn, 'This is a coup, a victory for enemies of democracy. If the roles were reversed there would be riots in the street, so we CAN'T let Brexit be derailed by this City slicker and a Brazilian crimper', *Daily Mail*, 3 November 2016, online at: https://www.dailymail.co.uk/debate/article-3903 236/We-t-let-Brexit-derailed-City-slicker-Brazilian-crimper-writes-RICHARD-LITTLEJOHN.html (last accessed 26 January 2022).

[17] D. Raab, 'Wrecking tactics will only backfire: Remain campaign is on a collision course with democracy that it can't win', *Daily Mail*, 4 November 2016, online at: https://www.dailymail.co.uk/news/article-3903682/Wrecking-tactics-backfire-Remain-campaign-collision-course-democracy-t-win-wri tes-DOMINIC-RAAB.html (last accessed 26 January 2022).

The *Telegraph*[18] took the same line as the *Mail* in describing Lord Justice Sales as 'a close friend of Tony Blair, the former Prime Minister who campaigned for Remain and wants a second vote on Britain's EU membership' and notes that 'Lord Thomas co-founded a Europhile legal group'. In the main body of its front-page article, it quotes six people opposed to the High Court's decision and not one in favour. Anti-juridicalism looms large in these quotations, with Ian Duncan Smith complaining that 'you now have the High Court telling government and Parliament how to go about their business. This is unprecedented', and Lord Tebbit claiming that 'judges are out of their boxes these days and need to be put back in', while Douglas Carswell, then UKIP's only MP, hit out at this 'shocking judicial activism', adding: 'These judges are politicians without accountability'.

Paradoxically, however, the *Telegraph*'s numerous comment columns, by, among others, Ian Duncan Smith and former *Telegraph* editor Charles Moore, entirely avoided calling into question the judges' independence and impartiality and thus are free of the elements of anti-juridicalism that inform its front-page news story. The same is true of the columns by its assistant editor and chief leader writer, Philip Johnston, and of its unsigned editorials, which take the line that the High Court should have declined to hear the Article 50 case because it concerned a political dispute that should be settled in Parliament and not by judges. One can disagree with such an approach, as did the Supreme Court, but reasoned criticism of the High Court on these grounds is of an entirely different order from the populist, anti-juridical discourse with which this article is primarily concerned.

'Political pygmies'

Unsurprisingly, the anti-juridicalism unleashed by certain newspapers and politicians in the wake of the High Court judgment attracted substantial criticism from the legal profession, but parliamentarians joined in too, including a number of notable Conservatives in both Houses. For example, the former Attorney General Dominic Grieve was quoted in the journalism trade paper, *Press Gazette*, on 7 November,[19] as condemning press criticism of the three judges as 'chilling and outrageous' and 'smack[ing] of the fascist state'; in his view, reading some of the newspaper coverage was like 'living in Robert Mugabe's Zimbabwe' and he warned of 'the danger of a sort of mob psyche developing'. From the legal side, the

---

[18] 'Judges vs the people: Government ministers resigned to losing appeal against High Court ruling', *Telegraph*, 3 November 2016, online at: https://www.telegraph.co.uk/news/2016/11/03/the-plot-to-stop-brexit-the-judges-versus-the-people/ (last accessed 26 January 2022).

[19] D. Ponsford, 'IPSO chair Sir Alan Moses: Lord Chancellor should do more to protect judges from "ignorant criticism"', *Press Gazette*, 7 November 2016, online at: https://www.pressgazette.co.uk/ipso-chair-sir-alan-moses-lord-chancellor-should-do-more-to-protect-judges-from-ignorant-criticism/ (last accessed 26 January 2022).

QC Lord Macdonald of River Glaven, a former Director of Public Prosecutions, addressed himself to some of the Brexit-supporting politicians quoted so enthusiastically by much of the press, stating that:

> These are risible and constitutionally illiterate attacks from politicians who should know better. The high court has reaffirmed the sovereignty of parliament within the rule of law. In other words, it has fulfilled precisely its most critical function in a democratic society. The idea that judges would be better employed kowtowing to the executive is shameful heresy from political pygmies.[20]

But, as far as the national press was concerned, such criticisms featured to any significant extent only in its liberal rump, namely the *Guardian/Observer*, the *Independent* and the *Financial Times*.

A little too late and quite a lot too little

This was only to be expected, but more disturbing was the distinct hesitancy of both the Prime Minister, Theresa May, and the Justice Secretary and Lord Chancellor, Liz Truss, to comment on these attacks on the judiciary, particularly as the latter's post carries with it a duty to 'respect the independence of the judiciary' and to 'uphold the rule of law' under Section 3(6) of the Constitutional Reform Act 2005. This hiatus, and the fact that they both equivocated when they finally did speak, reveals a great deal about the symbiotic relationship between the Conservative press and Conservative governments mentioned earlier.

On Friday 4 November, a previous Lord Chancellor, Lord Falconer, wrote an article for the *Guardian* headed 'The Vicious Assault on UK Judges by the Brexit Press is a Threat to Democracy'.[21] In it, he pointed out that:

> We trust our judges to uphold the law and the constitution impartially. This impartiality depends on judges not expressing views, so they can't defend themselves. That's why the government has an obligation to defend them and why the constitution places a duty on the lord chancellor to do so. The government needs to make it clear that they dissociate themselves from these attacks and come to the defence of the judges.

In particular, Falconer argued, Truss needed to 'make it clear immediately that the government has no quarrel with the judges and has total confidence in them. Disagreement with the judges is dealt with by appeal not by abuse'.

In the face of mounting criticism, including a resolution passed on Friday 5 November by the Bar Council regretting the Justice Secretary's lack of a public

---

[20] O. Bowcott and H. Stewart, 'MPs condemn newspaper attacks on judges after Brexit ruling', *Guardian*, 4 November 2016, online at: https://www.theguardian.com/media/2016/nov/04/labour-conde mns-newspaper-attacks-on-judges-after-brexit-ruling (last accessed 26 January 2022).
[21] C. Falconer, 'The vicious assault on UK judges by the Brexit press is a threat to democracy', *Guardian*, 4 November 2016, online at: https://www.theguardian.com/commentisfree/2016/nov/04/assa ult-uk-judges-brexit-press-judiciary-constitution (last accessed 26 January 2022).

statement and calling on her to condemn the attacks as a 'matter of urgency',[22] Truss put out a very brief statement on the same day (within 96 minutes of the resolution being passed, to be precise) to the effect that:

> The independence of the judiciary is the foundation upon which our rule of law is built and our judiciary is rightly respected the world over for its independence and impartiality. In relation to the case heard in the high court, the government has made it clear it will appeal to the supreme court. Legal process must be followed.[23]

However, this did little more than restate the principle of judicial independence and entirely failed to condemn the attacks on the judiciary. The former Lord Chief Justice, Lord Judge, interviewed on Radio 4 on the same day, expressed the view that her response was 'a little too late and I think it's quite a lot too little. Because it doesn't actually address the damage to public confidence consequent on [these] kind of headlines'.[24] Similarly, Chantal-Aimée Doerries QC, the chairman of the Bar Council, stated: 'We would wish her to go further. The resolution passed by the Bar Council called upon her to condemn the attacks on the judiciary and it is that we are still looking for. It is that which is so potentially damaging to the justice system in this country'.[25] And on Monday 7 November, 17 QCs from the eminent chambers 1 Crown Office Row wrote to Truss expressing their dismay at her 'inadequate' response to the attacks on the high court judges. They argued that:

> The ill-founded basis for the abuse which has followed this judgement has required firm correction. Your statement at the weekend failed to spell out in clear terms that the judges in question had simply been ruling on the dispute, had not been motivated by bias, and that to accuse them of trying to thwart the will of the people was dangerously to misrepresent what they had done.

The letter concluded: 'Without an independent judiciary, supported by the executive, and above all yourself, talk of the rule of law is empty'.[26]

'We don't kowtow here'

On Sunday 6 November, the *Guardian* reported that the Prime Minister, on a flight to Delhi for a trade mission, had told reporters merely that 'I believe in and value

[22] D. Boffey, 'Brexit: lawyers confront Liz Truss over "dangerous" abuse of judges', *Guardian*, 6 November 2016, online at: https://www.theguardian.com/politics/2016/nov/05/lawyers-war-liz-truss-over-abuse-judges-brexit-barristers (last accessed 26 January 2022).

[23] 'Liz Truss defends judiciary after Brexit ruling criticism', *Guardian*, 5 November 2016, online at: https://www.theguardian.com/law/2016/nov/05/barristers-urge-liz-truss-to-condemn-attacks-on-brexit-ruling-judges (last accessed 26 January 2022).

[24] R. Burgon, 'Liz Truss swore to defend the judiciary. But she stood by as they got a roasting', *Guardian*, 8 November 2016, online at: https://www.theguardian.com/commentisfree/2016/nov/08/liz-truss-defend-judges-article-50-stood-by (last accessed 26 January 2022).

[25] Boffey, 'Brexit: lawyers confront Liz Truss over "dangerous" abuse of judges'.

[26] J. Rozenberg, '17 silks from @1CrownOfficeRow tell @trussliz they are "dismayed" by her "inadequate defence" of the Brexit judges', *Twitter*, 7 November 2016, online at: https://twitter.com/JoshuaRozenberg/status/795738825133789184?s=20 (last accessed 26 January 2022).

the independence of our judiciary. I also value the freedom of our press. These both underpin our democracy'.[27] In response, Lord Falconer wrote to *The Times* on 9 November, stating:

> The prime minister emphasises the importance of freedom of the press and independence of the judiciary, and implies that to attack the press for their attacks of the Brexit judges is to attack the freedom of the press. She believes that saying she supports an independent judiciary is all that is required. She misses the point. The press must be free to say what they think. What gives the judges confidence their independence will be protected is that the government of the day will defend them against individual campaigns designed to influence them. That did not happen. No 10 refused to defend them despite being repeatedly invited to do so, and the lord chancellor has still not defended them. The most striking failure is the silence of the lord chancellor. It signals to the judges that they have lost their constitutional protector.[28]

On the other hand, May's few words earned her the headline in the *Mail*, 'May Backs Press in Judges Row' (although given that May's remarks were even-handed, the story – albeit in a paper of a different political complexion – could just as easily have been headlined 'May Backs Judges in Press Row').[29] The story also noted that Lord Patten, speaking on the previous day's ITV programme *Peston on Sunday*, had criticised the hostile press coverage of the High Court's decision, quoting him as saying that 'Theresa May should make it clear that she doesn't like the way that tabloid editors have been pushing this debate'. Patten's remarks immediately earned him a rebuke from the same day's *Mail*'s Comment column headed 'No Lord Patten. We Don't Kowtow Here'.[30] This described him as

> that perfect embodiment of the arrogant political class, who has enjoyed a life of opulent privilege at the taxpayer's expense since the voters had the good sense to sack him as an MP 24 years ago. Governor of Hong Kong. European Commissioner. Chancellor of Oxford University. Chairman of the BBC. And now this committed Europhile has assumed a new mantle – that of self-appointed Censor-in-Chief.

It continued:

> Is this a tip he picked up from the Chinese? Because this was a blatant call for the suppression of dissent. And as a former guardian of the BBC's editorial independence

---

[27] A. Asthana and H. Stewart, 'Theresa May defends newspapers over attacks on article 50 judges', *Guardian*, 6 November 2016, online at: https://www.theguardian.com/politics/2016/nov/06/labour-will-not-block-article-50-jeremy-corbyn-allies-confirm (last accessed 26 January 2022).

[28] 'Lord Chancellor's ability called into question', *The Times*, 9 November 2016, online at: https://www.thetimes.co.uk/article/lord-chancellors-ability-called-into-question-qps7zccjc (last accessed 26 January 2022).

[29] D. Martin and J. Slack, 'The press must be free to criticise: Theresa May backs newspapers after attacks on judges who ruled EU deal must go through Parliament', *Daily Mail*, 6 November 2016, online at: https://www.dailymail.co.uk/news/article-3910708/The-press-free-criticise-Theresa-backs-newspapers-attacks-judges-ruled-EU-deal-Parliament.html (last accessed 26 January 2022).

[30] 'Daily Mail Comment: No, Lord Patten. We don't kowtow here', *Daily Mail*, 7 November 2016, online at: https://www.dailymail.co.uk/debate/article-3911700/DAILY-MAIL-COMMENT-No-Lord-Patten-don-t-kowtow-here.html (last accessed 26 January 2022).

Lord Patten should be truly ashamed. The fact is that by scrutinising the backgrounds of the judges, the Press – which, thankfully, is still free in this country – is simply doing its job of holding the powerful to account. It's Lord Patten and his embittered Remainer friends who are failing to show respect – in this case, for the legions who voted for Brexit. Why on earth should the judiciary – one of the last great unreformed British institutions – be above criticism?

We shall return to the *Mail*'s views on the accountability of the judiciary towards the end of this chapter.

'A green light'

Meanwhile, criticism of Truss' refusal to condemn the anti-juridicalism of sections of the press (as well as of certain members of her own party) had continued apace. On 7 November,[31] a number of angry Conservative MPs, many of them senior lawyers, had confronted Truss at a private meeting and told her that there was 'huge' concern about the slowness of her response to the anti-juridical attacks by sections of the press and of their own party – including the Communities Secretary, Sajid Javid, who, on the BBC programme *Question Time* on 4 November, had criticised the judgment as 'a clear attempt to frustrate the will of the British people'.[32] One MP was quoted as stating that 'her job is to defend the judiciary from attack, and while she is not required to attack the *Daily Mail* she should have disassociated the government from their attacks', and when Truss argued that the job of defending the judiciary should fall to the Lord Chief Justice in the first instance, this also provoked criticism since Lord Thomas was one of those under attack for giving the judgment in the first place.

That Monday also saw three more high-profile attacks on the wave of anti-juridicalism and criticisms of Truss for her inaction in the face of it.[33] Thus the Law Society President, Robert Bourns, stated: 'Attacks on the judges simply because they were doing their jobs does our country no credit, and government ministers must be unequivocal in their support for the rule of law even if they disagree with the judgment'. Francis FitzGibbon QC, Chairman of the Criminal Bar Association, complained that:

> Neither the Lord Chancellor nor the Prime Minister have done what they ought to do, and unreservedly condemn both the calling of judges 'enemies of the people', the demands for their dismissal, and the making of their blameless personal lives into objects of reproach. Standing by and saying nothing may not be meant as such, but is likely to be seen as tacit approval for what has gone on, and encouragement for more

---

[31] J. Elgot, 'Liz Truss confronted by Tory MPs over handling of article 50 row', *Guardian*, 8 November 2016, online at: https://www.theguardian.com/politics/2016/nov/08/liz-truss-confronted-by-tory-mps-handling-of-article-50-row (last accessed 26 January 2022).

[32] 'Brexit case "attempt to block will of people" says Sajid Javid', BBC News, 4 November 2016, online at: https://www.bbc.co.uk/news/uk-politics-37866411 (last accessed 26 January 2022).

[33] O. Bowcott, 'Attorney general defends judges criticised over Brexit ruling', *Guardian,* 7 November 2016, online at: https://www.theguardian.com/politics/2016/nov/07/attorney-general-jeremy-wright-defends-judges-criticised-brexit-ruling (last accessed 26 January 2022).

of the same. In these disturbed times, dignified silence doesn't work because there are too many people who will see it as a green light.

And finally, demonstrating that the populist onslaught on the judges had caused concern beyond the confines of the UK, Nils Muižnieks, the commissioner for human rights at the Council of Europe, which oversees the European Court of Human Rights, criticised the 'blatant attacks on the independence of the judiciary designed to stir up popular hatred, not just against the so-called "enemies of the people" but also those who brought the claim to the courts'. He went on to argue that 'political leaders have a duty to stand up to those sectors of the media that are stirring up hatred. A stronger message is now needed from the UK government which clearly condemns the personal attacks on the judges and the targeting of those individuals who brought the challenge to the courts'.

The next day, on 8 November, the *Guardian*[34] reported that, in the House of Lords, the Conservative former Justice Minister, Lord Faulks, had questioned the Lords spokesperson for the Ministry of Justice, Lord Keen, about the issue. Referring to the 'disgraceful attack on the judiciary', Faulks asked: 'Would you take this opportunity to show the government's support for the entire cohort of the judiciary, whether it be the supreme court, the divisional court or the magistracy?' To which Keen responded:

> We have a judiciary of the highest calibre. We have a free press which is not always of the highest calibre. Sensationalist and ill-informed attacks can undermine public confidence in the judiciary. But our public can have every confidence in our judiciary and it is a confidence, I believe, that must be shared by the executive.

The article also reported that the Conservative Chair of the Commons Justice Select Committee, Bob Neil, had issued a statement noting that it condemned personal attacks on members of the judiciary. It stated that:

> Free debate should not be couched in terms of abuse of individuals who, by virtue of the oath they have taken and the role they discharge, cannot defend themselves publicly. It is quite wrong to vilify or attack judges or attempt to intimidate or undermine them. The right of the press to speak freely must be exercised responsibly; it is not a licence to attack judges in a personal manner or seek to undermine the constitutional principle of judicial independence, which is absolute.

Freedom to undermine democratic principles

Finally, on 10 November, Truss made a statement. This took the form of a letter to *The Times*[35] in response to that from Lord Falconer published the previous day.

[34] J. Elgot and O. Bowcott, 'Lords justice spokesman condemns "ill-informed" attacks on judiciary', *Guardian*, 8 November 2016, online at: https://www.theguardian.com/law/2016/nov/08/lords-justice-spokesman-condemns-ill-informed-attacks-on-judiciary (last accessed 26 January 2022).

[35] The bulging intray facing President Trump', *The Times*, 10 November 2016, online at: https://www.thetimes.co.uk/edition/comment/the-bulging-intray-facing-president-trump-62rxh35gs (last accessed 26 January 2022).

Like Theresa May's remark a few days earlier, this was as much a defence of the freedom of the press as of the independence of the judiciary. Thus, briefly noting that 'an independent judiciary is the cornerstone of the rule of law, vital to our constitution and freedoms' and that it was indeed her duty to defend it, she went on to say that she thought it unlikely that 'the high court is imperilled by the opinions of any newspaper' and to argue, at rather greater length, that 'there is another principle at stake here: the freedom of the press. I believe in a free press, where newspapers are free to publish, within the law, their views. It is not the job of the government or lord chancellor to police headlines, and it would be a dark day for democracy if that changed'. In this respect, it is also worth noting that when the Health Minister, Jeremy Hunt, appeared on the *Andrew Marr Show* on 6 December, he too brought up the question of press freedom, averring that 'I would defend to the hilt the right of newspapers within the law to write what they like and to criticise politicians'.[36] Similarly, on 5 November, Dominic Raab, the former Justice Minister, told the *Telegraph*: 'This is a hugely contentious ruling bound to provoke criticism and debate. Our judges are robust, not some precious shrinking violets. Frankly, the Bar Council sound like they want to gag debate, which is hardly democratic'.[37]

However, while no one would deny the importance of a free press to a democratic society, this leaves wide open the question of what actually constitutes such a press. In particular, if it is to be considered as free, what must it be free from, and what must it be free to do? A press may be free from control by the state, but not from owners with their own political agenda and governmental links. And if the function of a free press is to act as a Fourth Estate, striving in the public interest to uphold and protect democratic values, should it be free to undermine one of the cornerstones of democracy, namely the independence of the judiciary and, more generally, the principle of the separation of powers? Detailed discussions of these matters are beyond the scope of this article, but they do relate very closely to the questions raised earlier concerning the relationship between the press and government.[38] In this instance, the suspicion must remain that such invocations of press freedom on the part of the government serve the primary purpose of maintaining good relations with highly supportive newspapers, while those newspapers' defence of press freedom extends only to their freedom to follow a particular editorial line, even though this may be highly partisan, rooted in inaccuracies and untruths, and deeply damaging to the democratic process. Anyone remotely familiar with the manner in which the government and most of the national press acted in concert to ensure that none of the Leveson Inquiry's recommendations were ever put into practice and marshalled a

---

[36] Bowcott, 'Attorney general defends judges criticised over Brexit ruling'.

[37] Bowcott, 'Attorney general defends judges criticised over Brexit ruling'.

[38] For a more detailed discussion of this topic see J. Petley, 'The Leveson Inquiry: Journalism Ethics and Press Freedom', *Journalism*, 13 (2012), 529–538; G. Phillipson, 'Leveson, The Public Interest and Press Freedom', *Journal of Media Law*, 5 (2013), 220–240. See also my witness statement to the Leveson Inquiry: https://discoverleveson.com/evidence/Witness_Statement_of_Professor_Julian_Petley/11469/media

very particular conception of 'press freedom' in order to back up their arguments,[39] cannot fail to spot certain disturbing parallels here.

'The next lot'

Immediately after the High Court delivered its judgment in the Article 50 case, the government made clear its intention to appeal to the Supreme Court. Equally rapidly, sections of the press cast doubt on the integrity of several of its members. Thus, on 5 November, the *Telegraph* ran an article headed 'Four Judges to Rule on Brexit Have Previous Ties with Europe'.[40] In recent years, the *Telegraph* has increasingly aped the *Mail* (earning it the sobriquet the *Mailygraph* from *Private Eye*), and this article makes exactly the same use of highly selective capsule descriptions of judges as several *Mail* pieces discussed in this article. As it is hard to see what point these thumbnail sketches serve other than to cast doubt on the impartiality and independence of the judges in question, these can quite properly be considered as expressions of anti-juridicalism. Thus, for example, Lords Carnwath and Reed are identified as co-founders of the EU Forum of Judges for the Environment, 'a body that exists to promote the enforcement of national, European and international environmental law'. Of Lord Reed, it is further noted that he was a judge in the European Court of Human Rights, 'where he was on the panel that decided that Robert Thompson and Jon Venables, the child killers of toddler James Bulger, had not received a fair trial'. This is a cause very close to the *Telegraph*'s heart as the paper had played a highly significant role in demonising the two boys in the wake of their trial for the murder,[41] has a very long history (along with other Conservative newspapers) of attacking the Court,[42] and bitterly opposed its judgment in a subsequent action involving Thompson and Venables.[43] Thus this description, strictly factual though it may be, also carries a vast amount of negative baggage. Lord Kerr is identified as a former judge in the ECtHR, and, finally, we are informed that Lord Mance has, among other European achievements, 'served as a member

---

[39] S. Barnett and J. Townend, '"And What Good Came of It at Last?" Press-Politician Relations Post-Leveson', *The Political Quarterly*, 85 (2004), 159–169.

[40] G. Rayner, 'Four judges to rule on Brexit have previous ties to Europe', *Telegraph*, 4 November 2016, online at: https://www.telegraph.co.uk/news/2016/11/04/Four-judges-to-rule-on-Brexit-have-previous-ties-to-Europe/ (last accessed 26 January 2022).

[41] B. Franklin and J. Petley, 'Killing the Age of Innocence: Newspaper Reporting of the Death of James Bulger', in J. Pilcher and S. Wagg (eds), *Thatcher's Children? Politics, Childhood and Society in the 1980s and 1990s* (London, Falmer Press, 1996), pp. 134–154.

[42] J. Petley, 'Podsnappery: Or Why British Newspapers Support Fagging', *Ethical Space: The International Journal of Communication Ethics*, 3 (2006), 42–50; D. Mead, '"You Couldn't Make It Up": Some Narratives of the Media's Coverage of Human Rights', in K.S. Ziegler, E. Wicks and L. Hodson (eds), *The UK and European Human Rights: A Strained Relationship?* (Oxford, Hart Publishing, 2015), pp. 453–472.

[43] J. Petley, '"Kill a Kid and Get a House": Rationality versus Retribution in the Case of Robert Thompson and Jon Venables, 1993–2001', in S. Wagg and J. Pilcher (eds), *Thatcher's Grandchildren? Politics and Childhood in the Twenty-First Century* (Basingstoke, Palgrave Macmillan, 2014), pp. 1–26.

of a seven-person EU panel that helps select judges and advocates-general of the European Court of Justice and General Court'. Appearing as they do in a paper profoundly hostile to the EU and to the European Convention on Human Rights, these highly selective sketches are very far indeed from being neutral and purely factual descriptions.

An article by Andrew Pierce, published in the *Mail* on 7 November, headed 'And Now Here's the Next Lot Lining up to Have a Go',[44] repeats most of the points made about the judges in the *Telegraph* article above, but, significantly, adds that 'Britain's selection of Supreme Court justices is far more secretive than the process in the US' and that 'no public scrutiny is required'. This theme was also taken up by the paper on the same day in its article attacking Lord Patten, noted above.[45] This complained that the Supreme Court is a 'virtual closed shop' with the judges 'largely selected by their peers'. It noted that 'calls for public hearings to gauge candidates' views and any political leanings – as happens in the US – have been resisted', and asked rhetorically: 'Isn't it time for a change?'

That the *Mail* required just such a change becomes abundantly clear from the considerable vigour with which it would pursue this theme during the run-up to the Supreme Court judgment. Once again, this involved casting aspersions on the independence and impartiality of the judiciary in a fashion that can legitimately be described as anti-juridical.

This battle was re-joined in an article and leader column on 3 December. The former, entitled 'The Judges and the People',[46] by Guy Adams, revealed that:

> Four of the 11 members of the Supreme Court have formal links to either the EU, its courts or European institutions; five have publicly expressed views which appear to be sympathetic to the EU; while six have personal links with individuals who have been critical of the Leave campaign. Only four have no obvious associations with the Remain ethos.

Each of the 11 judges is then given a 'Europhile' rating from one to five and subjected to highly selective thumbnail sketch in the habitual *Mail* style noted above. In order to fully appreciate the importance of this form of innuendo-laden, join-the-dots 'journalism', the lengthy article (nearly 3,000 words) really needs to be read as a whole, but a few examples should give a clear idea of the kinds of tactics that it utilises and indicate that it is not an attack only on the Supreme Court judges but

---

[44] A. Pierce, 'And now here's the next lot lining up to have a go: judges who will rule on Brexit impact', *Daily Mail*, 7 November 2016, online at: https://www.dailymail.co.uk/news/article-3911656/And-s-lot-lining-EU-links-judges-rule-Brexit-impact.html (last accessed 26 January 2022).

[45] 'Daily Mail Comment: No, Lord Patten. We don't kowtow here', *Daily Mail*, 7 November 2016, online at: https://www.dailymail.co.uk/debate/article-3911700/DAILY-MAIL-COMMENT-No-Lord-Patten-don-t-kowtow-here.html (last accessed 26 January 2022).

[46] G. Adams, 'The judges and the people: Next week, 11 unaccountable individuals will consider a case that could thwart the will of the majority on Brexit. The Mail makes no apology for revealing their views – and many have links to Europe', *Daily Mail*, 2 December 2016, online at: https://www.daily mail.co.uk/news/article-3995754/The-judges-people-week-11-unaccountable-individuals-consider-case-help-thwart-majority-Brexit-Mail-makes-no-apology-revealing-views-links-Europe.html   (last accessed 26 January 2022).

a full-throated populist assault on what papers such as the *Mail* habitually label the 'liberal elite'. Thus, for example, Supreme Court president Lord Neuberger (five-star Europhile rating) 'has expressed views that betray an empathy with EU legal institutions' and stated that he 'would oppose withdrawal from the European Convention on Human Rights'. The fact that he was until recently a governor of the University of the Arts is dragged into service in order to draw attention to the fact that its vice-chancellor had 'emailed students on the day after the EU referendum to say that "the Leave vote breaks my heart", adding: "I make no apologies in sharing my shock and dismay"'. However, Lord Neuberger's fitness for the job in hand is questioned primarily by focusing on the allegedly left-wing views of his family and friends, allegations that are unworthy of repetition here. As for Lady Hale, also five-star rated, we are informed that 'they don't come more progressive', that she has made 'countless pronouncements said [not least by the *Mail*] to have undermined the institution of marriage', that she recently backed a European Court of Human Rights ruling over votes for prisoners, and that 'in a 2015 speech in Oxford spoke favourably about the process via which European courts can overrule British ones'. In the case of Lord Mance, we are told that he 'made a fawning speech in Luxembourg upon the retirement of Vassilios Skouris as president of the European Court of Justice, declaring that his presidency "has seen a powerful reaffirmation of the autonomous and binding nature of EU law"'. However, as with Lord Neuberger, it is his family, and indeed his family's friends and employers, that come in for the full *Mail* treatment here, providing the reader with a veritable galaxy of the 'liberal elite'. These smears and innuendos will not be repeated here, but needless to say, Lord Mance earns the full five stars.

'Unaccountable judicial power'

The lengthy leader,[47] entitled 'Why the Free Press Should Shine a Light on This Unelected Court', began by dismissing the criticism of the paper's 'Enemies of the People' article as 'an outburst of hysteria', argued that it had put 'the vital issue of unaccountable judicial power on the map', and claimed that the paper had 'every right to investigate the records of the 11 [judges] for clues to where they stand, both on the EU and the limits of judicial power to overrule MPs', particularly in the light of the 'disturbing' facts revealed by Adams' 'investigation'. Drawing on several of the thumbnail sketches in Adams' article, it singled out for criticism Lord Neuberger on account of his wife's support for remaining in the EU and Lady Hale as a judge who has 'repeatedly shown herself ready to overrule ministers and parliament'. This, in the paper's view, has been greatly facilitated by another of its favourite hate objects, namely the Human Rights Act 1998, because 'human

---

[47] 'Daily Mail Comment: Why the free Press must shine a light on this unelected court', *Daily Mail*, 3 December 2016, online at: https://www.dailymail.co.uk/debate/article-3996182/DAILY-MAIL-COMMENT-free-Press-shine-light-unelected-court.html (last accessed 26 January 2022).

rights laws [sic] are so broadly phrased that they allow judges considerable leeway to interpret them, often at the expense of the government of the day'. The result is, according to the *Mail*, that judges have become not only 'judicial activists' but have also 'progressively assumed the role of the overtly political Supreme Court in Washington'. However, and this for the paper is the nub of the matter, the US court's judges 'are appointed only after intensive public scrutiny of their personal and political views', whereas in Britain, the Supreme Court judges 'are selected by a cosy five-person special commission, out of public sight'. And that is why, in the *Mail*'s view, 'it is so essential for a free Press to subject judges – no less than politicians, civil servants or archbishops – to the scrutiny they would otherwise escape'. In true populist fashion, it concludes by promising that 'though Remainers and the Left may hurl abuse at us, this paper, for one, will always take seriously our role as the Champions of the People'.

Two days later, on 5 December 2016, Adams returned to the fray in an article headlined 'Quangocrats Who Choose Judges in Secret – and How it Puts Us to Shame'.[48] This decried the 'secretive and opaque' way in which the judges are selected for Britain's Supreme Court, comparing it unfavourably with the public selection of their US equivalents in which it is 'considered absolutely crucial and fundamental to the national interest that the people they govern are made familiar with every possible detail about who they are, and what motivates them'. This 'great exercise in democratic accountability' is then contrasted with the 'scandalous' way in which the British judges have been 'elevated to their current status without undergoing any public scrutiny whatsoever' and how 'the public has been told precious little about what shapes the Justices' view'. Details of some of the judges' links to the EU are reprised from the previous article, and the Selection Commission is criticised for being 'dominated by members of the legal profession', leading Adams to conclude that: 'Impressive though their CVs may be, it seems unlikely that this collection of high-powered quangocrats count many UKIP voters among their circle of close acquaintants. As to the whys and wherefores of their decision-making process in choosing Supreme Court judges, it's anyone's guess'.

The same day's *Mail* also carried a leading article headed 'Heat, Fury and a Very Political Judgement'.[49] This ridiculed the assumption that the judges are 'somehow able to be guided only by intellectual legalistic principles, divorcing themselves from the consequences of their decision', and argued that 'it is utterly impossible for them to deliberate in a vacuum, impervious to the political heat and fury surrounding their ruling'.

---

[48] G. Adams, 'The Brexit judges selected by quangocrats: How the Supreme Court justices who will decide the Article 50 case today are chosen in secret – and how the US puts us to shame', *Daily Mail*, 5 December 2016, online at: https://www.dailymail.co.uk/news/article-3999994/Quagocrats-choose-judges-secret-puts-British-shame.html (last accessed 26 January 2022).

[49] 'Daily Mail Comment: Heat, fury, and a very political judgment', *Daily Mail*, 5 December 2016, online at: https://www.dailymail.co.uk/debate/article-4000236/DAILY-MAIL-COMMENT-Heat-fury-political-judgement.html (last accessed 26 January 2022).

Harbingers of the future

These articles in the *Mail* about the Supreme Court judges, stretching from 7 November to 5 December 2016, raise as many important issues as those that appeared in the immediate aftermath of the High Court judgment on 3 November, and I want to conclude by considering their import and particularly their possible long-term implications.

First, the *Mail* singularly failed to acknowledge its own very considerable role in communicating, and indeed in helping to generate, the 'political heat and fury' that it mentioned. Ever since Stanley Baldwin famously remarked in 1931 that 'the newspapers attacking me are not newspapers in the ordinary sense' but 'engines of propaganda' for the views of their proprietors, Lords Beaverbrook and Rothermere, who were intent on exercising 'power without responsibility – the prerogative of the harlot throughout the ages', newspapers have been very wary of boasting of the political power that they undoubtedly wield.[50] However, this power is none-theless real for being largely unacknowledged – indeed, its invisibility is actu-ally a crucial aspect of its potency. For the most part, newspapers are the invisible actors in the stories that fill their pages: press power is simply assumed away, and journalists represent themselves as merely the people's proxies holding others to account. During the Article 50 furore, the *Mail* may have raged repeatedly against 'unaccountable judicial power' and claimed to speak on behalf of 'the people', but the sense in which its owner, the non-domiciled Lord Rothermere, its then editor, Paul Dacre, and its journalists are themselves publicly accountable is entirely unclear. When challenged on this issue, press barons and their senior employees habitually fall back on the argument that they speak for their readers, and that this gives them a mandate. However, according to the National Readership Survey covering the period in question, the *Mail* was read daily by about 3.35 million people. But given that the current UK population is 64 million, the *Mail* reached barely 5% of it. Thus, why it is any more publicly accountable than the judges it has in its sights is indeed hard to fathom.

Second, many would actually agree that greater transparency about how Supreme Court judges, and indeed judges in general, are chosen would be most welcome. However, the problem with the American system favoured by the *Mail* is that it involves a highly politicised judicial appointments process, which runs the risk of the Supreme Court being loaded with judges whose views echo those of the sitting president, as happened in the Nixon era in particular.

Third, if the appointments process did become politicised in this fashion, it would be absolutely inevitable that the newspapers considered in this article would

---

[50] Witness the furore following the famous, but atypical, boast by *The Sun*, 11 April 1992, in the wake of the General Election, that 'It's the *Sun* wot won it'. This was actually condemned by Rupert Murdoch himself when he appeared before the Leveson Inquiry in 2012 – see B. Dowell, 'Rupert Murdoch: "Sun wot won it" headline was tasteless and wrong', *Guardian*, 25 April 2012, online at: https://www.theguard ian.com/media/2012/apr/25/rupert-murdoch-sun-wot-won-it-tasteless (last accessed 26 January 2022).

become deeply enmeshed in it. Indeed, this is precisely what they have long desired to do. Of course, and as mentioned earlier, in democratic theory, newspapers act as members of the Fourth Estate, scrutinising every aspect of the democratic process – including the workings of the judicial system – in order to safeguard the public interest. The fundamental problem here, however, is that these papers are far too politically partisan, far too deeply embroiled in the political system over which, according to Fourth Estate principles, they are supposed to act as watchdogs, and far too committed to the political and ideological interests of those who own and run them, to count as members of the Fourth Estate as it is generally understood. Indeed, to use Baldwin's term, these are not 'newspapers in the ordinary sense', and it is extremely disturbing that by far the best-informed book on the real, as opposed to the idealised, relationship between the press and the political system in the UK should be entitled *Democracy Under Attack: How the Media Distort Policy and Politics*.[51] Anybody wishing to grant yet more political power to papers such as these would be well advised to read it.

The fourth and final point concerns the political consequences of the stories explored in this article (as well as those following the Supreme Court judgment on 24 September 2019 regarding Boris Johnson's prorogation of Parliament).[52] As noted earlier, while the argument that 'it's all got up by the press' should be avoided, it would equally be most unwise to underestimate the importance of the intimate and mutually reinforcing links between Conservative politicians and Conservative newspapers. Anyone inclined to do so should read the highly authoritative articles by the former *Telegraph* Political Editor and *Mail* Political Columnist Peter Oborne on this subject.[53]

Bearing these considerations in mind, then, it is worth turning to the Conservative election manifesto,[54] which was published on 24 November 2019. In the section entitled 'Protect Our Democracy', it states that: 'After Brexit we also need to look at the broader aspects of our constitution: the relationship between the Government, Parliament and the courts; the functioning of the Royal Prerogative; the role of the House of Lords'. More specifically, it promises that:

> We will update the Human Rights Act and administrative law to ensure that there is a proper balance between the rights of individuals, our vital national security and

---

[51] Dean, *Democracy under Attack: How the Media Distort Policy and Politics*; see also J. Petley, 'What Fourth Estate?', in M. Bailey (ed.), *Narrating Media History* (London, Routledge, 2009), pp. 184–195.
[52] J. Petley, 'The *Sun* still has the "enemies of the people" in its sights', *Inforrm*, 1 October 2019, online at: https://inforrm.org/2019/10/01/the-sun-still-has-the-enemies-of-the-people-in-its-sights-julian-pet ley/ (last accessed 26 January 2022).
[53] P. Oborne, 'British journalists have become part of Johnson's fake news machine', *openDemocracy*, 22 October 2019, online at: https://www.opendemocracy.net/en/opendemocracyuk/british-journalists-have-become-part-of-johnsons-fake-news-machine/?fbclid=IwAR1LQfC9PGgE2x4gl5_v6rqGj1W-srB9L5q6Sa63gy-LQP0MVszcxTtSlpM (last accessed 26 January 2022).
[54] Conservative and Unionist Party, *Get Brexit Done: Unleash Britain's Potential* (London, Conservative Party, 2019), online at: https://assets-global.website-files.com/5da42e2cae7ebd3f8bde353c/5dda924905 da587992a064ba_Conservative%202019%20Manifesto.pdf (last accessed 26 January 2022).

effective government. We will ensure that judicial review is available to protect the rights of the individuals against an overbearing state, while ensuring that it is not abused to conduct politics by another means or to create needless delays. In our first year we will set up a Constitution, Democracy & Rights Commission that will examine these issues in depth, and come up with proposals to restore trust in our institutions and in how our democracy operates.

Vague though much of this is, it would be impossible to miss the references to the subjects that so enraged the newspapers whose coverage is the subject of this chapter – in particular, the 'abuse' of judicial review 'to conduct politics by another means or to create needless delays', and the 'updating' of the Human Rights Act, for so long such a bugbear of significant sections of the Conservative press and party.

Moving on to the Queen's Speech on 19 December 2019, we find the briefing notes[55] returning once again to the subject of the Constitution, Democracy and Rights Commission, whose function is described variously as being 'to develop proposals to restore trust in how our democracy operates' and 'to consider the relationship between Government, Parliament and the courts', 'to explore whether the checks and balances in our constitution are working for everyone' and to 'examine the broader aspects of the constitution in depth and develop proposals to restore trust in our institutions and in how our democracy operates'. Again, the language is vague, but in the context of the events of the previous three years and the manner in which certain papers reported them, this raises significant fears about the independence of the judiciary. Unsurprisingly, then, Simon Davis, President of the Law Society of England and Wales, warned those drawing up the scope of the new commission to safeguard the 'delicate balance that underpins our unwritten constitution'. He continued:

> An independent legal profession and a government accountable to the people are fundamental elements of a nation rooted in the rule of law. We must preserve and protect these principles at all costs. Our court system and our judges are there so the law laid down by parliament can be interpreted. In a mature democracy, it is crucial that the independence of this process is maintained.

However, such a warning was to be conspicuously ignored – if not indeed snubbed. Thus, on 27 January, Suella Braverman, a former Chair of the European Research Group, a Junior Minister at the former Department for Exiting the EU and an MP with a consistent record[56] on voting against laws to promote human rights, wrote an article for the Conservative Home website in which she argued that:

> Restoring sovereignty to Parliament after Brexit is one of the greatest prizes that awaits us. But not just from the EU. As we start this new chapter of our democratic story, our Parliament must retrieve power ceded to another place – the courts. For too long,

---

[55] *The Queen's Speech 2019* (London, Prime Minister's Office, 2019), online at: https://assets.publishing.service.gov.uk/government/uploads/system/uploads/attachment_data/file/853886/Queen_s_Speech_December_2019_-_background_briefing_notes.pdf (last accessed 26 January 2022).
[56] *They Work for You: Suella Braverman*, online at: https://www.theyworkforyou.com/mp/25272/suella_braverman/fareham/votes (last accessed 26 January 2022).

the Diceyan notion of parliamentary supremacy has come under threat. The political has been captured by the legal. Decisions of an executive, legislative and democratic nature have been assumed by our courts. Prorogation and the triggering of Article 50 were merely the latest examples of a chronic and steady encroachment by the judges. For in reality, repatriated powers from the EU will mean precious little if our courts continue to act as political decision-maker, pronouncing on what the law *ought* to be and supplanting Parliament. To empower our people we need to stop this disenfranchisement of Parliament.[57]

On the grounds that 'traditionally, Parliament made the law and judges applied it', Braverman complained that 'today, our courts exercise a form of political power … Judicial review has exploded since the 1960s so that even the most intricate relations between the state and individual can be questioned by judges'. Entirely predictably, the culprit for this 'encroachment' is identified as the Human Rights Act and the 'prolific human rights industry which it has spawned', by means of which 'the concept of "fundamental" human rights has been stretched beyond recognition'. She concluded:

> I am pleased that the Government has promised to update the Human Rights Act to restore the proper balance between the rights of individuals, national security and effective government and to set up a Constitution, Democracy and Rights Commission to ensure that the boundaries of judicial review are appropriately drawn.

This sounded suspiciously like a job application, and unsurprisingly, on 13 February, Braverman was appointed as the new Attorney General of England and Wales. As Adam Wagner argued,[58] her appointment represented 'the opening salvo' from the illiberal, anti-human rights ideologues in the Conservative Party and signalled all too clearly the government's future direction in this area. The new Attorney General's 'wish list' for uncontested executive power, unencumbered by the checks and balances that have been so long taken for granted in Western democracies, is all too clearly a direct expression of the populist, anti-juridical ideology examined in this chapter. This puts the executive at the centre, 'freed' from the mechanisms of democratic accountability that the technocrats and post-democracy advocates in No.10 regard as anachronistic, and leaves it accountable only to the 'will of the people'. If anything proves that the government has declared war on the independence of the judiciary and on human rights, it is surely the appointment of an Attorney General who is given to ill-conceived attacks on the very concept of

[57] S. Braverman MP, 'People we elect must take back control from people we don't. Who include judges', *Conservative Home*, 27 January 2020, online at: https://www.conservativehome.com/platform/2020/01/suella-braverman-people-we-elect-must-take-back-control-from-people-we-dont-who-include-the-judges.html (last accessed 26 January 2022).

[58] A. Wagner, 'Suella Braverman's appointment as Attorney General spells danger for human rights', *New Statesman*, 14 February 2020, online at: https://www.newstatesman.com/politics/uk/2020/02/suella-braverman-s-appointment-attorney-general-spells-danger-human-rights (last accessed 26 January 2022).

judicial independence and is clearly opposed to both the Human Rights Act and the European Convention on Human Rights.

Sadly, the majority of the national press is far more likely to endorse Braverman's fetishisation of executive power than it is to answer Simon Davis' call to protect the independence of the judiciary. Indeed, as these newspapers played an active role in igniting the 'heat and fury' over the Article 50 judgments by both the High and Supreme Courts and then proceeded to give unqualified support to the Conservatives in the December 2019 election,[59] it would be entirely unrealistic to expect them to do anything other than to cheerlead for the government in what is clearly shaping up to be an all-out attack on judicial independence. Such behaviour is no more the mark of a Fourth Estate than are the government's manoeuvrings and veiled threats against the judiciary the mark of a mature democracy. But there again, without a properly functioning Fourth Estate acting as a watchdog on those who hold power in our society, governments have little to fear if they are determined to behave in an undemocratic, and indeed authoritarian, fashion.

[59] D. Jackson, E. Thorsen, D. Lilleker and N. Weidhase, *UK Election Analysis 2019: Media, Voters and the Campaign* (Bournemouth, Centre for Comparative Politics and Media Research, 2019), available online at: http://www.electionanalysis.uk/ (last accessed 26 January 2022).

Part II

Judicial Independence: International and Historical Perspectives

6

Judicial Independence and Two Visions
of American Democracy

DAVID ALAN SKLANSKY

To THINK CLEARLY about judicial independence, we need to be clear about its purposes. That, in turn, requires clarity about democracy. In the United States, as in much of the rest of the world today, two visions of democracy are in competition, one emphasising popular sovereignty and the other emphasising institutions and group politics. The choice between the two – roughly speaking, the choice between populism and pluralism – has implications for what judicial independence means, why it matters, and how it can best be preserved.

Following the election of Donald Trump as President in 2016, judicial independence in the United States became both more important and more threatened. This chapter will provide an overview of how judicial independence fared in the United States in the years following Trump's victory, and it will draw lessons about how judicial independence should be understood and defended in a time of widespread populist challenges to liberal democracy. The most obvious lesson, and the most important, is that judicial independence is a key battleground between populism and pluralism, whether those labels refer to rival theories of democracy or to opposing forms of politics. For populists, independent courts are inherently anti-democratic, a departure from rule by 'the people'. For pluralists, in contrast, independent courts are a democratic safeguard, a means for the fair and peaceful resolution of intergroup conflicts. From a pluralist perspective, judicial independence is both meaningful and feasible, but it needs defending. It is as much about prosecutors as it is about judges, and the threats it faces are as much about values as they are about rules.

The Trump administration in court

When Donald Trump was elected President of the United States in 2016, it was not obvious that courts would stand in the way of much of his agenda. A good number

Proceedings of the British Academy, **250**, 113–127, © The British Academy 2022.

of American legal scholars and political scientists, particularly in the 1980s, 1990s and early 2000s, had either called judicial independence a myth or cast serious doubt on its value.[1] These scholars reasoned that judges were human beings, susceptible to the same biases and social pressures as anyone else. And it is true that judges in the United States, including justices of the Supreme Court, have tended on the whole to reflect popular beliefs, and that judges in other countries have tended to go along with even the worst authoritarian regimes.[2] So there was reason to doubt that independent courts could be relied upon to safeguard individual rights and constitutional norms in the Trump era.

As it turned out, though, courts blocked, stalled or moderated a good deal of what the Trump administration tried to do. This began almost immediately after Trump took office when federal judges invalidated the first two versions of Trump's anti-Muslim travel ban.[3] The Supreme Court later upheld the third, scaled-back version,[4] but in the meantime, federal courts had stalled the administration's rescission of the Deferred Action for Child Arrivals programme, an Obama-era initiative that provided immigration relief to students who were brought to the United States without proper documentation when they were young children.[5] Federal trial judges around the country blocked deportations ordered by the Trump administration.[6] Federal courts also enjoined the Trump administration from preventing undocumented teenagers in custody from having abortions and struck down the administration's efforts to allow employer-funded health plans to exclude coverage for contraceptives.[7] A federal trial judge invalidated the Trump administration's decision to allow state and local officials to block refugees from being resettled in their jurisdictions.[8] In 2019, the Supreme Court struck down Trump's efforts to add a question about citizenship to the 2020 census.[9] By the end of that calendar year,

---

[1] E.g., E. A. Posner and A. Vermeule, *The Executive Unbound: After the Madisonian Republic* (New York, Oxford University Press 2011); F. C. Cross, 'Thoughts on Goldilocks and Judicial Independence', *Ohio State Law Journal*, 64 (2003), 195–219; P. S. Karlan, 'Two Concepts of Judicial Independence', 72 (1999), *Southern California Law Review*, 535–58 at 557; A. S. Miller, 'Myth and Reality in American Constitutionalism', *Texas Law Review*, 63 (2008), 181–206.

[2] H. P. Graver, *Judges Against Justice: On Judges When the Rule of Law is Under Attack* (New York, Springer 2015), p. 300; M. A. Livingston, *The Fascists and the Jews of Italy: Mussolini's Race Laws, 1938–1943* (Cambridge, Cambridge University Press 2014), p. 148; I. Müller, *Hitler's Justice: The Courts of the Third Reich*, trans D. L. Schneider (Cambridge (Mass.), Harvard University Press 1991), pp. 195–196; R. O. Paxton, *Vichy France: Old Guard and New Order, 1940–1944* (New York, Alfred A. Knopf 1972), p. 339; F. Maltzman, L. Sigelman and P. J. Wahlbeck, 'Supreme Court Justices Really Do Follow the Election Returns', *PS: Political Science and Politics*, 37 (2004), 839–42.

[3] *Hawaii v Trump*, 859 F.3d 741 (9th Cir. 2017); *International Refugee Assistance Project v Trump*, 857 F.3d 554 (4th Cir. 2017); *Washington v Trump*, 847 F.3d 1151 (9th Cir. 2017).

[4] *Trump v Hawaii*, 585 US ___ (2018).

[5] M. D. Schear and A. Liptak, 'Supreme Court Agrees to Hear "Dreamers" Case', *New York Times*, June 28, 2019, A1.

[6] Schear and Liptak, 'Supreme Court Agrees to Hear "Dreamers" Case'.

[7] *California v United States Department of Health & Human Services*, 941 F.3d 410 (9th Cir. 2019); *J.D. v Azar*, 925 F.3d 1291 (D.C. Cir. 2019).

[8] *HIAS, Inc. v Trump*, Civ. No. PJM 19-3346 (D. Md. Jan. 15, 2020).

[9] *Department of Commerce v New York*, 588 US ___ (2019).

states attorneys general had filed 98 lawsuits against the Trump administration – the majority challenging administration efforts to roll back environmental regulations – and more than three-quarters had been successful or were still pending, often with temporary stays in place.[10] Meanwhile, a defamation suit proceeded against Trump in a New York state court, brought by a woman Trump called a liar during the presidential campaign after she said he had sexually assaulted her in 2007.[11] The Supreme Court allowed the Trump administration to impose new restrictions on border seekers and to divert military funds for use in constructing a border wall while litigation over the legality of those actions continued in the lower courts.[12] But even when they proved temporary, court rulings against Trump and his administration often delayed and forced revisions of their plans.

If we define judicial independence to mean the integrity of court proceedings, encompassing the professional independence of prosecutors as well as of judges, then the significance of judicial independence in the Trump era becomes even clearer. Federal prosecutors doggedly pursued investigations into Russian efforts to tip the 2016 election in Trump's favour and into apparent obstruction of justice by Trump and his current and former associates. Several of those associates were convicted and sent to prison. Much of this work was done by Special Counsel Robert Mueller, who ran an independent investigation on behalf of the Department of Justice, but other parts of the work were carried out by other federal prosecutors, most notably the office of the United States Attorney for Manhattan.[13] After Mueller's investigation concluded, the bulk of his lengthy report was made public, documenting Russian interference in the 2016 election and setting forth evidence of the President's repeated, unsuccessful efforts to block the work of Mueller's team.[14] By 2019, New York state prosecutors were conducting their own investigations into Trump's business dealings and into allegations that he paid hush money and falsified business records in order to cover up extramarital affairs.[15]

More important, and notwithstanding the repeated, orchestrated chants of 'lock her up' at Trump's campaign rallies,[16] Trump's electoral victory in 2016 was not

[10] P. Nolette, State Attorneys General Data, attorneysgeneral.org, updated 31 December 2019.

[11] S. M. Nir, 'Trump Can Be Sued for Defamation by "Apprentice" Contestant', *New York Times*, 15 March 2019, A26.

[12] A. Liptak, 'Justice Permit US to Exclude Asylum Claims', *New York Times*, 12 September 2019, A1; A. Liptak, 'Ruling Allows Shift of Funds to Build Wall', *New York Times*, 27 July 2019, A1.

[13] S. LaFrancier, B. Weiser and M. Haberman, 'Prosecutors Say Trump Organized Illegal Payments', *New York Times*, 8 December 2018, A1.

[14] R. S. Mueller III, Report on the Investigation Into Russian Interference in the 2016 Presidential Election (Washington DC, Government Printing Office 2019).

[15] E. Durkin, 'The Thorn in Trump's Side', *Guardian*, 2 May 2019, online at: tinyurl.com/yxwg3qgk (last accessed 26 January 2022); B. Protess and W. K. Rashbaum, 'Trump Family Businesses Subpoenaed Over Hush Money', *New York Times*, 2 August 2019, A15; W. K. Rashbaum and B. Protess, 'D.A. Orders 8 Years of Trump Tax Returns', *New York Times*, 17 September 2019, A23.

[16] K. M. Kruse, 'How Trump Is Worse Than Wallace', *New York Times*, 28 July 2019, A21; P. W. Stevenson, 'A Brief History of the "Lock Her Up!" Chant by Trump Supporters Against Clinton', *Washington Post*, 22 November 2016, online at: tinyurl.com/hllgxa6 (last accessed 26 January 2022).

followed by criminal prosecutions of his opponent, Hillary Clinton, or any of his other political enemies. Trump himself repeatedly called on Twitter for his adversaries to be investigated and jailed. His targets included not only Hillary Clinton and her former aide Huma Abedin but also, significantly, lawyers in the Department of Justice and agents and supervisors in the Federal Bureau of Investigation whom Trump accused of being biased against him. For the most part, though, the Department of Justice resisted these calls. Trump's first Attorney General, Jeff Sessions, opened an inquiry into actions Hillary Clinton had taken as Secretary of State, but nothing came of it, and eventually the matter was dropped.[17] Moreover, Sessions, who had worked for Trump's election, recused himself from the Russia investigation, and Deputy Attorney General Rod Rosenstein – another Trump appointee – rebuffed Trump's efforts to terminate or circumscribe Mueller's probe.

However, Trump replaced Sessions with a new Attorney General, William Barr, in February 2019, and there soon were signs that Trump might be making progress towards turning the Department of Justice into a political weapon. Barr delayed the release of Mueller's report and misrepresented its findings in order to minimise its damage to Trump.[18] The Department of Justice opened an antitrust investigation of four major automakers – Ford, Volkswagen, Honda and BMW – that had embarrassed the President by striking a deal with the state of California to reduce their vehicles' emissions further than the Trump administration had announced it would require.[19] More ominously, the Department of Justice authorised prosecutors to seek a criminal indictment of Andrew McCabe, the dismissed former acting director of the FBI, for misleading the internal investigators about his role in authorising disclosure of an ongoing investigation of the Clinton family foundation shortly before the 2016 election. McCabe's misrepresentations, even if proven, were not of the kind that typically would lead to a prosecution, and Trump had long demonised McCabe and called for him to be fired and criminally investigated for his role in the Department of Justice probe into Russian influence in the 2016 election.[20] Several months later, the Department reportedly opened an investigation into whether James Comey, the former FBI director, had illegally leaked information to reporters two years earlier – the second investigation the Department had opened into possible leaks by Comey. Comey, like McCabe, had been ousted and vilified by Trump – despite the fact that it had been Comey who had publicised

---

[17] D. Barrett and M. Zapotosky, 'Justice Dept. Winds Down Clinton-Related Inquiry Once Championed by Trump. It Found Nothing of Consequence.", *Washington Post*, 9 January 2020, online at: tinyurl.com/t47sylk (last accessed 26 January 2022).
[18] D. Graham, 'Barr Misled the Public – And It Worked', *Atlantic*, 1 May 2019, online at: tinyurl.com/y42yaxvy (last accessed 26 January 2022).
[19] H. Tabuchi and C. Davenport, 'US Investigates Emissions Pledge', *New York Times*, 7 September 2019, A1.
[20] Q. Jurecic, 'Will Trump Succeed in Prosecuting Andrew McCabe?', *New York Times*, 28 August 2019, online at: nyti.ms/2Pk8oNU (last accessed 26 January 2022); M. Zapotosky and S. S. Hsu, 'Justice Department Authorized Prosecutors to Charge Andrew McCabe', *Washington Post*, 12 September 2019, tinyurl.com/yxwpjsm7 (last accessed 26 January 2022).

details about the criminal investigation into Hillary Clinton during the 2016 presidential election.[21] Comey apparently fell out of favour with Trump soon after Trump took office when Comey failed to promise personal loyalty to the new president.[22] The Department of Justice also launched a criminal probe into the initiation of the Department's own Russia investigation.[23] Meanwhile, Trump reportedly promised pardons to aides who violated any laws while helping him to fulfil his campaign promises,[24] and he tried, unsuccessfully, to have the chief lawyer for the White House order the Department of Justice prosecute both Clinton and Comey.[25]

Trump's repeated calls for the Department of Justice to pursue his political enemies were a marked departure from a long tradition requiring presidents to stay out of prosecutorial decision-making in order to keep those decisions apolitical. For that reason, they should be understood as attacks on the ideal of judicial independence. I will return to this point below, but for now, the important point is the striking degree to which judicial independence, defined to include the professional autonomy of prosecutors as well as judges, provided a significant check on the Trump administration, notwithstanding the longstanding arguments by many American scholars suggesting that judicial independence was chimerical or meaningless. What had those scholars missed?

Judicial independence under rival theories of democracy

The American academics who called judicial independence a myth[26] were not mistaken exactly, but they focused on a particular kind of independence. They thought the point of judicial independence was to provide a check on democracy, to prevent the majority from violating constitutional rights or short-circuiting constitutional requirements. So they thought judicial independence required the courts to stick to principles that the country as a whole was ignoring. And they thought that was unlikely because judges (and, we might add, prosecutors) are human beings. And it is true that when you look at history, in the United States or overseas, you do not find many examples of judges bucking the clear sentiments of their communities.

But that is not the only way to think of judicial independence. The kind of independence you want from judges – or from prosecutors – will depend on the threats you are trying to guard against. That will likely depend, in turn, on how you think about democracy and what you think threatens it. Suppose you think of

[21] A. Goldman, 'A Leak Inquiry May Put Focus Back on Comey', *New York Times*, 17 January 2020, A1.
[22] M. S. Schmidt, 'In a Private Dinner, Trump Demanded Loyalty. Comey Demurrred', *New York Times*, 11 May 2017, A1.
[23] K. Benner and A. Goldman, 'Barr Refocuses Russia Inquiry on His Own Agency', *New York Times*, 25 October 2019, A1.
[24] K. Rogers and Z. Kanno-Youngs, 'Trump Tells Aides "Take the Land" as Impatience Grows on Border Wall', *New York Times*, 28 August 2019, A17.
[25] Goldman, 'A Leak Inquiry May Put Focus Back on Comey'.
[26] See footnote 1.

democracy as a kind of conveyer belt that takes the pre-existing will of the majority and transforms it into policy. And suppose your main worry is that sometimes the majority will ride roughshod over one or more minorities or that the majority may overlook its own true, long-term interests. Then you might hope that the court system could stand apart from the wishes of the majority and faithfully apply some principles of fair dealing and farsighted statecraft. That is what you would mean by judicial independence.

The problem is that there is strong reason to doubt that human judges or human prosecutors really can stand apart from the wishes of the majority – or that, if they could, it would be safer to rely on their judgments about what counts as fair and farsighted than on the judgments of the majority. So if you have a conveyor belt understanding of democracy, you may well doubt that judicial independence is possible or that you want it.

But now suppose, instead, you have what is often called a 'pluralist' theory of democracy. You think of democracy as a system for allowing different groups to live together and govern themselves peacefully, or as Lord Sumption puts it in his 2019 Reith Lectures, 'a constitutional mechanism for arriving at collective decisions and accommodating dissent'.[27] And suppose your main worry is populism – not populism in the 19th century American sense of agrarian anti-elitism, but populism in the modern, European and Latin American sense – a 'moralized form of antipluralism' in which 'only some of the people are actually the real, authentic people'.[28] Trump is a classic populist in this sense. Suppose you believe that when populists of this kind win elections, they treat political opposition as illegitimate, they are hostile to civil liberties, and they move to colonise or to undermine any institutions that can challenge what they take to be self-evident – that they are the only true representatives of the people.

If you have a pluralist conception of democracy, and if you think the paramount threat to democracy is populism of this kind, then you will want courts to push back against the idea that 'only some of the people are really the people' and to guard against attacks on fair elections, freedom of expression, and political organising. You will want the courts to stand apart from tribe or faction – partly so that their judgments will be respected by all sides, partly as a barrier against politicised prosecutions and partly because you will want courts to help reinforce pluralist democratic values in the society as a whole. This is what you will mean by judicial independence. It will not seem unrealistic to you, at least in the short term. Once populists are in power, though, you will expect to see independent courts come under attack. That in fact happened in the United States following Trump's election, and I will discuss those attacks later in this chapter.

---

[27] J. Sumption, *Trials of the State: Law and the Decline of Politics* (Profile Books, 2019), p. 69.
[28] J.-W. Müller, *What is Populism?* (Penguin Books, 2017 ed.), pp. 20–21; see also, e.g., C. Mudde and C. R. Kaltwasser, *Populism: A Very Short Introduction* (New York, Oxford University Press, 2017); N. Urbinati, *We the People: How Populism Transforms Democracy* (Cambridge, MA, Harvard University Press, 2019).

First, though, I need to say a little more about populism and pluralism, What I have called 'the conveyer belt understanding' of democracy could also be called the populist or 'popular sovereignty' model because it places popular sovereignty and the 'will of the people' at the heart of its understanding of democracy. This was a common understanding, possibly the dominant understanding, of democracy among American academics from the 1980s through the early 2000s, and it was and remains central to many non-academic discussions of democracy.[29] The populist, or popular sovereignty, model of democracy is not the same thing as populism as a political style – a Manichean, 'moralized form of antipluralism'. One is a theory of democracy and one is a type of politics. They are connected, though. Populism as a Manichean, antipluralist form of politics depends upon and elevates a popular sovereignty view of democracy; populist politicians couple this theory of democracy with a divisive, moralised understanding of who constitutes 'the people'. Scholarly defences of the popular sovereignty model of democracy generally do not defend the sharp distinction that populist politicians draw between 'the pure people' and 'the corrupt elite'.[30] They do, though, tend to counterpose 'experts' and 'elites' against 'ordinary' people and to see democracy as in large part a matter of empowering the latter against the former.

From the late 1940s through most of the 1960s, the orthodox theory of democracy among American scholars, and to a great extent among popular writers, was different. It was explicitly pluralist. It understood democracy in the United States as a bottom up process of intergroup accommodation: neither majority rule nor minority rule, but 'minorities rule'.[31] This theory of 'democratic pluralism' fell out of favour in the late 1960s and the 1970s, in part because its academic proponents had coupled their ideas about how American democracy should and could work with a rosy, at times complacent, understanding of how well it actually did work. When the descriptive side of pluralism lost its credibility, the analytic side of the theory was discredited as well.[32] Recently, though, the rise of populist politics in the United States, Europe and Great Britain has brought renewed scholarly attention to, and renewed appreciation for, pluralist accounts of democracy.

There are, of course, many ways to divide up theories of democracy. Which taxonomy is most helpful depends on which threats are most pressing. Lord Sumption is particularly worried about an abandonment of politics in favour of judicial pronouncements, so he contrasts pluralism, his favoured account of democracy, with 'a system of values ... not chosen or necessarily supported by the people or

---

[29] C. H. Achen and L. M. Bartels, *Democracy for Realists: Why Elections Do Not Produce Responsive Government* (Princeton, Princeton University Press, 2016). For scholarly elaborations of the popular sovereignty understanding of democracy, see, e.g., L. D. Kramer, *The People Themselves: Popular Constitutionalism and Judicial Review* (New York, Oxford University Press, 2005); R. Parker, *Here the People Rule: A Constitutional Populist Manifesto* (Cambridge, MA, Harvard University Press, 1998).

[30] Mudde and Kaltwasser, p. 6.

[31] R. A. Dahl, *A Preface to Democratic Theory* (Chicago, University of Chicago Press, 1956), p. 133.

[32] Achen and Bartels, pp. 224–225.

even open to meaningful discussion among them'.[33] Academic defenders of the popular sovereignty model of democracy often contrast it with rule by elites; in fact, the post-war version of democratic pluralism, when it came under attack in the late 1960s and 1970s, was commonly described as the 'elite theory of democracy'.[34] That way of dividing up theories of democracy made sense, and continues to make sense, to scholars who view elites and self-appointed experts as the greatest threat to democracy. But for observers who now find the ascendance of illiberal populism as the paramount threat to democracy, it makes more sense to counterpose popular sovereignty with pluralism, as I have done, as the main rival accounts of democracy.

Threats to judicial independence in the Trump era

From the perspective of democratic pluralism – the perspective that sees democracy as a system for allowing a heterogeneous population govern itself and accommodate their differences – judicial independence is both feasible and important. It is important because independent courts provide a forum for resolving intergroup conflicts in fair and principled ways, and because if court proceedings are *not* independent, they can become a tool of intergroup oppression. It is feasible because it does not depend on judges or prosecutors setting themselves apart from or seeing the world differently than 'the people'. From the pluralist perspective, there is no such thing as 'the people'; there is a range of individuals and groups with different views. What we want judges and prosecutors to be 'independent' from are factions and other governmental officials.

In contrast, from the perspective of popular sovereignty, judicial independence is, at best, a problematic ideal. Neither its feasibility nor its desirability is self-evident. Judges and prosecutors are human, and they are part of society, so they cannot be relied upon to stand up to the 'will of the people'. Nor is it clear why we would want them to do so. Populists draw heavily on the popular sovereignty understanding of democracy; they take the whole point of democracy to be effectuating the 'will of the people'. When populists come to power, they therefore can be expected to be scornful of judicial interference with their agenda and hostile to the very idea that courts should be 'independent'.[35]

That was true of Donald Trump. Before and after his election as president, Trump repeatedly attacked judges and prosecutors he viewed as unfriendly. He did not call for, and did not try to implement, new rules or procedures restricting the

---

[33] Sumption, p. 69.

[34] E.g., K. Prewitt and A. Stone, *The Ruling Elites: Elite Theory, Power, and American Democracy* (New York, Harper & Row 1973); R. W. Krouse, 'Polyarchy and Participation: The Changing Democratic Theory of Robert Dahl', *Polity*, 14 (1982), 441–63 at 444.

[35] Müller, pp. 45, 65–66; S. Baer, 'The Rule of – and Not by Any – Law. On Constitutionalism', *Current Legal Problems*, 71 (2018), 335–68; N. Lacey, 'Populism and the Rule of Law', *Annual Review of Law and Social Science*, 15 (2019).

independence of court proceedings. Instead, the attacks took the form of efforts to undermine the legitimacy of court proceedings by claiming that judges and prosecutors who were not in Trump's camp were corrupt and illegitimate. Thus, for example, Trump called the judge who struck down the first version of the travel ban a 'so-called judge'.[36] Attorney General Jeff Sessions called it ridiculous that the second version of the ban could be invalidated by a judge 'sitting on an island in the Pacific' – the island in question being Oahu, the largest part of the state of Hawaii.[37] Trump's supporters repeatedly complained that the judges ruling against the administration were acting lawlessly, that they were in 'revolt' and had 'joined the "resistance"'.[38] And that is nothing compared to attacks that were mounted against career prosecutors in the Department of Justice, including, but not limited to, Robert Mueller and his staff. Trump regularly accused prosecutors and law enforcement agents involved in the Russia investigation of corruption and criminality; sometimes he went further and called them treasonous.[39]

The attacks on the judges were based on little more than that they ruled against Trump and that some, but certainly not all, were appointed by Democratic presidents. The attacks on the prosecutors were based on little more than that they were investigating Trump and his associates and that some of them – but certainly not all of them, and not Mueller – had contributed in the past to political opponents of Trump. Trump even attacked Sessions, his own Attorney General, for assigning a politically sensitive internal investigation to the Justice Department's Inspector General (IG) because the IG had been appointed by President Obama and was therefore, Trump said, 'an Obama guy'.[40] When Trump removed Sessions from office in 2019, he made clear that it was in large part because of the efforts that Sessions had taken to be impartial, in particular Session's decision to recuse himself from the Russia investigation on the grounds that Sessions himself had played key roles in Trump's re-election campaign and on his transition team. Trump also complained publicly that Sessions was not aggressively investigating and prosecuting Trump's opponents, in particular Hillary Clinton.[41]

---

[36] T. Fuller, 'Judge Denounced by Trump is Known for Independence', *New York Times*, 4 February 2017, A13.
[37] C. Savage, 'Sessions Dismisses Hawaii as "an Island in the Pacific"', *New York Times*, 20 April 2017, A15.
[38] E.g., J. Blackman, 'The Legal Resistance to President Trump', *National Review*, 11 October 2017, online at: tinyurl.com/yyqu4le5 (last accessed 26 January 2022).
[39] E.g., P. Baker and E. Sullivan, 'Trump Responds to Mueller Statement With Accusation of a Vendetta', *New York Times*, 30 May 2019, A16; K. Benner and A. Goldman, 'Darker Portrait Emerges Of a Justice Department Battered From On High', *New York Times*, 19 April 2019, A14; R. Thebault and M. Flynn, 'Trump Suggests Rosenstein, McCabe Are "Treasonous," Citing Fox News', *Washington Post*, 19 February 2019, online at: tinyurl.com/yyk68sv3 (last accessed 26 January 2022).
[40] P. Baker and K. Brenner, 'Trump Tears into Sessions Over Russia Investigation', *New York Times*, 28 February 2018, A1.
[41] P. Baker, K. Brenner and M. D. Shear, 'Trump Replaces Sessions with a Loyalist; Vows "Warlike" Stance on House Inquiries', *New York Times*, 7 November 2018, at A1.

The fixation on loyalty and on the party affiliation of the judges and prosecutors standing in Trump's way was of a piece with Trump's harping, during the campaign, on the ethnic background of Gonzalo Curiel, the federal district judge who presided over a fraud lawsuit brought against Trump in California.[42] It fit, as well, with another important attack Trump and his supporters mounted on independent courts: the effort to pack the courts with judges who were selected on nakedly partisan grounds and who would see themselves as partisans even when deciding cases. Federal judges in the United States, including justices of the Supreme Court, serve for life. They are appointed by the President and then confirmed by the Senate after hearings at which the nominees are questioned under oath. Observers in Britain are right to see this selection process as a 'particular vulnerability' of judicial independence in the United States,[43] and it is a vulnerability that Trump and his supporters exploited dramatically.

Trump was hardly the first President to care about the ideology of the judges he appointed, but the process became much more openly and unabashedly partisan under his administration. What was new was the triumphalism, the dropping of any pretence – let alone a genuine belief – that courts, or the judicial selection process, should be nonpartisan. The White House and its supporters in Congress crowed about their success in installing 'conservative' judges and 'holding' the Supreme Court.[44]

At times, the judges Trump appointed made clear that they, too, saw themselves as partisans. For example, Don Willett, a former member of the Texas Supreme Court appointed by Trump to a federal court of appeals, boasted that he had 'built a record that is widely described – well, universally described – as the most conservative of anybody on the Supreme Court', that he accepted that label with 'gladness and gusto', that there was 'no ideological daylight' to his right, and that he had 'garnered support from every corner of the conservative movement.'[45] Brett Kavanaugh, appointed to the United States Supreme Court by President Trump, used the opening statement of his confirmation hearing before the Senate Judiciary Committee to lash out at Democrats on the committee and 'left-wing' opponents of his nomination.[46]

---

[42] A. Rappeport, 'Judge Faulted by Trump Has Faced a Lot Worse', *New York Times*, 3 June 2016, A12.
[43] Lacey; see also O. Bowcott, 'Lady Hale Warns UK Not to Select Judges on Basis of Political Views', *Guardian*, 18 December 2019, online at: tinyurl.com/uy2r5sp (last accessed 26 January 2022).
[44] E.g., K. Freking, 'Pace of Confirmations Gives McConnell Chance to Bask in Wins', *Seattle Times*, 6 December 2017, online at: tinyurl.com/y5tqdx6m (last accessed 26 January 2022); A. Liptak, 'Nonpolitical Justices? A Case May Test That', *New York Times*, 16 September 2019, A15; T. McCarthy, 'All the President's Judges: How Trump Can Flip Courts at a Record-Setting Pace', *Guardian*, 11 May 2019, online at: tinyurl.com/y6kcon8c (last accessed 26 January 2022); D. Victor, 'McConnell Says Republicans Would Fill a Supreme Court Vacancy in 2020, Drawing Claims of Hypocrisy', *New York Times*, 29 May 2019, online at: nyti.ms/2Wc76at (last accessed 26 January 2022).
[45] N. Cobler, 'Tweet-Loving Justice Don Willett Confirmed for Federal Appeals Court', *Dallas Morning News*, 13 December 2017, online at: tinyurl.com/y469rsyq (last accessed 26 January 2022); L. Greenhouse, 'Why Judges Matter', *New York Times*, 21 December 2017, online at: nyti.ms/2DkCd6T (last accessed 26 January 2022).
[46] 'Brett Kavanaugh's Opening Statement: Full Transcript', *New York Times*, 26 September 2018, online at: nyti.ms/2NItSCM (last accessed 26 January 2022).

Beyond attacking judges and prosecutors as partisan and biased when they did not appear to be on his side, and beyond making judicial appointments into nakedly partisan exercises of power, Trump also sought to use criminal investigations and prosecutions as weapons against his political opponents. The President of the United States heads the executive branch of the government, which includes the Department of Justice. Traditionally, though, presidents have taken pains to avoid the perception that they are trying to influence investigatory or prosecutorial decisions. Trump took a very different approach, calling publicly for the Justice Department to investigate and jail Hillary Clinton, her former aide Huma Abedin, and prosecutors and FBI agents involved in the Russia investigation. Trump also sought to weaponise foreign investigations and prosecutions, pressuring the government of Ukraine to investigate his political opponents, including former Vice President Joseph Biden and his family.[47] This was the step that eventually led the House of Representatives to adopt the first articles of impeachment against Trump formally seeking his removal from office.[48]

Lessons from the American experience

Under President Trump, independent courts in the United States became particularly important, and the very idea of independent courts came under multipronged attack. How should that idea be defended – in America or anywhere else it faces similar challenges?

One important lesson of the American experience following 2016 is that to defend judicial independence, we need to defend against populism of the kind that Donald Trump exemplifies: an antipluralist form of politics organised around morally circumscribed understanding of 'the people'. That means, as many have pointed out, working to address some of the very real grievances about elitism, stunted opportunity and governmental unresponsiveness that can help to fuel populism.[49] But we also need to understand the nature of what we are protecting when we protect judicial independence. And in that regard, the first thing to say is that judicial independence is not, as Americans often tend to think, a matter of isolating the judicial and the executive functions of government from each other.[50] The standard explanation of judicial independence in the United States (the explanation generally favoured, that is to say, by people who do not believe judicial independence is

---

[47] J. E. Barnes et al., 'President Asked Ukraine's Leader for Biden Inquiry', *New York Times*, 21 September 2019, A1; K. P. Vogel, 'Behind Phone Calls, Long-Held Grudge Toward Ukraine', *New York Times*, 21 September 2019, A1.

[48] House Resolution 755, *Congressional Record*, 165, 18 December 2019, H12130-H122206.

[49] Mudde and Kaltwasser, pp. 108–112; Müller, pp. 76–79, 103.

[50] More generally, as Daniel Epps argues in an important recent article, the rule of law in a system of criminal adjudication depends institutional checks and balances, not on separation of powers. Daniel Epps, 'Checks and Balances in the Criminal Law', *Vanderbilt Law Review*, 74 (2021), 1–84.

a myth) has to do with the separation of powers. But the Department of Justice and the FBI are not part of the Judicial Branch; they are part of the Executive Branch, the branch headed by the President. And the Department of Justice and the Federal Bureau of Investigation were as important as the courts as checks on the Trump administration. Moreover, the attacks on judicial independence during the Trump administration were accompanied by virtually identical attacks on the independence of federal prosecutors and the FBI.

In any legal system that gives prosecutors significant power and discretion – and the American legal system goes very far in that regard – you cannot have independent courts without prosecutors who have a degree of independence. Otherwise you wind up with what scholars of authoritarianism call 'discriminatory legalism' – summed up in the reputed maxim of the Peruvian strongman Oscar Benevides, 'For my friends, everything; for my enemies, the law!'[51] That is why President Richard Nixon was rightly seen to have crossed a red line with the so-called Saturday Night Massacre – Nixon's effort to shut down the Watergate investigation being run by a special prosecutor appointed by the Attorney General.[52] And that is why maintaining the integrity and independence of prosecutors, and insulating the Department of Justice from White House pressure to investigate and jail the president's enemies, is as important as preserving the independence of judges.

A second lesson to draw from the recent American experience is that defending the independence of judges and prosecutors today means defending norms and values, not just written rules. The most significant attacks on judicial independence in the Trump era did not take the form of changes in legal mandates; they consisted, instead, of assaults on norms and values. Some of this was 'convention-trashing':[53] open violation of longstanding but unwritten rules against, for example, the naked politicisation of judicial appointments, or direct presidential influence on prosecutorial decision-making. But the threats to judicial independence in the Trump administration also included attacks on some deeper commitments. These included pluralism, professionalism and the idea of objective truth.

By 'pluralism', I mean not just the theory of democracy that stands opposed to populism, but also, and more importantly, that theory's underlying values of tolerance and compromise. In defending pluralism in both of these senses, we can draw some lessons – both positive and negative – from the post-war scholars who made pluralism, for several decades, the dominant account of American democracy. These scholars were admirably disdainful of the romantic ideal of a unified public. They had seen that ideal in action in Germany, in Italy, in the Soviet Union. They grimaced every time they saw someone writing about 'the People' with a capital P, and they were right to do so. On the other hand, the democratic pluralists in

---

[51] K. Weyland, 'The Threat from the Populist Left', *Journal of Democracy*, 24 (2013), 18–32 at 23.
[52] E.g., W. B. Wendel, 'Government Lawyers in the Trump Administration', *Hastings Law Journal*, 69 (2017), 275–352 at 329–30.
[53] Lacey.

mid-20th century America were unduly complacent about how democracy actually functioned in the United States. In particular, they were inattentive to the special poison of racism in American society and to the dangers of trusting too heavily in elites as the lubricant of a plural society. They produced an account of American democracy that depended on most people staying uninvolved in politics and leaving government to the experts. That was never a particularly appealing vision, and in an era of social media and the interactive web, it seems increasingly implausible. The half-century-old writings of the democratic pluralists deserve to be dusted off, but their analysis also needs to be retooled and adapted for the 21st century. That is a vital project, and it is well underway.[54]

The retooling of democratic pluralism should incorporate more caution about reliance on elite expertise, but it will need to leave a large role for professionalism. The history of authoritarianism in Europe, in Latin America and elsewhere provides ample evidence of the role of professionalism in sustaining democracy and the rule of law – and the importance of judges and lawyers, in particular, seeing themselves as bound together by ethical rules and shared occupational standards. It is a fallacy to think that judges and prosecutors have to be driven first and foremost by their partisan affiliations, but it is a fallacy that, if repeated often enough, can begin to make itself true. So one other important role for scholars at this moment, especially legal scholars, is to help clarify, for the bench and the bar and the public, what a credible form of professionalism looks like for judges, for prosecutors and for lawyers more generally. In pursuing this inquiry, the United States has a good deal to learn from the United Kingdom and from Europe, where traditions of professionalism for judges and lawyers run deeper than in the United States.[55] But there is also important work to be done in reconfiguring ideals of legal professionalism so that they will work in the American cultural context while being significantly stronger than those the country currently has.

Finally, defending judicial independence today necessarily goes hand in hand with defending the idea of objective truth. Or rather, it is connected to the idea that truth can be determined in a neutral and nonpartisan manner. The ideal of judicial independence is often discussed today in connection with constitutional courts: that is, courts that sit in judgment on the permissibility of actions taken by government officials and laws enacted by democratically elected legislatures. The most fundamental task of courts, though, is to resolve more mundane legal disputes – including, importantly, allegations of criminal conduct. Courts deciding criminal cases often need to interpret legal rules, but their most basic task is to assess factual truth: whether the defendant did what the charges allege. The same can be said about courts deciding most cases seeking to impose civil liability for

---

[54] E.g., Achen and Bartels; Mudde and Kaltwasser; Müller; Urbinati.
[55] E.g., E. Luna and M. L. Wade, 'Looking Back and at the Challenges Ahead', in E. Luna and M. L. Wade (eds.), *The Prosecutor in Transnational Perspective* (New York, Oxford University Press, 2012), pp. 424–444.

civil wrongs. The point of making court proceedings independent – of insulating judges and prosecutors from political pressures – is to ensure that those decisions are made objectively so that courts do not become weapons of persecution and can function as neutral, trusted forums for resolving disputes between people no matter their ideologies or group affiliations. At least, that is much of the point of judicial independence if democracy is understood from a pluralist rather than populist perspective.

The Manichean anti-elitism of populist politics, however, is in strong tension with the idea that truth can or should be sought in a neutral, nonpartisan manner. If society is divided between corrupt elites and the pure, genuine 'people', then judges and prosecutors – like anyone else – can only be trusted if they are from the latter camp. There is no common ground of neutral fact-finding; the question is whose 'facts' should be treated as true, and this boils down to who is in power. If there is no such thing as neutral, objective fact-finding, then the pluralist argument for independent courts begins to fall apart.

Conclusion: Populism, pluralism and judicial independence

The phrase 'judicial independence' is doubly ambiguous. In order to give it content, we need to decide what the 'judiciary' consists of and also determine how and from what it should be 'independent'. To answer those questions intelligently, we need to be clear about what judicial independence is for – why we care about it in the first place. For most people, the value of judicial independence is tied up with ideas about democracy. So what judicial independence means and how it should be defended will vary depending on how you understand democracy.

If democracy means popular sovereignty – effectuating the 'will of the people' – then judicial independence is a problematic ideal, justifiable only as a limitation on democracy, a way of imposing side constraints, and it is unclear how much independence we can realistically expect from courts even if we want it. Popular sovereignty, as a theory of democracy, is not the same thing as populist politics, but there is an affinity between the two. The rise of disturbing forms of populism in the United States, as well as in the United Kingdom and Europe, has renewed the attraction of a rival theory of democracy built around the idea that society consists of a wide range of individuals and groups with different aspirations, and that the point of democratic governance is to allow them to accommodate their differences peacefully and equitably.

From that perspective – the perspective of democratic pluralism – judicial independence is not a check on democracy but a constituent part of democracy; it is a mechanism of principled accommodation between different kinds of people, a way of preserving trust and cooperation. It is also a necessary safeguard against one group using criminal investigations and judicial processes as a tool of persecution. It requires the independence of prosecutors as well as the independence of judges, and it depends on informal norms as much as on written rules. Fortunately, from that perspective, democratic pluralism is not just important, it is also feasible, in part because the kind of 'independence' it requires is a degree of institutional insulation, not hermetic isolation from prevailing opinions. Judicial independence of this kind will not take care of itself, though, particularly when it is under serious attack, as it was in the United States during the presidency of Donald Trump and may continue to be in the years ahead. It needs defending.

7

Is There a French *Habeas Corpus*? Thinking About the Control by an Independent Judicial Authority Over the Deprivation of Liberty Before Criminal Trials

RAPHAËLE PARIZOT

THINKING ABOUT CONTROL over the deprivation of liberty before criminal trials in France is just another way of thinking about the existence of a 'French *habeas corpus*'. The aim of the *habeas corpus* doctrine, an English invention born with the Magna Carta of 1215 and developed in other acts such as the Habeas Corpus Act of 1679, is to protect against arbitrary detentions by the state. It means that every deprivation of liberty must be controlled. It supposes that deprivation of liberty is subject to an independent, effective control by the judge.[1]

In France, for a long time, such a control did not exist. Of course, the French Declaration of the Human and Civic Rights of 1789 provides in Article 2 the right to safety[2] and stresses, in Article 7, that 'No man may be accused, arrested or detained except in the cases determined by the Law, and following the procedure that it has prescribed. Those who solicit, expedite, carry out, or cause to be carried out arbitrary orders must be punished; but any citizen summoned or apprehended by virtue of the Law must give instant obedience; resistance makes him guilty'. But first, the Declaration does not directly provide for a control of the deprivation of liberty, and second, this text has had constitutional status only since 1971.[3]

---

[1] J. Farbey, R. J. Sharpe and S. Atrill, *The Law of Habeas Corpus* (Oxford, Oxford University Press, 3rd edn, 2011). In French, see D. Baranger, '*Habeas Corpus*', in J. Andriantsimbazovina, H. Gaudin, J.-P. Marguénaud, S. Rials, F. Sudre (ed.), *Dictionnaire des droits de l'homme* (Paris, Puf, 2008); G. Cuniberti, '*Habeas Corpus*', in L. Cadiet (ed.), *Dictionnaire de la Justice* (Paris, Puf, 2004).

[2] Art. 2 of the Declaration of the human and civic rights: 'The aim of every political association is the preservation of the natural and imprescriptible rights of Man. These rights are Liberty, Property, Safety and Resistance to Oppression'.

[3] Cons. Const., Decision No. 71–44 DC, 16 July 1971.

Proceedings of the British Academy, **250**, 128–137, © The British Academy 2022.

In reality, the first productive initiative to introduce a form of *habeas corpus*[4] at the highest level in France was made after the Second World War, during the discussion about the Constitution of the Fifth Republic. The result was the introduction in the Constitution of 1958 (posterior – it is important to stress – to the adoption of the European Convention on Human Rights that provides for such a control in Article 5§3)[5] of Article 66: 'No one shall be arbitrarily detained. The Judicial Authority, guardian of the freedom of the individual, shall ensure compliance with this principle in the conditions laid down by statute'.[6] However, this Article cannot be considered conclusive. On the contrary, it opened a strong period of political invocation and juridical evolution on the question of *habeas corpus* in France and on the control of the freedom of the individual by the judicial authority.

At a political level, *habeas corpus* appears to have emerged as something of a magic bullet; a 'recurrent slogan'[7] that allows politicians to show their interest in the rights of the individual deprived of liberty during the criminal process.[8] At a

---

[4] For a long time, the French doctrinal has been interested in the English *habeas corpus*. For example, with several references, E. Sallé de la Marinière, '*L'Habeas corpus anglais et la liberté individuelle en France*', *Revue critique de législation et de jurisprudence* (1934), pp. 570–617.

[5] Art. 5 of the European Convention on Human Rights 'Right to liberty and security':

'1. Everyone has the right to liberty and security of person. No one shall be deprived of his liberty save in the following cases and in accordance with a procedure prescribed by law: (…)

(c) the lawful arrest or detention of a person effected for the purpose of bringing him before the competent legal authority on reasonable suspicion of having committed an offence or when it is reasonably considered necessary to prevent his committing an offence or fleeing after having done so; (…)

3. Everyone arrested or detained in accordance with the provisions of paragraph 1 (c) of this Article shall be brought promptly before a judge or other officer authorised by law to exercise judicial power and shall be entitled to trial within a reasonable time or to release pending trial. Release may be conditioned by guarantees to appear for trial'.

[6] About the birth of the article 66 of the Constitution, see D. Maus, '*Regards sur l'écriture de l'article 66 de la Constitution de 1958: un Habeas Corpus à la française?*', in *L'homme et le droit. Mélanges en hommage à Jean-François Flauss* (Paris, Pedone, 2014, pp. 571–585); D. Salles, '*Michel Debré et la protection de la liberté individuelle par l'autorité judiciaire*', *Cahiers du Conseil constitutionnel* (No. 26, August 2009).

[7] F. Terré, '*Habeas corpus, habeas animum*', in *Mélanges en l'honneur du professeur Jacques-Henri Robert* (Paris, LexisNexis, 2012, p. 753).

[8] Several political speeches show a strong interest for a real French *habeas corpus*, classifying under this 'label' elements sometimes far from the English institution (right of access to a lawyer, right to a remedy against the decision on the pre-trial detention…): the programme of Blois, presented the 9 January 1978 by Raymond Barre, then Prime Minister, proposes to think about the introduction of an *habeas corpus* in France and nominates a commission directed by prof. Jean Rivero (*Le Monde*, 11 January 1978; see also M. Simon, '*Habeas corpus. Droit anglo-américain, droit français*', *Gazette du Palais* (1978, 2e sem., pp. 421–424)); declarations in April 1984 of Robert Badinter, then Minister of Justice, about a government bill (that will become the Act No. 84–576 of 9 July 1984 about the rights of individuals during the pre-trial detention) presented as introducing a procedure of *habeas corpus* in France (*Le Monde*, 26 April 1984); the declaration of the 20 May 1988 of Pierre Arpaillange, then Minister of Justice, supporting the creation of a 'French *habeas corpus*' (*Le Monde*, 24 May 1988); the speech of the 7 January 2009 of Nicolas Sarkozy, President of the Republic, at the *Cour de cassation*'s

juridical level, if the Constitution establishes the judicial authority as the guardian of the freedom of the individual, the Constitutional Council reads this principle in a strict way.

In order to understand this evolution, it is necessary to recall some fundamental elements of the French legal system. Since an Act of August 1790, the French justice system contains two branches: the judicial branch (with judges competent for private or criminal matters, and at the top, the *Cour de cassation*) and the administrative branch (with administrative judges competent for public administration matters, and at the top, the *Conseil d'État*).[9] Of course, each branch bears responsibility for the protection of fundamental rights. Since 1980, the administrative branch has been considered independent as the judicial branch.[10] However, in line with Article 66 of the Constitution, only judicial authorities have jurisdiction relating to issues affecting the freedom of the individual.

This raises an issue of how the domain that relates to 'the freedom of the individual' should be delineated. The *Conseil constitutionnel* initially adopted a broad interpretation that not only related to the deprivation of liberty but also extended to breaches of the right to private life.[11] But at the end of the 1990s, it opted for a more restrictive approach, considering that the freedom of the individual was affected only by decisions related to the deprivation of liberty (e.g., police custody, detention, involuntary hospitalisation).[12] So, decisions on deprivations of liberty had to be taken by judicial authorities, but decisions on restrictions of liberty could come under the control of administrative authorities.[13]

This case law, which can be considered to be stripping the judicial authority of powers relating to the freedom of the individual, is far from being over and

---

opening session, repeating an element of the programme of his candidacy to the presidential elections (*Le Monde*, 8 January 2009) and supporting the creation of a committee of reflexion about criminal justice, named Committee Léger (name of the president) with the particular mission to examine 'if a French *habeas corpus* could be justify that a judge only dedicated to the defence of liberties should be created'.

[9] D. Truchet, 'Dualisme juridictionnel', in Dictionnaire de la Justice, *op. cit.*

[10] Cons. Const., No. 80-119 DC of 22 July 1980, §6.

[11] Cons. Const., No. 83-164 DC of 29 December 1983: regarding to the possibility to searches by the tax administration, '*si les nécessités de l'action fiscale peuvent exiger que des agents du fisc soient autorisés à opérer des investigations dans des lieux privés, de telles investigations ne peuvent être conduites que dans le respect de l'article 66 de la Constitution qui confie à l'autorité judiciaire la sauvegarde de la liberté individuelle sous tous ses aspects, et notamment celui de l'inviolabilité du domicile*'.

[12] Cons. Const., No. 98-405 DC of 29 December 1998; Cons. Const., No. 99-411 DC of 16 June 1999; Cons. Const., No. 2003-467 DC of 13 March 2003.

[13] See strong opinions of two First Presidents of the *Cour cassation* and of the vice-president of the *Conseil d'Etat*: G. Canivet, '*Pathologie de la garantie de la liberté individuelle. Le syndrome de confusion. Examen de la jurisprudence du Conseil constitutionnel relative à l'interprétation de l'article 66 de la constitution*', in *Humanisme et Justice. Mélanges en l'honneur de Geneviève Giudicelli-Delage* (Paris, Dalloz, 2016, pp. 323–347); B. Louvel, '*L'autorité judiciaire, gardienne de la liberté individuelle ou des libertés individuelles?*', Réflexion à l'occasion de la rencontre annuelle des premiers présidents de cour d'appel et de la Cour de cassation (2 February 2016), https://www.courdecassation.fr/publicat ions_26/discours_publications_diverses_2039/discours_2202/premier_president_7084/gardienne_ liberte_33544.html; J.-M. Sauvé, 'Quel juge pour les libertés?', Recueil Dalloz (2016, pp. 1320–1328).

knows new expressions with the state of emergency that came into force in France after the terrorist attacks in Paris between 14 November 2015 and 1 November 2017. As part of the law on the state of emergency, the Minister of the Interior has the power to order a person against whom 'there is strong reasons to believe that his/her comportment constitutes a threat for the public security and order'[14] to stay at home for a maximum of 12 hours per 24 hours for a maximum of 12 months, renewable for three months. Questioned about the conformity of this power to impose house arrest with Article 66 of the Constitution, the *Conseil constitutionnel* opined that this obligation to stay at home for 12 out of every 24 hours was not really a deprivation of liberty, concluding that it could therefore be decided by an administrative authority (the Minister).[15] In other words, it determined that a partial deprivation of liberty was not a deprivation of liberty under Article 66. One might expect that the end of the state of emergency period on 1 November 2017 would also have been the end of the application of such provisions. Unfortunately, the main provisions of the state of emergency law of 1955 were integrated into common law by a Law of 30 October 2017.[16] Since the adoption of this Law,[17] in order to prevent terrorism, the Minister of Interior has the power to force persons suspected to pose a particularly serious threat to public order and security to stay in a determined geographic area and to present themselves each day to a police officer or be placed under electronic supervision.[18] This measure may not necessarily amount to a deprivation of liberty, but it is an important restriction of liberty. Its imposition is justified on the basis of a risk (not the suspected commission of an offence), the restrictive measure is ordered by the administrative authority (the Minister of Interior), and without the control – *a priori* – of the judicial authority (but with the possible control – *a posteriori* – of the administrative judge).[19]

Moreover, even if limited to 'classical' deprivations of liberty (e.g., police custody, pre-trial detention), the question of the control of the judicial authority has considerably evolved under the Code of Criminal Procedure;[20] in particular with

[14] Art. 6 of the Law No. 55-385 of the 3 April 1955 on the state of emergency.
[15] Cons. Const., No. 2015-527 QPC of 22 December 2015.
[16] Law No. 2017-1510 of 30 October 2017 strengthening the internal security and the fight against terrorism.
[17] Until July 2021, several provisions were provisional; since a law of 30 July 2021, all provisions are definitive.
[18] Art. L. 228-1 of the Internal security code (Code de la sécurité intérieure).
[19] Beyond the Law on the state of emergency of 1955 and the following provisions in the antiterrorist French law, one may wonder about the texts on the sanitary state of emergency adopted in order to face the epidemic of Covid-19 and about their conformity to the Constitution. Regarding the pre-trial deprivations of liberty, the Ordinance No. 2020-3030 of 25 March 2020 for the adaptation of provisions of criminal procedure on the basis of the Law No. 2020-290 of 23 March 2020 of emergency to face the epidemic of Covid-19 provides for that prolongations of police custodies in the field of organised crime can 'intervene without the presentation of the person before the competent magistrate' (art. 14); it also provides for that maximum periods for pre-trial detention and for home arrests under electronic supervision are '*ipso jure*' extended of two or three months for *délits* and of six months for *crimes* (art. 16).
[20] The French Code of criminal procedure of 1959 substituted the Code of criminal instruction of 1808.

the Law of 15 June 2000,[21] which provides that 'the coercive measures to which a person suspected or prosecuted may be subjected are taken by or under the effective control of judicial authority. They should be strictly limited to the needs of the process, proportionate to the gravity of the offence charged and not such as to infringe human dignity'.[22] According to this provision, the judicial authority is the liberties and custody judge (*juge des libertés et de la détention*), which is also a creation of the Law of 15 June 2000. For a long time, this judge's role was limited to the external supervision of pre-trial detention (the judge was initially named, in the preparatory debates, 'judge of the pre-trial detention'). As shall be argued below, this judge was a kind of '*trompe-l'oeil*' institution, lacking in the ability to exercise effective control.[23] The weight of this judge's role has, without doubt, increased in recent years, but there remains some way to go before this judge can be considered as an effective body of control for the coercive measures decided during the criminal pre-trial. Moreover, it is worth recalling that the judicial authority competent to order coercive measures is, if the defendant is in police custody, the public prosecutor, with the unavoidable question of their independence.

The effectiveness of control by the liberties and custody judge

During the course of the criminal process, all decisions (definitive as well as provisional) about deprivation of liberty are in principle taken by a judge. Definitive detention (i.e., the penalty of imprisonment) must be pronounced by a judge or, to be more precise, judges (correctional court or assize court). Pre-trial detention (*détention provisoire*), since the Law of 15 June 2000, is no longer decided by the investigating judge (*juge d'instruction*) but by the liberties and custody judge (*juge des libertés et de la détention*). This judge is in charge, during the investigation stage, of most issues pertaining to pre-trial detention. He or she considers the necessity to order or extend pre-trial detention and decides about release applications[24]

---

[21] Law No. 2000-516 of 15 June 2000 strengthening the protection of the presumption of innocence and the rights of victims.

[22] Preliminary article III alinea 4 of the Code of Criminal Procedure. This article has been recently completed, with the Law No. 2019-222 of 23 March 2019 of programme 2018-2022 and reform for the justice, with a paragraph providing for the same type of control for measures breaching the private life: 'During the criminal procedure, measures against the private life of a person must be taken, by or under the effective control of judicial authority, only if they are, relating to the circumstances of the case, necessary to the discovery of the truth and proportionate to the gravity of the offence'.

[23] On the uncomfortable part of the *juge des libertés et de la détention*, see B. de Lamy, 'Le juge des libertés et de la détention: un trompe l'œil?', Droit pénal (2007, étude n°13); G. Giudicelli-Delage, '*La figure du juge de l'avant procès entre symboles et pratiques*', in *Le droit pénal à l'aube du troisième millénaire. Mélanges offerts à Jean Pradel* (Paris, Cujas, 2006), p. 335 et seq.

[24] Art. 137-1 Code of criminal procedure. An appeal is possible against these decisions (art. 185 et 186 Code of criminal procedure).

when an investigating judge has denied them.[25] The liberties and custody judge's competences are not limited to pre-trial detention; he or she is also in charge of several acts relating to restriction or deprivation of liberty during the police inquiry (e.g., extension of the police custody after 48 hours when the Law provides for it,[26] authorisation of some searches[27] and special investigative techniques to fight the organised crime).[28] This judge appears ever more as the guardian of the freedom of the individual over the strict reading of Article 66 of the Constitution by the *Conseil constitutionnel.*

Nevertheless, practice quickly stressed the imperfections of this new judge's role, status and function. Little by little, some of these defects have been corrected, but there is still room for improvement.

First, relating to the judge's status, legislation enacted on 8 August 2016[29] gives the *juge des libertés et de la détention* a more protected status: this judge was previously a judge with a high rank but simply appointed by the president of the district court of first instance. Since the August 2016 legislation, the judge is nominated by an Order of the President of the Republic.[30]

Second, relating to the judge's function, progress must be highlighted, both on the duties *of* this judge and the duties *to* him or her, in order to make judicial control more effective. In relation to the first of these elements, the *juge des libertés et de la détention* is required to explain his or her decision with reasons. This stems from two important decisions of 2016 when the Criminal Chamber of the *Cour de cassation* noted that it would no longer accept a simple reference to the reasons developed in the request of the public prosecutor and instead required the judge to give real written reasons for his or her decision. The Chamber noted:

> [T]his requirement of detailed written reasons is required under the European Convention on Human Rights and taking into account the evolution of the status and the jurisdictional role of the liberties and custody judge, imposed by the legislator. Written reasons are an essential guarantee against the risk of a disproportionate breach of the freedom of the concerned person and must allow the defendant to know the precise reasons [for the decision].[31]

---

[25] If the investigating judge can no longer decide about a pre-trial detention, he can still decide about release application (art. 144-1 Code of criminal procedure).

[26] Art. 706-88 Code of criminal procedure in the case of organised crime.

[27] Art. 76 Code of criminal procedure to authorise searches during the preliminary police inquiry (i.e., which is not the flagrance police inquiry) without the consent of the person concerned; art. 706-89 and 706-90 Code of criminal procedure to authorise searches outside the legal times (6 a.m. – 9 p.m.) in the field of the organised crime.

[28] Art. 706-95 and s. Code of criminal procedure.

[29] Organic Law No. 2016-1090 of the 8 August 2016 concerning statutory guaranties, deontological obligations and the recruitment of magistrates as well as the High Council of the Judiciary.

[30] Art. 28-3 of Ordinance No. 58-1270 of 22 December 1958 concerning the Organic law on the status of the judiciary. With this way of nomination (which is the same way provided for the investigating judge, the judge for children and the judge for the execution of penalties), this judge is protected against any possibility from removal.

[31] Crim., 23 November 2016, No. 16-81904. See also Crim., 23 November 2016, No. 15-83649 to allow a search in a preliminary police inquiry without the consent of the person.

While this seems like a positive development, it must be noted that this obligation can be respected merely with the reproduction *in extenso* of the request of
the public prosecutor if it answers point by point the requirements of the Code.[32]
It will be important to keep a careful eye on the position of the *Cour de cassation*
and to monitor that this obligation will not transform the expected control in a kind
of 'lip-sync ... of others',[33] and that the judge expresses a personal point of view
about the case file.

On the other hand, the judge must be practically enabled to achieve his or her
mission. He or she needs to be given the means to exercise the requested control
in practice. This necessity has been stressed by the *Conseil constitutionnel*, which
considered that, where the liberties and custody judge lacks access to all of the
materials of the case, the judge cannot exercise effective control over the protection
of suspects' liberty.[34] In other words, an effective control needs both an 'illuminating' decision (founded on strong reasons) and an 'illuminated' decision (with
access to all of the relevant materials). On this last point, further reform is needed
in order to make the control an effective control and in order to allow the judicial
authority to exercise a materially independent control.

By contrast, as shall be seen, the control currently exercised by the public prosecutor could be deemed materially complete (insofar as he or she has access to all the
relevant material) but statutory problematic (owing to the absence of judicial control).

Control by the public prosecutor

During the police inquiry stage of the criminal process, a police officer can decide to
place a suspect in police detention for the purposes of questioning (*garde à vue*) if

---

[32] Crim., 21 January 2020, No. 18-84899. In a preliminary police inquiry, to allow a search without the
consent of the person concerned, it is necessary that 'on pain of nullity, the custody judge's ruling states the
qualification of the offence for which the evidence is being sought, as well as the address of the places in
which these operations may be carried out. This decision is reasoned with reference to the legal and factual
matters, which justify the necessity for these measures' (art. 76 Code of criminal procedure). The *Cour
de cassation* considers that reasons could be only 'the reproduction *in extenso* of the request of the public
prosecutor' if the judge 'refers to article 76, to suspected offences and to the fact that they are punished by
a prison sentence of five years or more and if he takes into consideration the risk of the loss of the evidence
regarding to the gravity and the number of the offences, the personality of the suspected person'.

[33] P. Truche, *L'anarchiste et son juge. A propos de l'assassinat de Sadi Carnot*, Paris, Fayard, 1994,
p. 181 (in the conclusion, the author, former General Prosecutor at the Court of Appeal of Lyon and at
the Court of Appeal of Paris, and former Prime President of the *Cour de cassation*, gives his remarks
about the way to write a request and advises to *'ne pas faire de play-back sur les disques des autres'*).

[34] The legislator tried to extend the field of some special investigative techniques, at the moment
limited to the fight against organised crime, to all crimes. But the *Conseil constitutionnel* (Cons. Const.,
Decision No. 2019-778 DC of 21 March 2019) considered such provisions unconstitutional because
crimes, contrary to offences regarding organised crime, are not necessarily serious *and* complex to
justify the application of these techniques particularly intrusive and because the control by the judge is
deficient: he has no access to all the materials of the procedure (for example, he has no access to reports
that he would not order). The provisions are contrary to the Constitution.

there is one or more plausible reasons for suspecting that the person concerned has committed or attempted to commit an offence.[35] In France, there are two types of investigation: the judicial investigation (*instruction*), led by the investigating judge (*juge d'instruction*), and the inquiry (*enquête*), led by the district prosecutor (*procureur de la République*), which is the most common form of investigation.[36] During the inquiry, police custody is subject to the supervision of the district prosecutor for the first 48 hours with control transferring to the liberties and custody judge if, in exceptional cases, police custody is extended beyond 48 hours.

As a deprivation of liberty, police custody must be submitted to a control by the judicial authority (Art. 66 Const.). Is the public prosecutor effectively a member of the judicial authority? The question is hard because the function of public prosecutor is assumed by magistrates who are members of the judicial authority[37] without being independent,[38] whereas independence is a main feature of the judicial authority.[39] This institutional paradox – of a judicial role without a judicial status – has been read in different ways. On the one hand, the *Conseil constitutionnel* has expressed the view that the public prosecutor is a full member of the judicial authority, with sufficient guarantees of independence. In a December 2017 decision,[40] the *Conseil* held that, on the basis of Articles 16 of the Declaration of Human and Civic Rights,[41] Article 20 of the Constitution[42] and Articles 64 and 65 of the Constitution, 'the Constitution grants independence to the *Magistrats du Parquet* (i.e., prosecutors), from which flows

---

[35] Art. 62-2 and s. Code of criminal procedure.

[36] Historically, the judicial investigation was the only type of investigation available. That is the practice (prosecutors) who developed the use of an inquiry before to apply to an investigating judge. This practice was finally recognised in the code of criminal procedure of 1959 (ever in force) and became the common frame. Today, the judicial investigation is ever required for the most serious offences (criminal offences), though it may be ordered for less serious offences in particularly complex cases (art. 79 Code of criminal procedure), and it concern less than 3% of the judicial cases. As developed above, during the judicial investigation, it is the JLD who has responsibility for ordering and extending pre-trial detention (*détention provisoire*) (art. 137-1 c. proc. pén.).

[37] The judicial authority is composed of judges and public prosecutors. According to Article 65 of the Constitution, 'the High Council of the Judiciary shall consist of a section with jurisdiction over judges and a section with jurisdiction over public prosecutors'.

[38] Art. 5 of Ordinance No. 58-1270 of 22 December 1958 concerning the Organic law on the status of the judiciary: 'The *Magistrats du Parquet* [public prosecutors] are placed under the management and supervision of their managers and under the authority of the *Garde des Sceaux*, Minister of Justice. At the hearing, they are free to speak'.

[39] Art. 64 of the Constitution: 'The President of the Republic shall be the guarantor of the independence of the Judicial Authority.

He shall be assisted by the High Council of the Judiciary.

An Institutional Act shall determine the status of members of the Judiciary.

Judges shall be irremovable from office'.

[40] Cons. const., No. 2017-680 QPC, 8 December 2017.

[41] Art. 16 of the Declaration of Human and Civic Rights: 'Any society in which no provision is made for guaranteeing rights or for the separation of powers, has no Constitution'.

[42] Art. 20 of the Constitution: 'The Government shall determine and conduct the policy of the Nation' (which includes the power to determine the prosecution policy).

the free exercise of their legal activity, that this independence must be reconciled with the Government's prerogatives and that it is not ensured by the same guarantees as those applicable to *Magistrats du Siège* (i.e., judges)'. The Court of Justice of the European Union agrees with this conclusion in the context of the European arrest warrant. In its decision of 12 December 2019, the Court of Justice held that 'in France, public prosecutors have the power to assess independently, in particular in relation to the executive, the necessity and proportionality of a decision to issue a European arrest warrant and exercise that power objectively, taking into account all incriminatory and exculpatory evidence'.[43] On the other hand, the European Court of Human Rights held that owing to their status, public prosecutors in France did not satisfy the requirement of independence from the executive, which, according to its well-established case-law, was, like impartiality, one of the guarantees inherent in the autonomous notion of 'officer' within the meaning of Article 5§3.[44] This position has been supported by the domestic case law of the *Cour de cassation*. First, in a 2010 decision, the Criminal Chamber held that the public prosecutor could not be considered 'a judicial authority according to the meaning of Article 5§3 of the European Convention of Human Rights, since he doesn't have the guarantees of independence and impartiality required by this text and he is a prosecuting party'.[45] Second, in speeches delivered in 2018, at the formal event that marks the beginning of the judicial year, the higher *magistrats* of the *Cour de cassation* expressed the same opinion before the President of the Republic.[46]

These decisions raise the issue of compatibility between French law and the European Convention of Human Rights. The Convention requires that every person deprived of his or her liberty shall be brought 'promptly' ('*aussitôt*') before a judge or other officer authorised by law to exercise judicial power. According to the European Court, this condition of promptness is interpreted as four days or a little less;[47] this is later than provided for in French law, which requests a presentation before a judge

---

[43] CJEU, 12 December 2019, C-566/19 PPU and C-626/19 PPU (to answer to two requests for a preliminary ruling from a Court of Appeal of Luxembourg and the Rechtbank Amsterdam concerning procedures of European arrest warrant), §55.

[44] ECtHR, *Moulin v France*, 23 November 2010, §. 57; see also, ECtHR (Gd. ch.), *Medvedyev v France*, 29 March 2010.

[45] Crim., 15 December 2010, No. 10-83674.

[46] See in particular the speech of Jean-Claude Marin, General Prosecutor at the *Cour de cassation*, of the 15 January 2018: '*il se trouve qu'au sein même de cette autorité judiciaire indépendante, il existe une catégorie de magistrats, eux-mêmes indépendants comme membres de cette autorité, ainsi que l'a rappelé à plusieurs reprises le Conseil constitutionnel, qui sont placés sous l'autorité du Garde des Sceaux, membre de l'exécutif. Pour ces magistrats, ainsi institutionnellement écartelés, s'agit-il d'une indépendance à mi-temps, d'une indépendance à éclipses ou d'une indépendance dépendante?*' (https://www.courdecassation.fr/IMG/Rentrée2018_Discours%20Procureur%20général%20Jean-Claude%20Marin.pdf).

[47] ECtHR, *Brogan v United Kingdom*, 29 November 1988. For a shorter period, see ECtHR, *Gutsanovi v Bulgaria*, 15 October 2013, and the interesting comment of Prof. Damien Roets, '*Quel « aussitôt » pour l'*habeas corpus *européen?*', *Revue de science criminelle et de droit pénal comparé* (2014) p. 169.

after two days if the deprivation of liberty is to be extended.[48] On this basis, French law is probably not contrary to the European Convention. Nevertheless, the French public prosecutor cannot be understood as a judicial authority according to Article 5§3 of the European Convention; thus, it remains problematic that he or she exercises control over a suspect's deprivation of liberty.

Furthermore, the question of the control of the *garde à vue* is not completely dissociable from the question of the control of the inquiry. In France, the institution that controls the inquiry (the district prosecutor) is the institution that manages it. Can the district prosecutor continue both to manage the judicial police[49] and supervise the inquiry[50] (in particular, during its police custody (*garde à vue*) stage)?[51,52] This is an area that requires serious consideration and one where there is scope for change. Indeed, we are already witnessing the slow emergence of judicial control over the inquiry (*juridictionnalisation de l'enquête*) in France. Its main significance pertains for the time being to police searches,[53] but its reach must extend to pre trial deprivation of liberty. The 'French *habeas corpus*' still has a road to travel.

---

[48] In 1978, J. Carbonnier already wrote: '*La France, rêvant d'*Habeas corpus, *aligne, faute de mieux, les garanties qui peuvent y ressembler: (...) la règle des vingt-quatre heures qui exige que, passé ce délai, l'individu arrêté ou gardé à vue soit exhibé à la lumière judiciaire (...). Cette dernière garantie est du reste assez illusoire. L'irréparable peut être accompli en beaucoup moins de temps. Une journée compte une nuit, et la véritable liberté individuelle est de dormir dans son lit. En vingt-quatre heures, par la sueur et la barbe, la nature se charge de faire perdre la face aux innocents aussi vite qu'aux coupables*' (*Sociologie juridique* (Paris, Puf, 1ère édition 1978, 1ère édition Quadrige, 1994), p. 402).

[49] Art. 12 Code of criminal procedure: 'Judicial police operations are carried on under the direction of the district prosecutor by the officers, civil servants and agents designated by the present Title'.

[50] Art. 39-3 Code of criminal procedure: 'In their attributions of direction of the judicial police, the district prosecutor can address general or particular instructions to the investigators. He controls the legality of the means used by the investigators, the proportionality of their acts of investigation regarding the nature and the gravity of the facts, the orientation given to the inquiry as well as its quality (...)'.

[51] Art. 62-2 Code of criminal procedure: 'Police custody is a coercive measure decided by the police officer under the control of the judicial authority (...)'.

[52] About these questions, see in particular C. Ribeyre, 'Le contrôle de l'enquête par le procureur de la République', ed. M. Nicolas, Conference Les mutations du Parquet, Lexbase Pénal (No. 22, 19 December 2019).

[53] Since the Law No. 2019-222 of 23 March 2019 of programme 2018-2022 and of reform for justice, the Code of criminal procedure provides for the possibility to introduce before the liberties and custody judge a request for cancelling a search if the person is not prosecuted six months after this operation (art. 802-2).

8

Judicial Independence and the Prevention of Atrocity Crimes in Myanmar

DANIEL AGUIRRE

IN AUGUST 2017, the international community looked on as international atrocity crimes in Myanmar unfolded. Hundreds of thousands of Rohingya Muslims fled Northern Rakhine State into Bangladesh from a systematic military campaign targeting civilians, burning villages and using sexual assault as a weapon of war. At the same time, the military conducted campaigns in the Northern Shan and Kachin states characterised by violations of international law. Myanmar's judiciary and the international community failed to prevent these atrocity crimes. The horrific nature of the crimes committed against the Rohingya are the culmination of myriad other human rights violations in the country fuelled by long-standing impunity.[1] Despite all the warning signs – the lack of judicial independence, the unfair trials and routine human rights violations committed by state security forces with impunity – the international community was unable to foresee and prevent these escalating to atrocity crimes.[2] How did Myanmar's 'Remarkable Journey'[3] to democracy get so off track?

International law's approach to atrocity crimes is largely reactionary, emphasising intervention and deterrence through prosecution. The International Criminal Court

[1] All five United Nations Special Rapporteurs on the human rights situation in Myanmar identified systemic impunity as a critical obstacle to the realisation of human rights in Myanmar. Detailed findings of the Independent International Fact-Finding Mission on Myanmar, UN Doc. A/HRC/42/CRP.5, para. 1538; International Commission of Jurists, 'Myanmar: Rakhine State crisis demands full government commitment to protecting human rights of all', (Bangkok, 11 September 2017).

[2] Since this chapter was completed and submitted for publication, the Myanmar Military staged a coup, deposing the elected legislative and executive members of government while shutting down any semblance of an independent judiciary. See, United Nations, 'Statement attributable to the Spokesperson for the Secretary General – on Myanmar' (1 February 2021), online at: https://www.un.org/sg/en/content/sg/statement/2021-01-31/statement-attributable-the-spokesperson-for-the-secretary-general-myanmar (last accessed 26 January 2022).

[3] J. Burke, Obama Praises Burma's Remarkable Journey, *Guardian*, 19 November 2012, online at: https://www.theguardian.com/world/2012/nov/19/obama-burma-remarkable-journey-democracy (last accessed 26 January 2022).

Proceedings of the British Academy, **250**, 138–159, © The British Academy 2022.

(ICC) has begun an investigation into crimes against humanity and Myanmar has been brought before the International Court of Justice (ICJ) by The Gambia for alleged violations of the Genocide Convention. In 2020, the ICJ imposed provisional measures on Myanmar, including prevention,[4] that reiterate the Genocide Convention's focus on the prohibition and prosecution of alleged perpetrators.[5] Since the drafting of this article, a military coup installed an illegal junta that has waged a war against the people of Myanmar resulting in thousands of deaths and hundreds of thousands of people displaced. The junta has arrested and imprisoned activists, journalists and peaceful protesters while criminalising freedom of speech and assembly. The campaign is characterised by widespread torture and other ill-treatment during periods of detention and attacks that may constitute crimes against humanity and/or war crimes. The Special Rapporteur on the situation in Myanmar has criticised the lack of a coordinated response from the international community.[6] This confirms the opportunity lost to prevent human rights abuses that escalate to atrocities during a brief period of partial reform. This chapter argues that prevention of atrocity crimes depends on an independent judiciary and that judicial independence in Myanmar is so compromised that it is unable to act as a safeguard against human rights abuses, let alone prevent atrocity crimes like war crimes, crimes against humanity and genocide.

An obligation to prevent?

International law's preventative approach is inadequate where a national judiciary lacks the independence to hold the state accountable for routine human rights abuses before they escalate into atrocity crimes. Fulfilling an obligation to prevent atrocity crimes requires the rule of law and restraints on arbitrary state power[7] at the national level. In Myanmar, there are no national mechanisms in place willing or able to prevent routine human rights violations, let alone provide accountability for atrocity crimes like genocide. Analysis of the rule of law in Myanmar[8] demonstrates

---

[4] International Court of Justice, Order: Application of the Convention on the Prevention and Punishment of the Crime of Genocide (The *Gambia v Myanmar*) Request for the Indication of Provisional Measures, January 2020, General List No. 178, at paras. 86 (1) and (2).

[5] International Court of Justice, Order: The *Gambia v Myanmar*, at para. 51.

[6] Report of the Special Rapporteur on the situation of human rights in Myanmar, Thomas H. Andrews, A/HRC/49/76 at para 18.

[7] R. Peerenboom, 'Varieties of rule of law: An introduction and provisional conclusion', in R. Peerenboom (ed.) *Asian Discourses of Rule of Law* (London, Curzon Routledge, 2004) pp. 1–53.

[8] N. Cheesman, 'Thin rule of law or un-rule of law in Myanmar?', *Pacific Affairs* 82 (2009) pp. 597–613; N. Cheesman, 'What does the rule of law have to do with democratization (in Myanmar)', *South East Asia Research* 22.2 (2014) pp. 213–232; N. Cheesman, *Opposing the Rule of Law: How Myanmar's Courts Make Law and Order* (Cambridge, Cambridge University Press, 2015); N. Cheesman, 'That signifier of desire, the rule of law', *Social Research* 82(2) (2015) pp. 267–290; N. Cheesman, 'Rule-of-law lineages in colonial and early post-colonial Burma', *Modern Asian Studies* 50.2 (2016) pp. 564–601; N. Cheesman, 'Taking the rule of law's opposition seriously', *Hague Journal on the Rule of Law* 9.1(2017) pp. 29–44; E. Prasse-Freeman, *Conceptions of Justice vs. the Rule of Law. Myanmar: The Dynamics of an Evolving Polity* (Boulder, Lynne Rienner Publishers, 2014).

the inability or unwillingness of legal norms or institutions to restrain arbitrary state power, rendering it both functionally absent and used to justify authoritarian state power.[9] Rule of law rhetoric masks a law-and-order governance that imposes stability rather than accountability to the law. Imposing law and order through the courts undermines the balance of powers and judicial independence and prevents us from stopping international atrocity crimes before they happen.

International opprobrium following the commission of international atrocity crimes eclipses its failure to recognise the warning signs – such as the lack of an independent judiciary capable of holding state actors accountable and preventing these crimes – and act upon them. These warning signs were long highlighted by human rights organisations but were not heeded by the international community, who instead rushed to engage for strategic and economic reasons. Nevertheless, Myanmar's reform process was embraced and legitimised by the international community eager to engage economically and strategically. This allowed for routine patterns of human rights abuse and unfair trials, and ensured that security forces remained unaccountable. A judiciary lacking independence facilitated the commission of international atrocity crimes by failing to pre-empt them: it was unwilling and unable to hold perpetrators accountable for systematic human rights violations and other crimes inchoate to atrocity.

This chapter looks at the role of the judiciary in the prevention of international crimes by ensuring accountability for human rights abuses at the national level. It argues that without the rule of law and an independent judiciary, a state cannot prevent international crimes. Part one explains how Myanmar's judiciary was developed by successive authoritarian regimes to impose stability on the public rather than uphold the rule of law. It argues that judicial independence is not under threat in Myanmar because the judiciary was not designed to be impartial and independent – it is there to impose law and order, not hold authorities accountable. Part two examines the obligation to prevent atrocity crimes and argues that prevention should include implementing human rights law and requires an independent judiciary to ensure accountability before atrocity crimes or their inchoate forms are committed. It argues that there are clear warning signs that atrocities will be committed and that the international community ignored them, particularly the lack of judicial independence, while pursuing a policy of economic, political and development engagement.

Ruling by law in Myanmar's 'disciplined' democracy

Myanmar has never known the rule of law or had an independent judiciary capable of restraining arbitrary state power. Just because the term rule of law is used does not equate to the concept that prevails at the international level.[10] The rule of law

---

[9] A. Batesmith and J. Stevens, 'In the Absence of the Rule of Law: Everyday Lawyering, Dignity and Resistance in Myanmar's "Disciplined Democracy"' *Social & Legal Studies* 28 (2019) 573–599, 574.
[10] B. Z. Tamanaha, *On the Rule of Law: History, Politics, Theory* (Cambridge, Cambridge University Press, 2004).

did not emerge with what Melissa Crouch terms the 'big bang' of reforms since 2011.[11] Nor did it appear at the release of Aung San Suu Kyi in 2010 or the partial election of her National League for Democracy in 2015. It has been used since colonial times to describe systems designed to enforce law and order in which the judiciary never conducted fair trials and was never fully independent.[12]

Background: Colonialism and military dictatorship

British colonialism sacrificed individual and community rights to law and order, providing a bureaucratic system of executive power and surveillance, prone to discrimination, emergency measures and police power, administered by the judiciary to ensure stability and public order.[13] It used law to dominate people and extract resources.[14] The Courts granted leeway for the police and powerful actors while ethnic and gender-based discrimination was common.[15] The maintenance of law and public order took precedence over the rule of law and judicial independence.[16] The independence Constitution of 1947 included provisions for an independent judiciary. But Nick Cheesman argues that an independent judiciary and a rights-based approach to law was in regular conflict with upholding law and order.[17] Callahan agrees that an independent judiciary was stifled, not instilled, by the inherited colonial legal system.[18]

By 1962, even this flourishing of independence was over: Myanmar's Chief Justice was arrested in a military coup.[19] Military rule destroyed the procedural and substantive aspects of the rule of law, especially judicial independence.[20] Law became a way of maintaining control.[21] The military staffed the courts and decided cases within the framework of the public order programme.[22] In the 1970s, the military established people's courts and administrative bodies

[11] M. Crouch, 'The Layers of Legal Development in Myanmar', in M. Crouch and T. Lindsey (eds.) *Law, Society and Transition in Myanmar* (Bloomsbury, 2014) p. 33.

[12] Crouch, 'Layers of Legal Development' p. 34.

[13] For a full discussion on the development of law in colonial Burma, see Cheesman, *Opposing the Rule of Law*, pp. 39–60.

[14] Crouch, 'Layers of Legal Development', p. 34.

[15] Cheesman, *Opposing the Rule of Law* pp. 57–60.

[16] M. Aung-Thwin, 'Discourses of Emergency in Colonial and Post Colonial Burma', in V. Ramraj and A.K. Thiruvengadam (eds.) *Emergency Powers in Asia: Exploring the Limits of Legality* (Cambridge, Cambridge University Press, 2010) pp. 187–210.

[17] Cheesman, *Opposing the Rule of Law* pp. 65–72; For more on the origins of the Public Order (preservation) act see: U. H. Aung, 'The Law of Preventative Detention in Burma', *Journal of the International Commission of Jurists*, 3.1 (1961) p. 47.

[18] M. P. Callahan, 'State Formation in the Shadow of the Raj: Violence, Warfare and Politics in Colonial Burma', *Southeast Asian Studies* 39.4 (2002) p. 535.

[19] M. W. Charney, *A History of Modern Burma* (Cambridge, Cambridge University Press, 2009) pp. 75–90; See: Declaration No. 22 of the State Revolutionary Council, 7 March 1962.

[20] Cheesman, 'Rule-of-law lineages' p. 568; Crouch, 'Layers of Legal Development', p. 41.

[21] Cheesman, N. 'Rule-of-law lineages' p. 568.

[22] Cheesman, *Opposing the Rule of Law*, p. 88.

staffed by the executive based on military policy rather than the law.[23] The 1974 Constitution rejected the separation of powers: judges were considered members of the legislature, with varying legal qualifications and no power to interpret the law or constitution.[24]

Economic crises and military crackdowns in the 1980s led to democracy protests, and political turmoil ended with one military government replaced by another, the State Law and Order Restoration Committee (SLORC). SLORC dispensed with any political or legal pretences and implemented a market-orientated authoritarian system that entrenched wealth, land and resources in the hands of the military and their families.[25] Failed economic reforms inspired democracy movements and the 1988 student-led uprising that resulted in a military crackdown. An election in 1992 saw the National League for Democracy win a majority, but SLORC refused to step down and members of parliament were prevented from taking their seats, arrested and imprisoned.

SLORC emphasised a rule of law based on upholding law and order, peace and tranquillity.[26] The Office of the Attorney General was revised, giving it sweeping powers of law reform and control of the Bar Council, compromising the independence of lawyers.[27] The courts functioned but without legal transparency or accountability, and corruption became rife.[28] Legal education was undermined as law departments were closed or decentralised to new universities far from city centres or conducted through distant education programmes.[29]

What followed was nearly two decades of authoritarian military rule under SLORC and then the State Peace and Development Council (SPDC). The judiciary was regularly used to stifle opposition by imposing law and order with unfair trials. Lawyers were routinely jailed. In a 2006 report, UN Special Rapporteur Paulo Sergio Pinheiro demonstrated how the regime misused the legal system and lack of judicial independence to authorise and sanction human rights violations by law.[30]

This period coincided with economic collapse, sanctions and, bizarrely, constructing a new capital city far from populated areas called Nay Pyi Taw, where the Supreme Court of the Union now sits. Repression continued to characterise political events like the 'Saffron Revolution' in 2007 and natural disasters such as the 2008 Nargis Cyclone that killed hundreds of thousands.

---

[23] Cheesman, *Opposing the Rule of Law*, pp. 87–94.
[24] Crouch, 'Layers of Legal Development', p. 43.
[25] Crouch, 'Layers of Legal Development', p. 44.
[26] See State Law and Order Restoration Council Declaration No. 2/88, 18 September 1988; No. 6/88, 24 September 1988.
[27] Attorney-General Law (State Law and Order Restoration Council Law No. 3/88) See International Commission of Jurists, 'Right to Counsel: The Independence of Lawyers in Myanmar' (Geneva, 2013). Online at: https://www.icj.org/wp-content/uploads/2013/12/MYANMAR-Right-to-Counsel-electronic. pdf (accessed 20 October 2020).
[28] N. Cheesman, 'Myanmar's Courts and the Sounds Money Makes', in N. Cheesman, M. Skidmore and T. Wilson (eds.) *Myanmar's Transition: Openings, Obstacles and Opportunities* (Singapore, ISEAS, 2012) 231–248, at pp. 237–240.
[29] Crouch, 'Layers of Legal Development', p. 4.
[30] A/61/369, paras. 27–34. See also A/62/233, para. 30.E/CN.4/1999/35.

Armed conflict with and suppression of minority groups continued unchallenged by the courts. Many of the same judges, prosecutors, clerks and administrative personnel staff the judicial system today. Given this history, it is not surprising that the judiciary has been unable or unwilling to intervene to hold state actors accountable. Stephen McCarthy argues that Myanmar's legacy of military rule is 'reflected in the state of its current legal system, the judiciary and the rule of law.'[31]

Crisis, what crisis? Imposing law and order through the judiciary

The rule of law requires an independent judiciary to provide a check and balance on other branches of government and to protect human rights. But what if this is not the goal of governance? There is an emerging regional understanding in Southeast Asia where states apply a proceduralist interpretation of the rule of law emphasising security, property rights and the promotion of economic growth[32] without limiting state power or protecting human rights.

Myanmar's courts impose law and order.[33] This rule by law system contradicts the rule of law that protects human rights, ensures judicial independence, and makes the state and its agents subject to the law.[34] Therefore, judicial independence in Myanmar is not in crisis – the judiciary is functioning precisely as intended: it enforces law and order on the public and legally discriminates against minorities without holding authorities accountable. Where there is no judicial independence, no fair trials, no effective review of arrest and detention, no checks on the arbitrary use of force by the police and military, on torture or discrimination, atrocity crimes are possible.

Myanmar has adopted a constitution, reformed law and opened its economy for investment without an independent judiciary and institutions to promote justice, equality and human rights.[35] Myanmar's reforms, directed by the military, omit key rule of law content associated with human rights, justice and equality while remaining referential to the rule of law in order for legitimacy. The focus has been on reforming company law, investment law and land law, and improving domestic arbitration. They were not new initiatives designed to break with the past;[36] they

---

[31] S. McCarthy, 'Rule of Law Expedited: Land Title Reform and Justice in Burma (Myanmar)', in *Asian Studies Review*, 42(2) (2018) p. 233.

[32] For more on regional interpretations of the rule of law see: Curley, Dressel and McCarthy, 'Competing Visions of the Rule of Law in Southeast Asia: Power, Rhetoric and Governance', *Asian Studies Review* 42.2 (2018) pp. 192–209; J. Rajah, *Authoritarian Rule of Law: Legislation, Discourse and Legitimacy in Singapore* (Cambridge, Cambridge University Press, 2012).

[33] Law and order is often conflated with the rule of law in Myanmar. This is unsurprising given the convergence of the two concepts in popular culture, United Nations and academic discourse. What is surprising is the use of the two concepts in Myanmar's laws and jurisprudence given that there is no semantic overlap as there is in English. For an excursus on language see: Cheesman, *Opposing the Rule of Law*, pp. 29–33.

[34] For more on the rule of law under authoritarian regimes and Rule by Law in Asia, see: Ginsburg and Moustafa, (eds.) *Rule by law: The politics of courts in authoritarian regimes* (Cambridge: Cambridge University Press, 2008); Rajah, *Authoritarian rule of law*.

[35] Cheesman, 'Thin rule of law or un-rule of law', pp. 597–613.

[36] Crouch, 'Layers of Legal Development', p. 46.

were the culmination of years of planning by the dictatorship to rule by law, to retain powers in transition and to prevent their accountability for past and future human rights violations.[37]

Reform and the rule of law in the absence of an independent judiciary

The rule of law is an easy rhetorical device for politicians and the military to court national and international support during a transition. Authoritarian governments often seek to invoke rule of law rhetoric when in reality they are enforcing law and order through repression.[38] The authoritarian legal powers of the executive are quietly retained by undermining the independence of the judiciary and the legal profession while formally aligning with international standards.[39]

The Union Attorney General's Office (UAGO),[40] the Office of the Supreme Court of the Union (OSCU)[41] and the governing National League for Democracy (NLD)[42] have all signalled their commitment to reform in line with the rule of law and rights. While adherence to the rule of law rhetoric is required to engage with Western countries and the international organisations,[43] Myanmar's commitments have little human rights content. For example, in 2012, a new Rule of Law and Tranquillity Committee was created with a mandate that specifically excluded human rights.[44] The rule of law is pursued to promote stability and economic growth through investment law, property rights and contract enforcement rather than democracy, justice and human rights.[45] Law and order governance has always been concerned with using law to impose 'tranquillity', stability or order, often at the expense of human rights and judicial independence.[46]

---

[37] The author of this chapter has heard the reform process referred to as the 'retirement plan for the generals' on numerous occasions.

[38] T. Moustafa, 'Law and courts in authoritarian regimes', *Annual Review of Law and Social Science* 10(2014), p. 283.

[39] Batesmith and Stevens, 'In the Absence of the Rule of Law', p. 576.

[40] Union Attorney General's Office, *Moving Forward to the Rule of Law: Strategic Plan* (2015–2019).

[41] Office of the Supreme Court of the Union, 'Advancing Justice Together: Judiciary Strategic Plan 2015–2017'.

[42] National League for Democracy, Election Manifesto, 2015.

[43] For example, rule of law is one of the World Bank's six broad dimensions of governance as well as one of the Worldwide Governance Indicators (WGI) developed by a research team at the World Bank in 1996. See: A. Kraay, D. Kaufmann and M. Mastruzzi, *The Worldwide Governance Indicators: Methodology and Analytical Issues,* Policy Research Working Paper 5430 (Washington, DC, The World Bank, 2010).

[44] N. Nyien, 'Suu Kyi to Head "Rule of Law" Committee', *Irrawaddy magazine*, 7 August 2012. Online at: https://www.irrawaddy.com/news/burma/suu-kyi-to-head-rule-of-law-committee.html (last accessed 26 January 2022).

[45] S. McCarthy, 'Rule of Law Expedited: Land Title Reform and Justice in Burma (Myanmar)', *Asian Studies Review* 42:2 (2018) p. 235.

[46] See: N. Engelhart, 'Is regime change enough for Burma? The problem of state capacity' in *Asian Survey,* 45(4) (2005) pp. 622–644.

Myanmar's legal reforms reflect an understanding of the rule of law as maintaining law and order.[47] Stability is imposed, and law and order upheld, by a state relatively unencumbered by rule of law. Cheesman argues that the rule of law in Myanmar means law and order through administrative mechanisms – themselves not subject to judicial review – that subordinate and keep people quiet.[48] Legal reforms have not deposed the previous regime: the polity, economy and society are still largely controlled by the military. It retains legal, political and economic power over key ministries and departments within the government and the judiciary. It holds 25% of parliamentary seats – giving it a veto power on constitutional change – as well as control of the state's security apparatus. It controls the Ministry of Home Affairs, through which it controls civilian interaction with government to the local level, without civilian oversight.[49]

Myanmar's judiciary, aside from a brief flourishing of independence in the 1950s, has never been an independent institution capable of balancing power. Built on a colonial administration model, its role in imposing law and order and facilitating a rule by law governance has been perfected by successive military dictatorships. Reforms post 2010 have not addressed the logic of impunity underpinning rule by law and order governance and did not create an independent judiciary.[50]

Immunity provisions in the 2008 Constitution enable state actors to evade accountability for international crimes by prohibiting the prosecution of government and military officials for 'any act done in the execution of their respective duties' before March 2011.[51] It allows the military to independently administer all affairs of the armed forces,[52] using permanent military tribunals with the Commander-in-Chief exercising appellate power and ultimate authority,[53] despite international standards on impunity.[54] The Special

---

[47] Cheesman, *Opposing the Rule of Law*, pp. 16, 29–33.

[48] Cheesman, *Opposing the Rule of Law*, p. 35.

[49] For more details on the Ministry of Home Affairs and its local interaction with civilians through the General Administration Department see: K. K. P. Chit Saw and M. Arnold, *Administering the State in Myanmar: An Overview of the General Administration Department* (Asian Foundation, 2014).

[50] See Cheesman, *Opposing the Rule of Law*.

[51] Constitution of the Union of Myanmar, Article 445.

[52] Article 20(b) of the Constitution establishes that "The Defence Services has [sic] the right to independently administer and adjudicate all affairs of the armed forces".

[53] According to Articles 201 and 342 of the Constitution, the Commander-in-Chief is appointed by the 11-member National Defence and Security, of which six members are appointed by the military. Articles 293(b) and 319 establish permanent military tribunals. Article 343(b) of the Constitution further makes decisions of the Commander-in-Chief concerning military justice matters "final and conclusive", with no right of appeal. This effectively means that the Commander-in-Chief can also pardon anyone convicted by a military tribunal.

[54] Principles to Combat Impunity, principle 29; United Nations Commission on Human Rights, Draft Principles Governing the Administration of Justice Through Military Tribunals (E/CN.4/2006/58); F. Ni Aolain, 'Principle 29. Restrictions on the Jurisdiction of Military Courts', in F. Haldemann and T. Unger (eds.), *The United Nations Principles to Combat Impunity – A Commentary* (Oxford, Oxford University Press, 2018), p. 322: 'When military courts are deployed in fragile, transitional, and post-conflict states there is a clear and present danger that the modality of trial may compound rather than address serious human rights violations and the deficiencies of the rule of law.'

Rapporteur has called for the amendment of the Constitution to promote accountability.[55]

The government's special inquiries into allegations of human rights violations are not independent and impartial and do not provide access to remedies and reparation.[56] Reforms have not addressed the practical limits on the independence, competence and capacity of the judiciary that combine to undermine its ability to balance power with the other branches of government, administer justice and hold human rights violators accountable.[57] The judiciary lacks the willingness to assert independence in sensitive cases. There are still no fair trials in Myanmar according to international standards, and the powerful are not held accountable for their violations of rights.[58] As such, there are no effective avenues for justice within the civilian administration.

Melissa Crouch explains that 'the constitution is designed in such a way as to ensure strong executive oversight over judicial affairs, to the detriment of judicial independence.'[59] It limits judicial review of government decisions.[60] It grants the President the authority to appoint and impeach the Chief Justice of the Supreme Court[61] and the Chief Justices of the High Courts of the state and the regions.[62] The President is also involved in the appointment and impeachment of the Chairperson of the Constitutional Tribunal.[63]

There is no system of administrative law in Myanmar. The use of constitutional writs is restricted both through constitutional provisions limiting their scope and in practice by executive and military influence over the judiciary.[64] The Supreme Court has consistently refused to issue or even consider constitutional

---

[55] Report of the Special Rapporteur on the situation of human rights in Myanmar, UN Doc A/HRC/22/58 (2013), para 76.

[56] International Commission of Jurists, 'Achieving Justice for Gross Human Rights Violations' p. 34.

[57] See, e.g., International Bar Association, *The Rule of Law in Myanmar: Challenges and Prospects* (London, December 2012); K. Min San, 'Critical Issues for the Rule of Law in Myanmar', in N. Cheesman, M. Skidmore, T. Wilson (eds.) *Myanmar's Transition: Openings, Obstacles and Opportunities*, (Singapore, Institute of Southeast Asian Studies, 2012) pp. 217–229; N. Cheesman, "Myanmar's Courts and the Sound Money Makes", in *Myanmar's Transition: Openings, Obstacles and Opportunities*, N. Cheesman, M. Skidmore, T. Wilson, eds (Singapore, Institute of Southeast Asian Studies, 2012), pp. 231–248; N. Cheesman, *Opposing the Rule of Law*; Justice Base, *Monitoring in Myanmar – An Analysis of Myanmar's Compliance with Fair Trial Rights* (Yangon, 2017); International Commission of Jurists, *Achieving Justice for Gross Human Rights Violations*.

[58] International Commission of Jurists, Achieving Justice for Gross Human Rights Violations.

[59] Crouch, 'The Layers of Legal Development', p. 49.

[60] On the problems associated with the 2008 Constitution see: D. C. Williams, 'What's So Bad About Myanmar's Constitution: A Guide for the Perplexed', in M. Crouch and T. Lindsey (eds.) *Law, Society and Transition in Myanmar* (Bloomsbury, 2014) pp. 117–140.

[61] It suffices that the President is of the opinion that the person is 'an eminent jurist'; a law degree or legal practice is not required. Constitution of the Union of Myanmar 2008 art. 299, 302.

[62] Constitution of the Union of Myanmar 2008 art. 308, 311.

[63] Constitution of the Union of Myanmar 2008 art. 327,334.

[64] See: International Commission of Jurists, *Handbook on Habeas Corpus in Myanmar* (Geneva, 2016), online at: https://www.icj.org/myanmar-writ-of-habeas-corpus-can-help-protect-human-rights/ (last accessed 26 January 2022).

writ cases that deal with cases involving human rights violations, particularly habeas corpus.[65] Habeas corpus is derogable in emergencies and petitions have never been successful; as a result, lawyers have largely ceased applications to the Supreme Court.[66] Civil and criminal cases involving the military or police are referred to military courts and police courts, themselves lacking effective independence, bypassing civilian justice.[67]

The impartiality and independence of judges is further undermined by their perceived allegiance to the executive and their opaque appointment process.[68] The criteria for the appointment of judges does not include requirements to have a law degree or judicial experience.[69] Some judges of the Supreme Court are military appointees with military backgrounds contributing to a perception of undue influence from state authorities in politically sensitive cases.[70]

Most judges are not accustomed to holding the government accountable. Judges outside the Supreme Court are poorly paid and are considered quasi-civil servants asked to fulfil government administrative tasks rather than members of an independent judiciary. Supreme Court Judges are sometimes summoned to Parliament to explain controversial decisions. Many judges are often unfamiliar with the law and court procedures and lack the knowledge and experience to conduct fair trials.[71] They fail to correct the police and prosecution while allowing courtroom delays, politically motivated prosecutions and fabrications of evidence.[72] In some types of cases, there is a presumption of guilt and predetermined results, and regular court procedures are not followed.[73] In others, judges render decisions based on orders coming from government officials.[74] This all impedes the administration of justice, making sensitive cases difficult and dangerous.[75]

---

[65] International Commission of Jurists, *Handbook on Habeas Corpus in Myanmar*; M. Crouch 'The Common Law and the Constitutional Writs in Myanmar' in M. Crouch and T. Lindsey (eds) *Law, Society and Transition in Myanmar* (Oxford: Hart Publishing, 2014); M. Crouch, *Access to Justice and Administrative Law in Myanmar* (Promoting the Rule of Law Project, UNDP, 2014), online at: https://www.myjusticemyanmar.org/sites/default/files/Access%20to%20Justice%20and%20Administrat ive%20Law%20in%20Myanmar.pdf (last accessed 26 January 2022); M. Crouch, 'The Prerogative Writs as Constitutional Transfer', *Oxford Journal of Legal Studies*, 38.4, (2018) pp. 653–675.

[66] International Commission of Jurists, *Handbook on Habeas Corpus in Myanmar.*

[67] Detailed findings of the Independent International Fact-Finding Mission on Myanmar – A/HRC/42/CRP.5. paras. 1578–1582.

[68] International Commission of Jurists, 'Myanmar: end practice of appointing military officers to judiciary', (Bangkok, 16 September 2016), online at: https://www.icj.org/myanmar-end-practice-of-appoint ing-military-officers-to-judiciary/ (last accessed 26 January 2022).

[69] International Commission of Jurists, *Achieving Justice for Gross Human Rights Violations.*

[70] Detailed findings of the Independent International Fact-Finding Mission on Myanmar – A/HRC/42/CRP.5. Para. 1587.

[71] International Commission of Jurists, *Achieving Justice for Gross Human Rights Violations*, p. 33.

[72] International Commission of Jurists, *Achieving Justice for Gross Human Rights Violations*, p. 33.

[73] International Commission of Jurists, *Achieving Justice for Gross Human Rights Violations*, p. 33.

[74] International Commission of Jurists, *Handbook on Habeas Corpus in Myanmar*, p. 20.

[75] International Commission of Jurists, *Right to Counsel: The Independence of Lawyers in Myanmar* (Geneva 2013) p. 13, online at: https://www.icj.org/wp-content/uploads/2013/12/MYANMAR-Right-to-Counsel-electronic.pdf. (last accessed 26 January 2022).

As member of the executive branch of government, the UAGO is essentially a ministry of justice with the power to review all proposed laws and to advise the government on the legality of its actions.[76] The Attorney General is also the President of Myanmar's only officially recognised Bar Association, undermining the independence of lawyers.[77] The UAGO does not exercise functional independence or prosecutorial discretion fairly: it brings the full force of the law against those opposing the government, the military or well-connected crony businessmen while refusing to hold those same actors accountable for human rights abuses.[78] It regularly prosecutes journalists, human rights defenders and activists on spurious grounds,[79] resulting in low public confidence.[80]

Legal officers and prosecutors are generally not considered to have the independence and capacity to prosecute acts constituting human rights violations.[81] Similarly, the Myanmar Police Force lacks public confidence. It has no institutional independence and is corrupt.[82] The head of the Myanmar Police Force has a military background and the Police Force falls under the Ministry of Home Affairs, one of the military-controlled ministries. It lacks the technical capacity to undertake complex investigations in line with international standards and does not conduct credible, independent investigations into human rights violations.[83]

The legal profession in Myanmar has low public and professional standing.[84] Government officials and security actors continue to intimidate, harass, monitor and limit the independence of lawyers, causing fear of reprisals or sanctions, especially in cases involving the government or their vested interests, human rights defenders or human rights. In these cases, the state fabricates evidence and courts

---

[76] See: International Commission of Jurists, *Myanmar: newly appointed Attorney General should commit to reform, rule of law and human rights* (Bangkok, 6 April 2016), online at: https://www.icj.org/myanmar-newly-appointed-attorney-general-should-commit-to-reform-rule-of-law-and-human-rights/ (last accessed: 13 May 2021); D. Aguirre and V. Sathisan, "Rule of law depends on reform of Union Attorney General's Office", *Myanmar Times* (Yangon, 27 January 2016).

[77] International Commission of Jurists, *Achieving Justice for Gross Human Rights Violations*, p .34.

[78] International Commission of Jurists, *Achieving Justice for Gross Human Rights Violations*, p. 33.

[79] Detailed findings of the Independent International Fact-Finding Mission on Myanmar – A/HRC/42/CRP.5. Para. 1590.

[80] Detailed findings of the Independent International Fact-Finding Mission on Myanmar – A/HRC/42/CRP.5. Para. 1590.

[81] See, e.g., International Commission of Jurists, *Achieving Justice for Gross Human Rights Violations*; D. Aguirre and V. Sathisan, 'Rule of law depends on reform of Union Attorney General's Office'; See also Union Attorney General's Office, *Moving Forward to the Rule of Law – Strategic Plan 2015–2019*, (Naypyidaw, 2015).

[82] A. Selth, *Police reform in Burma (Myanmar): aims, obstacles and outcomes*, Regional Outlook Paper: No. 44, (Griffith Asia Institute, 2013).

[83] Detailed findings of the Independent International Fact-Finding Mission on Myanmar – A/HRC/42/CRP.5. Para. 1589.

[84] International Commission of Jurists, *Right to Counsel*.

decide the judgment before trial.[85] A traditionally hierarchical status-based cultural order also undermines the concept of the rule of law.[86]

The lack of judicial independence undermines a wide range of fair trial standards and the public's perception of the rule of law.[87] Corruption is prevalent.[88] The people do not believe they will receive a fair trial and view the prosecutors and judges as part and parcel with the government and military. Civil society has yet to embrace the judicial system as a venue to challenge policy and defend the rights of people and communities. They turn to any other form of dispute resolution alternatives.

The absence of judicial independence also enables the adoption of discriminatory law and policy. The constitution itself sends a contradictory message: in Article 347, it allows access to justice for everyone, but throughout the rest, rights are restricted to citizens only. The process of gaining citizenship has been criticised as discriminatory. The 1982 Citizenship Act creates arbitrary categories of citizenship and renders large sections of the population, including the Rohingya, effectively stateless. Its implementation mechanisms are opaque and burdensome, and in violation of the principle of legality. Right to review administrative decisions within this process are unduly restricted.[89]

The 2015 Race and Religion laws discriminate based on religion, sex and ethnicity (e.g., the Religious Conversion Law and Buddhist Women's Special Marriage Law) despite the constitution's prohibition of discrimination. Lawyers do not challenge law through the courts as the judiciary has demonstrated itself unwilling to hear constitutional arguments or to refer such disputes to the constitutional court for clarification. Bringing situations directly before the constitutional court is onerously prohibitive for citizens. As such, the constitutional provisions that (albeit inadequately) protect rights are unenforceable, allowing for law and policy to be adopted and implemented in contradiction to its provisions, and are not subject to review by the courts.

The courts are capable of enforcing law when it is in favour of the government. For example, colonial-era blasphemy laws contained in the Criminal Code are applied arbitrarily.[90] Laws related to freedom of expression such as defamation

---

[85] International Commission of Jurists, *Achieving Justice for Gross Human Rights Violations*, p. 35.

[86] M. M. Gyi, *Burmese political values: The socio-political roots of authoritarianism* (New York, Praeger Publishers, 1983).

[87] For more on the dearth of Fair Trials in Myanmar see Justice Base, *Monitoring in Myanmar: An Analysis of Myanmar's Compliance with Fair Trial Rights* (Justice Base, Yangon, 2017).

[88] See World Bank, *Worldwide governance indicators: Country data report for Myanmar, 1996–2012* (Washington, DC, World Bank, 2013); World Justice Project *Rule of Law Index 2014* (Washington, DC, The World Justice Project, 2014).

[89] See International Commission of Jurists, Challenges to Freedom of Religion or Belief in Myanmar: A Briefing Paper (Bangkok, October 2019).

[90] See International Commission of Jurists, Challenges to Freedom of Religion or Belief.

and freedom of assembly are similarly flouted in their application before the courts. The prosecution's discretion is exercised in favour of government proponents and against its detractors. The criminal law concept of intent is rarely discussed, and convictions occur in the absence of proven intent.

The deliberate design of an inadequate legal system and judiciary incapable of balancing power and upholding accountability for human rights violations constitutes a human rights violation in itself[91] and perpetuates impunity. A judiciary designed to enforce law and order at the expense of the rule of law and human rights will not prevent international crimes such as war crimes, crimes against humanity or genocide – instead, it justifies them. Myanmar's military now justifies 'clearance operations' characterised by the targeting of civilians, sexual violence and rape as a weapon of war, indiscriminate and disproportionate violence, and forced relocation as being conducted 'according to the rule of law'.[92] It is highly unlikely that this judicial system can prevent atrocity crimes or will be able to adequately fulfil the provisional measures recently imposed by the ICJ.

Judicial independence and the duty to prevent

An independent and impartial judiciary is the first line of defence against international atrocity crimes, not because it can always hold perpetrators responsible for these crimes, but because it can hold them accountable to human rights violations before they escalate and prevent an entrenched pattern of human rights violations. State authorities get used to regularly having their practice and policy reviewed for law-fulness and being held accountable for their actions. By the time atrocity crimes have been committed – even inchoate crimes considered by the Genocide Convention – it is likely too late for national-level accountability. States that commit atrocity crimes against their own populations lack an independent judiciary. Rule of law has broken down or never existed; there is no access to justice for victims or accountability for perpetrators.

The legal obligations associated with prevention of international crimes focus on intervention[93] or on holding perpetrators criminally accountable to deter future international crimes.[94] The ICJ, in imposing provisional measures on Myanmar,

---

[91] E.g., United Nations Human Rights Committee, General Comment No. 31 (CCPR/C/21/Rev.1/Add.13), para. 15.

[92] Various news media reported government and military spokesmen justifying actions as according to the rule of law. The Office of the President issued a similar line, but the webpages are no longer available.

[93] *2005 World Summit Outcome*, UN Doc. A/RES/60/1, 24 October 2005 ('World Summit Outcome'), § 138.

[94] Convention on the Prevention and Punishment of the Crime of Genocide, (1951) 78 UNTS 277; International Convention on the Suppression and Punishment of the Crime of Apartheid, (1986) 1015 UNTS 243, Art. I(1); International Convention for the Protection of All Persons from Enforced Disappearance, (2010) 2716 UNTS 3; Convention against Torture and Other Cruel, Inhuman or

summarises the obligation to prevent and punish genocide set out in Article I of the Convention as follows:

> The obligation to prevent and punish genocide set out in Article I of the Convention is supplemented by the distinct obligations which appear in the subsequent articles, especially those in Articles V and VI requiring the enactment of the necessary legislation to give effect to the provisions of the Convention, as well as the prosecution of persons charged with such acts. In so far as these provisions concerning the duty to punish also have a deterrent and therefore a preventive effect or purpose, they too meet the obligation to prevent genocide.[95]

In 2007, the ICJ held Serbia responsible for its failure to prevent the Srebrenica genocide that occurred in Bosnia in 1995.[96] Even though the judgment concerns extraterritorial application, it contains relevant interpretation of national obligations. It established that prevention is not synonymous with prosecution and entails separate obligations broadly defined.[97] It interprets the reference to prevention in the Genocide Conventions as entailing obligations for state parties when they 'learn of, or should normally have learned of, the existence of a serious risk that genocide will be committed' to 'employ all means available to them, so as to prevent genocide so far as possible.'[98]

Beyond genocide, the International Law Commission's discussion on the development of an obligation to prevent crimes against humanity goes further and includes 'effective legislative, administrative, judicial or other preventive measures'[99] and educating government officials and law enforcement officers on investigating and prosecuting offenders.[100] This approach pays more attention to judicial independence, impunity and preventing international atrocity crimes before they happen. It is an extension of the obligations to prevent atrocity crimes

---

Degrading Treatment or Punishment, (1987) 1465 UNTS 85 ('Convention Against Torture'); *Application of the Convention on the Prevention and Punishment of the Crime of Genocide (Bosnia and Herzegovina v Serbia and Montenegro)*, Judgment of 26 February 2007, ICJ Reports (2007) 429; International Convention on the Elimination of All Forms of Racial Discrimination, (1969) 660 UNTS 195, Art. 3.

[95] International Court of Justice, Order: The *Gambia v Myanmar* at 51; See also: Application of the Convention on the Prevention and Punishment of the Crime of Genocide (*Bosnia and Herzegovina v Serbia and Montenegro*), Judgment, I.C.J. Reports 2007 (I), p. 109, para. 159 and p. 219, para. 426.

[96] International Court of Justice, *Bosnia and Herzegovina v Serbia and Montenegro*, Merits, 26 February 2007, ICJ Report 2 (Genocide 2007) paras 438 and 450.

[97] International Court of Justice, *Bosinia and Herzegovina v Serbia and Montenegro*, Merits: para 427.

[98] International Court of Justice, *Bosinia and Herzegovina v Serbia and Montenegro*, Merits: paras 427, 430.

[99] *Report of the International Law Commission on the work of its Sixty-ninth session (1 May–2 June and 3 July–4 August 2017)*, UN Doc. A/72/10 at 45. Draft article 4 is as follows:

> 1. Each State undertakes to prevent crimes against humanity, in conformity with international law, including through: (a) effective legislative, administrative, judicial or other preventive measures in any territory under its jurisdiction or control; and (b) cooperation with other States, relevant intergovernmental organizations, and, as appropriate, other organisations.

> 2. No exceptional circumstances whatsoever, such as armed conflict, internal political instability or other public emergency, may be invoked as a justification of crimes against humanity.

[100] *Report of the International Law Commission on the work of its Sixty-ninth session* at 51–52.

to include the obligation to protect human rights at the national level. But what does that mean in practice, and does routine impunity for human rights violations and a lack of an independent judiciary count?

The primary responsibility remains with each state to build national resilience against atrocity crimes by implementing human rights law at the national level.[101] It must uphold the rule of law and protect human rights. Myanmar has a legal obligation to ensure accountability and access to effective remedies for violations of human rights,[102] including a duty to investigate, prosecute and punish gross human rights violations and serious violations of international humanitarian law.[103] Investigations into allegations of violations and all crimes must be prompt, thorough and effective, independent and impartial, and transparent.[104] The obligation to prevent rights violations entails: long-term obligations to introduce legislative and administrative frameworks capable of deterring violations; short-term

---

[101] Office on Genocide Prevention and the Responsibility to Protect (2014) Framework of the Analysis for Atrocity Crimes – A Tool for Prevention, p. 3.

[102] B. Ramcharan, 'The Law-Making Process: From Declaration to Treaty to Custom to Prevention', D. Shelton (ed.) *The Oxford Handbook on International Human Rights Law*, (Oxford, Oxford University Press, 2013), p. 512. The Universal Declaration of Human Rights (art. 8), the ASEAN Human Rights Declaration (art. 5), and several international treaties (e.g., art. 2 of the International Covenant on Civil and Political Rights; article 6 of the International Convention on the Elimination of All Forms of Racial Discrimination; art. 14 of the Convention against Torture and Other Cruel, Inhuman or Degrading Treatment or Punishment; art. 39 of the Convention on the Rights of the Child; art. 3 of the Hague Convention respecting the Laws and Customs of War on Land of 18 October 1907; art. 91 of the Protocol Additional to the Geneva Conventions of 12 August 1949, and relating to the Protection of Victims of International Armed Conflicts (Protocol I) of 8 June 1977; and arts. 68 and 75 of the Rome Statute of the International Criminal Court). It is also further developed in the United Nations Basic Principles and Guidelines on the Right to a Remedy and Reparations for Victims of Gross Violations of International Human Rights Law and Serious Violations of International Humanitarian Law, adopted and proclaimed by General Assembly resolution 60/147 of 16 December 2005, hereafter "Basic Principles and Guidelines on the Right to a Remedy and Reparation".

[103] E.g., A/HRC/27/56, para. 27. See also, e.g., Genocide Convention, art. 1; U.N. Human Rights Committee, General Comment No. 31 (CCPR/C/21/Rev.1/Add.13); J. M. Henckaerts and L. Doswald-Beck, 'Customary International Humanitarian Law. Volume I: Rules' (Cambridge, ICRC/Cambridge University Press, 2005), rules 150, 158 (hereinafter "ICRC/Customary IHL"); Basic Principles and Guidelines on the Right to a Remedy and Reparation (principles 1-5); and the Principles to Combat Impunity.

[104] Also, Principles to Combat Impunity, principle 19; Minnesota Protocol on the Investigation of Potentially Unlawful Death (2016), The Revised United Nations Manual on the Effective Prevention and Investigation of Extra-legal, Arbitrary and Summary Executions (New York and Geneva, United Nations, 2017) (hereafter 'Minnesota Protocol'); International and domestic courts have recognised this obligation on governments to prevent, investigate and, if necessary, prosecute. Inter-American Court of Human Rights, *Velasquez Rodriguez v Honduras*, Judgment of 29 July 1988, Ser. C, No. 4, which held that states had an obligation, as a corollary to their obligation to ensure rights, to investigate and, if warranted, prosecute and punish violations and to provide remedies to victims. Other regional human rights bodies, as well as United Nations treaty bodies, have all reaffirmed this principle. E.g., European Court of Human Rights, *Case of Benzer and others v Turkey*, App No. 23502/06, 24 March 2014; African Commission on Human and Peoples' Rights, *Zimbabwe Human Rights NGO Forum v Zimbabwe*, Communication No. 245/2002 (2006); U.N. Human Rights Committee, *Observations on Algeria*, CCPR/C/109/D/1874/2009, 7 January 2014, para. 7.10.

obligations to take measures to prevent violations; obligations to halt continuing violations; and obligations to prevent reoccurrence by investigating, prosecuting and punishing perpetrators. An independent judiciary fulfils short- and long-term obligations to deter and prevent reoccurrence. Neither of these accountability functions is performed by the judiciary in Myanmar.[105]

The Responsibility to Protect doctrine links preventative action to national law and human rights. It emphasises the primary responsibility of the state, but when that fails it promotes a preventative approach aimed at the international community.[106] While these UN statements link human rights abuses with atrocity crimes and focus on state responsibility to protect rights,[107] in practice, the emphasis has been on intervention. They remain non-binding policy guidelines and unimplemented unless political will to intervene exists.[108]

Prevention must be seen as a process implemented by independent and account-able national institutions before atrocity crimes are committed. Simply legislating against atrocity crimes does not prevent them if the judiciary cannot restrain state power. The content of an obligation to prevent international crimes must include addressing impunity and routine human rights violations before they become wide-spread and systematic. William Schabas argues that 'the prevention of crimes against humanity involves addressing violations of human rights that may not yet warrant qualification as "gross and systematic"'.[109] He asserts that, for example, the ILC's Draft Paper on Preventing Crimes Against Humanity does not go far enough to address the issue of inchoate crimes.[110] Instead, international law should develop to reflect and expand upon Article III of the Genocide Convention, which includes inchoate, or incomplete crimes, aside from Genocide,[111] such as conspiracy, public incitement and attempted genocide, which happen before the act takes place.[112]

While this approach is welcome, it does not go far enough, as in order to commit these inchoate crimes, the rule of law has ceased as the state is exercising

[105] International Commission of Jurists, 'Achieving Justice for Gross Human Rights Violations'.

[106] International Commission on Intervention and State Sovereignty (2001). The Responsibility to Protect; UN General Assembly (2005) Resolution 60/1, 2005 World Summit Outcome. UN Doc: A/RES/60/1 (2005 World Summit Outcome).

[107] Secretary General Ban Ki Moon (2009) Implementing the Responsibility to Protect. UN Doc: A/63/677; Office on Genocide Prevention and the Responsibility to Protect Framework of the Analysis for Atrocity Crimes – A Tool for Prevention (2014).

[108] A. J. Bellamy, The Responsibility to Protect – Five Years On, *Ethics and International Affairs* 24.2 (2010) pp. 160–166.

[109] W. Schabas, 'Prevention of Crimes Against Humanity' in *Journal of International Criminal Justice*, 16.4 (2018) p. 705.

[110] For a full analysis of the ILC Draft Papers regarding the Missing Inchoate Crimes see William Schabas, 'Prevention of Crimes Against Humanity', pp. 721–725.

[111] Convention on the Prevention and Punishment of the Crime of Genocide, (1951) 78 UNTS 277. Article III.

[112] The inchoate crimes were incorporated into the Ad Hoc Tribunals for the Former Yugoslavia and Rwanda (Art. 4(3) ICTYSt.; Art. 2(3) ICTRSt.) but were limited further in the Rome Statute of the International Criminal Court (2002) 2187 UNTS 3. Art. 25.

arbitrary power without balance. Prevention must begin before the inchoate crimes are committed. International atrocity crimes are not random events and neither are their inchoate crimes: perpetrators take advantage of the limitations and dysfunctions of state institutions. International crimes are foreshadowed by myriad warning signs and indicators – many of them human rights violations – are permitted by a dependent judiciary. Myanmar does not have an independent judiciary that can provide adequate access to remedy for victims of human rights abuses, let alone atrocity crimes or their inchoate forms. This has encouraged security actors to go further and impose systematic, widespread campaigns targeting their opponents.

It is clear that in practice, prevention requires an effective and independent judiciary to disrupt impunity. The United Nations Office on the Prevention of Genocide and the Responsibility to Protect identifies a defective national legal framework and a lack of an independent and impartial judiciary as a key risk factor for international crimes.[113] The UN's Set of Principles for the Protection and Promotion of Human Rights through Action to Combat Impunity recognises the reform of state institutions to ensure conformity with the rule of law as key to this process. With respect to the judiciary, Article 36 parts b) and c) are relevant:

> (b) With respect to the judiciary, States must undertake all other measures necessary to assure the independent, impartial and effective operation of courts in accordance with international standards of due process. Habeas corpus, by whatever name it may be known, must be considered a non-derogable right;

> (c) Civilian control of military and security forces as well as of intelligence agencies must be ensured and, where necessary, established or restored. To this end, States should establish effective institutions of civilian oversight over military and security forces and intelligence agencies, including legislative oversight bodies.[114]

Myanmar's culture of impunity

The collective actions of the government undermine the rule of law and result in what Cheesman calls routine impunity in practice.[115] This routine impunity should have been a warning to the international community, given Myanmar's history of human rights abuse and atrocity crimes. Yet routine impunity seems to be ignored until it escalates and results in massive human rights violations or atrocity crimes. The prominence of rule of law rhetoric and an emphasis on judicial reform seemed to mask a logic of impunity permeating all branches of government.

---

[113] United Nations Office for the Prevention of Genocide and the Responsibility to Protect, Framework for Analysis of Atrocity Crimes: A Tool For Prevention (United Nations, 2014) Risk Factor 3.
[114] Updated Set of Principles for the Protection and Promotion of Human Rights through Action to Combat Impunity (E/CN.4/2005/102/Add.1), art. 36 b and c.
[115] N. Cheesman, 'Routine Impunity as Practice (in Myanmar)', *Human Rights Quarterly* 41 (2019) 873–892, at 874.

Myanmar has not fulfilled its obligation to ensure accountability for international atrocity crimes such as genocide, war crimes or crimes against humanity. The Penal Code does include other serious crimes, but they are inconsistent with international standards.[116] While Myanmar has said it would not condone impunity 'where there is concrete evidence',[117] it does not promptly, thoroughly, independently and impartially investigate allegations.[118] This has more than legal ramifications: the United Nations Independent International Fact-Finding Mission on Myanmar explains that impunity for gross human rights violations enables their reoccurrence and emboldens perpetrators while silencing victims.[119] The United Nations Independent International Fact-Finding Mission on Myanmar has examined the infringement of human rights that enabled the international crimes. It cites the pervasive 'culture of impunity at the domestic level' as contributing to the commission of international crimes. It explains that:

> Justice has remained elusive for victims in Myanmar for decades, with the authorities systematically failing to condemn, investigate and prosecute perpetrators. Thirty years of United Nations resolutions and reports, as well as those from civil society, have identified impunity as a root cause of continued human rights violations in Myanmar.[120]

The UN Special Rapporteur, Yanghee Lee, identified the impunity and dominance of the military and other security forces over the judiciary as the main causes of recurrent human rights violations. She noted that allegations of violations were met by a government policy 'quick to resort to its standard position of "defend, deny and dismiss"'.[121] Beyond government denial, the UN Independent Fact-Finding Mission has found that 'impunity for human rights violations in Myanmar – especially where committed by security forces – is largely structural. It is built into the legal framework and the system of governance.'[122] The military does not answer to the judiciary and instead runs its own system of accountability beyond civilian oversight and under laws that do not contemplate human rights abuses.

Violations of international criminal law prompt responses based on holding those accountable through international criminal law. The United Nations Human

---

[116] Detailed findings of the Independent International Fact-Finding Mission on Myanmar – A/HRC/42/CRP.5, para. 1566; For example, The Penal Code provisions for rape and sexual violence are too restrictive. See CEDAW/C/MMR/CO/4-5, para. 27(a).

[117] H. E. Mr Kyaw Tin, "Statement at the High-Level Segment 4th Meeting, 37th Regular Session of the Human Rights Council" (27 February 2018).

[118] Detailed findings of the Independent International Fact-Finding Mission on Myanmar – A/HRC/42/CRP.5, para. 1564.

[119] Detailed findings of the Independent International Fact-Finding Mission on Myanmar – A/HRC/42/CRP.5, para. 1565.

[120] Detailed findings of the Independent International Fact-Finding Mission on Myanmar – A/HRC/42/CRP.5, para. 1537.

[121] A/HRC/34/67, para. 83. Also A/HRC/28/72, para. 57.

[122] Detailed findings of the Independent International Fact-Finding Mission on Myanmar – A/HRC/42/CRP.5, para. 1577.

Rights Council mandated an International Fact-Finding Mission to investigate 'the facts and circumstances of the alleged recent human rights violations by military and security forces... with a view to ensuring full accountability for perpetrators and justice for victims'.[123] This has now been replaced by the Independent Investigative Mechanism for Myanmar (IIMM).[124] The ICC will conduct an investigation into cross-border crimes affecting state party Bangladesh. The ICJ is examining allegations of genocide. But these constitute reactions to atrocity crimes rather than preventative measures. They do not replace independent national courts or prevent human rights violations from reoccurring like a competent, independent judiciary. All states, particularly Myanmar, must hold criminal trials, in competent jurisdictions, in line with international standards. It is only through concrete action to counteract decades of military impunity for human rights violations, including the establishment of independent courts, that crimes against humanity can be prevented in Myanmar.

Failure of the international community

The international community has failed to meet its responsibility to protect civilian populations from human rights violations and the commission of international crimes, including possibly genocide.[125] The UN Fact-Finding Mission points out that the international community had, through the UN, 'the responsibility to use appropriate diplomatic, humanitarian and other peaceful means and, through the Security Council, other collective measures to help to protect populations from atrocity crimes.'[126] The well documented human rights violations and international crimes – particularly in Rakhine State – occurred with a large UN presence throughout the country.

The United Nations adopted a 'Rights up Front' initiative in December 2013 to address the 'systemic failure' identified by an Internal Review Panel in meeting UN responsibilities to prevent and respond to serious violations of human rights and humanitarian law.[127] The UN vowed to put human rights first in all its operational and strategic decisions, a call heard loud and clear by civil society and NGOs in Myanmar. In 2014, the UN drafted its Framework of Analysis for Atrocity Crimes meant as a tool for prevention. In its foreword, the then Secretary

---

[123] UN Human Rights Council resolution 34/22 (2017), para 10.
[124] UN Fact-Finding Mission on Myanmar Hands Over to Independent Investigative Mechanism for Myanmar. https://www.ohchr.org/EN/HRBodies/HRC/Pages/NewsDetail.aspx?NewsID=24960&LangID=E
[125] A/RES/60/1 (2005 World Summit Outcome), para. 139.
[126] Detailed findings of the Independent International Fact-Finding Mission on Myanmar – A/HRC/42/CRP.5, para. 1557.
[127] UN Secretary-General (UNSG), *The Secretary-General: Renewing our commitment to the peoples and purposes of the United Nations*, 21 November 2013.

General, Ban Ki Moon, calls on the international community to 'pay attention to the warning signs.'[128]

The Framework lists common and specific factors that read like a description of human rights events in Myanmar from 2011 to 2019. Common risk factors include, among others: armed conflict; serious violations of international human rights and humanitarian law; weakness of state structures; capacity to commit atrocity; and enabling circumstances and preparatory action.[129] Specific factors, among others, include: intergroup tensions or patterns of discrimination; plans to attack, of an intent to destroy, or of widespread or systematic abuses; and threats to humanitarian or peacekeeping operations.[130] Given how obvious all these factors were during this period, the failure to prevent international crimes shows the systemic and structural failings of the United Nations system.[131]

Ban Ki Moon notes how important the Framework is given the UN's simultaneous reform and adoption of the Human Rights up Front policy that commits it to upholding the promise of 'never again' and to the prevention of rights violations and atrocity crimes at the centre of its work.[132] The UN Fact-Finding Mission itself argues that the Human Rights up Front policy was never implemented, that it was 'business as usual' engagement on development and humanitarian assistance only, leaving human rights advocacy to the externally based OHCHR and the Special Rapporteur.[133] The in-country UN presence dealt inadequately with human rights violations through 'quiet diplomacy', and its self-censorship undermined its position as rights violations escalated to international crimes.[134]

Few members of the international community were willing to publicly acknowledge that the failure to address widespread human rights abuses indicates an impunity that can escalate quickly into atrocity crimes. Instead, the international community seemed convinced that the ongoing armed conflicts and violations of all types of human rights across the country would change through engagement and economic development. Even the arrest and detention of hundreds of Rohingya men and boys without trials or representation in late 2016 and early 2017 did

---

[128] United Nations Office for the Prevention of Genocide and the Responsibility to Protect, *Framework for Analysis of Atrocity Crimes: A Tool for Prevention*, Foreword.

[129] United Nations Office for the Prevention of Genocide and the Responsibility to Protect, *Framework for Analysis of Atrocity Crimes: A Tool for Prevention*, pp. 10–18.

[130] United Nations Office for the Prevention of Genocide and the Responsibility to Protect, *Framework for Analysis of Atrocity Crimes: A Tool for Prevention*, pp. 10–18.

[131] The UN Commissioned its own 'lessons learned' document. G. Rosenthal, 'A Brief and Independent Inquiry into the Involvement of the United Nations in Myanmar from 2010 to 2018' (May 2019), online at: https://www.un.org/sg/sites/www.un.org.sg/files/atoms/files/Myanmar%20Report%20-%20May%202019.pdf (last accessed 26 January 2022).

[132] United Nations Office for the Prevention of Genocide and the Responsibility to Protect, *Framework for Analysis of Atrocity Crimes*, Foreword.

[133] Detailed findings of the Independent International Fact-Finding Mission on Myanmar – A/HRC/42/CRP.5, paras.1559–1560.

[134] L. Mahoney, 'Time to break old habits: Shifting from Complicity to Protecting the Rohingya', *Fieldview Solutions*, July 2018.

not dissuade the international community from its policy of engagement despite constant warning from human rights organisations.

Many diplomats refrained from calling the Rohingya by their name so as not to jeopardise relations with the government. NGOs engaged in human rights issues were cautioned by donors about upsetting the government. The international community seemed to want to talk rule of law but not to mention topics that were off-limits, such as human rights violations themselves. This legitimised the rule by law approach to governance and a legal system designed to impose law and order rather than protect rights. The first line of defence against international crimes was sacrificed for broader political and economic engagement. Despite these human rights failings, this approach continues as human rights remain missing from agreements between Myanmar, the United Nations agencies and international donors.[135] It seems clear that the need to secure strategic interests and investment opportunities remain paramount considerations for the international community.

Conclusion

While economic reform happens rapidly and political change is incremental, the reform and development of an impartial and independent judiciary is a transformative process requiring more than quick fixes.[136] There have been many rule of law training programmes that replicate Western liberal traditions or promote developmental policy without attempting to address the local political, economic and historical/cultural dimensions of judicial reform.[137] Judicial independence, for example, cannot just be declared after a series of successful workshops and training. It will take time to educate and train the next generation of the legal profession about the role of an independent judiciary. No amount of capacity building can work without commitments from the executive and the military to apply the rule of law. Civil and political gains are ephemeral if not protected by law and justiciable before the courts. An independent and impartial judiciary, aside from ensuring fair trials and access to justice, can provide a bulwark against the impunity that underlies international atrocity crimes.

The palpable optimism of the international community following the reforms from 2011 should have been tempered by a better understanding of what a rule by law-and-order governance or disciplined democracy actually means. A rule by law-and-order approach fails to recognise the link between an independent judiciary capable of upholding human rights law as a safeguard for preventing international crimes. The rule by law-and-order authority does not see the benefit of judicial

---

[135] Detailed findings of the Independent International Fact-Finding Mission on Myanmar – A/HRC/42/CRP.5, para. 1561.
[136] T. Carothers, 'Rule of Law Temptations', in *Fletcher Forum of World Affairs*, 33: 1 (2009), pp. 58–60.
[137] E. Prasse-Freeman, 'Conceptions of justice and the rule of law', in D. Steinberg (ed.), *Myanmar: The dynamics of an evolving polity* (Boulder, CO, Lynne Rienner, 2015), pp. 89–114.

independence, it sees it as a hindrance. It does not connect unchecked power characterised by human rights abuses and international crimes with instability and the deterioration of the law and order it so craves.

The failure of the government in Myanmar to uphold the rule of law and the international community's acquiescence provide important lessons for states undergoing transition, transitional justice, development cooperation, and economic and political engagement. Crimes against humanity do not occur without warning. The recent coup by the military demonstrates the failure of a strategy based on economic engagement at the expense of human rights and the rule of law.

When human rights violations without accountability become routine, a logic of impunity is confirmed. When powerful actors are not reigned in, they are emboldened to exert their will with no regard to human rights. The purpose of governance becomes ruling by law rather than upholding the rule of law. Human rights lawyers and activists in Myanmar repeatedly point to the lack of competence, mandate and the independence of the judiciary as a barrier to accountability and as an essential component to a system of impunity that emboldens the security forces. A state that denies access to justice, effective remedies and accountability for human rights violations contribute to their perpetuation with the potential for them to become atrocity crimes.

9

Identifying Dangers to Democracy: Fascism, the Rule of Law and the Relevance of History

STEPHEN SKINNER

WHILE STATES THE world over were trying to tackle the Covid-19 coronavirus, the political and legal problems of recent years appear to have been overshadowed by new and rapid governmental interventions in daily life. Yet this international emergency should not cause us to forget that, before it started, the political and constitutional orders of democratic states already appeared to be facing crises of a different sort, as they were rocked by instability and uncertainty, and their governments lurched onto unpredictable paths.[1] In the United Kingdom, the populist wave that gained momentum with the Brexit referendum and the subsequent claims about giving effect to 'the will of the British people' (more precisely, 51.9% of them in the 2016 referendum)[2] involved the infamous media attack on the judiciary,[3] as well as the willingness of some Conservative MPs to bypass democratic debate via an unusually long prorogation of Parliament.[4] In Hungary, the Fidesz government of Viktor Orbán revised the constitution and attacked judicial independence

---

[1] On the various concepts used to analyse this situation see T. G. Daly, 'Democratic Decay: Conceptualising an Emerging Research Field', *Hague Journal of the Rule of Law*, 11 (2019), 9–36 and G. A. Tóth, 'Constitutional Markers of Authoritarianism', *Hague Journal of the Rule of Law*, 11 (2019), 37–61 at 40–43.

[2] House of Commons Library, *Research Briefing: Analysis of the EU Referendum Results 2016*, online at: https://commonslibrary.parliament.uk/research-briefings/cbp-7639/ (last accessed 26 January 2022).

[3] J. Slack, 'Enemies of the People: Fury over "out of touch" judges who have "declared war on democracy" by defying 17.4m Brexit voters and who could trigger constitutional crisis', *Daily Mail*, 24 July 2019, online at: https://www.dailymail.co.uk/news/article-3903436/Enemies-people-Fury-touch-jud ges-defied-17-4m-Brexit-voters-trigger-constitutional-crisis.html (last accessed 26 January 2022).

[4] J. Elgot, 'What is prorogation and why is Boris Johnson using it?', *Guardian*, 28 August 2019, online at: https://www.theguardian.com/politics/2019/aug/28/what-is-prorogation-prorogue-parliament-boris-johnson-brexit (last accessed 26 January 2022).

in order to enact his vision of populist democracy and make it less liberal, supposedly to protect what he claims to be 'true' national values.[5] In Poland, the ruling Truth and Justice party mounted similar assaults on the judiciary to remove what it perceived to be obstacles to governmental power.[6] In Italy, under the 2018–2019 governing coalition comprising the nationalist Lega party and the populist Five Star Movement, the interior minister and Lega leader, Matteo Salvini, attacked judicial criticism of his anti-immigration policies,[7] echoing former Prime Minister Silvio Berlusconi's criticisms of the 'red robes', supposedly left-wing judges using the law to 'harass' mandated politicians.[8] In the US, Donald Trump made numerous attacks on the judiciary and their supposed bias against him and his associates.[9] In Turkey, Recep Erdoğan sought to strengthen the government by purging the judiciary and leaving the justice system 'in crisis' due to a 'climate of fear'.[10]

That apparent crisis of liberal democracy and the separation of powers was also a crisis of the rule of law, which is likely to be exacerbated as governments increase their emergency powers to tackle the current threat to public health. A mutable and elusive concept, the rule of law is generally understood to be a focal point of liberal democratic society, a touchstone in democratic discourse and a keystone of democratic practice, which supposedly protects against non-democratic developments and ties its politico-legal structures together.[11] It is foundational to

---

[5] Freedom House, *Hungary: Freedom in the World 2019*, 24 July 2019, online at: https://freedomho use.org/country/hungary/freedom-world/2019 (last accessed 26 January 2022). Section F1; see also C. Dupré, 'Unconstitutional Constitutions: a Timely Concept' in A. von Bogdandy and P. Sonnevend (eds), *Constitutional Crisis in the European Constitutional Area: Theory, Law, Politics in Hungary and Romania* (Oxford, Hart Publishing, 2015), pp. 351–370. Orbán's powers increased further with coronavirus pandemic measures: E. Zerofsky, 'How Viktor Orbán Used the Coronavirus to Seize More Power', *New Yorker*, 9 April 2020, online at: https://www.newyorker.com/news/letter-from-europe/how-viktor-orban-used-the-coronavirus-to-seize-more-power (last accessed 26 January 2022).

[6] T. Koncewicz, 'Farewell to the Separation of Powers – On the Judicial Purge and the Capture in the Heart of Europe', *Verfassungsblog*, 19 July 2017, online at: https://verfassungsblog.de/farewell-to-the-separation-of-powers-on-the-judicial-purge-and-the-capture-in-the-heart-of-europe/ (last accessed 26 January 2022); J. Berendt, 'In Poland, A Stubborn Defender of Judicial Independence' *New York Times*, 10 January 2020, online at: https://www.nytimes.com/2020/01/10/world/europe/poland-judges-tuleya. html (last accessed 26 January 2022).

[7] For example, A. Giuffrida and L. Tondo, 'Italy's far-right interior minister, Matteo Salvini, escalates attack on judges', *Guardian*, 6 June 2019, online at: https://www.theguardian.com/world/2019/jun/06/ salvini-steps-up-attacks-on-italian-judges-who-challenge-him (last accessed 26 January 2022).

[8] 'Silvio Berlusconi e la magistratura: 18 anni di processi e polemiche', *Huffington Post*, 24 December 2012, online at: https://www.huffingtonpost.it/2012/10/24/silvio-berlusconi-e-la-ma_n_2011278.html (last accessed 26 January 2022).

[9] For example, D. Smith, 'Roger Stone case: chief justice urged to step in as Trump's 'abuse of power' condemned', *Guardian*, 13 February 2020, online at: https://www.theguardian.com/us-news/2020/feb/ 13/roger-stone-case-trump-democrats-supreme-court (last accessed 26 January 2022).

[10] For example, C. Gall, 'Erdoğan's Purges Leave Turkey's Justice System Reeling', *New York Times*, 21 June 2019, online at: https://www.nytimes.com/2019/06/21/world/asia/erdogan-turkey-courts-judici ary-justice.html (last accessed 26 January 2022).

[11] H. P. Graver, *Judges Against Justice: On Judges When the Rule of Law is Under Attack*, (Berlin, Springer, 2015), pp. 15–17.

liberal democracy because it represents and at least in principle ensures the limitation of governmental power, the legitimation of that power as lawful authority, the prevention of arbitrariness through universalised principles of justice and accountability, and the protection of rights.[12] Even so, the rule of law can be perceived as a spectrum, in the sense of the concept's 'thin' (merely formal and/or procedural) and 'thick' (encompassing substantive, institutional, normative and cultural) meanings, the technical and nuanced variations on its general theme in the civil law theories of *Rechtsstaat* and *État de droit*, and differing degrees of adherence to its components across systems and over time.[13] Just as democracies vary in their emphasis on liberal values or the importance of representation and the popular mandate, so they vary in their respect for law, legality and legal principles and processes.[14] Even where a state claims to rely on law and legality, that reliance can be ambivalent and not in and of itself a positive force or value-neutral mechanism of governance.[15] A meaningful 'thick' concept of the rule of law requires close integration of legal principle, substance and procedure, together with actual practice and more intangible dimensions of institutional and individual culture. Despite these variations, or perhaps because of them, the rule of law has been proclaimed to be part of the common heritage of European states, as a semi-mythical narrative of their lineage and shared values, and as the idealised core of their supposed development and aspiration towards common goals.[16] It is also a contested and elusive benchmark of European democratic credentials, non-compliance with which – or 'backsliding' – is a ground for transnational institutional and procedural censure.[17]

The claimed common heritage of democracy under the rule of law in Europe is predominantly a post-war and post-communist construction, involving a positively prospective formulation of values and objectives and a negatively retrospective

---

[12] Note T. Bingham's influential summary in *The Rule of Law* (London, Allen Lane, 2010) and European Commission for Democracy through Law, *Report on the Rule of Law*, adopted by the Venice Commission at its 86th plenary session (Venice, 25–26 March 2011) Study No. 512/2009, CDL-AD (2011) 003rev (Strasbourg, Council of Europe, 2011).

[13] D. Fairgrieve, 'État de droit and Rule of Law: Comparing Concepts: A Tribute to Roger Errera' (2015) Public Law, 40–59; P. Costa and D. Zolo, *The Rule of Law: History, Theory and Criticism* (Berlin, Springer, 2007); N. Lacey, 'Populism and the Rule of Law', *Annual Review of Law and Social Science*, 15 (2019), 79–96, 81–84.

[14] D. Grimm, 'Types of Constitutions', Part IV 'Constitutions as Expressions of Political Ideas', in M. Rosenfeld and A. Sájo (eds), *The Oxford Handbook of Comparative Constitutional Law* (Oxford, Oxford University Press, 2012), pp. 115–128.

[15] K. L. Scheppele and L. Pech, 'Is the Organisation of National Judiciaries a Purely Internal Competence?', *Verfassungsblog*, 4 March 2018, https://verfassungsblog.de/is-the-organisation-of-natio nal-judiciaries-a-purely-internal-competence/ (last accessed 26 January 2022).

[16] Statute of the Council of Europe (1949) Preamble and Article 1; European Convention on Human Rights (1950), Preamble; Treaty on European Union (2007, post-Lisbon Treaty), Preamble and Articles 1a, 6 and 61.

[17] K. L. Scheppele and L. Pech, 'What is Rule of Law Backsliding?' (2 March 2018) and 'Was the Commission Right to Activate pre-Article 7 and Article 7(1) Procedures Against Poland', *Verfassungsblog*, 7 March 2018, https://verfassungsblog.de/category/debates/protecting-the-rule-of-law-in-the-eu/ (last accessed 26 January 2022).

rejection of the abuse and oppression that characterised the totalitarian regimes that existed across the continent for much of the 20th century. Current tectonic shifts in politics and related threats to the rule of law, in terms of contextual conditions (e.g., economic fragility, population movements and concerns about national security) and their socio-political side-effects (e.g., populism, creeping authoritarianism, nationalistic identities and challenges to liberalism) are sometimes said to echo the beginnings of those past totalitarian experiences. In other words, the crisis affecting judicial independence and the rule of law today seems to raise the spectre of periods of European history that were generally considered to be temporally specific anomalies, brought to a close by the end of the Second World War and the Cold War, and prevented from recurring by post-1945 and post-1989 democratic reconstruction at the national and international levels.[18]

This chapter considers the apparent echoes of a past time of crisis in the populist attacks on constitutionalism and peers back into the darkness at an example of totalitarianism, namely Italian Fascism, and its impact on law. First, the chapter discusses the nature and impact of populism and the extent to which it is appropriate to compare it with historical Fascism. Second, the chapter outlines some of the main features of politico-legal ideology under the Italian Fascist regime in the 1920s–40s, focusing on the field of criminal law and the regime's relations with the judiciary. Third, the chapter argues that an analysis of historical Fascism can ground evaluation of recent developments in political discourse relating to the rule of law. This does not necessarily mean that they herald a return to Fascism in its past form, but that historical experience offers some key indicators of when a similarly dangerous assault on the rule of law is occurring, albeit in a new guise, and could be about to shift from crisis to catastrophe.

Current concerns and legal history

The possible echoes of the anti-democratic past have been a significant point of reference in recent commentaries on populism and the apparent authoritarian turn in several countries. Common considerations in these works are conceptual, namely the perennial problem of definition, and practical, namely whether, and if so, to what extent, connections or parallels can be drawn between the past and the present. The latter point involves the question of relevance, in the positive sense of the

---

[18] For example R. Primus, 'A Brooding Omnipresence: Totalitarianism in Postwar Constitutional Thought', *Yale Law Journal*, 106 (1996–97), 423–457; C. Joerges and N. S. Ghaleigh (eds), *Darker Legacies of Law in Europe: the Shadow of National Socialism and Fascism over Europe and its Legal Traditions* (Oxford, Hart Publishing, 2003); C. Dupré, *The Age of Dignity: Human Rights and Constitutionalism in Europe* (Oxford, Bloomsbury-Hart, 2015), pp. 57–62; and C. Cercel, *Towards a Jurisprudence of State Communism: Law and the Failure of Revolution* (Abingdon, Routledge, 2018), pp. 5–12, 204. Between those two waves of post-totalitarian reform came the military dictatorships and their democratic replacement in Portugal, Spain and Greece.

usefulness of bringing to light what past experience can tell us, and in a more negative or cautious sense of awareness of the risk of potentially problematic occultation or distraction, in that an over-hasty or over-dramatic link with historical totalitarianism can conceal or divert attention from matters of real concern today. An outline of some of these commentaries serves to highlight the key issues in this area.

Two recent studies of the phenomenon of populism have engaged broadly with its political significance in relation to democracy. In Jan-Werner Müller's influential discussion of populist movements and governments, he defines them as anti-elitist, antipluralist, and rooted in a form of identity politics that seeks to legitimate and ground authority in distorted claims to represent the will of 'the people'.[19] This is not in a democratic sense of the majority of an electorate, but an almost mystical and certainly mythical and inaccurate appeal to an exclusionary notion of the 'authentic people' that the populists claim only they know and understand. Noting the tendency of populist governments to curtail freedoms and gradually restrict the functioning of democratic institutions and civil society, Müller argues that they undermine democratic values and practices but do not quite press ahead with full-blown authoritarianism. For that reason, Müller argues that populist governments form 'defective' democracies rather than the 'illiberal' democracies that some populist leaders proclaim.[20]

In their recent work, Roger Eatwell and Matthew Goodwin have argued that populism should more accurately be referred to as 'national populism'.[21] Observing that national populist movements are generally not entirely anti-democratic but 'opposed to certain *aspects* of liberal democracy',[22] Eatwell and Goodwin focus on the socio-political roots of national populist movements around the world and propose four main explanatory factors. These are distrust of politicians and established political institutions, fear of destruction of national historic identity, a sense of relative deprivation in the face of economic inequality, and de-alignment from prior forms of stable political identity.[23] These authors argue that national populism has been developing since before the 2008 global financial crisis, comprises concerns that are not restricted to only some sectors of society,[24] and promises to reorient democracy to focus on the popular will, to defend ordinary people and to replace out-of-touch elites.[25] Their analysis of populism usefully explains how it stems from conditions of disruption and destabilisation, and dislocates the bases of government away from previous models of representative democracy.[26]

---

[19] J.-W. Müller, *What is Populism?* (Penguin Books, 2017) pp. 2–4; see also J.-W. Müller, 'Parsing Populism: Who Is and Who Is Not a Populist These Days?', *Juncture*, 22.2 (2015), 80–89.

[20] Müller, *What is Populism?*, pp. 44–60.

[21] R. Eatwell and M. Goodwin, *National Populism: The Revolt Against Liberal Democracy* (Pelican Books, 2018).

[22] Eatwell and Goodwin, *National Populism*, p. xi.

[23] Eatwell and Goodwin, *National Populism*, pp. xxi-xxiii and chapters 3–6.

[24] Eatwell and Goodwin, *National Populism*, pp. 8–25.

[25] Eatwell and Goodwin, *National Populism*, pp. 54–57.

[26] See also Lacey, 'Populism and the Rule of Law', 84–85.

In that regard, populist political leaders and governments have shown their willingness to bend or subvert previously respected democratic principles and institutions, and some commentators have pointed explicitly to the legal and constitutional dimensions of these approaches. For example, David Landau has examined how governments that can be seen to fit within the mould of populism have tended to undertake quite sweeping constitutional reforms, such as the changes passed under Viktor Orbán's government in Hungary and Recep Erdoğan's in Turkey.[27] For Landau, these revisions of the constitutional order have three essentially populist functions, namely 'deconstructing the existing political regime, serving as an ideological critique that promises to overcome flaws in the prior constitutional order, and consolidating power in the hands of the populist leadership'.[28] While he notes that such radical reorganisations of political power can highlight weaknesses in existing liberal democratic systems and the need to address them, this populist approach to constitutional reform can also lay the groundwork for a dangerous concentration of power and its long-term retention.[29]

This tendency to use law to effect structural and institutional change in order to strengthen governmental power or push through an illiberal agenda has been analysed by Ozan O. Varol in terms of 'stealth authoritarianism'[30] and by Kim Lane Scheppele as 'autocratic legalism'.[31] Varol's study draws attention to the use of formal mechanisms of control, especially legal, rather than informal or overt measures of repression. Although considering the use of such mechanisms in non-democratic systems, Varol also points to their deployment in democratic systems, including the United States, in order to demonstrate 'the limits of democratic processes and their vulnerability to abuse.'[32] Scheppele focuses on the example of constitutional reform in Hungary, which has included eroding the independence of the judiciary as well as electoral reform that strengthens the position of the governing party,[33] and argues that by 'attacking the very basis of a constitutional order while using the methods made possible by that constitutional order, the new illiberals may be cheered on at first by the adulating crowds who sought change, but those same crowds will find these illiberals impossible to remove once they have destroyed the constitutional system that could have maintained their democratic

---

[27] D. Landau, 'Populist Constitutions', *The University of Chicago Law Review*, 85 (2018), 521–543.

[28] Landau, 'Populist Constitutions', 522.

[29] Landau, 'Populist Constitutions', 541–543.

[30] O. O. Varol, 'Stealth Authoritarianism', *Iowa Law Review*, 100 (2015), 1673–1742, see 1678–79 and at 1684 note his emphasis on the use of law to erode the possibility of cyclical power transfers among political parties. See also H. A. García and G. Frankenberg (eds), *Authoritarian Constitutionalism: Comparative Analysis and Critique* (Cheltenham, Edward Elgar, 2019) and on populism's authoritarian tendency in East Central Europe see B. Bugaric and A. Kuhelj, 'Varieties of Populism in Europe: Is the Rule of Law in Danger?', *Hague Journal of the Rule of Law*, 10 (2018), 21–33.

[31] K. L. Scheppele, 'Autocratic Legalism', *The University of Chicago Law Review*, 85 (2018), 545–83, 561–62.

[32] Varol, 'Stealth Authoritarianism', 1680.

[33] Scheppele, 'Autocratic Legalism', 549–53.

accountability over the long run.'[34] That is, 'by consolidating power under the guise of legality (often constitutional legality), the autocrats set the stage for snapping the trap of democratic pretence when the tide of public opinion turns against them.'[35] Both studies show how changes to the legal and constitutional fabric, often carried out on a populist platform, can appear to use the tools of the rule of law to introduce covertly a systemic reality that is deeply out of alignment with that concept's liberal democratic objectives.

However, it is important to note that the influence of populism on law is not only a question of direct constitutional revision. Nicola Lacey has argued that populist politics can potentially affect law in discursive as well as substantive ways and that the extent to which changes in respect for the rule of law are in fact attributable to populism is contingent on a system's social and institutional conditions.[36] As Lacey shows, in addition to direct governmental law reform, there are four main pathways between populist politics and law, including what she calls 'agenda setting', or shaping the direction and content of political debate; influencing the formulation of actual policies; affecting the exercise of discretionary executive powers; and 'convention trashing', that is, a shift in attitude of office holders that leads to disregard for established norms of governmental conduct.[37] Alongside these overlapping layers of what is said and what is done, it is also important to recall their concomitants of what is not said and not done, a political absence that can be just as problematic.[38] Consequently, while constitutional reform can be the most evident form of 'stealth authoritarianism' or 'autocratic legalism', the rule of law can be eroded through other routes of political influence as well.

The issue of the nature and degree of shift in a system's legal fabric brings us to the question of historical comparison. Some of the above studies of populist politics and their effects, as well as other works, have included reflection on populism's possible relationship with, and differences from, historical forms of authoritarianism and fascism.[39] While it is important to note that fascism is a deeply contested concept, it generally signifies an extreme form of political regime based on a belief in a uniquely important national or racial community, an ideology of national destiny and regeneration, a singular model of state power centred on a charismatic leader, opposition to both the perceived weaknesses of democracy and the threat of socialism and communism, and a reliance on and fascination with

---

[34] Scheppele, 'Autocratic Legalism', 548.

[35] Scheppele, 'Autocratic Legalism', 582. On the erosion of constitutional democracy in the United States, see S. Levinson and J. M. Balkin, 'Constitutional Dictatorship: Its Dangers and Its Design', *Minnesota Law Review*, 94 (2010), 1789–1866.

[36] Lacey, 'Populism and the Rule of Law', 81.

[37] Lacey, 'Populism and the Rule of Law', 86–90.

[38] On the then Lord Chancellor's silence during the 'enemies of the people' furore, see 'Lord Chancellor bows to Pressure to Support Brexit judges', *Financial Times*, 5 November 2016, online at: https://www.ft.com/content/5fa3c042-a369-11e6-8898-79a99e2a4de6 (last accessed 26 January 2022).

[39] Non-capitalised 'fascism' is used here to refer to a more generic concept while capitalised 'Fascism' is used to refer specifically to the Italian regime.

violence.[40] Roger Griffin's influential 'new consensus' model of fascism as a generic ideological type defines it as a 'palingenetic form of populist ultranationalism', situating fascism beyond mere nationalism or populism and characterising it by its radical focus on national rebirth.[41]

With regard to these definitional issues, Müller distinguishes current populism from the extremes of historical German National Socialism and Italian Fascism in terms of their 'racism, a glorification of violence, and a radical "leadership principle"',[42] which indicate some of the deeper ideological aspects differentiating fascism from 'defective democracy'. Eatwell and Goodwin similarly distinguish national populism from fascism, which they argue had more fundamentally transformative aims. These they summarise as the construction of a new spiritual community demanding total adherence, the creation of a new model of man under the direction of strong leaders, and the development of a new sort of economic system oriented between socialism and capitalism.[43] According to Federico Finchelstein's recent study of the history of populism and fascism, these two are distinct because of the former's roots in democracy, even though it subverts it and may turn towards authoritarianism, while fascism is a form of 'ultraviolent dictatorship' that is fundamentally anti-democratic.[44] Populists reconceptualise the electorate as 'the people' and claim that governmental interpretation of its wishes is unquestionable, emphasising the need for governmental freedom of action without interference from other systemic institutions, such as the judiciary. For Fascism, the leader supposedly acted in the interests of the people, but any representative links between them were insubstantial, and elections were replaced by a dictatorship. In contrast to the above studies, Madeleine Albright has (controversially) argued that current populist leaders, in their rhetorical and reformist attacks on democratic institutions, are directly adopting fascist tactics and are explicitly echoing, if they are not already replicating, past fascist regimes.[45]

Considering the impact of populist developments on the rule of law raises concerns about their similarity to past erosions of democracy but, apart from Albright's book, these studies stress that populism cannot be equated with fascism. It is also important to be aware that an over-simplified reference to historical fascism can be counterproductive. Scheppele cautions that thinking of fascism and authoritarianism solely in reductive or stereotyped terms of Hitler's or Stalin's brutal

---

[40] S. G. Payne, *Fascism: Comparison and Definition* (Madison, University of Wisconsin Press, 1980); Z. Sternhell with M. Sznajder and M. Ashéri, *The Birth of Fascist Ideology: From Cultural Rebellion to Political Revolution* (D. Maisel trans) (Princeton, NJ, Princeton University Press, 1994); and R. O. Paxton, *The Anatomy of Fascism* (London, Penguin Books, 2005). See also E. Traverso, *The New Faces of Fascism: Populism and the Far Right* (London, Verso, 2019), pp. 97–127 and S. Garau, *Fascism and Ideology: Italy, Britain and Norway*, (Abingdon, Routledge, 2015), pp. 1–3.

[41] R. Griffin, *The Nature of Fascism* (London, Routledge, 1993), p. 26; contrast Paxton, *The Anatomy of Fascism*, p. 221.

[42] Müller, *What is Populism?*, p. 93.

[43] Eatwell and Goodwin, *National Populism*, pp. 58–64; see also Paxton, *The Anatomy of Fascism*, p. 143.

[44] F. Finchelstein, *From Fascism to Populism in History*, (University of California Press, 2017), pp. 3–5.

[45] M. Albright (with B. Woodward), *Fascism: A Warning*, (London, William Collins, 2018).

regimes can desensitise critical awareness and distract attention from insidious decline. As she puts it, the 'bite-sized takeaway lessons from the two signature authoritarians of the twentieth century constitute the modern repertoire of signals that the public will recognize as dangerous. The problem is that people overlearn the simple lessons and believe that unless those precise things happen, the danger is not very great.'[46] She warns that:

> The takeaway lessons of the twentieth century prepare people for different sorts of threats to liberalism: pervasive ideological appeals that justify the destruction of institutions, the invocation of total emergency, mass violations of human rights, and tanks in the streets. By contrast, the new autocrats come to power not with bullets but with laws. They attack the institutions of liberal constitutionalism with constitutional amendments. They carefully preserve the shell of the prior liberal state – the same institutions, the same ceremonies, an overall appearance of rights protection – but in the meantime they hollow out its moral core.[47]

In that light, this chapter turns to the historical example of Italian Fascism, not as a direct parallel or provocative reading grid for sensationalising current concerns, but as a cautiously constructed comparator to support evaluation of the degree of danger represented by populist interventions in politico-legal discourse and practice, as well as their possible direction of travel. This discussion of Fascism is partly based on the need to incorporate historical awareness of past oppression in, and acknowledge the influence of such awareness on, public discussion about the public sphere,[48] but mainly due to the need to be aware of history's potential lessons. The example of Italian Fascism has also been selected because Mussolini's government consolidated its power by turning Fascism into a regime based on a special relationship with law. It is thus important to recognise that law represents an element of continuity and commonality between democratic and non-democratic systems over time and in divergent contexts, that the relationship between a political system and law can reveal key aspects of that system's identity, and that law can be the medium through which that identity shifts. Consequently, this reflection on the rule of law and its crises can usefully consider historical Fascism by remaining within the legal field and can draw informative lessons from it, without implying (as per Scheppele's warning) that they are restricted to that regime's more extreme attributes and their reproduction.

Fascism, law and the judiciary

The political movement led by Benito Mussolini in Italy became a regime that lasted from 1922 to 1943 and was the first to go by the name 'Fascist'.[49] It was

---

[46] Scheppele, 'Autocratic Legalism', 572–573.
[47] Scheppele, 'Autocratic Legalism', 582.
[48] Traverso, *The New Faces of Fascism*, pp. 59–60; see also S. Skinner, 'Tainted Law? The Italian Penal Code, Fascism and Democracy', *International Journal of Law in Context*, 7.4 (2011), 423–446 at 433, 436–439.
[49] On the origins of the term 'fascist' see Paxton, *The Anatomy of Fascism*, p. 4 and R. J. B. Bosworth, *Mussolini's Italy: Life Under the Dictatorship* (London, Penguin Books, 2006), pp. 121–22.

also the first regime to adopt the term 'totalitarian', taking the adjective used by its critics and using it to describe its methods and aims.[50] The generic term 'fascist' is nowadays sometimes too lightly used to indicate extreme, authoritarian or intransigent political views, but historically the term 'Fascist' relates specifically to the Italian dictatorship and its particular, albeit loose, bundle of ideological tenets. Italian Fascism was always a rather eclectic and unclear political movement, but it is nevertheless possible to outline some of its main components and features.

As a movement, Fascism was originally born from a range of interests and influences. These included frustrated former soldiers in the aftermath of the First World War who were angry with the Italian Liberal government that seemed to have let them down; the philosophical and artistic movement known as the Futurists, who were fascinated by modernity, mechanisation, speed and the glories of war; Nationalists and socialists; and an acute sense of wounded and resurgent masculinity and national pride, which manifested itself as a desire to improve Italy's fortunes against its regional rivals and to revive the glory of ancient Rome.[51] In other words, the Fascists wanted to make their country great again. Among this mixture of influences, efforts were made to articulate the foundations and aims of Fascism as a system. However, it is important to note that those purporting to do so expressed an awkward relationship with the ideas they sought to convey, in that while setting out an ideological view, they denied the importance of ideas and theories, claiming instead that Fascism was primarily based on action.[52] More problematic is the fact that proponents of Fascism sought to present themselves, and their movement, as revolutionary, although as subsequent analyses have underlined, the regime's politico-legal programme was in many ways continuous with that of the preceding Liberal order in Italy,[53] and its success was partly attributable to its ability to draw on pre-existing political ideas and concerns.[54] Linking both of these issues is the concern that by focusing on Fascist expressions of political doctrine, too much weight might be given to rhetoric and propaganda, which is not the same

[50] According to S. G. Payne, *A History of Fascism, 1914–1945*, (Madison, The University of Wisconsin Press, 1995), p. 121, the term 'totalitarian' was first used pejoratively by an anti-Fascist politician, Giovanni Amendola (killed by Fascist thugs in 1925), then adopted by the Fascist philosopher, G. Gentile, 'The Philosophic Basis of Fascism', *Foreign Affairs*, 6.2 (1928), 290–304 at 299 to refer to the 'comprehensive' scope of Fascist doctrine, 'which concerns itself not only with political organization and political tendency, but with the whole will and thought and feeling of the nation'. It was subsequently embraced by Mussolini in his famous statement that Fascism meant 'Everything within the state, nothing outside the state, nothing against the state', which is said to have been first published in his entry on 'Fascist Doctrine' in the *Enciclopedia Italiana* (1932).

[51] Griffin, *The Nature of Fascism*, pp. 63–76.

[52] Gentile, 'The Philosophic Basis of Fascism', 300–301.

[53] S. Cassese, *Lo Stato Fascista*, (Bologna, Il Mulino, 2010), pp. 13–15, 82; L. Klinkhammer, 'Was There a Fascist Revolution? The Function of Penal Law in Fascist Italy and Nazi Germany' *Journal of Modern Italian Studies*, 15.3 (2010), 390–409; M. Sbriccoli, 'Caratteri originari e tratti permanenti del sistema penale italiano (1860–1990)', in L. Violante with L. Minervini (eds), *Storia d'Italia, Annali 14, Legge Diritto Giustizia*, (Turin, Giulio Einaudi, 1998), pp. 487–551.

[54] Garau, *Fascism and Ideology*, p. 4.

as the regime's reality.[55] With those problematic parameters in mind, the intention here is to underline some of the main claims and stated aims of Fascism in relation to law, as well as aspects of actual practice.

The major figure in the expression of Fascism's objectives was a former nationalist politician and professor of commercial law, Alfredo Rocco, who was Mussolini's Minister of Justice from 1925 to 1932 and came to be known as the architect of the Fascist state.[56] In a speech in Perugia on 30 August 1925, subsequently published in 1926 under the title of 'The Political Doctrine of Fascism', and in his 1930 address to the King to present the final text of the new Italian Penal Code, Rocco set out his vision for law and the state under the Fascist regime.[57] This can be distilled into three main points. The first and perhaps most important of these is that the Fascist system was to be focused on the centrality and paramountcy of the state. The state had to be strong and, in Rocco's view, was to be understood as having its own identity. It was to be led by a small elite, supposedly acting for the good of the people. Although the Fascist movement originally included some apparently 'populist' elements in that Rocco sought to emphasise the genius of the Italian people, its glorious Roman past and its special destiny, the Fascist state and its exercise of power were not to be based on claims about popular will but on a concept of society 'juridically organized as a state'.[58] Also, as a crucial part of that ideological focus on the strong state, individuals were said not to matter. In an explicit rejection of Kant's famous maxim, Rocco declared that individuals were means to the ends of the strong state.[59] Individual rights were unwanted constraints on the state, limiting its freedom of action so that for Rocco, only the state was to have rights and individuals only duties; and while Rocco declared that individual liberty existed under Fascism, it was liberty for the individual to fulfil himself in the interests of the state.[60] Subsequently, despite the appearance of Rocco's claims, the Fascist regime did not try to assume total control over all institutions, but Mussolini's government did strengthen its powers in successive stages, merging the Fascist party and its high officials with many pre-existing state structures, replacing elected offices with party appointments,

---

[55] Garau, *Fascism and Ideology*, p. 19.
[56] A. J. Gregor, *Mussolini's Intellectuals: Fascist Social and Political Thought*, (Princeton, Princeton University Press, 2005), pp. 38–60 and F. Lanchester, 'Alfredo Rocco e le Origini dello Stato Totale', in E. Gentile, F. Lanchester and A. Tarquini (eds), *Alfredo Rocco: dalla Crisi del Parlamentarismo alla Costruzione dello Stato Nuovo*, (Rome, Carocci, 2010), pp. 15–38.
[57] Alfredo Rocco, 'The Political Doctrine of Fascism', *International Conciliation*, (1926) 393–415; A. Rocco, 'Relazione a sua Maestà il Re del Ministro Guardasigilli (Rocco) Presentata nell'udienza del 19 Ottobre 1930-VIII per l'approvazione del testo definitivo del Codice Penale', in Ministero della Giustizia (ed), *Lavori Preparatori del Codice Penale e Del Codice di Procedura Penale, Vol. VII, Testo del Nuovo Codice Penale con la Relazione a Sua Maestà il Re del Guardasigilli*, (Rome, Tipografia delle Mantellate, 1930) pp. 7–28.
[58] Rocco, 'The Political Doctrine of Fascism', 405.
[59] Rocco, 'The Political Doctrine of Fascism', 402–403.
[60] Rocco, 'The Political Doctrine of Fascism', 403–404.

and seeking to increase the pervasive influence of Fascism and party institutions in all aspects of society.[61]

The second main point about Rocco's outline of the Fascist state, and the regime's practices, concerns the importance of law. The legal history of the Mussolini regime shows that a form of 'rule of law', and even a foundational concept of justice, were important in Fascism.[62] Both law and justice were central elements of Fascist self-representation and symbolism, and law was central to the regime's consolidation, expression and exercise of power. The so-called ultra-fascist laws of 1926 reinforced the Fascists' grip on government and to some extent replaced the violence of the 'Black Shirts' (or *squadristi*, followers of Mussolini who would physically attack their political opponents) with mechanisms of state repression.[63] The new Penal Code and Penal Procedure Code of 1930-1931, as well as the Civil Code and Civil Procedure Code of 1942, also demonstrated the regime's efforts to construct its new order through legal means. Underpinning these developments was an adherence to legality, the requirement for there to be legal norms satisfying criteria of certainty, which in liberal systems reflects the importance of a legal foundation for state power and of the guarantees that come with duly enacted law.[64] However, this concept of legality was reconceptualised as an expression of the will of the strong state, with respect and obedience for the law demanded on the basis that it was an emanation of the state, rather than the prescriptive and protective mechanism advocated and supposedly adhered to in liberal democracies.[65] In this concept of legality, law was to be focused on upholding and enforcing state interests and shaping society. In other words, the Fascist form of rule of law was really an expression of 'rule by law'.

Third, perhaps unsurprisingly, criminal law was one of the principal instruments of state power and control, with its provisions likened to the state's war power. Justice Minister Rocco declared that the 'power to punish is in fact one of the

---

[61] Cassese, *Lo Stato Fascista*, pp. 16–21; Garau, *Fascism and Ideology*, p. 112 and 117–122.

[62] L. Lacchè, "'Also and Above All a Regime of Justice." Criminal Law and the Aesthetics of Justice Under the Italian Fascist Regime: The Role of Architecture', in S. Skinner (ed), *Ideology and Criminal Law: Fascist, National Socialist and Authoritarian Regimes*, (Oxford, Hart Publishing, 2019), pp. 9–32 at 10–22.

[63] Lacchè, "'Also and Above All a Regime of Justice,"' p. 10.

[64] For example, Article 1, 1930 Penal Code prohibiting punishment without a basis in law.

[65] M. A. Cattaneo, 'Il Codice Rocco e l'Eredità Illuministico-Liberale', in *La Questione Criminale*, 7.1 (1981), 99–110; S. Vinciguerra, 'Dal codice Zanardelli al codice Rocco. Una panoramica sulle ragioni, il metodo e gli esiti della sostituzione', in S. Vinciguerra (ed), *Il Codice Penale per il Regno d'Italia (1930) Codice Rocco*, (Milan, CEDAM, 2010), pp. xi–xxxviii, xxvii; see also F. Bricola, 'Teoria generale del reato' in A. Azara and E. Eula (eds), *Novissimo Digesto Italiano* vol XIX (Turin, UTET, 1979), pp. 7–38, 32–33. On the ambivalence at the heart of liberal concepts of legality see M. Sbriccoli, 'La penalistica civile. Teorie e ideologie del diritto penale nell'Italia unita', in A. Schiavone (ed), *Stato e Cultura Giuridica in Italia dall'Unità alla Repubblica*, (Editori Laterza, Roma-Bari, 1990), pp. 147–232 and L. Lacchè, 'The Shadow of the Law: The Special Tribunal for the Defence of the State between Justice and Politics in the Italian Fascist Period', in S. Skinner (ed), *Fascism and Criminal Law: History, Theory, Continuity*, (Oxford, Hart Publishing, 2015), pp. 15–33 at 17.

greatest attributes of sovereignty.'[66] According to Rocco, criminals were to be considered internal enemies of the state, to be fought and vanquished like any other foe.[67] Although the new 1930 Penal Code reflected some significant continuities with criminal law in pre-Fascist, Liberal Italy, it also showed the Fascist regime's reordered priorities and ideological objectives. These were apparent in the Code's structure, with crimes against the state coming before other offences; its repressive aims, with harsher punishments for many offences than in previous criminal laws; and the ways in which its style and content reflected the regime's intention for criminal law to serve state interests first and foremost, including a reliance on flexible concepts to ensure interpretive adaptability and the formulation of offences designed to protect Fascist values, such as the family.[68]

Alongside these theoretical and substantive aspects of law under Fascism, it is important to note the regime's interaction with the legal system. The Fascist regime used the same measures as previous governments of the Liberal period to exert executive control over the judiciary, such as through the control of disciplinary processes, allocation of positions and career progression.[69] Although according to Justice Minister Rocco judges were not supposed to become mere puppets of the state but to remain independent in the name of justice, they were expected to support the regime. In a parliamentary speech on 19 June 1925, Rocco declared that 'the judiciary must not engage in politics of any kind. We do not want them to be on the side of government or Fascism, but we firmly insist that they must not engage in anti-government and anti-Fascist politics.'[70] For Rocco, judicial independence was not to be taken literally as indicating a complete separation of the judge from governmental influence, but should be understood instead to indicate the special nature of the judicial role, which was detached but essentially public in character.[71] As that role was inherently political, Rocco felt sure that the judiciary would align itself with the regime, although he still needed to issue a series of circulars to point judges in the right direction.[72] The exertion of political control was reinforced by measures such as the prohibition of judicial associations

---

[66] Rocco, 'Relazione a sua Maestà il Re del Ministro Guardasigilli', 7.

[67] S. Skinner, 'Violence in Fascist Criminal Law Discourse: War, Repression and Anti-Democracy', *International Journal for the Semiotics of Law*, 26.2 (2013), 439–458.

[68] G. N. Modona and M. Pelissero, 'La politica criminale durante il fascismo' in L. Violante (ed), *Storia d'Italia, Annali 12, La criminalità*, (Turin, Einaudi, 1997), pp. 759–847; P. Garfinkel, *Criminal Law in Liberal and Fascist Italy*, (Cambridge, Cambridge University Press, 2016), pp. 389–456.

[69] Lacchè, 'The Shadow of the Law', p. 25; on the treatment of judges generally under authoritarian regimes see Graver, *Judges Against Justice*, p. 39.

[70] A. Rocco, *Discorsi parlamentari* (Bologna, Il Mulino, 2005), p. 213, cited in Riccardo Cavallo, 'The Judiciary and Political Power Under the Fascist Regime in Italy', in Skinner, *Ideology and Criminal Law*, pp. 165–186 at 174.

[71] On the similar approach in Nazi Germany see H. P. Graver, 'Why Adolf Hitler Spared the Judges: Judicial Opposition Against the Nazi State', *German Law Journal*, 19.4 (2018), 845–877 at 846 and H. P. Graver, 'Judicial Independence Under Authoritarian Rule: An Institutional Approach to the Legal Tradition of the West', *Hague Journal of the Rule of Law*, 10 (2018), 317–339 at 331–35.

[72] Cavallo, 'The Judiciary and Political Power Under the Fascist Regime in Italy', pp. 173–174.

and the requirement for all prospective judges to be members of the Fascist party, which together demonstrated the regime's efforts to anchor professional identity and allegiance in Fascism.[73]

The reform implemented by the subsequent Fascist Minister of Justice, Dino Grandi, in 1941 increased governmental influence over the judiciary under the guise of consolidating the rules on the judicial career structure, which meant greater ministerial control. This reform also included making changes to the Supreme Court, the highest judicial body in Italy, in order to ensure respect for legality in the sense of 'uniform interpretation' of the law in line with 'national aims', thereby influencing how lower courts applied the law.[74] At the same time, while the regime sought to exert control over the judiciary, the latter readily aligned itself with the regime, continuing a certain tendency towards complicity with the government already demonstrated by judges in the pre-Fascist era, and avoided interpretive tension by claiming to respect the letter of the law as it was enacted.[75] The Fascist regime did not directly seek to end the independence of the judiciary but took steps to curtail it and, in any case, benefited from judicial adherence to the Fascist line. Consequently, as these examples demonstrate, law and the legal system became key parts of the Fascist regime's mechanisms of control.

Lessons from historical fascism

As discussed in the first part of this chapter, some populist governments are already undermining the legal fabric of liberal democracy through direct measures,[76] while in other systems, as discussed by Lacey, apparent assaults on the rule of law involve contextually contingent interactions between politics and law at several discursive and substantive levels.[77] Such an inclination away from previous liberal democratic standards raises questions about the degree of that inclination and whether it represents a proverbial 'slippery slope' towards a form of fascism, or a new sort of anti-democratic regime that resembles it. To consider these issues, this section focuses on political discourse relating to the rule of law and argues that the above outline of Italian Fascism can provide useful indications of when changes in a system's politico-legal identity might be moving beyond populism and into a more dangerous phase.

Political discourse, involving the form and content of political debate, is one of the first aspects of a political system to undergo significant shifts, which can

---

[73] Cavallo, 'The Judiciary and Political Power Under the Fascist Regime in Italy', p. 176.
[74] Cavallo, 'The Judiciary and Political Power Under the Fascist Regime in Italy', p. 175 and 185.
[75] Cavallo, 'The Judiciary and Political Power Under the Fascist Regime in Italy', p. 186. On judges and the acceptance of authoritarian legality more generally see Graver, *Judges Against Justice*, p. 53 and on judges in Nazi Germany more specifically see Graver, 'Why Adolf Hitler Spared the Judges', 846–847.
[76] Tóth, 'Constitutional Markers of Authoritarianism', 46–59.
[77] Lacey, 'Populism and the Rule of Law'.

in turn lead to changes in policy, practice and wider behaviour.[78] The relationship between populism and fascism at the discursive level has already received critical attention, showing that echoes of fascism and its ideology can take various forms. For example, Enzo Traverso has argued that historic forms of fascism, although not the same as current forms of populism and far-right politics, still resonate directly in some groups that openly claim a descent from past fascist movements ('neofascism') and indirectly in those groups that reproduce aspects of fascism in disguised forms ('postfascism').[79] 'Postfascism', he argues, involves a covert adoption and repackaging of fascistic nationalism, xenophobia and identity politics in the guise of a populist reform agenda.[80] This process of adopting coded echoes of fascist ideology in far-right and populist discourse has also been underlined by Ruth Wodak and John Richardson, who point to the need to trace political themes across 'text and talk' in order to identify not only their historical origins but also importantly their implicit references, or resonances.[81] In addition to these direct and conscious, as well as covert and implicit, connections with fascist ideology in political discourse, it is important to note that some populist discursive themes reflect or reproduce elements of fascism in non-deliberate ways that nevertheless indicate disturbing historic resonance through a lack of awareness of, or careless indifference to, their implications. These sorts of connections can be just as dangerous by allowing fascistic components to enter public debate and setting it onto an anti-democratic trajectory. In order to identify and assess some of the most disturbing discursive resonances, three metaphorical 'red flags' are proposed here.

The first relates to Fascism's driving ideological foundation. Populist claims about the 'will of the people' and measures to curtail judicial 'interference' with governmental activity reflect populism's foundational opposition between its supposed mandate and the established elite. This emphasis on governmental freedom of action would arguably start to tilt at a dangerous angle if political discourse were to meld the populists' dubious representative assertions with declarations about the restoration of past glory, the paramountcy of the state – and especially its leader – as the embodiment and sole guardian of the nation's interest,[82] and a re-conceptualisation of law as being first and foremost a means for state action, to be shaped solely to suit the political will of government. This would be indicative of an absolute belief in the presumed legitimacy, purpose and authority of a government that cannot countenance the idea of being thwarted. Glorifying redemptive justice as an instrument of its new political order, and

---

[78] R. Wodak and J. E. Richardson, 'European Fascism in Talk and Text: Introduction', in R. Wodak and J. E. Richardson (eds), *Analysing Fascist Discourse: European Fascism in Talk and Text*, (Abingdon, Routledge, 2013), pp. 1–16 at 7.

[79] Traverso, *The New Faces of Fascism*, pp. 6–7.

[80] Traverso, *The New Faces of Fascism*, pp. 32–33 and 186.

[81] Wodak and Richardson, 'European Fascism in Talk and Text', pp. 1–3.

[82] Compare Graver, 'Why Adolf Hitler Spared the Judges', p. 868.

relying on law as an emanation and tool of the strong state, the Fascist regime accepted the need for judges as a core part of the legal system, but only if they were compliant with its aims. Populist assaults on judicial independence because of judges' perceived resistance to a government's supposedly unbounded mandate echo that past approach to the monopolisation of power. Attacking the judiciary as a public institution and undermining its independence are not only an erosion of the rule of law but also a gateway to dictatorship.[83]

Such an approach would be especially alarming if accompanied by the other two discursive red flags suggested here. With reference to Alfredo Rocco's statements of Fascist ideology, the second of these involves the rejection, even the vilification, of human rights and their portrayal as negative constraints on state action that need to be reconfigured as a selective benefit to be earned, rather than a universally inherent attribute of humanity. In that vein of politico-legal discourse, the state is portrayed as embodying the superior, collective interest, and rights are portrayed as an obstructive, self-indulgent fiction that should be at least restricted, if not disposed of. This is because rights are seen as being relied on by the wrong sort of individuals, or more generally, because the idea of rights is replaced by a focus on responsibilities to state and society. This is not to say that critical reflection on the appropriate scope of rights is never acceptable, as human rights require protection in the context of proportionate balancing of conflicting interests. However, an emphasis on rights as obstacles to the state, on the state as the focus of politics and society, and on individuals as lacking inherent worth, were key elements of Fascist doctrine, which sought to replace individual rights with loyal citizens' duties. As above, such a rejection of rights is grounded in an absolute belief that government and the state know best. It diminishes or denies the importance of individuals in favour of the perceived needs of a majority, sweeping aside the weak and the marginalised.[84]

The third red flag in the area of political discourse is the predominance of a language of violence. This involves various elements. One is the perception of 'others' (be they criminals, foreigners, political opponents, the poor or unemployed, or people of different racial backgrounds, sexualities or religious beliefs) as inferior or threatening to a perceived national norm, and their portrayal as enemies against whom resistance is not only required but also justified. Another is the recasting of political debate and disagreement in belligerent or militarised language through an aggressive rhetorical style that emphasises terms and metaphors of combat and inflates argument into conflict. A third indicator involves disregard or disrespect for, even denigration of, women and what are perceived to be feminine attributes. Fascism, and specifically Rocco's claims about law and the state, emphasised these sorts of language and imagery. This reflected Fascism's genesis from the First World War, its glorification of military might and Rocco's

---

[83] See footnotes 4, 6–11 above and related text.
[84] Paxton, *The Anatomy of Fascism*, p. 142.

metaphorical connections between the state's power in war and its power in law. It also reflected Fascism's inherent masculine bias and emphasis on male strength, which appeared, for example, in Rocco's assertion of the nation's 'recovered virility and energy' and the importance of the 'strong state' as contrasted with liberal democracy and its perceived (effeminate) weaknesses.[85] Explicitly and implicitly expressing both martial and gender violence, this sort of inflated discourse can appear as over-enthusiastic or heavy-handed rhetoric, but its adoption can entail not only a coarsening of political exchanges, but also an erosion of democratic values and standards of behaviour in institutions of state and a threat to society more generally.

These three metaphorical red flags, separately and together, indicate the presence of dangers to democracy. Fascism as it developed in early 20th-century Italy, with its uniforms, rallies and neo-imperialism, is unlikely to return, but these historical lessons from it can serve to highlight when a shift in discourse enters what can be called a zone of potentiality that could signal the start of new and dangerously restrictive and repressive assaults on the rule of law. Whether or not they mean that a system is becoming 'fascist' in a generic sense is, however, open to varying interpretations,[86] which largely depend on whether discourse is matched by significant alterations in practice.[87] For example, Donald Trump infamously based his initial political campaign on the premise that he would 'make America great again', an apparent promise of national rebirth that he has accompanied with xenophobic promises to 'build a wall' to keep out the sorts of foreigners he considers undesirable. Parts of the rhetoric around Brexit in the UK have likewise included allusions to a supposedly noble past and claims about a dynamised nation in the future. Attacks on the judiciary in both systems have come against this political backdrop and seem intended to free government from constitutional constraint.[88] Similarly, the direct assaults on judicial independence in Hungary and Poland have been accompanied by nationalistic rhetoric about revitalising each country and reaffirming true national values. Human rights have also been in the firing line, with political opposition to them apparently expressed without consideration of the historical resonances and implications of their proposed abandonment.[89] Rhetorical

---

[85] Rocco, 'Relazione a sua Maestà il Re del Ministro Guardasigilli', 25; Skinner, 'Violence in Fascist Criminal Law Discourse', 449. See further on the Fascist cult of masculinity L. Benadusi, *Il Nemico dell'uomo nuovo: L'omosessualità nell'esperimento totalitario fascista* (Milan, Feltrinelli, 2005), pp. 30–34.

[86] Note for example the American Historical Association's January 2020 annual conference plenary debate entitled 'Resolved: Fascism is Back', online at: https://aha.confex.com/aha/2020/webprogram/ Session20131.html (last accessed 26 January 2022).

[87] Finchelstein, *From Fascism to Populism in History*, pp. 5–6.

[88] Note the UK government's 'frustration' with 'excessive' recourse to judicial review that overturns ministerial decisions: O. Bowcott, 'What is judicial review and why doesn't the government like it?', *Guardian*, 11 February 2020, online at: https://www.theguardian.com/law/2020/feb/11/what-is-judicial-review-and-why-doesnt-the-government-like-it (last accessed 26 January 2022).

[89] Compare elements of Conservative Party opposition to human rights in the UK, for example: R. Merrick, 'Theresa May to consider axeing Human Rights Act after Brexit, minister reveals',

violence has at the same time increased, especially in racist and misogynistic terms, leading in some instances to real violence.[90] Incidents of each of these red flags could prove to be short-lived and, although alarming while they last, could fade into the background of political turbulence that democratic societies go through periodically and that vary according to their institutional cultures. Yet when populist discourse about law involves one or more of them and accompanies endeavours to change the constitutional order or the substance and culture of the rule of law, the crisis arguably demands urgent critical attention.

Conclusion

We are not living in the 1920s 1930s there are contextual echoes today, but also contextual and systemic differences. Fascism is not immediately on our doorsteps, although in some parts of Europe its descendants are close to re-entering mainstream politics and parties echoing its style and language already have seats in some legislative assemblies. While pluralism must allow space for a range of perspectives from across the political spectrum, it does not necessarily mean that anti-democratic discourse can safely be accommodated, although to the extent that pluralism is able to foster informed public debate and support effective parliamentary processes, it can in many countries still dilute and oppose such tendencies. Even though populism is not the same as fascism, populist erosions of liberal-democratic principles can pave the way for an authoritarianism that will most probably entrench itself further if unopposed and could lead to something more extreme.

It is essential to analyse and conceptually differentiate these various trends, and to monitor actively the forms and content of politico-legal discourse, as well as the changes in practice that follow. Fascism came to power by degrees, and changed from its early manifestation as a movement into a regime,[91] following a trajectory that spanned insertion into mainstream politics, reliance on authoritarian law, merger of party with state, deprivation of liberties and attempts at socio-political

---

Independent, 18 January 2019, online at: https://www.independent.co.uk/news/uk/politics/theresa-may-human-rights-act-repeal-brexit-echr-commons-parliament-conservatives-a8734886.html (last accessed 26 January 2022).

[90] On the connections between Donald Trump's political discourse and 'white nationalist' violence see: D. Schnazer, 'We must call the El Paso shooting what it is: Trump-inspired terrorism', *Guardian*, 5 August 2019, https://www.theguardian.com/commentisfree/2019/aug/05/trump-inspired-terrorism-el-paso (last accessed 26 January 2022). On the dangers of 'violent and dehumanising' language and inflammatory rhetoric in UK politics see: 'Theresa May: "Be careful about language" on Brexit', *BBC News*, 22 October 2018, https://www.bbc.co.uk/news/uk-politics-45938754 (last accessed 26 January 2022) and B. Quinn and V. Dodd, 'Heated rhetoric by politicians "risks triggering violence"', *Guardian*, 26 September 2019, online at: https://www.theguardian.com/uk-news/2019/sep/26/heated-rhetoric-by-politicians-risks-triggering-violence (last accessed 26 January 2022).

[91] Paxton, *The Anatomy of Fascism*, p. 23.

totalisation. Recent experience in Central Europe and elsewhere has shown that, just as in the early 20th century, constitutional law and legal culture alone cannot always protect liberal democracy.[92] It is therefore important to be aware of the nature and possible implications of political and legal changes as they start to happen if they are to be resisted more effectively.

[92] Graver, *Judges Against Justice*, p. 276; note also Graver, 'Why Adolf Hitler Spared the Judges', 874–77 on the potential strengths of attachment to the rule of law and judicial independence in the Western legal tradition.

Part III

Judicial Independence in Context: From Criminal Justice to 'Law and Emotions' Studies and Looking to the Future of Judicial Independence

10

Judicial Independence and Countering Terrorism in the UK

JOHN D. JACKSON

TERRORIST VIOLENCE CAN lead not only to dreadful loss of life and physical destruction, but also to states taking disproportionate measures that threaten core principles and values that have long been held dear, such as the independence of the judiciary.[1] In the aftermath of 9/11, a number of states resorted to declarations of war and permanent states of emergency to counter terrorism that were validated by reference to a series of UN Security Council resolutions that have recognised that terrorism constitutes a threat to international peace and security.[2] One of the consequences has been the establishment of special courts and military commissions to try civilians charged with acts of terrorism, the military commissions in Guantánamo Bay being perhaps the most infamous example of this. Although international human rights bodies have not gone so far as to prohibit such courts as a rule, they rarely pass muster because they fail to achieve the independence, impartiality and judicial guarantees required by human rights and humanitarian law.[3] In a number of contexts in which military courts have been established, judges have been given temporary or provisional appointments, or they have been in a direct chain of command with the forces who have captured, detained and interrogated those before the court. Some human rights bodies have gone further and extended the protections of independence beyond the separation of powers and judicial conditions of service. One

---

[1] Cf. the comment of Lord Hoffmann in *A v SSHD* [2004] UKHL, [2005] 1 AC 68 [96]-[97] that serious terrorist violence in the UK has not threatened the institutions of government or our existence as a civil community; the real threat to the life of the nation comes from anti-terror laws such as the power of indefinite detention.

[2] Security Council resolutions 1373 (2001), 1456 (2003), 1566 (2004), 1624 (2005), 2178 (2014), 2341 (2017), 2354 (2017), 2368 (2017), 2370 (2017), 2395 (2017) and 2396 (2017).

[3] D. Weissbrodt and J. C. Hansen, 'The Right to a Fair Trial in an Extraordinary Court' in F. Ní Aoláin and O. Gross (eds.), *Guantánamo and Beyond: Exceptional Courts and Military Commissions in Comparative Perspective* (Cambridge, Cambridge University Press, 2013), p. 314.

Proceedings of the British Academy, **250**, 181–199, © The British Academy 2022.

particular example is the approach the Inter-American Court of Human Rights adopted towards the faceless Peruvian military courts that were set up in 1992 to try civilians charged with terrorist activities.[4] The Court rejected Peru's argument that the courts had been lawfully established and their independence was guaranteed under the Constitution by saying that the military tribunals were not the tribunals previously established by law for civilians. According to the Court, '[a] basic principle of the independence of the judiciary is that every person has the right to be heard by regular courts, following procedures previously established by law'.[5] It was therefore a violation of the right to an independent tribunal to try a civilian in an extraordinary military court for a matter that a regular court should hear.

Human rights instruments permit states in time of 'war or other public emergency threatening the life of the nation' to take measures derogating from their human rights obligations 'to the extent strictly required by the exigencies of the situation'.[6] It is accepted that some terrorist acts and the actions of terrorist organisations can create necessary and sufficient conditions to activate the threshold of emergency under both national and international law.[7] However, although states are given a certain margin of appreciation over the declaration of an emergency, they have clear obligations under international law, especially international human rights law, refugee law and humanitarian law. The UN Special Rapporteur on the Protection of Human Rights and Fundamental Freedoms has stressed that the declaration of an emergency does not give states 'carte blanche' to do whatever they wish.[8] Although the rights to liberty and to a fair trial are not formally non-derogable rights, international bodies such as the UN Human Rights Committee are increasingly moving to close a perceived weakness in the derogation system by declaring that certain aspects of due process protections such as guarantees of judicial independence are effectively non-derogable whatever the emergency.[9] In two Advisory Opinions dating back to 1987, the Inter-American Court of Human Rights found that certain derogable rights under the Convention are effectively rendered non-derogable by giving an expansive interpretation to the meaning of 'judicial guarantees' in Article 27(2) so that even when persons are detained and denied a fair trial, they still have a right to be brought before a court and to challenge the lawfulness of their detention before an independent and impartial judge.[10]

---

[4] *Castillo Petruzzi v Peru*, Judgment, Inter-AmCtHR (ser. C) No. 52 (1999).

[5] *Castillo Petruzzi v Peru*, para. 129.

[6] European Convention on Human Rights Art. 15(1); cf. American Convention on Human Rights Art. 27(1).

[7] UN Rapporteur, *Report of the Special Rapporteur on the promotion and protection of human rights and fundamental freedoms while countering terrorism on the human rights challenge of states of emergency in the context of countering terrorism* (2018) A/HRC/37/5.2, para. 3.

[8] UN Rapporteur, *Report*, para. 66.

[9] UN Rapporteur, *Report*, para. 42.

[10] Inter-American Court of Human Rights, Judicial Guarantees in States of Emergency (Arts. 27(2), 25 and 8 of the American Convention on Human Rights), Advisory Opinion OC-9/87 (October 1987) (OEA/Ser.L/VI/111.9, doc. 13), p. 40; and Habeas Corpus in Emergency Situations (Arts. 27(2), 25(1) and 7(6)

Human rights bodies therefore recognise the fundamental importance that must be attached to the independence of the judiciary whether states declare a state of emergency or not. With its wealth of experience of conflicts involving terrorism throughout the 20th century,[11] the UK has not recently resorted to special or military courts and has instead used the ordinary judiciary to review executive action and to try terrorist cases.[12] But this strategy poses its own challenges for the judiciary. The more the ordinary judiciary is employed to implement controversial special measures and procedures designed to counter terrorism, the greater the risk that their independence will be impugned. The UN Special Rapporteur has praised the UK for establishing an Independent Reviewer of Terrorism Legislation to keep terrorism legislation under review.[13] But we shall see that this does not mean that the legislation enacted has been uncontroversial.

This chapter seeks to review how the judiciary has risen to the challenge of maintaining its independence in the face of the measures taken to counter terrorism in the UK over the past 50 years. It will be argued that while judicial independence has managed to remain unscathed throughout both recent phases of terrorism, there is a danger that the secret judicial processes that are now used to assess whether individuals pose a risk of terrorism propagate a perception that behind closed doors, judges are deferring too readily to the executive. Before coming to the issues of judicial independence, however, we need to consider what the terrorist threat has been and how the UK has reacted to it.

UK terrorism and counter-terrorism: Two phases

Over the past 50 years or so, there have been two main phases of terrorist activity within the UK: Northern Irish, or so-called Troubles-based terrorism dating back to the beginning of the 1970s; and more recently since 9/11, global Islamist or so-called jihadi-based terrorism.[14] Although some terrible atrocities have been inflicted in the more recent phase of terrorism and much fear has arisen because of the indiscriminate way in which it is carried out with the potential for massive casualties, it is important not to lose a sense of perspective in terms of the actual fatalities caused by this terrorism in comparison with those that have arisen out of Northern Irish terrorism. Figures show that from 1970 until the end of 2017 there have been 3,410 fatalities caused by terrorism in the UK, but 85.66% of these were due to

---

of the American Convention on Human Rights), Advisory Opinion OC-8/87 (January 1987) (OEA/Ser.L/V/111.17, doc. 13), p. 33.

[11] D. Bonner, *Executive Measures, Terrorism and National Security* (Aldershot, Ashgate, 2007).

[12] Cf. the use of military courts to try Irish civilians during the First World War. See S. Enright, *The Trial of Civilians by Military Courts in Ireland 1921* (Salins, Irish Academic Press, 2012).

[13] UN Rapporteur, *Report*, para. 75.

[14] S. Greer, 'Terrorism and Counter-Terrorism in the UK: From Northern Irish Troubles to Global Islamist Jihad' in G. Lennon, C. King and C. McCartney (eds.), *Counter-terrorism, Constitutionalism and Miscarriages of Justice* (Oxford, Hart Publishing, 2019), pp. 45–62.

Troubles-based Northern Ireland terrorism from 1970 to 1990.[15] From 9/11 until the end of 2017, there were 127 fatalities in the UK, mostly (but not exclusively) at the hand of 'jihadi-based' terrorists – that is an annual average of eight deaths.

In each of these phases of terrorism, the UK's early reaction was to resort to draconian executive measures. The Northern Ireland government's response to the rise in IRA terrorist violence in 1971 was to introduce internment under special emergency powers legislation dating back to the origins of partition, which represented the primary method of dealing with terrorism in Northern Ireland throughout its history.[16] The strategy badly misfired as it had the effect of escalating the violence instead of reducing it and proved to be a 'recruiting sergeant' for further IRA volunteers.[17] When the violence spread to mainland Britain, most dramatically in the Birmingham pub bombings that killed 21 people in 1974, the UK government revived a measure that had previously been used in the Second World War to exclude suspected Irish terrorists from the mainland by empowering the Secretary of State to make exclusion orders prohibiting suspected terrorists from being in Great Britain.[18] Like internment, this strategy also proved counterproductive as exporting terrorism to Northern Ireland was not an effective means of preventing it altogether.[19]

Although these measures remained on the statute book for many years, it was clear that another strategy would have to be found to contain the violence, and members of the judiciary played a part in developing a new approach. When the British government took over direct control for the affairs of Northern Ireland in 1972, it commissioned the Diplock Commission under the chairmanship of Lord Diplock, a Lord of Appeal in Ordinary, to consider 'whether changes should be made in the administration of justice in order to deal more effectively with terrorism without using internment under the Special Powers Act'.[20] This was the first in a long line of independent reports and reviews of counter-terrorism measures within the UK undertaken by both serving or retired members of judiciary that paved the way slowly towards more proportionate and human rights compliant methods for dealing with terrorism through the ordinary judicial system. The Diplock report marked the beginnings of a strategy that became known as 'criminalisation', which gradually superseded the internment approach for dealing with terrorism. The report considered that any criminalisation through the ordinary courts should comply with the minimum requirements for a criminal trial laid down in Article 6

---

[15] See the University of Maryland's Global Terrorism Database, online at: https://www.start.umd.edu/gtd/ (last accessed 26 January 2022).

[16] Civil Authorities (Special Powers) Act (NI) 1922.

[17] Bonner, *Executive Measures*, p. 90 citing Standing Advisory Commission on Human Rights, *Report* (1976–77) ch. 4.

[18] Prevention of Terrorism Act 1974, s. 3(3((b).

[19] C. Walker, *The Prevention of Terrorism in British Law*, 2nd edn (Manchester, Manchester University Press, 1992), pp. 88–89.

[20] Lord Diplock, *Report of the Commission to consider legal procedures to deal with terrorist activities in Northern Ireland* (London, HMSO, 1972) Cmnd 5185.

of the ECHR – although as we shall see, the jury-less Diplock courts that it recommended were controversial and the emergency legislation that resulted gave sweeping powers of arrest and questioning to the security forces.[21] Long before the enactment of the Human Rights Act 1998 that effectively incorporated the European Convention on Human Rights (ECHR) into UK law, however, the report's reference to the ECHR set an important baseline against which all future legislation directed at containing Northern Ireland terrorism could be judged.

Later independent reviews paid even more regard to the ECHR. Three years later, the Gardiner Committee, under the chairmanship of Lord Gardiner, a former Labour Lord Chancellor, sitting with two Northern Ireland judges, was specifically commissioned to consider measures to deal with terrorism 'in the context of civil liberties and human rights'.[22] Although, like Diplock, the Committee did not feel able to recommend an immediate end to internment, it further entrenched the criminalisation policy by asserting that executive detention could not remain as a long-term policy. As Northern Ireland terrorism declined and momentum built towards the peace process that culminated in the Belfast peace agreement,[23] the process of criminalisation was given unqualified approval in the Lloyd report in 1996, which made a number of recommendations for dealing with terrorism within the ordinary law.[24] This led to the enactment of the Terrorism Act 2000, which saw an end to internment and exclusion orders, and to this day remains the foremost piece of counter-terrorist legislation in the UK.

The events of 9/11 marked a shift in turning attention away from Northern Ireland terrorism towards global 'international' terrorism, which was said to pose a terrorist threat 'quite distinct from anything that we have previously faced'.[25] Rather than sticking to an exclusive policy of criminalisation in combatting this threat, the government reverted to a policy of exclusion and indefinite detention by enacting the Anti-terrorism, Crime and Security Act 2001 and entering a derogation under Article 15 of the ECHR because such detention failed to comply with Article 5(1)(f). The Act empowered the Secretary of State to issue certificates for the indefinite detention of suspected international terrorists when it was not possible to deport or remove them from the UK because subjecting them to the threat of persecution abroad would breach Article 3 of the ECHR. In the new era of human rights compliance under the Human Rights Act, however, the judiciary played a greater role in constraining the government's inclination towards draconian measures in this phase of terrorism than it did in the Northern Ireland phase. When the UK's

---

[21] Northern Ireland (Emergency Provisions) Act 1973.
[22] Lord Gardiner, *Report of a Committee to consider, in the context of civil liberties and human rights, measures to deal with terrorism in Northern Ireland* (London, HMSO, 1975) Cmnd 5847.
[23] *The Belfast Agreement: an agreement reached at the multi-party talks on Northern Ireland* (London, Stationery Office, 1998) Cm 3883.
[24] Lord Lloyd, *Inquiry into Legislation Against Terrorism* (London, HMSO, 1996) Cm 3420.
[25] Hansard (HL) vol 629, col 142 (27 November 2001) (Lord Goldsmith) cited in C. Walker, *Blackstone's Guide to the Anti-Terrorism Legislation* (Oxford, Oxford University Press, 2014) p. 30.

derogation was challenged by a number of persons who had been detained under the 2001 Act, the House of Lords, by a majority of 8–1, declared the legislation to be incompatible with the ECHR because the measures taken were disproportionate and discriminatory, as they were directed at non-nationals only.[26]

Rather than release those subject to indefinite detention unconditionally, the government responded by enacting further executive measures known as control orders that imposed severe restrictions on the movement and association of suspected terrorists and were later replaced by somewhat less draconian 'terrorism prevention investigation measures' (TPIMs).[27] After the events of 7 July 2005, when bombs killed 52 people on the London Underground and Tony Blair famously announced that the 'rules of the game' were changing, foreign suspects were subjected to new measures relating to deportation, exclusion and nationality.[28] At the same time, the realisation that a number of terrorists were not foreign but 'homegrown' led to a renewed emphasis on criminalisation.[29] A number of new terrorist offences and investigative powers, notably 28-day detention before charge (since reduced to 14 days),[30] were contained in the Terrorism Act 2006. The shift towards criminalisation can be seen by comparing the figures for terrorism-related prosecutions against the number of TPIMs in force from 2012 until 2016. As shown in Table 10.1, there have been many more terrorism-related prosecutions than TPIMs. What then have been the challenges to judicial independence posed by these measures? We shall first look at judicial review of executive measures before coming to judicial involvement in criminal cases.

Judicial review of executive measures

Judges can face challenges to their independence when they are co-opted into reviews of executive measures that require them to apply procedures that fall short of recognised due process standards. A good example of this was when 'quasi-judicial' hearings were convened to review detentions in order to present internment without trial with a 'better face' after the British imposed direct rule on Northern Ireland in March 1972.[31] In order to protect the security and safety of sources who gave information to the authorities, the review procedures fell short of fundamental guarantees of due process. The hearings were in private, normal rules of evidence

---

[26] *A v SSHD* [2004] UKHL 56, [2005] 1 AC 68.

[27] Prevention of Terrorism Act 2005, Terrorism Prevention Investigation Measures Act 2011.

[28] Specifically, a new approach was taken towards deportation whereby the government would seek diplomatic assurances that deportees would not be subjected to ill-treatment by the countries to which they returned. See J. Tooze, 'Deportation with assurances' [2010] PL 362.

[29] C. Walker, 'Terrorism Prosecution in the United Kingdom' in Ní Aoláin and Gross, *Guantánamo and Beyond*, pp. 246–248.

[30] Protection of Freedoms Act 2012, s. 57.

[31] Bonner, *Executive Measures*, p. 91.

were waived, screens were used to protect the identity of witnesses and parts of the hearing could be held in the absence of the detainee or his legal representative in the interests of public safety or the safety of any persons.[32] Judges were co-opted from outside Northern Ireland – from Scotland, England and Wales, and even Nigeria – and the appeal tribunal was chaired by a former England and Wales Court of Appeal judge. The proceedings were by no means 'rubber-stamps', and figures showed that a number of releases were ordered.[33] But the procedures were phased out after Lord Gardiner made stringent criticism of them. Although the criticism was not directed at the judicial commissioners themselves, the procedures were described as a 'veneer' to an enquiry that bore no relationship to common law procedures, and their apparent similarity to ordinary judicial processes was bringing the ordinary processes of law in Northern Ireland into disrepute.[34]

In many ways, these proceedings can be seen as the 'forerunner' of the 'open' and 'closed' session procedures that take place in the Special Immigration Appeals Commission (SIAC), which sits to hear secret evidence in immigration cases and also heard appeals by foreign nationals against certificates issued by the Secretary of State under the 2001 Act.[35] Similar procedures were later introduced in High Court hearings established to review those who had been subject to control orders and later TPIMs by the Home Secretary.[36] One difference between these procedures and those used in the Northern Ireland secret procedures is that security-cleared lawyers, known as special advocates, are appointed to represent the interests of detainees in the closed proceedings. Although the use of special advocates was prompted by the ECtHR decision in *Chahal v UK*,[37] which appeared to endorse the view that they provide a substantial measure of procedural fairness, there has been much unease about their use within the judiciary. In one case, Lord Steyn described the special advocate procedure as completely lacking the essential characteristic of a fair hearing.[38] Later, a majority of the Supreme Court in *Al Rawi v The Security Service*[39] considered that the courts had no inherent power to authorise closed procedures with special advocates in a common law civil claim because such procedures undermined the key tenets of justice that the courts had spent centuries defending.

---

[32] Detention of Terrorists (Northern Ireland) Order (1972 No. 1632 NI 15) Arts. 14-17 later incorporated in the Northern Ireland (Emergency Provisions) Act 1973. For a description of the procedures see K. Boyle, T. Hadden and P. Hillyard, *Law and State: The Case of Northern Ireland* (London, Martin Robertson, 1975), pp. 59–61, R. J. Spjut, 'Internment and Detention without Trial in Northern Ireland 1971–1975: Ministerial Policy and Practice' (1986) 49 MLR 712, Bonner, *Executive Measures*, pp. 93–94, L. Donohue, *Counter-Terrorist Law and Emergency Powers in the United Kingdom 1922–2000* (Dublin, Irish Academic Press, 2001).

[33] Boyle, Hadden and Hillyard, *Law and State*, p. 70. Bonner, *Executive Measures*, p. 94.

[34] Lord Gardiner, *Report* [152]-[154].

[35] Bonner, *Executive Measures* pp. 93–94.

[36] Civil Procedures Rules Pt 76, Pt 80.

[37] (1996) 23 EHRR 413.

[38] *Roberts v Parole Board* [2005] UKHL 45, [2005] 2 AC 738 [88].

[39] *Al Rawi v The Security Service* [2011] UKSC 34, [2012] 1 AC 531.

When closed procedures were challenged by appellants who had been detained under the 2001 Act on the ground they did not measure up to the requirements of Article 5(4) of the ECHR, the ECtHR in a unanimous Grand Chamber ruling in *A v UK*[40] considered that the special advocate procedure could perform an important role in counterbalancing the lack of a full, adversarial hearing by testing the evidence and putting arguments on behalf of the detainee. But the Court held that the special advocate could not perform this in any useful way unless the detainee was provided with sufficient information about the allegations against him to give effective instructions to the special advocate. The need for a core gist of the allegations against one has since been made a requirement for all cases affecting the liberty of the individual, including those subjected to control orders and TPIMs.[41] But this has not ended the controversy about special advocates. Lord Bingham summed up the continuing unease about them when he said that the right of those in jeopardy to know the case against them has not perhaps been 'effectively gutted' by the special advocate procedures but has been severely restricted in cases where the authorities are unwilling to disclose sensitive security information to those in jeopardy, and this was not a situation that proponents of the rule of law could view without unease.[42]

When judges are seen to be involved in procedures that lack the hallmark of the rule of law, there is a danger that their reputation for independence and impartiality can become sullied. The intelligence information that is relied on by the state in these proceedings may lack the robustness of evidence that is put before an open court, and the courts are consequently asked to accept evidence of a quality that would not be accepted in a public proceeding. It is also the case that the threshold evidential test that must be met by the government is very much lower than in a conventional civil or criminal trial. But a survey of SIAC cases suggests that it is possible for appellants to mount successful challenges.[43] As Table 10.2 shows, in a survey of 107 substantive appeals, reviews or bail applications between 2003 and 2017 reported on SIAC's database of open judgments where special advocates were involved and there was therefore some closed evidence, it was found that 21 were successful outcomes for the appellants, a headline success figure of 19.6%. Where it was possible from the open judgments to make some estimate of whether the outcomes were based on mainly open or closed evidence, it was estimated that 9 out of 19 successful outcomes (47%) were based on closed or a mix of open and closed evidence. Although this shows that SIAC is not simply 'rubber-stamping' government cases when the case is based on closed evidence, the question remains whether the secrecy of the process and the fact that justice is not being seen to be done undermines trust in the whole process, including the trust in the judiciary to

[40] *A v UK* (2009) 49 EHRR 29.
[41] *SSHD v AF* [2009] UKHL 28, [2010] 2 AC 269.
[42] T. Bingham, *The Rule of Law* (London, Penguin, 2011), p. 151.
[43] J. Jackson, *Special Advocates in the Adversarial System* (Abingdon, Routledge, 2019), pp. 214–217.

act independently. We will come back to this question when we have looked at the challenges judges have faced in criminal cases.

The Diplock courts

The shift towards criminalisation that has characterised British policy in both phases of terrorism over the past 50 years has presented more challenges for judges in terms of maintaining their independence from the executive than the policy of executive intervention. For the policy of criminalisation shifts the focus for dealing with terrorist activities away from the executive towards the criminal trial. This was to prove a particular challenge for judges in the so-called Diplock trials in Northern Ireland.

The non-jury Diplock courts were not special courts in the sense that they involved any derogation from the ordinary fair standards set out in Article 6. We have seen that Lord Diplock set these standards as the baseline. Nor were they special in the sense that they co-opted special judges who had special terms and conditions from other judges. The Diplock trials were heard in Belfast Crown Court and the judges who sat in them were ordinary judges who continued to preside in jury trials for what were known as 'ordinary decent criminals'. Nevertheless, the absence of the jury in the Diplock trials was very significant.[44] Although it required no derogation from Article 6 of the ECHR, the jury has long been a symbolic centrepiece of British justice, giving ordinary citizens the function of determining guilt or innocence in serious cases. In the absence of the jury, judges had to combine their traditional role of umpiring a contest between the state and the accused with a new fact-finding role. This meant being put in the front line of maintaining law and order as it was ultimately their responsibility to decide whom to convict and whom to acquit.[45]

In this situation, it was perhaps inevitable that judges would attract criticism. At first, many of the Diplock cases relied heavily on the use of confessions, and there were grave concerns about the way in which these had been obtained at designated interrogation terrorist centres (at Castlereagh and Gough). In particular, there were credible reports conducted by Amnesty International, among others, that there had been maltreatment of suspects at these centres.[46] The courts became tainted with these allegations when they were seen to uphold confessions obtained at these centres. A combination of a more relaxed standard of admissibility for confessions imposed by Parliament,[47] the difficulty of deciding who to believe when allegations

---

[44] For a full comparison between 'Diplock' trials and jury trials, see J. Jackson and S. Doran, *Judge without Jury; Diplock Trials in the Adversary System* (Oxford, Clarendon, 1995).

[45] For discussion of this invidious role and how it impacted on attitudes towards the judiciary, see S. Doran and J. Jackson, 'The judicial role in criminal cases' in N. Dawson, D. Greer and P. Ingram (eds.), *One Hundred and Fifty Years of Irish Law* (Belfast, SLS Publications, 1996), p. 69.

[46] *Report of an Amnesty International Mission to Northern Ireland* (London, Amnesty International, 1978).

[47] Northern Ireland (Emergency Provisions) Act 1978, s. 8.

of ill-treatment were made and the absence of a jury that meant judges had to decide themselves on the truth of confessions all conspired to damage the judiciary's reputation for independence. Instead of being associated with a relatively benign criminalisation policy that was different in kind from internment without trial, the Diplock courts and the judges alongside them became associated with a security strategy of putting people behind bars on the basis of dubious confessions. The courts then suffered a further blow to their reputation when suspects were used to become informants – 'supergrasses', as they were known – against their former paramilitary associates. Suspects were rounded up on the word of these informants and detained for long periods pending trial. When judges began to convict on this basis, criticism inevitably followed.[48]

But then, just as large numbers of supergrasses and supergrass trials threatened to overwhelm the courts and engulf them in a major crisis of legitimacy, the Lord Chief Justice, Lord Lowry, in a landmark case in 1983, quoted Lord Atkin's famous dictum in *Liversidge v Anderson*[49] involving executive power at the height of the Second World War that:

> In this country, amid the clash of arms, the laws are *not* silent. They may be changed, but they speak the same language in war as in peace. This war is being waged by organisations that style themselves as armies and observe military procedures, but it has not invaded and will not be allowed to invade the courts. The rule of law has prevailed and will continue to prevail there.[50]

It would be wrong to characterise this judgment as marking a dramatic shift in judicial attitudes. Even in their darkest hour – during the confessions era of the 1970s and the supergrass era of the 1980s – the statistics did not bear up the charge that the courts were a mere 'rubber-stamp' for security strategies.[51] But there is no doubt that this intervention by the judiciary's most senior figure sent out a strong signal of the importance of the rule of law even in times of the gravest emergency and that the courts would not succumb to executive pressure. Convictions on the basis of uncorroborated 'supergrass' testimony came to a halt. The judgment marked a turning point in rehabilitating the reputation of the Diplock courts at just the moment when their credibility was being questioned as never before. The courts continued to operate beyond the Northern Ireland conflict and survived the post-conflict peace process. After the Belfast/Good Friday Agreement, many of the trappings of the emergency system that were put in place in the 1970s – special rules governing the admissibility of confessions, the presumption against jury trial in respect of many offences – were reversed, but Diplock trials remained intact. They continue to be

---

[48] S. Greer, *Supergrasses: Informers and anti-terrorist law enforcement in Northern Ireland* (Oxford, Clarendon, 1995).

[49] *Liversidge v Anderson* [1942] AC 2016, 244.

[50] *R v Gibney and others* [1983] 13 NIQB 8.

[51] For discussion of the claim that Diplock judges became 'case-hardened', see Jackson and Doran, *Judge without Jury*, pp. 33–36.

deployed in a small number of cases involving dissident republican or loyalist para-militaries, and there is very little pressure for them to be abolished.[52]

The ordinary criminal courts

Just when the reputation of the Diplock courts was beginning to be rehabilitated in the late 1980s, across the water, a crisis of confidence in the ordinary courts was sparked when the Court of Appeal was forced to quash a number of convictions arising out of IRA bombings on the mainland in the 1970s. The cases of the Birmingham Six, the Guildford Four, the Maguire Seven and Judith Ward led to the establishment of a Royal Commission on Criminal Justice to address the failings that led to such miscarriages of justice.[53] It was not the judges who were responsible for the convictions but juries, and the fault for the miscarriages of justice lay largely in the investigation processes of the police and forensic scientists in the way confessions were extracted and scientific evidence was handled, and in the failures in disclosure of evidence.[54] But the cases betrayed attitudes on the part of certain judges that showed undue deference towards police evidence, of which the most famous example was Lord Denning's statement in 1980 upholding an appeal by West Midlands police against a civil action that those convicted of the Birmingham pub bombings were seeking to bring against the police for injuries they received in police custody. In his words:

> If the action were to proceed and the six men won, that would mean the police were guilty of perjury, that they were guilty of violence and threats, that the confessions were involuntary and that the convictions were erroneous, all of which would be such an appalling vista that every sensible person in the land would say: 'it cannot be right that these actions should go any further'.[55]

Looking back now at these words, they seem very much the product of a bygone age. Lord Denning himself later admitted that he was wrong and that the West Midland detectives had 'let us all down'.[56] It is inconceivable today that judges would express such unreserved confidence in police evidence. Too many failings in police investigations have since come to light, a long-standing one being the non-disclosure of police evidence.[57]

[52] J. Jackson, 'Many years on in Northern Ireland: the Diplock legacy' (2009) 60 *Northern Ireland Legal Quarterly* 213.

[53] Royal Commission on Criminal Justice, *Report* (London, HMSO, 1990) Cm 2263.

[54] S. Poyser, A. Nurse and R. Milne, *Miscarriages of Justice: Causes, consequences and remedies* (Bristol, Polity Press, 2018).

[55] *McIlkenny v Chief Constable of West Midlands Police Force* [1980] 2 All ER 227, 239–240.

[56] C. Dyer, 'Lord Denning, controversial people's judge, dies aged 100', *Guardian*, 6 March 1999, online at: https://www.theguardian.com/uk/1999/mar/06/claredyer1 (last accessed 26 January 2022).

[57] HMCPSI and HMIC, *Making it Fair; A Joint Inspection of the Disclosure of Unused Material in Volume Crown Court Cases* (2017) online at: https://www.justiceinspectorates.gov.uk/cjji/wp-content/uploads/sites/2/2017/07/CJJI_DSC_thm_July17_rpt.pdf (last accessed 26 January 2022).

Today, the judges presiding over terrorist trials are very experienced. The 2015 Criminal Practice Directions on the case management of terrorism cases state that all indictable terrorism cases will be managed by High Court judges nominated by the President of the Queen's Bench Division.[58] If the number of terrorist cases was to rise significantly, this could lead to a concern that certain judges were spending so much of their time in terrorist cases that they were effectively becoming specialist national security judges. There is, however, little sign of this happening, and for the moment, reliance on experienced High Court judges for dealing with these cases seems sensible.

The challenge of secrecy

This does not mean that there are not some concerns about how the judiciary is perceived when the principle of open justice is departed from in terrorist trials. We earlier raised the question of whether judicial scrutiny of executive measures in secret hearings undermines trust in the independence of the judiciary. Criminal proceedings can be characterised as the archetypal dispute between the state and the individual requiring proceedings to be as transparent as possible. But the growing trend in the use of secret evidence in national security law appears to be seeping into criminal proceedings as well as other proceedings. It is true that the Justice and Security Act 2013, which was enacted in reaction to the decision in *Al Rawi*, authorises the use of closed procedures in any type of civil proceeding but specifically excludes proceedings 'in a criminal cause or matter' from its remit.[59] It is not (yet) possible to withhold any of the evidence the prosecution intends to rely upon at trial against a defendant. But it has for some time been open to the prosecution to make what is known as a Public Interest Immunity (PII) application to the court before trial in the absence of the defence that it should be exempted in the public interest from having to make full disclosure of material that would otherwise have to be disclosed. Although, like closed procedures, this departure from open justice was originally conceived as a procedure to be adopted in only exceptional cases, it has been argued that there has been a degree of normalisation in the use of PII claims.[60]

In such cases, it is for the judge to make an independent decision as to whether the public interest in non-disclosure is outweighed by the public interest in securing justice.[61] But the difficulty is that he or she is determining an issue behind closed doors in the absence of one of the parties, which may have a material bearing on the overall outcome of the case and create a risk of a miscarriage of justice. In *Edwards*

---

[58] Criminal Practice Directions 2015 [2015] EWCA Crim 1567, CPD XIII Listing, Annex 4: Case Management of Terrorism Cases.

[59] Justice and Security Act 2013, s. 6(11).

[60] S. McKay, 'The Doctrine of Public Interest Immunity and Fair Trial Guarantees' in Lennon *et al, Counter-terrorism*, p. 209.

[61] *R v Chief Constable of West Midlands Police, ex parte Wiley* [1995] 1 AC 274, 280.

and Lewis v UK,[62] the ECtHR held that there was a breach of Article 6 of the ECHR in two cases where the material that was not disclosed to the defence after a PII hearing related to an issue that the judge had ultimately to decide, namely the issue of entrapment. As the defence had been denied access to the material, in the court's opinion, it was not possible for them to argue the entrapment point fully before the judge. In the aftermath of this case, the House of Lords accepted it may in an exceptional case be necessary in the interests of justice to appoint a special counsel to be appointed who would represent the interests of the defence in the PII hearing.[63] This may help to obviate the risk of a miscarriage of justice, although much will depend on the degree of access the special counsel is given to what the accused's defence is. Like special advocates, special counsel are barred from communicating with defendants and their legal representatives once they are given access to sensitive information. But it does not deal with the point that justice is still being dispensed behind closed doors. The concern is particularly acute in national security cases. Here the judge is presented with a ministerial certificate that requires the relevant minister to be satisfied that any disclosure 'would cause real risk of serious prejudice to an important public interest'.[64] Lawyers on behalf of the executive then make arguments about disclosure of the material in private. However independent the judge's decision, the lack of transparency does not help to instil confidence that justice has been done.

The principle of open justice is undermined even more when trials themselves are heard in private. Under section 8 of the Official Secrets Act 1920, any part of a trial involving offences under the Act may be held in camera when publication of any evidence would be 'prejudicial to the national safety'.[65] But a new precedent seemed to be set a few years ago when a trial judge in a terrorist case involving two defendants made an order that the entire trial be held in private (i.e., in-camera, with the public and the media excluded) and that the publication of reports of the trial would be prohibited, including the names and identities of the defendants. On an appeal lodged by media groups, the Court of Appeal in *Guardian News and Media and others v Incedal and Rarmoul-Bouhadjar*[66] limited the judge's order somewhat by ruling that certain parts of the trial could be heard in public (such as the swearing-in of the jury, the reading of the charges, some of the judge's introductory remarks to the jury, parts of the prosecution opening and the verdicts and sentence) and that the defendants could be named. But the court ordered that the core of the trial would be held in private, although this did not preclude a review by the prosecution and the judge in the course of the trial and in the event, at the

---

[62] *Edwards and Lewis v UK* (2005) 40 EHRR 24.
[63] *R v H; R v C* [2004] UKHL 3, [2004] 2 AC 135: See J. Jackson, 'Is There a Need for Special Counsel in Criminal Proceedings?' [2020] Crim LR 772.
[64] CPS, *Disclosure Manual*, online at: https://www.cps.gov.uk/legal-guidance/disclosure-manual (last accessed 26 January 2022), chapter 34.
[65] Official Secrets Act 1920, s. 8(4).
[66] *Guardian News and Media v Incedal and Rarmoul-Bouhadjar* [2014] EWCA Crim 1861.

behest of the prosecution, substantially more of the trial was held in open court than the Court of Appeal had directed.[67] After the trial, the media applied to have the reporting restrictions lifted, the judge dismissed the application, and the Court of Appeal dismissed the appeal.[68] The Lord Chief Justice, Lord Thomas, took the opportunity to set out the principles at stake. He said the principle of open justice is fundamental to the rule of law and to democratic accountability, but he went on to cite a passage from Lord Diplock's judgment in *Attorney General v Leveller Magazine Ltd*,[69] that it was sometimes necessary to depart from this principle where 'the nature or circumstances of the particular proceedings are such that the general rule in its entirety would frustrate or render impracticable the administration of justice'. However, he repeated Lord Diplock's important words that:

> Apart from statutory exceptions, however, where a court in the exercise of its inherent power to control the conduct of proceedings before it departs in any way from the general rule, the departure is justified to the extent and to no more than the extent that the court reasonably believes it to be necessary in order to serve the ends of justice.[70]

The other important point that Lord Thomas stressed was a constitutional one that has a particular bearing on the independence of the judiciary. He made it clear that where the reason for departing from the principle of open justice is based on reasons relating to national security, it is for the court and the court alone to determine if this strict necessity test has been met. The reasons will often be contained in a certificate submitted to the court by the Director of Public Prosecutions (DPP) on behalf of the Secretary of State. While the court will pay the highest regard to what is stated in the certificate and should not depart from the view of the Secretary of State on national security issues provided there is an evidential basis for it, the court is always free to depart from the views set out in the certificate as to the weight to be attached to the national security interests because it is always for the court to make the decision on whether those interests necessitate the departure from the principle of open justice. Furthermore, the DPP's view as to whether or not the prosecution will continue if the evidence is to be heard in public is not the determining factor because there is an important distinction in the constitutional functions of the court and the prosecutor. Determining the matter on the basis of the DPP's view would remove from the court its proper constitutional function of determining whether a departure from the principle of open justice is justified, as the decision would rest on the implicit threat of the DPP not to prosecute unless the court were to defer to the view of the DPP.

While this is an admirable attempt to uphold the independence of the judiciary and the separation of functions between the prosecution and the court, when it comes to determining whether the evidence in issue should be heard in open court

---

[67] As reported in *Guardian News and Media Ltd v R & Incedal* [2016] EWCA Crim 11 [28].
[68] *Guardian News and Media Ltd v R & Incedal* [2016] EWCA Crim 11.
[69] *Attorney General v Leveller Magazine Ltd* [1979] AC 440, 450.
[70] *Attorney General v Leveller Magazine Ltd* [1979] AC 440, 450.

or not, in practice, it would seem to take a very brave judge to rule in favour of open justice where the evidence in issue affects national security, and the result of such a ruling will deter the prosecution from prosecuting the case where otherwise it should do so. The judge may in effect feel he or she has no choice but to order that the evidence be heard in private with the risk that he or she is seen as siding with the executive in prioritising national security over the demands of open justice.

It is true that some ameliorating steps were taken in this case to mitigate the effect of any departure from open justice and others were proposed by the Lord Chief Justice in his judgment. In the first appeal, the Court of Appeal broke new ground by permitting a small number (up to 10) of accredited journalists to be invited to attend the bulk of the trial on terms that compelled confidentiality. Although the motive of advancing public scrutiny by these means was laudable, there are questions about this policy.[71] It is not clear what the criteria should be for deciding who should be invited to attend and for deciding 'accreditation'. Furthermore, journalists may be disposed to moderate what they may report subsequently so as not to lose their accreditation. A further question is why other bodies such as the Law Society, the Bar Council or certain NGOs working in the area should not also be invited to attend. Another point made by the Lord Chief Justice is that the presence of accredited journalists during significant parts of the trial makes the management of the trial much more demanding than if the in-camera parts of the trial were simply conducted in the absence of the media.[72] This led the Court of Appeal to the firm view that a court should 'hesitate long and hard' before it makes an order similar to that made in this case.[73] Even when an order is made, journalists may continue to be prevented from publishing reports long after the trial, in which case, how does this really promote open justice? The Court of Appeal accepted that there will be cases where the need for public accountability cannot be achieved through the press in its function as 'watchdog' of the public interest, but on issues relating to terrorism it would be open to the Intelligence and Security Committee of Parliament to consider any issues it considers need to be examined and for public accountability to be achieved in that way. While this Committee may perform such a role, however, this would be very much an ex post facto review conducted perhaps long after the trial and would be unable to address lingering suspicions that justice behind closed doors may not have been done.

Another step mentioned by the Lord Chief Justice was that in determining whether to hear evidence in camera when the DPP makes an application, a trial judge might be greatly assisted in national security cases by an independent lawyer

---

[71] L. Woods, L. McNamara and J. Townsend, *Response to Law Commission Consultation (on the Protection of Official Data* (CP 230 (2017)), online at: https://binghamcentre.biicl.org/documents/14_law-commission-consultation-on-the-protection-of-official-information-woods-mcnamara-townend-09062017-final-online.pdf (last accessed 26 January 2022).

[72] *Guardian News and Media Ltd v R & Incedal* [2016] EWCA Crim 11 [68].

[73] *Guardian News and Media Ltd v R & Incedal* [2016] EWCA Crim 11 [69].

assigned to provide assistance.[74] This would seem to be akin to the appointment of an amicus to assist the judge, perhaps, although this is not mentioned, taking on the role of a special advocate or special counsel by putting countervailing points to those made by the DPP. Although this may assist the judge in coming to a truly independent decision on whether to order an in-camera hearing, it does not deal with the perception that if such a hearing is ordered, justice may be losing out to national security considerations.

Finally, the Lord Chief Justice in his judgment referred to the fact that, as a consequence of these procedures, it was likely that judges would for some time be faced with determining applications for parts of the trial to be held in camera for reasons of national security and there will be appeals to the Court of Appeal that will result in closed judgments that give the courts' reasoning.[75] The Lord Chief Justice was here referring to another downside to secret justice, namely that it results in closed judgments that are never exposed to the public. Apart from the closed judgments that the Court of Appeal had to issue in this case explaining why a departure from open justice was necessary, there have been other examples in terrorist cases of parts of judgments of the Court of Appeal being closed or redacted. In one case where the defendants with alleged links to Al-Qaeda were convicted of making fertiliser-based bombs to attack shopping centres, parts of the judgment of the Court of Appeal were redacted.[76] In another Northern Ireland case, virtually all of the Court of Appeal judgment quashing the conviction of a leader of Sinn Fein for being an accomplice in the kidnapping of a police informant was suppressed.[77] The danger here, and the same applies to the secret judgments in SIAC and other cases where closed procedures are ordered, is that a growing body of secret case law develops that is accessible only to the government and to certain security-cleared advocates. In the *Incedal* case, the Lord Chief Justice revealed that these judgments may not be accessible to anyone at all if they are not retained within court files with the result that they are lost for future reference. This led him to ask the Registrar of the Court of Appeal to set up a working party to see how closed judgments might be retained within the court files. Such files, of course, would remain closed to the public, including lawyers who are not security-cleared, which raises the further question of whether there should be somebody responsible over time for reviewing the necessity for keeping such judgments closed.

All these ameliorating steps are a poor second-best substitute for open justice.[78] *Incedal* was undoubtedly a very exceptional case and it seems that there has been no case like it since. But in the first appeal, the Court of Appeal seemed to brace itself for further cases when it declared that a necessary corollary of the policy of criminalisation (dealing with terrorists through the Criminal Justice System) was that the Crown should not be deterred from prosecuting cases of suspected

---

[74] *Guardian News and Media Ltd v R & Incedal* [2016] EWCA Crim 11 [66].
[75] *Guardian News and Media Ltd v R & Incedal* [2016] EWCA Crim 11 [77]-[78].
[76] *R v Omar Khyam* [2008] EWCA Crim 1612.
[77] *R v Morrison* [2009] NICA Crim 1.
[78] Woods *et al*, *Response to Law Commission Consultation* [4.14].

terrorism by the risk of material, properly secret, becoming public through the trial process.[79] This inevitably meant that there would be tensions between the principle of open justice and the needs of national security and, all the more so, as the security agencies come out of the shadows and cooperate closely with the police in the criminal justice system.[80]

In its consultation paper on the effectiveness of criminal law provisions that protect official information, the Law Commission provisionally concluded that it was necessary to undertake a separate review to consider whether the powers to order secret proceedings in civil cases in order to protect sensitive information could be 'tailored' for use in criminal cases.[81] But it is suggested that we should be very wary of any curtailment of open justice in criminal terrorist cases where it is vitally important to show, as Lord Lowry put it, that unlike terrorists we operate within the rule of law. In a memorable passage in a landmark decision some years ago, upholding the media's ability to be given access to court documents, Lord Justice Toulson made a vital connection between open justice and the rule of law when he said:

> The rule of law is a fine concept but fine words butter no parsnips and it can only be achieved through open justice which lets in the light and allows the public to scrutinise the workings of the law for better or for worse.[82]

Conclusion

It is time to draw to a close this retrospective analysis of whether the UK's counter-terrorism measures over the past 50 years have dented the judiciary's reputation for independence. Although the UK has eschewed the use of special military commissions or courts, which human rights bodies have claimed directly erode the principle of judicial independence, we have seen that the judiciary has been used to review executive measures by means of procedures that undermine core principles of due process and open justice. The use of blatantly unfair secret procedures to review detention measures in Northern Ireland in the early 1970s is an example of how such procedures can undermine trust in the judicial process. As a result of its ruling in *A v UK*, those subjected to control orders and TPIMs must at least be given notice of the core allegations against them, and special advocates act on their behalf in closed procedures. But concerns over the secrecy of these procedures raise questions about the damage that they could do to the reputation of the judicial process if they were to be deployed on a much greater scale than they have been.

The displacement of executive intervention in favour of criminalisation as the primary means of combatting terrorism has been hailed as a welcome trend as a

---

[79] *Guardian News and Media v Incedal and Rarmoul-Bouhadjar* [2014] EWCA Crim 1861 [14].
[80] *Guardian News and Media v Incedal and Rarmoul-Bouhadjar* [2014] EWCA Crim 1861 [15].
[81] Law Commission, *The Protection of Official Data: A Consultation Paper* (2017) CP 230.
[82] *R (Guardian News and Media Ltd) v City of Westminster Magistrates* [2012] EWCA Civ 420 [1].

criminal justice approach more consistent with legitimacy and fairness.[83] But, as we have seen, it has exposed the judiciary to challenges in terms of the need to preserve independence as the courts are put in the front line of both protecting the community from terrorism and respecting human rights and the rule of law. Over time, the judiciary in Northern Ireland weathered the controversies surrounding the Diplock courts by asserting the importance of the rule of law even in times of grave emergency. Judges in mainland Great Britain have not had to face anything like the number of terrorist cases that threatened to overwhelm the criminal courts in the darkest days of the 'Troubles', but they had to come to terms with the spectre of miscarriages of justice in Irish terrorism cases and, more recently, as we have seen, to deal with tensions between upholding the principle of open justice and the needs of national security. No one in recent years has questioned the commitment of the judiciary towards upholding their independence and the rule of law. The danger is more that secrecy prevents the public from seeing justice being done and risks undermining confidence in the judicial process.

This raises questions about the wisdom of resorting to criminal prosecution in national security cases where the evidence is intertwined with the need to protect sources with the result that parts, if not the entire core, of the trial may have to be heard in secret. Where the evidence that an individual poses a real threat to public safety cannot be made public, it may be preferable to proceed by resorting to executive measures such as TPIMs than contaminating the criminal process with secret trials. This is not to endorse a greater use of TPIMs but to make the point that it may be necessary to keep this kind of executive intervention on the statute book as a last resort for protecting the public in exceptional cases where it is not possible to proceed by means of open evidence. The secrecy involved in these review processes may itself diminish confidence in them, but at least it is confined to exceptional measures and may do less damage to confidence than diluting fundamental safeguards such as open justice long associated with the criminal trial.

The difficult challenge of how to proceed in a manner that both protects the public without diluting public confidence in the courts highlights the need to deploy other strategies in countering terrorism that go beyond law enforcement. Countering terrorism is a multi-faceted enterprise requiring a multi-layered approach. After the events of 7/7, there was not only a renewed emphasis on criminalisation but also a recognition of the need for a broader counter-terrorism strategy, known as CONTEST, which combined four strands, namely pursue, prevent, protect and prepare.[84] This strategy evolved against the background of a realisation that it is not possible to resolve the new threats of global terrorism by simply 'arresting and prosecuting more people'.[85] One of the shifts of policy has been to reduce

---

[83] Walker, *Anti-Terrorism Legislation*, p. 277, 'Terrorism Prosecution', p. 264.
[84] Home Office, *CONTEST: The United Kingdom's Strategy for Countering Terrorism* (London, TSO, 2011) Cm 8123.
[85] Home Office, *CONTEST*, p. 11.

the risk of terrorism by much earlier interventions through countering radicalisa-
tion and violent extremism. This prevent strategy has itself provoked much controversy and sparked debate about how to provide strong security in ways that do not
compromise the core values in a liberal democracy.[86] The experience of the past
50 years suggests that an undue focus on using suspect or secret evidence in the
judicial process risks undermining one of these core values, which is the need to
uphold confidence in the independence of the judiciary.

Table 10.1 Number of TPIMs and terrorism-related prosecutions (2012–2016)

	Prosecutions *	TPIMs +
2012	51	8
2013	65	8
2014	101	1
2015	81	3
2016	33	7
Total	331	27

* Source: Home Office 2017
+ Source: G. Allen and N. Dempsey, *Terrorism in Great Britain: The Statistics* (House of Commons Library 2018)

Table 10.2 Outcome of substantive appeals or reviews in SIAC cases (2003–2017)

Type of case	Successful	Unsuccessful	% success
Appeals against certification under ATCSA 2001	1	17	5.5
Appeals against deportation	8 (2 mixed)	23	25.8
Appeals against refusal of entry	1	8	11.1
Appeals against deprivation of citizenship	0	6	0
Claims to asylum	0	2	0
Reviews of refusal to grant naturalisation	2	16	11.1
Reviews of exclusion of non-EEA nationals from UK	1	1	50
Bail applications	8 (2 mixed)	13	38.1
Total	21	86	19.6

Source: J. Jackson, *Special Advocates in the Adversarial System* (2019)

---

[86] J. Richards, *A Guide to National Security: Threats, Responses and Strategies* (Oxford, Oxford University Press, 2012) chapter 10.

11

The Parole Board as an Independent Judicial Body, and Challenges to Its Independence

HIS HONOUR JEREMY ROBERTS QC*

THE PAROLE BOARD for England and Wales (the Board) occupies a small but important place in our criminal justice system. It is now, though it was not always, a judicial body whose independence should be respected by the executive.

Its decisions are always important: it is important not only that the public should be protected by the imprisonment of those whose risk of serious harm to other people requires it, but also that prisoners are not kept in prison when there is no good reason for that to happen.

The first part of this paper will examine the stages by which the Board acquired its present status as an independent judicial body; the second part will examine some of the challenges to its independence which it has faced thus far; and the final part will look into the future.

I have been a member of the Board since 2010, but any opinions expressed in this paper are my own personal ones, written in my capacity as an occasional contributor to academic papers and discussions. They are not written on behalf of the Board and should not be understood to represent the opinions of the Board or its other members.

The stages by which the Board acquired its present status

The creation of the Board and the reasons for it

The Board was created in 1967 in the wake of the abolition of the death penalty for murder and the consequent substantial increase in the number of people in prison serving life sentences.

* Since this paper was written there have been further challenges to the independence of the Parole Board, which will no doubt be the subjects of debate and discussion.

Proceedings of the British Academy, **250**, 200–222, © The British Academy 2022.

If you were convicted of murder before 1957, the mandatory sentence was death. The judge had no discretion about that. His clerk would get out what was called the black cap (in fact, it was a square piece of black cloth) and put it on top of the judge's wig: the judge would then look down at you and tell you that you would be taken from court to a place of execution where you would be hanged by the neck until you were dead.

That did not take place immediately, as it had done in days past. You would be taken back to the prison where you had been detained, and there you would stay until your appeal rights had been exhausted and (if your conviction was not quashed on appeal) the Home Secretary of the day had decided whether to reprieve you: that meant commuting the death sentence to one of life imprisonment, something the Home Secretary had power to do by exercising the royal prerogative of mercy on behalf of the Sovereign.

If any appeal was dismissed and there was no reprieve, your execution would take place in a shed in the prison yard. The hangman would do his job and there would then be no need for any further decision to be made in your case.

If you were reprieved, all subsequent decisions in your case fell within the administrative remit of the Home Secretary, as the Secretary of State responsible for the criminal justice system. The judiciary had no further part to play. The Home Secretary would decide such matters as:

- the prison at which you should be detained at any time;
- whether you should be transferred to a secure psychiatric hospital (something that happened to many reprieved prisoners who had mental health problems but not such as to escape the death penalty on the ground of insanity);
- whether (and if so when) you should be released on licence;
- whether (and if so when) you should be recalled to prison because of a perceived increase in your risk; and
- if so, whether (and if so when) you should be re-released on licence.

No doubt in making those decisions the Home Secretary would usually act on the advice of his officials in the Home Office, but ultimately the decision was his.

Reprieved murderers ('mandatory lifers') were not the only people serving life sentences. There were also (as there still are) 'discretionary lifers', people who have committed other very serious offences for which the maximum penalty is life imprisonment and whose crimes are regarded by the sentencing judge as requiring such a sentence. Back in the days of the death penalty, the criteria for imposing discretionary life sentences were quite restrictive, so the number of discretionary lifers was limited. The Home Secretary had the same administrative powers and responsibilities in their cases as in the cases of mandatory lifers.

The death penalty was abolished by two stages. By section 7 of the Homicide Act 1957, it was abolished in all but a few specified types of case (one of which was the murder of a police officer or prison officer acting in the course of his duty), and by section 1 of the Murder (Abolition of Death Penalty) Act 1965, it was abolished in those cases too.

When the death penalty was abolished, life imprisonment became the mandatory sentence for murder, just as death by hanging had previously been. This naturally resulted in a substantial increase in the number of lifers in prison. The Home Secretary's administrative powers and responsibilities in their cases remained unchanged.

Under the Criminal Justice Act 1967, the Board was set up as a purely advisory body to make recommendations to the Home Secretary about his decisions in this area. The statutory requirements were that the Board should consist of a chairman and at least four other members, including a judge, a psychiatrist, a probation officer with experience of supervising prisoners released on licence and a person who had made a study of the causes of delinquency and the treatment of offenders. The initial number of members was 17.

The members would make their recommendations jointly, and largely on the basis of reports from prisons about the prisoner's progress (though at some stage a system was introduced by which one of the members would actually go to the prison where the prisoner was detained to interview him and report back).

Over the years that followed, an administrative practice was developed by successive Home Secretaries that was eventually formalised in a Ministerial Statement made by the then Home Secretary in 1983. Under that practice, there were two stages to the process of deciding when, if at all, a prisoner should be released on licence.

Stage 1 occurred soon after the sentence was passed. The Home Secretary of the day would then specify a minimum period that the prisoner would have to serve before being considered for release on licence. That period came to be known as the prisoner's 'tariff'. It was intended to reflect the seriousness of the crime: the more serious the Home Secretary believed the crime to be, the longer would be the tariff. In deciding on the tariff, the Home Secretary would consult the trial judge and the Lord Chief Justice for their views but was in no way bound by them.

Stage 2 occurred after the prisoner's tariff had expired. The decision about release on licence would be made by the Home Secretary at that time (almost certainly a different person from the one who had fixed the tariff) and would be based on what he believed to be the level of the prisoner's current risk of serious harm to the public. Only if he believed that risk to be sufficiently low to be manageable on licence in the community would the Home Secretary release the prisoner. In reaching his decision on that point, the Home Secretary would consult the Parole Board and take into account its recommendation, but he was free to depart from it as he thought fit (which he quite often did).

Challenges to the UK parole system in the European Court of Human Rights

The first successful challenge to the legality of the UK parole system was brought in 1987 in the European Court of Human Rights (ECtHR) in Strasbourg by lawyers acting for a Mr Weeks. Mr Weeks was a discretionary lifer who had been released on licence but recalled to custody by the Home Secretary, who had then declined to follow the recommendation of the Board for re-release.

The argument successfully advanced on his behalf in Strasbourg was that decisions about release or re-release on licence should be made by a court and not by a politician. That argument was based on Article 5(4) of the European Convention on Human Rights. Article 5(4) provides that:

> Everyone who is deprived of his liberty by arrest or detention shall be entitled to take proceedings by which the lawfulness of his detention shall be decided speedily by a court and his release ordered if the detention is not lawful.

The Convention had not itself become part of UK law at that time. However, the UK was a signatory to it (UK lawyers had played a major part in its drafting), and since 1960 it had been open to a UK citizen to take proceedings against the UK in the ECtHR: if he or she could establish a breach of the Convention that affected him or her, he or she might obtain payment of compensation and expenses. There was an understanding that if the UK was found to be in breach of the Convention, Parliament would change the law so as to bring it into compliance.

In Mr Weeks' case, the ECtHR accepted that Article 5(4) applied not only when a citizen is first arrested and/or imprisoned, but at any time subsequently when he continues to be detained; and that in the event of a challenge to the lawfulness of his continued detention the matter should be decided by a court.

The ECtHR further decided that the Board, if it was given the responsibility for making parole decisions, might qualify as a 'court' for the purposes of Article 5(4), but only if: (a) it was independent of the executive and the parties, and (b) it had in place an appropriate set of judicial procedures to ensure fairness to both parties. There are two parties to parole proceedings: the prisoner and the Secretary of State, who represents the interests of the public and the victims. Under the original system, the Board did not make the decisions, so that system obviously did not comply with Article 5(4) as interpreted in Strasbourg.[1]

This was clearly a decision to be welcomed. Courts can be expected to reach their decisions by an objective application of the relevant legal principles to the facts as established by the evidence. Politicians, with the best will in the world, are liable to be influenced by public opinion – or what they believe public opinion is likely to be. Public opinion is not a safe or reliable basis for making decisions affecting the liberty of a subject. The public are unlikely to have an accurate and complete understanding of the relevant facts and legal principles: they may also be easily influenced by extensive publicity given to views expressed by those with particular interests.

The decision of the judges in Strasbourg does not seem to have done Mr Weeks himself much good. He did not obtain any compensation from the UK government,

---

[1] *Weeks v United Kingdom* (1987) 10 EHRR 293.

and the ECtHR did not have the power to direct his release or to change UK law, which remained unchanged for another four years.

During that time, another case had been taken to Strasbourg on behalf of three discretionary lifers, Messrs Thynne, Wilson and Gunnell.[2] Their case was decided in 1991, and the court affirmed its previous decision in *Weeks*.

The decisions in these ECtHR cases were confined to discretionary lifers. The view seems to have been taken that there was a material distinction, for the purposes of Article 5(4), between discretionary lifers and those serving mandatory life for murder. The distinction was thought to be that a mandatory life sentence reflected the extreme seriousness of the crime of murder and meant that in principle the offender had been ordered to spend the rest of his life in prison so that his release on licence could be thought to be an act of mercy that could properly be left to the discretion of a government minister. Conversely, under the approach laid down by the Court of Appeal at that time, a discretionary life sentence would only be imposed in practice where, irrespective of the seriousness of the actual offence, the defendant suffered from a mental or psychological abnormality that made him a danger to the public and that might or might not be cured by appropriate treatment. It was therefore thought to be appropriate that an assessment of his continuing risk should be made by a court.

UK law was eventually changed by Parliament in the Criminal Justice Act 1991 to bring the law in relation to discretionary lifers into compliance with the Convention as interpreted by the ECtHR in *Weeks*. The 1991 Act transferred the power to fix a discretionary lifer's tariff from the Home Secretary to the sentencing judge, and the power to direct release or re-release after expiry of the tariff from the Home Secretary to the Board (the Home Secretary being obliged to comply with the Board's decision even if he disagreed with it). Both stages of the decision-making process had therefore been transferred from the executive to the judiciary (of which the Board now formed part in discretionary lifer cases). For the next few years there were therefore two parallel systems for the release of lifers. In the system that applied to mandatory lifers the decisions were all made by the Home Secretary, while in the system that applied to discretionary lifers they were made by the judiciary in the form of the Board.

That state of affairs came to an end as a result of another decision of the ECtHR in 2002, by which time the Human Rights Act 1998 had incorporated the Convention into our law so that it was open to our courts to find breaches of its provisions. The decision in 2002 was in the case of a Mr Stafford, who was a convicted murderer. In his case, the UK Courts followed the decision of the ECtHR in *Weeks* and *Thynne*, but when the case was taken to Strasbourg, the ECtHR effectively reversed those decisions and decided that there was no real distinction between discretionary and mandatory lifers and that the *Weeks* principle should apply to both. In both types of case, the seriousness of the offence was reflected in the tariff, and continued

---

[2] *Thynne, Wilson and Gunnell v United Kingdom* (1990) 13 EHRR 66.

detention after the tariff expired could only be justified if the prisoner's risk of serious harm to the public was such as to make it necessary to keep him in prison.

In consequence of the ECtHR decision in *Stafford*[3] and a further decision of the House of Lords that followed it, the Criminal Justice Act 2003 brought the position in murder cases into line with that in discretionary lifer cases. As in murder cases, the trial judge was made responsible for fixing the tariff and the Board was made responsible for deciding whether to direct release on licence once the tariff had expired: if it decided to do so, the Home Secretary was placed under a legal duty to comply with that direction.

That remains the position today, though in 2007, the criminal justice functions of the Home Secretary were transferred to the Secretary of State for Justice (a newly created position). Since the 2003 Act, there has been a single regime for all lifers, murderers and others alike. In both types of case, the powers and responsibilities of the executive have been transferred to the judiciary. The process of change has largely been brought about as a result of the efforts of lawyers representing prisoners, who have seen the independent Parole Board as a more reliable arbiter of risk and its manageability than a politician.

The substantial expansion of the Board's remit and caseload has inevitably led to an increase in its size. It now has more than 250 members (judicial members, psychologists, psychiatrists and others – the others being known as 'independent members') supported by a secretariat of similar size.

The transformation of the Board into a judicial body, and problems associated with it

The transition of the Board from being a purely advisory body to being one whose primary function is judicial has not been without its complications and potential sources of difficulty. The complex relationship between the Board and the Secretary of State is one such potential source of difficulty. The Secretary of State is at one and the same time a party to proceedings to decide whether a prisoner should be released on licence, and the government minister responsible to Parliament for the activities of the body responsible for making those decisions.

In relation to release on licence, the Board's decisions are binding on the Secretary of State, but in another important area (deciding whether a prisoner should be moved from a closed prison to an open one), the Board's role is purely advisory. Despite the transfer to the Board of the Secretary of State's responsibility for making decisions about release on licence, the latter remains responsible for deciding where a prisoner should be detained while he is still in prison. If the prisoner is in a closed prison, the referral of his case by the Secretary of State to the Board will typically ask it to decide whether to direct his or her release on licence

---

[3] *Stafford v UK* (2002) 35 EHHR 32.

and, if it does not do that, to advise the Secretary of State whether the prisoner is ready to be moved to an open prison: the roles of the Board and the Secretary of State are therefore reversed in the two decisions which have to be made. There are also cases where the Board is asked to advise about the suitability for a move to open conditions of a prisoner whose tariff has not yet expired.

Both in his capacity as a government minister and in his capacity as a party to parole proceedings, the Secretary of State is, of course, under a duty to respect the independence of the Board.

As regards the Board's status when making decisions about release on licence, in 1996, Sir Thomas Bingham (as he then was) described the Board as 'an independent quasi-judicial body'.[4] Several years later (as Lord Bingham), he accepted that it was more accurate to describe it as 'a judicial body and a court within the meaning of Article 5(4)'.[5]

Although the Board has been given the status of a court, it lacks the powers and resources that most other courts have in order to fulfil their judicial functions. There is no requirement under Article 5(4) that the Board's procedures should be the same as those of other courts, though of course the overall requirement of fairness to both parties applies to it as it does to all courts.

Because of the special nature of the work that it does, the Board operates in several respects in a different way from most other judicial bodies. Its procedures are, for the most part, specified in the Parole Board Rules (made by the Secretary of State but usually after consultation with the Board) and in the Board's own guidance to its members.

Although the Board holds oral hearings, in normal times these take place either in prisons or by video link between prisons and the Board's headquarters in London. During the Covid-19 pandemic, they have taken place remotely by video or telephone link with the prisoner, and usually the Prison Offender Manager (formerly called the Offender Supervisor) at the prison and the panel members and other witnesses at their homes or offices.

The Parole Board Rules formerly imposed a blanket ban on disclosure of any information about parole proceedings. That rule has now been relaxed to the extent that summaries of decisions can be provided in certain circumstances, as provided for in the current Parole Board Rules.[6] The complete secrecy that previously surrounded parole proceedings did not help to inform the public about the Board's role and the rules under which it is required to operate.

Another respect in which the Board's procedures differ from those of other judicial bodies is that its proceedings are not wholly adversarial. Because of the particular issues that the Board has to decide, the proceedings are in fact hybrid – a mixture of adversarial and inquisitorial elements. They are adversarial in that there

---

[4] *R v Parole Board* ex parte *Watson* (1996) 1 WLR 906.
[5] *R v Parole Board* ex parte *Giles* (2004) AC 1.
[6] The Parole Board Rules 2019 (S.I. 2019 No. 1038), Rule 27.

are two parties and each can present evidence, test the other side's evidence by questioning and make written and oral representations to the panel hearing the case. They are, however, inquisitorial in two respects.

First, in a purely adversarial system, it is the parties who decide what evidence to place before the court. In the parole system, the bulk of the written evidence is presented on behalf of the Secretary of State by the Public Protection Casework Section of the Ministry of Justice (PPCS). The prisoner and his or her legal representative can present further written evidence if they wish. The Board itself can and usually does direct the production of any further evidence that it believes it needs in order to make its decision, and it is the responsibility of PPCS on behalf of the Secretary of State to obtain and present that evidence.

Second, in a purely adversarial system, it is the parties or their representatives who question the witnesses at the hearing, and although the judge or jury can ask some questions in a criminal or civil trial, they are encouraged not to ask too many (and indeed, if the judge asks too many questions, that may provide a ground of appeal). In the parole system, it is the panel members who are in charge of the presentation of the evidence: they decide which witnesses should be called to give oral evidence, they decide on the order in which the witnesses give evidence, and they normally question the witnesses first and ask most of the questions.

The starting point in the panel's assessment of risk is the prisoner's previous behaviour, and in particular his or her record of offending. The Board's limited powers and resources mean that it has to rely on the decisions of criminal courts to establish what offences the prisoner has or has not committed. If the prisoner was convicted of an offence, the Board must proceed on the basis that he or she committed that offence even if he or she is still denying it many years later: the Board has neither the authority nor the resources to go behind the conviction and decide whether the jury's verdict was correct. Similarly, if the prisoner was acquitted of an offence, the Board must proceed on the basis that he or she did not commit it, though evidence of the circumstances surrounding the incident in question may be relevant to the Board's assessment of risk. There may obviously be difficulties if an allegation of a criminal offence was made but, for whatever reason, was not the subject of a criminal trial and thus was not the subject either of a conviction or of an acquittal.

Like other courts, panels of the Board sometimes have to resolve conflicts of fact for the purpose of their decisions. It is for the party seeking to rely on any assertion of fact to prove that fact. Because parole proceedings are regarded as civil rather than criminal, the standard of proof is the civil standard (balance of probabilities), though it has been said that the more serious an allegation is, the greater is the need for cogent evidence to prove it.[7] In reality, panels, like civil courts, are usually able to reach conclusions one way or the other on disputed facts without resorting to applying the burden of proof.

[7] *R v D* (2008) UKHL 33.

Much of the information presented to the panel usually takes the form of hearsay evidence contained in reports prepared by professional witnesses. These always include the Prison Offender Manager (who is responsible for supervising the prisoner while he or she is in prison) and the Probation Practitioner (formerly known as the Community Offender Manager and before that simply as the Offender Manager), who will be responsible for supervising the prisoner if he or she is released on licence. They may also include one or more psychologists and/ or psychiatrists. The professional witnesses will normally rely on a great many hearsay statements of fact appearing in previous reports or records. Where such statements are disputed, it is often difficult to assess their reliability.

Hearsay evidence is in principle always admissible in parole proceedings: Rule 24 (6) of the Parole Board Rules 2019 (reproducing the corresponding provision in previous rules) states that:

> An oral panel may produce or receive in evidence any document or information whether or not it would be admissible in a court of law

That sounds straightforward enough but is, of course, subject to the overall requirement of fairness. It is self-evident that there may be some cases in which it is fair to make findings of fact on the basis of hearsay evidence and others in which it is not. The Rules do not contain any guidance on the question when it is or is not fair to rely on hearsay evidence to establish disputed facts.

The Court of Appeal has held that what is or is not fair in any individual case will depend on all the circumstances of that case and is a matter for the panel itself to decide: the panel should consider the evidence and decide whether it is fair to rely on it and, if so, how much weight to place on it (taking into account that it has not been tested by questioning).[8]

This principle is easily stated but not always easy to apply in practice. Particular problems arise in relation to hearsay allegations of misconduct or criminal behaviour on the part of the prisoner (whether before or during the sentence). While there can be no general rule, it would obviously very often be unfair to rely on a disputed allegation that the prisoner committed a criminal offence for which he or she could have been but was not prosecuted. The criminal courts are normally the proper place for the determination of criminal allegations to take place. There are safeguards built into the procedures of the criminal courts (such as the prosecution's duty to disclose anything which undermines their case) that do not exist in the parole system; that, and the lack of the opportunity for the prisoner or his or her legal representative to test the evidence of a person making an allegation, is likely in many cases to mean that it could not be fair for the panel to rely on hearsay evidence.

Despite all these difficulties, and the fact that ministers and their officials are not always quick to adjust to changes that they may not have welcomed, I believe it is fair to say that the system has on the whole worked well since the Board was

---

[8] *R (on the application of Sim v Parole Board) (2003) EWCA Civ 1845* and *R (on the application of Brooks) v Parole Board (2004) EWCA Civ 80.*

made responsible for making decisions about release on licence, and that it has achieved its objective of protecting the public while giving a chance for a fresh start to prisoners whose continued imprisonment is not necessary. The system is probably not the one that we would have devised if we had been starting from scratch, but (like many things in the UK!) that has not prevented it from being a fair and effective one.

Risk assessment is not, of course, an exact science, and a prisoner who is well motivated to avoid a return to offending may find it difficult – after being released and finding it impossible to obtain a job – to resist the temptation to solve his or her problems by re-offending. It is inevitable in any parole system that there will be some instances of prisoners on parole licence committing further offences (some of them serious), but such instances have been relatively rare. The only way of preventing them would be to abolish parole altogether or to adopt an unduly risk-averse approach that would result in the unnecessary and unfair incarceration of many prisoners.

It is perhaps not surprising, given the unusual and complex nature of the relationship between the Board and successive Secretaries of State, that there have been a (very) few instances of the latter losing sight of the Board's status as an independent judicial tribunal and seeking to encroach on its judicial functions. These have been recognised by the courts and corrected insofar as that was possible. They will be discussed in the next section of this chapter.

Challenges to the Board's independence

From the outset of its time as a court for the purposes of Article 5(4), there have been concerns that the Board was not truly independent of the executive and the parties. Indeed, one of the arguments deployed in the ECtHR in 1987 on behalf of Mr Weeks, in challenging the lawfulness of the UK's then parole system, was based on the suggested lack of independence of the Board. The ECtHR, while its judgment in that case meant that the Board could not qualify as a court unless and until it made the actual decisions about the release on licence of discretionary lifers, did not – on the information then available to it about how the system operated – accept that it lacked the necessary impartiality and independence.

In 2000, a further challenge to the UK system was mounted in the ECtHR on behalf of a Mr Hirst, whose lawyers argued that the Board could not be regarded as independent because (a) its members included former employees of the prison service and members of the Board of Visitors and (b) there were structural links between the Board's secretariat and funding body and the prison service. That argument was, again, not accepted: indeed, it was rejected at the admissibility stage.[9]

---

[9] *Hirst v UK* (App No. 40787/98).

The case of Brooke and others

In 2008, the lawyers for four prisoners (Messrs Brooke, O'Connell, Murphy and Ogannisyan) brought judicial review proceedings against the Board and the Secretary of State for Justice in which they successfully advanced fresh arguments that the Board was not truly independent of the executive and the parties. They argued that the way the system was operated – and in particular, certain things that the Home Secretary had done before the transfer of his responsibilities to the Secretary of State for Justice – amounted to interference with the Board's independence and an attempt to influence its decisions in a manner adverse to prisoners seeking release. The Board adopted a neutral stance in the proceedings. The Secretary of State disputed the claim, but the Divisional Court upheld it and the Court of Appeal upheld the Divisional Court's decision.[10]

The judgments of the Divisional Court and the Court of Appeal are quite complex and well worth studying in detail. The Secretary of State relied on the decisions of the ECtHR in *Weeks* and *Hirst,* but in the Divisional Court Lord Justice Hughes (as he then was) pointed out that the ECtHR had had far less information available to it about the workings of the system than was by then available to the UK courts.

The Court of Appeal summarised, as follows, the position as it emerged from the evidence available to it and the Divisional Court:

> Neither the Secretary of State nor his Department has adequately addressed the need for the Parole Board to be and to be seen to be free from influence in the performance of its judicial functions. Both by Directions and by the use of his control over the appointment of members the Secretary of State has sought to influence the manner in which the Board carries out its risk assessments. The close working relationship between the Board and the unit acting as its sponsor has tended to blur the distinction between the executive role of the latter and the judicial role of the former.

Both courts held that the fact that the Secretary of State appoints the members of the Parole Board was not in itself objectionable provided that they are selected on the basis of their independence and impartiality as well as their qualifications. However, it was clear from the evidence that the Home Secretary had proposed to control the appointment of new members with the express purpose of making the Board less likely to direct release on licence. The evidence was summarised as follows by the Divisional Court in its judgment:

> In Spring 2006 the annual round of [the selection process] was well advanced, and the short-listing had been finished, when it was overtaken by a ministerial initiative. This had been signaled in advance to the Board by the Department, and was announced publicly when on 22 May 2006 the then Home Secretary delivered the Board's annual lecture. It came at a time when there was public anxiety about re-offending by released prisoners, particularly because of two very high-profile murders committed by such persons. The import of the lecture was that there could be no excuses for a system which did not prevent such events, that the safety of the public must outweigh the rights of the offender, and that anyone serving an indeterminate sentence could be released only if the panel members were 'absolutely satisfied' that it was safe to do so.

[10] *R (Brooke and others) v Parole Board and Secretary of State for Justice* (2008) EWCA Civ 29.

The Secretary of State went on to announce that by June he intended to appoint new members of the Board with experience either of being a victim of crime or of involvement with a victim support organisation. The purpose of these appointments, he said, was to 're-balance the whole system in favour of victims'. In order to accommodate this new initiative, there had had to be put in train a separate and parallel selection process, involving the targeting of suitable persons, superimposed on the existing appointment round and after the short-listing had already been done.

It is no part of a court's function to make any finding about the merits of the proposed alteration to the selection criteria, for which the case may or may not have been strong. But it came from the minister of the Crown whose task it is, in every disputed case before the Board, to present the case against release. It was an explicit exercise by that party of the power of appointment, alongside exhortation to require a near guarantee of future behaviour in released prisoners, with a view to changing what was perceived to be over-readiness to release. It was designed to alter, to some extent at least, the outcome of cases before the Board. Whatever the merits of the then current debate about parole, this exercise of that power can only be inconsistent with the objective appearance of the Board's independence from the Executive and from one party to its proceedings. We have little doubt that it came the more easily to hand because the Board exists as a sponsored unit within the appointing minister's Department of State, which arrangement induces the appearance of direct ministerial responsibility for it.

In addition to this point, both courts identified other aspects of the system, as it had been operated by the Home Secretary and his ministers and officials, that were found to involve encroachment on the Board's independence. These included:

- The fact that the Board as an executive non-departmental public body was sponsored and funded by a body (the Sentencing Enforcement Unit of the National Offender Management Service) that could not be said to be independent of the executive and the parties.
- The refusal of the sponsoring unit to provide funding for a process that the Board considered to be essential for the purpose of its judicial functions. The Board proposed that a Board member should interview any prisoner who was to be denied an oral hearing, but ministers decided only to provide funding for about 10% of such interviews.
- The issuing by the Home Secretary to Board of documents described as 'Directions'. The Court of Appeal, in a previous case brought on behalf of a Mr Girling,[11] had held that this practice was not open to criticism provided that the directions did not seek to influence the Board in its judicial functions but were confined to identifying matters that the Board would need to take into account, where relevant, in making its decisions. Mr Girling's case showed, however, that the Secretary of State had not always appreciated that distinction and on one occasion at least had issued a direction seeking to influence the Board's decisions.
- The limited tenure of membership of the Board coupled with the power of the Secretary of State to terminate a member's appointment without any procedure being in place to ensure that termination could only take place for good cause and subject to fair process.

[11] *R (Girling) v Parole Board* (2006) EWCA Civ 1779.

As a result of the decision in *Brooke*, a number of changes were made to the system, including the transfer of sponsorship of the Board to another department of the Ministry of Justice (the Arm's Length Body (ALB) Governance Division), which it was hoped could be regarded as genuinely independent of the executive and the parties. Concerns remained, however, about the closeness of the working relationship between the Board and PPCS, and also about the Secretary of State's power to terminate a member's appointment without any process being in place to ensure fairness. This latter concern came to the fore in 2018 when, in the wake of the quashing by the Administrative Court of the Board's widely unpopular decision to direct the release on licence of a Mr John Worboys, the then Secretary of State effectively dismissed the Board Chair, Professor Nick Hardwick, without any good reason, thereby clearly encroaching on the independence of the Board.

The case of John Worboys

Mr Worboys had been a 'black cab' driver in London and had been convicted of 19 sexual offences (including one rape) committed against 12 women in the back of his taxi. He was sentenced to an indeterminate sentence ('imprisonment for public protection') with a 'tariff' of eight years before he could be considered by the Board for release on licence. His tariff expired on 14 February 2016. On 26 December 2017, a panel of the Board directed his release on licence. That direction was quashed by the Administrative Court on 28 March 2018.

In quashing the direction, the Court acknowledged that the case was exceptional. It was exceptional because the offences for which Mr Worboys was prosecuted related to only 14 of about 80 women who had apparently made complaints to the police that he had sexually assaulted them (this was because of the established practice in the criminal courts that an indictment to be tried by a jury should not be overloaded by including too many charges for them to disentangle and consider separately). In the result, he was convicted of offences against 12 of the 14 women and acquitted in relation to the other two.

It is not unreasonable to suppose that the prosecution had chosen what they perceived to be their strongest cases to put on the indictment. The acquittals demonstrated that the safeguards provided by the criminal justice system (including the opportunity to test the complainants' evidence by cross-examination) operated effectively. They also demonstrated that the jury heeded the judge's warning (equally applicable to parole proceedings) that it is impermissible to lump all the allegations together and it is necessary to examine each allegation separately.

This is particularly so in sexual cases, where the issue of consent usually has to be considered. Even where, as in Mr Worboys' case, evidence of the defendant's behaviour towards other women may be admissible as demonstrating a systematic course of conduct on his part, it by no means followed that none of the women consented to his approaches.

The fact that Mr Worboys was convicted of only a relatively small proportion of the offences that the police believed he had committed meant that the judge had to fix the sentence by reference only to those offences of which he had been convicted. It is unclear whether the judge was aware of the other allegations, but if so, he could not lawfully take them into account when fixing the sentence.

When the Board was faced many years later with the task of assessing Mr Worboys' current risk to the public, the situation was a highly unusual one. In a case of this kind, there are normally sufficient charges ('counts') on the indictment to give an adequate overall picture of the defendant's offending. But the facts of this exceptional case threw into sharp focus the question of how the Board should approach the use of hearsay evidence to prove past offences of which the prisoner had been accused but never convicted.

The PPCS and the panel to which the case was allocated understandably proceeded on the basis that it would not be fair or safe for the Board to rely on hearsay evidence of sexual allegations for which Mr Worboys could have been prosecuted but had not been. Thus it was that, although there were some references in the dossier prepared by PPCS to the existence of a large number of allegations that had not resulted in convictions:

- the Secretary of State's officials in PPCS who prepared the dossier for the Board did not think it appropriate to include evidence relating to those other allegations;
- the psychologists who carried out risk assessments for the purpose of the parole review did not think it appropriate to take the other allegations into account in their assessments: they no doubt took the sensible view that the validity of their assessments would be compromised if they took into account something that the Board itself could not lawfully use as evidence;
- the Board member who conducted the initial paper review of the case ('MCA assessment') did not direct that information about how the other allegations should be obtained and added to the dossier;
- the experienced chair of the panel to which the case was allocated did not, in her Panel Chair Directions, make any such direction;
- the experienced Secretary of State's representative, who presented his case at the parole hearing, while opposing release on the basis of the evidence before the panel, did not suggest (either in written representations before the hearing or in oral representations at the hearing) that information about the other allegations should be obtained and considered by the panel; and
- the officials who advised the Secretary of State after the hearing, when it was certainly known that a good deal of information about the other allegations was available, did not suggest (as they could have done) that the Secretary of State should invite the Board to re-open its review of the case so that that information could be considered.

In short, all these professionals who were involved in the case shared the unanimous understanding that it would not be permissible for the panel to rely on hearsay evidence about the other allegations in order to make findings of 'wider offending'. Furthermore, when the Secretary of State sought legal advice from a senior independent lawyer or lawyers about whether there were any grounds for him to challenge the panel's decision by way of an application for judicial review, he was clearly advised that there was no such ground.

The Administrative Court, however, took a different view when two of the victims brought their own judicial review proceedings against the Board and the Secretary of State. Its judgment repays careful study.

Mr Worboys had consistently stated that the only sexual offences he had committed were those of which he had been convicted. Ms Philippa Kaufmann QC, on behalf of the claimants, drew the court's attention to the existence of hearsay evidence that suggested that he had committed many more sexual offences than those which he admitted. She submitted, first, that the panel had erred in failing to obtain that evidence and second, that even without that evidence, the panel's decision to direct release was irrational.

The court did not accept the second of those arguments. It did, however, while acknowledging that there were powerful arguments on both sides, accept the first argument. It appears to have accepted that PPCS and the panel had been justified in concluding that hearsay evidence of 'unconvicted' offences could not have been used as a basis for finding that Mr Worboys had committed such offences. It did, however, accept Ms Kaufmann's argument that the panel should have obtained information about the alleged further offences, 'not necessarily for the purpose of proving that [Mr Worboys] had committed other offences, but as a means of testing the account he was advancing and the evidential premises of the psychologists' reports'. In adopting that argument, the court stated that 'this evidence or material could have been used as a means of probing and testing the honesty and veracity of [Mr Worboys'] account'. It therefore quashed the direction for release, and the case had to be considered afresh by another panel, applying the approach suggested by the court. In fact, Mr Worboys did not seek to renew his application for release on licence, and the case was decided with a negative decision on the papers.

It will be apparent from the above that the *Worboys* case raised complex and difficult points of law on which, as often happens, views could and did reasonably differ. The approach taken by the panel, though the Administrative Court ultimately took a different one, was certainly a reasonable and defensible one.

The panel's decision to direct Mr Worboys' release on licence was greeted with fury in some sections of the media. The use in their reports of such expressions as 'scandal' or 'outrage' betrayed a complete lack of awareness of the legal complexities of the case and, probably, of the fact that the panel was a judicial tribunal required to apply the law as it understood it to be. That lack of awareness was not, perhaps, surprising given the veil of secrecy behind which the Board had at that time been required to carry out its tasks. The Board had been anxious for some time to be able to lift the veil to some extent, but the Secretary of State had resisted that (and indeed his counsel on his instructions argued unsuccessfully against it in the Divisional Court in *Worboys*). Secrecy is a fertile breeding ground for misunderstanding and misconceived criticisms.

What is disappointing is that the ignorance of the sections of the media that were so vociferous in their criticism of the panel's decision in *Worboys* was evidently shared by the then Secretary of State. On the day before the Administrative Court's judgment was delivered in open court, copies of it were (as is normal practice) given to the parties, who of course included the Secretary of State. It is a matter of record that later that day there was a meeting between the Secretary of State and the Chairman of the Board, Professor Nick Hardwick, in which the former effectively demanded the latter's resignation, telling him that his position had become untenable. Professor Hardwick did not agree but bowed to the Secretary of State's demand and resigned.

In his letter of resignation, Professor Hardwick acknowledged, in light of the Administrative Court's decision, that the panel had been mistaken in its approach to the unconvicted allegations, and went on to state: 'I am sorry for the mistakes that were made in this case but I have always made it clear that I will support the members and staff of the Board in the very difficult individual decisions which they have to make and I will accept responsibility for the work of the Board. I will not pass the buck to those who work under me. In these circumstances I inform you of my decision to resign with immediate effect.'

In his public statement following Professor Hardwick's resignation, the Secretary of State stated: 'I accept Professor Hardwick's resignation and believe that this is the correct decision in the light of the serious failings outlined in today's judgment.'

It is highly unlikely that the Secretary of State could have regarded Professor Hardwick's position as untenable or believed that his resignation was appropriate if he had been aware of the full facts of the case and the legal issues involved. If he had had time to make enquiries and ascertain the true position, he might well have been made aware by his officials and legal advisers of the complexities and difficulties of the case and of the fact that the panel had not been guilty of *'serious failings'* but had been conscientiously trying to apply the relevant legal principles.

However, there was no doubt perceived to be a political imperative that *'something had to be done'* (and to be done very quickly) in the light of the quashing of the panel's widely unpopular decision and the public's likely perception (erroneous as it can now be seen to be) that the Board under Professor Hardwick's leadership had made a serious blunder and could not be trusted to make appropriate decisions in future.

The Secretary of State's hasty and ill-informed intervention in this case clearly amounted to a significant interference with the independence of the Board. Like any other judicial tribunal, a panel of the Board must be free to make the decisions that it conscientiously believes to be the correct ones. Sometimes its decisions are very difficult and involve issues on which views may reasonably differ. Sometimes they are bound to be unpopular. Sometimes the tribunal's views may not coincide with those of a higher court. That is why we have a system of appeals and judicial reviews, which provides the proper route for correcting decisions that are found (in the opinion of a higher court) to have been mistaken.

All judicial tribunals make mistakes from time to time (or perhaps it would be better to say that they make decisions with which a higher tribunal disagrees). When they do, that does not mean – even in a high profile case – that their position has become untenable or that they should be expected to resign: it can hardly be suggested that, if a High Court or Circuit Judge makes a decision that is overturned on appeal, the Lord Chief Justice and/or the Secretary of State should be expected to ask them to tender their resignations.

It is possible to envisage (though it is to be hoped that they will be very rare) cases where a judge or member of a judicial tribunal is guilty of an error of judgment (or more likely a series of errors of judgment) so grave as to put in question their suitability to continue to serve in a judicial capacity, and thus to make it appropriate for them to be asked to resign. However, the decision as to whether that is the case ought clearly to be made by a proper disciplinary process in which the facts can be carefully examined, and not by a politician's hasty response to the quashing of an unpopular decision.

Politicians are, as pointed out above and as the *Worboys* case graphically demonstrates, unlikely to have the necessary knowledge of the relevant facts and legal issues, and are liable to be swayed into hasty action by public opinion (which may itself be based on ignorance of those matters). It is difficult to see how any properly informed and fair-minded member of the public could have thought for one moment that the *Worboys* panel's approach to the case was a serious blunder of a kind requiring anybody's resignation.

Furthermore, the Secretary of State's intervention must have had unfortunate consequences. It must have sent out two unfortunate messages, one to the public and the other to future panels.

By effectively aligning himself with the public's erroneous perception of what had happened in the *Worboys* case, the Secretary of State can only have reinforced that perception and caused significant but unwarranted damage to the public's confidence in the system.

Future panels will sometimes (as in the *Worboys* case) be faced with situations where it is obvious that what they believe to be the correct decision will be deeply unpopular with the public and sections of the media. Central to the independence of the Board is the principle that in such a situation, the panel must make the decision that, applying the legal principles as it believes them to be, it considers to be the correct one. The message sent out by the forced resignation of Professor Hardwick was that if the panel did that and the decision was then overturned by the High Court, a dismissal or forced resignation might follow. That would clearly increase the pressure on panels to make the popular decision rather than the correct one.

The *Wakenshaw* case and its consequences

In the light of Professor Hardwick's forced resignation, judicial review proceedings were instituted against the Secretary of State by the lawyers acting for a prisoner unconnected with the *Worboys* case (a Mr Wakenshaw). The lawyers applied for permission to seek a number of declarations to the effect that in several respects, the current parole system failed the test of objective independence.

The application was considered on 7 August 2018 by Mr Justice Mostyn, who granted permission to seek a declaration, in the following terms, on one of the grounds put forward by the lawyers:

> That the period of appointment (three or four years, renewable for three or four years) of Parole Board members, coupled with the power of the Secretary of State to remove a member if he is satisfied that he or she has failed without reasonable excuse to discharge the functions of his or her office for a continuous period of at least three months, or is unable to discharge the functions of the office, without recourse to any procedure or machinery to determine the merit of a decision to remove him or her on one or other of those grounds means that the provisions for tenure of Parole Board membership fail the test of objective independence,

Mr Justice Mostyn went into the matter in some detail and was clearly of the view that the claim for judicial review should succeed.[12]

Although the application had been triggered by the effective dismissal of the Board Chair, the lawyers' criticism of the system related to the positions of all Board members. It emerged at the hearing that Professor Hardwick's terms of appointment, drafted since the decision in *Brooke*, differed from those of all other Board members (which were still in the pre-*Brooke* form) but still left the decision whether to remove the Board Chair in the hands of the Secretary of State without any procedure to enable him to challenge it. That meant that those terms still fell foul of the decision in *Brooke*.

The judge was told by counsel for the Secretary of State that the terms of Professor Hardwick's appointment were 'generic' and would have applied to all members. Investigation showed that not to be the case. The judge observed that, remarkably, the terms of appointment for members other than the Board Chair had remained exactly as they were at the time of the *Brooke* case, in which they had been a key reason leading to the declaration that the provisions for tenure failed the test of objective independence. He was told by counsel for the Secretary of State that the failure to amend the terms was an 'oversight' and that it was proposed to bring other members' terms of appointment into line with those of the Board Chair. The judge proceeded, for the purposes of his judgment, on the basis of that happening, but was clearly of the view that the failure to include any machinery for challenging a removal decision by the Secretary of State (whether relating to the Board Chair or any other member) would be incompatible with the objective independence of the Board.

In light of Mr Justice Mostyn's ruling, it was very sensibly agreed between the Secretary of State's representatives and Mr Wakenshaw's lawyers that the judicial review proceedings should be adjourned for three months to give the Secretary of State the opportunity to change the system so as to bring it into compliance with the law.

---

[12] *R (on the application of Wakenshaw) v Secretary of State for Justice and Parole Board* (2018) EWCC 2089 (Admin).

The Secretary of State duly agreed with the Board, in a document entitled 'Agreed Protocol for Termination of Membership of the Parole Board', a procedure by which, on the application of the Secretary of State or the Chair of the Board, a Panel may be appointed to decide whether a member of the Board (including the Board Chair) has met one of the specified grounds for termination of his or her appointment, and if so whether to recommend to the Secretary of State that the appointment of that member should be terminated. The Secretary of State agreed that a member's appointment should only be terminated if the Panel so recommended.

The specified grounds for members other than the Board Chair are: that the member in question has become for any reason incapable of carrying out their duties, has failed to comply with the Board's Quality Assurance Framework or the Board's Code of Conduct, has been convicted of any criminal offence or is an undischarged bankrupt. There are slightly different grounds in the case of the Board Chair. There can be no doubt that if this Protocol had been in place at the time of Professor Hardwick's dismissal, he could never have been dismissed.

Any Panel appointed under the Protocol will be made up of a member of the Board (usually the Judicial Vice-Chair), a representative of the Secretary of State (usually a Director from the Justice and Courts Policy Group in the Ministry of Justice) and somebody independent of the Secretary of State or the Board. The independent member will chair the Panel and the decision will (in the event of disagreement) be a majority one.

These changes should certainly be effective to prevent a repetition of the unfortunate and unwarranted dismissal of Professor Hardwick. They should repair some but not all of the damage caused by the Secretary of State's intervention. Some of the pressure on panels to make the popular decision rather than the one that the panel believes to be correct should be relieved. The damage to public perception of the system cannot be repaired, nor can the unwarranted damage to the career of a conscientious and well-regarded public servant.

The future

It is of course not possible to predict with accuracy what the future may hold for the Board and for prisoners whose future currently depends on it.

Possible reform of the system

Various suggestions have been made in the past for reform of the system, and since this chapter was written, a 'Root and Branch' review of the Parole system has commenced. The suggestions for reform over the years have included:

a)   that the Board should be removed from the control of the Secretary of State and moved into HM Courts and Tribunals Service;

b)   that the Secretary of State's role as a party to parole proceedings should be transferred to the Crown Prosecution Service;

c)   that the Board should be abolished and an entirely new system introduced to decide on the release of prisoners on licence;

d)   that the Board should remain in its present form but be given additional powers and resources, and

e)   that changes should be made to its current procedures.

As indicated above, I believe it is fair to say that the system has on the whole worked well since the Board was made responsible for making decisions about release on licence. The changes put in place (in one case belatedly) as a result of the decision in *Brooke* have ensured the Board's structural independence. The occasional instances of the executive interfering in the Board's performance of its judicial role have been few and far between: they have been recognised by the courts and not repeated. Prison lawyers will no doubt continue to be vigilant in the future to identify any further such instances and to take appropriate action through the courts to remedy them.

While the relationship between the Board and the Secretary of State is unusual and has had the potential to cause significant problems, that has happened only rarely, and there is much to be said for applying the principle, 'If it ain't broke, don't fix it'. I have seen first hand that there is a good working relationship between the Board and PPCS and that there is a general recognition of and respect for the Board's independence. Matters of possible concern are discussed regularly between the managements of both organisations.

In specific cases, the Secretary of State, though a party to the proceedings, usually adopts a neutral stance and does not seek to put forward any arguments for or against release on licence. In high-profile or particularly sensitive cases, he will often instruct one of his team of representatives to present written representations in advance of the hearing and to attend the hearing to ask questions of the witnesses (including the prisoner) and make oral representations at the close of the evidence. The 'house style' of any representations on behalf of the Secretary of State is generally restrained and constructive, and his or her representatives usually do not ask many questions (if any) but focus on any additional points that have not been covered in questioning by the panel.

The idea of transferring the Secretary of State's role to the Crown Prosecution Service is an interesting one, but it is doubtful whether anything would be gained by it. The Crown Prosecution Service will of course have access to a great deal of information about the prisoner's offence(s), but that can always be obtained from them by PPCS (if necessary, at the direction of the panel). Most of the evidence to be considered by the panel will relate to the prisoner's progress in custody and will come from employees of the Secretary of State (probation officers, prison officers or prison psychologists). PPCS are experienced in obtaining and presenting this evidence to the Board.

Some changes to the Board's procedures have been made since the decision of the Divisional Court in *Worboys*. These are still 'bedding down', and it remains to be seen whether further changes are required.

Disclosure of information about parole proceedings

The relaxation of the prohibition on disclosure of information relating to parole proceedings seems to have been generally welcomed. Summaries of decisions are now provided if requested by a victim (or victim's family), by the media or anyone else with a legitimate interest. Feedback about this system appears thus far to have been positive.

In some jurisdictions, parole hearings are open to the public, or at least to anybody (such as a victim) with a legitimate interest in the case. In the UK at present, victims can normally attend the initial part of a parole hearing to read their 'victim personal statements' (setting out the impact which the prisoner's crime has had on them) to the panel before the hearing begins, but they have to withdraw after doing so. The debate continues about whether they should be allowed to observe the remainder of the proceedings.

The reconsideration procedure

A new system has been introduced whereby, to avoid the time and expense of an application for judicial review, an application can be made by the prisoner or by the Secretary of State (usually at the request of a victim) for reconsideration of a decision to direct or not to direct release on licence. Such decisions are now provisional for 21 days, during which an application for reconsideration can be made.

There are only two grounds for such an application: (a) that the decision was irrational and (b) that it was procedurally unfair. There is a screening process, and any eligible application is referred to a judicial member of the Board. The judicial member will consider the application, the dossier, the panel's decision and any representations submitted by either party, and may then either refuse the application or grant it. If it is granted, the judicial member will direct that the case should be reconsidered by the same or a different panel, and if appropriate a further hearing will be directed.

The decisions of judicial members on reconsideration applications are published but anonymised so that a body of case law is being built up. If either party wishes to challenge the judicial member's decision, an application may be made to the Administrative Court for judicial review of that decision.

This system (a kind of in-house judicial review process) is still in its early stages. By 4 December 2020, there had been 285 eligible applications for reconsideration, and 222 decisions had been issued. In 42 of those decisions, reconsideration was directed. This is, I believe, a slightly higher 'success rate' than the rate of successful applications to the Administrative Court for judicial review.

The system seems to be working well but obviously may need some fine-tuning as further experience is built up. There have been no concerns about the Secretary of State's role in the process.

Additional powers

There are some things that could be done to reduce some of the difficulties caused by the Board's limited powers and resources. For example, at present, a panel of the Board cannot enforce the attendance of a reluctant witness to attend the hearing and give evidence: it has to direct the Secretary of State to apply to the High Court or County Court under the Civil Procedure Rules[13] for a witness summons requiring the witness to attend. This rather cumbersome way of going about things should really not be necessary. Increased use of the video link facility might enable some witnesses whose presence at the hearing in person is undesirable to give oral evidence to panels, thereby reducing the need to consider hearsay evidence.

Use by the CPS and the courts of a procedure to avoid future *Worboys*-type problems

The *Worboys* case exposed a weakness in the system. PPCS and the panel were clearly right in concluding that it could not be fair, in the circumstances of that case, for the panel to rely on hearsay evidence as a basis for a finding of 'wider offending'. The 'half-way house' solution proposed by the Administrative Court is not without its difficulties and not really a satisfactory way of establishing relevant facts. It is to be hoped that cases like *Worboys* will be extremely rare. If they should occur, there is in fact a procedure available to avoid similar problems arising. It is, however, a procedure that can only be used by the Crown Prosecution Service and the courts, and liaison between the various authorities may be helpful.

This procedure was introduced by sections 17–20 of the Domestic Violence, Crime and Victims Act 2004 to cater for cases where a large number of offences are alleged and it is difficult to frame an indictment that reflects the totality of the defendant's offending. The procedure involves a 'two stage trial'. In such a trial, the indictment will contain a large number of counts, but some of those will be treated as samples to be tried by the jury: if the jury convicts on any or all of the sample counts, any others that appear to relate to the same course of criminal conduct will be tried by the judge alone. The judge will of course be required to give a detailed judgment setting out the reasons for his or her decision.

This procedure became available in January 2007, which was before Mr Worboys was arrested and charged. With all the benefit of hindsight it can be seen

---

[13] Civil Procedure Rules, Rule 34.4.

that, if the 'two stage trial' procedure had been used in his case, it would have had a number of advantages.

First, verdicts would have been obtained (some from the jury and some from the judge) on each of the many allegations against Mr Worboys. The judge would then have been able to pass a sentence that reflected the totality of his offending. Second, the Parole Board would have had a sound basis on which to make a fully informed assessment of his current risk, and last but not least, all those who could be proved to have been victims of Mr Worboys would have had the opportunity of giving their evidence in court – instead of, as happened to many of them, being thanked for their cooperation but told that no action was going to be taken on their complaints because there were already enough counts on the indictment.

It would be unfair to the CPS to criticise them for not seeking to use this procedure in Mr Worboys' case. It was a relatively new procedure and they can be forgiven for not anticipating the problems that were to arise in the case, as explained in this article. However, the experience of the *Worboys* case has demonstrated that in any future similar case, the use of the procedure would merit serious consideration.

12

The Judge Under Pressure: Fostering Objectivity by Abandoning the Myth of Dispassion

MOA BLADINI AND STINA BERGMAN BLIX*

THE INHERENTLY COERCIVE nature of law makes its enforcement the most intrusive form of state power. To secure legitimacy and reproduce trust in the legal system, it is crucial that judicial activities are performed objectively and impartially. Traditionally, the ideal of objectivity has been closely associated with dispassion; a judge that can put her emotions and values, implicitly emotional drives and motivations aside under 'the veil of ignorance', as suggested by Rawls, and evaluate the case before her in a rational way.[1] The ideal of the dispassionate judge has a long tradition in Western democracy; 400 years ago, Hobbes argued for such an ideal and it is still as vivid today.[2]

Two narratives that question judicial independence and the objective judicial process are rapidly gaining ground.[3] First, populist movements portray elite decision-making as distanced, alien to, and 'out of touch' with, the concerns of the

* The writing of this chapter was made possible thanks to the Swedish Research Council (VR 2016-01218) and the European Research Council (ERC) under the European Union's Horizon 2020 research and innovation programme (757625, JUSTEMOTIONS).
[1] J. Rawls, *A Theory of Justice* (Cambridge, The Belknap press of Harvard University Press, 1999), T. A. Maroney, 'The Persistent Cultural Script of Judicial Dispassion', *California Law Review*, 99 (2011), 629–681. M. Bladini, *I objektivitetens sken. En kritisk granskning av objektivitetsideal, objektivitetsanspråk och legitimeringsstrategier i diskurser om dömande i brottmål. (In the semblance of objectivity – a critical review of objectivity claims and legitimation strategies in criminal trial discourses)* (Göteborg, Makadam förlag, 2013).
[2] T. Hobbes, *Leviathan* (Oxford, Oxford University Press, 2008). Note the rise and demise of the emotional judge in Europe, especially in German free law and in Soviet Russia during the period of 1880–1930. An in depth discussion on emotions in the judiciary in modern Europe is found in Pavel Vasilyev, 'Beyond Dispassion: Emotions and Judicial Decision-Making in Modern Europe', *Journal of the Max Planck Institute for European Legal History*, 25 (2017), 277–285.
[3] 'Introduction', in this volume.

people they should serve. This narrative has led to the curtailment of judicial discretion in some European countries.[4] A second narrative that increasingly attracts the interest of governments is the appeal of automation through different forms of artificial intelligence (AI). AI appears to offer a less expensive and more efficacious way of guaranteeing greater predictability and control over legal decision-making.[5] Legislative measures and more formal responses (*de jure* protections) are one way to meet these challenges. At the same time, research emphasises that other, more informal and cultural factors are crucial to understanding how to deal with the practical challenges of protecting judicial independence.[6]

Both narratives are based on the supposition that legal decision-making is performed by a dispassionate and therefore objective decision-maker. However, research on emotions and rational decision-making from several disciplines show the opposite, that reason and emotion are in fact inevitably intertwined.[7] One way to approach the challenges of these narratives is to seek to understand and elucidate the reality of decision-making; to identify the subtle emotional processes and emotion management that guide the logical application of abstract principles as well as the everyday interaction of legal proceedings.

This chapter scrutinises the criminal procedure and decision-making processes through an emotion lens and shows how emotions are necessary both for an objective decision-making process as well as for legitimating criminal procedure. By identifying the role of emotions in legal procedure, we aim to show how human, passionate judges can serve as gatekeepers both in relation to the populist portrayal of judges as detached from the reality of everyday life and to the idea of AI replacing judges in legal decision-making.

---

[4] Here the UK, Poland and Hungary can serve as examples, although it takes different shapes in the states mentioned. See European Commission, 'Rule of Law: European Commission takes new step to protect judges in Poland against political control', 17 July 2019, online at: https://ec.europa.eu/com mission/presscorner/detail/en/IP_19_4189 (last accessed 26 January 2022) and Amnesty International, 'Continued Attacks against the Independence of the Judiciary in Hungary', 23 September 2019, online at: https://www.osce.org/odihr/431879?download=true (last accessed 26 January 2022) respectively.
[5] Several countries have initiated projects on AI taking part in judicial decision-making, some of these will be discussed below. A report from Partnership on AI presents benefit and risk analysis and points out the judiciary as an area of high risk assessment. See Partnership on AI, *Report on Algorithmic Risk Assessment Tools in the US Criminal Justice System* (2019), online at: https://www.partnershiponai.org/ report-on-machine-learning-in-risk-assessment-tools-in-the-u-s-criminal-justicc-system/ (last accessed 26 January 2022).
[6] See the conclusion, 'On Crisis', to this volume. Note that emotions in law, or 'emotionalization of law', has had a specific impact on the change of criminal laws. This chapter, however, has a different focus, emotions in legal decision-making, i.e., in legal procedure, see S. Karstedt, 'Emotions and Criminal Justice' *Theoretical Criminology* 6, (2002) 299–317. Emotions are also fundamental in the populistic discourse on criminal law, but will not be discussed here.
[7] R. de Sousa, *The Rationality of Emotion* (Cambridge, MA, MIT Press, 1987), A. Etzioni, 'Normative-Affective factors: Toward a New Decision-Making Process', *Journal of Economic Psychology*, 9 (1988) 125–150, A. R. Damasio, *Descartes Error: Emotion, Reason and the Human Brain* (New York, Avon Books, 1994), Jack Barbalet, *Emotion, Social Theory and Social Structure – A Macrosociological Approach* (Cambridge, Cambridge University Press, 1998).

Law and emotions

Law and emotions as an academic subject has developed quickly during the past two decades and now covers numerous fields of research, including theoretical as well as empirical studies and a diversity in choice of foci.[8] While the field of law and emotions in general, and emotions in judicial decision-making in particular, is a fast-developing field, it is less well-known by legal practitioners and legal scholars and hence needs to be properly introduced.

Law and emotion research spans several disciplines, such as sociology, psychology, law, history, philosophy and neuroscience, and the diversity of the field is augmented by the various legal systems concerned, including common law, civil law and mixed legal systems.[9] The role of emotions in law can also be examined from several perspectives: in relation to victims, offenders, jurors, legal actors such as police officers, prosecutors, lawyers or judges, and the law itself, as well as legal institutions.[10] So far, most research on law and emotion has been conducted within common law traditions.[11] In a civil law context, German historians have recently started to explore the field.[12] In the Scandinavian context, the main contributions have been made by primarily Swedish researchers of sociology and criminology.[13] In this chapter, the authors will focus on the role of emotions in criminal procedure,

---

[8] J. E. Stannard, 'How to do Law and Emotion' *Civil & Legal Sciences,* 2 (2013). For a brief history of the field of law and emotions, see K. Abrams and H. Keren, 'Who's Afraid of Law and the Emotions?' *Minnesota Law Review,* 94 (2010), 1997–2074.

[9] T. A. Maroney 'Law and Emotion: A Proposed Taxonomy of an Emerging Field', *Law and Human Behaviour,* 30 (2006), 119–142, B. H. Bornstein and R. L. Weiner, *Emotion and the Law. Psychological Perspectives* (Springer, New York, 2006) and S. A. Bandes, 'Introduction to The Passions of Law' *The Passions of Law* (New York, New York University Press, 1999).

[10] S. A. Bandes and J. A. Blumenthal, 'Emotions and the Law', *The Annual Review of Law and Social Science,* 8 (2012) 161–181.

[11] See, for example, the work by Terry Maroney, Professor of Law and Professor of Medicine, Health and Society at Vanderbilt Law School in USA, Susan Bandes, Emeritus Centennial Distinguished Professor of Law at De Paul College of Law in USA, Sharyn Roach-Anleu, Matthew Flinders Distinguished Professor at the College of Humanities, Arts and Social Sciences, Flinders University in Australia, Bettina Lange, Associate Professor of Law and Regulation at the Centre for Socio-Legal Studies, Faculty of Law, Oxford University in the UK.

[12] D. Ellerbrock and S. Kesper-Biermann, 'InterDisciplines'. *Journal of History and Sociology,* 2 (2015) 1–15, H. Landweer and D. Koppelberg, *Recht und Emotion I. Verkannte Zusammenhänge* (Verlag Karl Alber 2016) and H. Landweer and F. Bernhardt, *Recht und Emotion II. Sphären der Verletzlichkeit* (Verlag Karl Alber, 2017).

[13] S. Bergman Blix and Å. Wettergren, 'A Sociological Perspetive on Emotions on the Judiciary', *Emotion Review,* 8 (2016) 32–37, S. Bergman Blix and Å. Wettergren, *Professional Emotions in Court. A Sociological Perspective* (New York, Routledge 2019), N. Törnqvist, *Att göra rätt. En studie om professionell respektabilitet, emotioner ochstricta linjer bland relationsvåldsspecialiserade åklagare* (*Doing just right: A study on professional respectability, emotions and narrative lines among prosecutors specialised in relationship violence*) (Stockholm, Department of Criminology 2017), L. Flower, 'Doing Loyalty: Defence Lawyers' Subtle dramas in the Court-room', *Journal of Contemporary Ethnography,* 6 (2018) 226–254.

i.e., in relation to legal decision-making in criminal processes, building on two ongoing research projects.[14]

Emotion and rationality

So, emotions are not just mindless; they embody thoughts. Therefore, we cannot dismiss them from judicial reasoning and writing just by opposing them in an unreflective way to reasoning and thought.[15]

The quote from Nussbaum discussing emotions and judicial decision-making from a philosophical perspective illustrates the idea of emotion and reasoning as intertwined in a mutual interplay. Emotions are in general associated with internal reactions that interfere with the activities carried out due to, for example, unreasonable and strong excitement or irrational distraction.[16] There is a strand of empirical research within social psychology where more subtle emotions in legal decision-making have been examined: how jurors' emotions affect their attribution of responsibility,[17] as well as how emotions affect how people understand information.[18] Studies within this field also investigated how police officers were affected by their emotions in investigative processes, showing that sad officers were more thorough when carrying out the investigation compared to angry police officers.[19] All these examples portray emotion in the legal decision-making process as having a biasing effect and being opposite to rationality.[20] However, as substantiated by research from several disciplines, emotions must also be understood as a fundament of the human predisposition to act, as the fuel of action. If one had no emotions, one would lack motivation to act (and, in the end, to live).[21] Thus a fundamental starting point in current theories

---

[14] Bergman Blix is the principal investigator and Bladini is participating in both the interdisciplinary project *Emotions in judicial decision-making*, carried out in Swedish courts from 2017–2019 funded by the Swedish Research Council (2016-01218), and the comparative interdisciplinary project Justemotions, carried out in Sweden, Scotland, Italy and the US during 2018–2023, funded by the European Research Council (grant agreement No. 757625).

[15] M. Nussbaum, 'Emotions in the Language of Judging', *St. John's Law Review*, 70 (1996), 23–30, p. 25.

[16] J. Barbalet, 'A Characterization of trust. And its consequences', *Theory and Society*, 38 (2009), 367–382.

[17] N. Feigenson and J. Park, 'Emotions and Attributions of Legal Responsibility and Blame: A Research Review', *Law and Human Behaviour*, 30 (2006), 143–161.

[18] K. Ask and A. Pina, 'On Being Angry and Punitive: How Anger Alters Perception of Criminal Intent', *Social Psychological and Personality Science*, 2 (2011), 494–499 and J. S. Lerner and L. Z. Tiedens, 'Portrait of The Angry Decision Maker: How Appraisal Tendencies Shape Anger's Influence on Cognition', *Journal of Behavioural Decision Making*, 19 (2006), 115–137.

[19] K. Ask and A. Granhag, 'Hot cognition in investigative judgments: the differential influence of anger and sadness', *Law and Human Behaviour*, 31 (2007), 537–551.

[20] Barbalet, *Emotion, social theory and social structure. A macrosociological Approach*.

[21] Barbalet, *Emotion, social theory and social structure. A macrosociological Approach*. 'For in action the whole person participates, and science, then, requires that 'intellect, will, taste, and passion co-operate just as they do in practical affairs' (James 1987[…])'. Quote from J. Barbalet, 'Science and Emotion', *Sociological Review*, 50 (2002), 132–150.

of emotions is that the traditional view of emotion and rationality as mutually exclusive categories is erroneous: emotions rather play a crucial role for rational action.[22] Three aspects of the relationship between rationality and emotion have previously been examined within various disciplines.[23] In philosophy, emotions have been discussed as a supplement to reason, and the use of factual knowledge has been scrutinised in relation to emotions, leading to the conclusion that cognition is not enough to decide what one needs to know and what to ignore. Damasio has shown that people who suffered from brain damage and lost contact with the emotional parts of the brain, but with a preserved cognitive capacity, found it difficult to make decisions. They got stuck in the reasoning: 'on the one hand... but on the other hand, on the one hand...'. Damasio's conclusion is that the ability to make decisions needs to involve emotions because one needs to 'feel' the consequences.[24]

A second aspect of emotions in rational processes, hence, decision-making, is that emotions guide attention: what to notice, what to attend to and what to inquire about. Emotions might also serve to motivate interest and confidence in a process of gathering information or solving a problem, pride in expertise, and/or aversion to waste of time and efficiency. These emotions work with cognition to further rational action and most often stay outside our conscious awareness, therefore not reflected upon as emotions.[25]

A third aspect is that the relation between emotions and rationality is culturally embedded; the understanding of the role of emotions for rational action varies across time and space.[26] In court, people's tragedies are often the subject of a trial and hence there are lots of emotions involved. Outside the court, it would seem rational to react emotionally and, for example, comfort someone who was sharing a tragedy. In court, there are other emotional regimes at play. A judge is expected not to seem affected by a crying victim; an unemotional display is considered rational in the context of the judiciary. What would seem like a rational emotional response in one setting can be deemed irrational in another. This last aspect puts focus on the importance of contextualising the role of emotions in court. Emotions might be expressed or displayed in different ways in different situations due to specific emotional regimes or feeling rules, concepts that will be introduced and further developed below.

---

[22] Barbalet, 'A Characterization of trust. And its consequenses', E. Illouz and S. Finkelman, 'An Odd and Inseparable Couple: Emotion and Rationality in Partner Selection' *Theory and Society,* 38 (2009), 401–422 and Bergman Blix and Wettergren, *Professional Emotions in Court A Sociological Perspective.*

[23] The authors refer to a Weberian definition of *rationality* as pervasive, calculating, reflexive consciousness, as described by Illouz and Finkelman in 'An Odd and Inseparable Couple: Emotion and Rationality in Partner Selection'.

[24] Damasio, *Descartes Error: Emotion, Reason and the Human Brain.*

[25] De Sousa, *The Rationality of Emotion.* A. Morton, 'Epistemic Emotions' in P. Goldie (ed.), *The Oxford Handbook of Philosophy of Emotion* (New York, Oxford University Press, 2010), 385–399, J. Barbalet, 'Emotions beyond Regulation: Backgrounded Emotions in Science and Trust', *Emotion Review,* 3 (2011), 36–43. These emotions might also be acknowledged as epistemic emotions, and discussed more in dept in the section on background emotions below.

[26] Illouz and Finkelman 'An Odd and Inseparable Couple: Emotion and Rationality in Partner Selection'.

Emotions and judging

> *'remember stone face!' (Asta, judge, 60+)*

Legal decision-making comprises decisions of procedural character, as well as of substantive law. Hence, the conception of decision-making in the context of criminal law involves a variety of decisions such as questions concerning how to deal with an annoying defence lawyer or a sobbing victim; how best to assess a witness' credibility; and how to decide whether a certain document should be obtained or not. Some of these decisions might not be formal ones, but they are of importance in the process of being objective and displaying objectivity.

The quote above comes from an experienced judge who in an interview explained how to display an objective image of herself as a judge. She told the interviewer that she, as a novice judge, had to put a sticker in her law book to remind herself to 'put on the stone face'.[27] A crucial part of legitimating the judiciary is to display objectivity,[28] and, as the ideal of the judge is a dispassionate one, the 'stone face' is an important feature of the emotion work judges do in court. Not only is the judge supposed to represent justice showing a stone face, but she is also expected to be just by making rational decisions, hence putting her emotions aside.[29] But a vast amount of research has shown that these presuppositions are inaccurate. As we demonstrate below, emotions make a crucial contribution to procedural justice and hence legitimacy.

Judges are, as discussed above, exposed to highly emotional situations on a daily basis and to actively prevent them from taking over is part of their emotional management. The management of emotions in court is three-fold: it includes handling others' emotions, one's own emotions, and the way these are displayed or not.

In the following, four theoretical concepts from sociological emotion theory are presented and described in the context of the judiciary: foreground as well as background emotions, emotion management and empathy.

Foreground emotions

> *'Sexual assaults, especially when there are children involved... I allow myself to be sad then. And if I become so sad that it affects me, both the way I look and how I think, then I have to take a break.'* (Karin, judge, 50 +)

The above quote is a typical example of foreground emotions. Judge Karin discusses a type of case that judges typically find to be emotionally straining and that she knows might affect her so pervasively that she has to deal with her emotions for

---

[27] Quotes used in this chapter come from the ongoing research project *Emotions in judicial decision-making*.

[28] Bladini, *I objektivitetens sken*.

[29] Å. Gunnarsson, E.-M. Svensson, J. Käll and W. Svedberg, *Genusrättsvetenskap* (Studentliteratur 2018). Maroney, 'The Persistent Cultural Script of Judicial Dispassion'.

them not to interfere with her professional activities. Strong emotion shifts the judge's focus from the trial to her own internal state. If her sadness threatens her ability to both display objectivity and think objectively, she takes a break to calm down and refocus. What is most often conceptualised as emotions are those that end up in the foreground and interrupt our actions, expressed both cognitively and physically. Foreground emotions force the emotional subject to reflect and react upon them.[30]

The quote also highlights the situational bearing of feelings rules. In society in general, sexual assault on children is anticipated to instigate strong emotional reactions, but the rules of the court, with their emphasis on professionalism and impartiality, imply that the judge must not experience nor express sadness.[31] As noted above, one of the strongest commitments of the emotional regime for judges in court is the display of unemotional rationality, i.e., a stern face.[32]

Background emotions

'My impression is that both of them have taken this seriously, if I may say so. And spent quite a lot of time, energy and professional knowledge on this case. So, it differs from many other cases, and is kind of a prestigious case.' (Peter, judge, 45 +)

The quote comes from an interview with a judge when a trial was finished in a district court in Sweden. He discusses the other legal actors and praises them for their professionalism in this case. He appreciates their engagement and good work and makes the reflection that it might depend on the fact that it was a prestigious case. What he does is comment on the backgrounded emotions that motivated the prosecutor and defence lawyer to make an extra effort in the case. In contrast to the foregrounded emotions, backgrounded emotions are subtle, cooperating with the actions carried out instead of disrupting them. They are typically invisible and unconscious or on the border of one's consciousness.[33] Pride in the profession is seen as a driving force in legal actors' work. Other background emotions important in the legal professions are curiosity in the facts of the case, a blasé feeling towards non-legally relevant facts, the feeling of uncertainty driving the process of evaluating evidence forwards, and the feeling of certainty that will stop the process of

[30] Barbalet, 'Emotions beyond Regulation: Backgrounded Emotions in Science and Trust'.
[31] E. Goffman, *Frame Analysis: An Essay on the Organizational of Experience* (Boston, MA, Northeastern University Press, 1974). A. R. Hochschild, 'Emotion work, feeling rules, and social structure', *American Journal of Sociology*, 3 (1979), 551–575, W. M. Reddy, *The Navigation of Feeling – A Framework for the History of Emotions* (Cambridge, Cambridge University Press, 2009).
[32] Note that this analysis is made in a Swedish context. Even though research shows that the script of rational and unemotional decision-making makes a claim of display dispassion also applies to other Western courts, see Bergman Blix and Wettergren, *Professional Emotions in Court. A Sociological Perspective* and K. Mack and S. Roach Anleu, 'Performing Impartiality: Judicial Demeanor and Legitimacy', *Law and Social Inquiry-Journal of the American Bar Foundation*, 35 (2010), 137–173.
[33] Barbalet, 'Emotions beyond Regulation: Backgrounded Emotions in Science and Trust'.

inquiry. The examples mentioned show how background emotions cooperate with and underpin the cognitive processes one is engaged in and since they are below the threshold of awareness, they might not be named and reflected upon.[34]

Background emotions are thus necessary to rational action: they inform, guide and support one's focus, help to distinguish important from less important details and do so in a quicker way than a cognitive evaluation would. Hence, background emotions typically operate in knowledge seeking processes and are relevant in a discussion on legal decision-making.

A group of background emotions that are associated with decision-making in particular are epistemic emotions.[35] Epistemic emotions are linked to cognitive evaluation by providing information about the quality of one's knowledge and motivating certain kinds of mental action.[36] There is an ongoing discussion on which emotions can be considered epistemic, but they most often include feelings of certainty, understanding, curiosity, epistemic anxiety and uncertainty. All of these feelings affect deliberation; 'a feeling of certainty freezes inquiry', while curiosity opens up for further examination.[37] As we saw above in the section on foreground emotions, these also influence cognitive processes but are often seen as disruptive of a rational process. However, as we will see below in relation to AI in judging, this contention needs qualification.

Emotion management

Several studies have focused on emotion management in court, scrutinising the professional emotional regimes of the defence lawyer, the prosecutor and the judge.[38] Emotional regimes, from a judge's perspective, regulate the task of managing the emotions of others as well as one's own.[39] As discussed above, the emotional regime

---

[34] Barbalet, 'Science and Emotion', p. 147.

[35] S. Arango-Muñoz, 'The nature of epistemic feelings', *Philosophical Psychology*, 27 (2014), 193–211, R. de Sousa, 'Epistemic Feelings' in G. Brun, U. Doğuoğlu and D. Kuenzle (eds) *Epistemology and Emotions* (Aldershot, Ashgate, 2008), 185–204. Morton, 'Epistemic Emotions'.

[36] Arango-Muñoz, 'The nature of epistemic feelings'.

[37] de Sousa, 'Epistemic Feelings', p. 191.

[38] Criminologist Nina Törnqvist has explored the emotion rules of a trial and the 'emotional ideals' that the professional identity rests on in particular regarding prosecutors. Törnqvist, *Att göra rätt*, p. 297. Flower has explored the emotional regimes of defence lawyers in 'Doing Loyalty: Defence Lawyers' Subtle dramas in the Court-room', and the emotional regimes of judges has been investigated by Bergman Blix and Wettergren *Professional Emotions in Court. A Sociological Perspective*. See also S. Roach Anleu and K. Mack, 'Magistrates' Everyday Work and Emotional Labour', *Journal of Law and Society*, 32 (2005) 590–614, S. Roach Anleu and K. Mack, *Performing Judicial Authority in the Lower Courts* (London, Palgrave Socio-Legal Studies, 2017), K. Jacobsson, '"We Can't Just Do It Any Which Way": Objectivity Work among Swedish Prosecutors', *Qualitative Sociology Review*, IV (2008), 46–68.

[39] Management of the judge's own as well as the parties' emotions in the court has been explored by Roach Anleu and Mack, 'Magistrates' Everyday Work and Emotional Labour', P. Darbyshire, *Sitting in Judgment: The Working Lives of Judges*, (Oxford, Hart Publishing, 2011), J. A. Scarduzio, 'Maintaining Order through Deviance? The Emotional Deviance, Power, and Professional Work of Municipal Court Judges', *Management Communication Quarterly*, 25(2) (2011), 283–310, M. Herzog-Evans, *French*

regulating judges in court is the non-expressive, stone-faced one. When practising the display of the stone face, the judge engages in a sort of 'double agency': she acts upon emotions while simultaneously observing and regulating their display. To display an emotion other than the experienced one or absence of the same (dispassion) demands that the judge decouples the expression of emotion from the experience of it.[40] Sometimes it is necessary, or expected, to show or display emotions, even though the judge does not experience such emotion.

Empathy

Empathy is an important part of the judiciary and has been explored and discussed in research on legal decision-making and in relation to the parties.[41] Empathy is not an emotion such as sympathy and compassion, but a capacity.[42] It is a tool to tune in with others, a crucial resource both in evaluating hearings and other evidence and in emotion management.[43] It might be described as the emotional and cognitive capacity to imagine how a situation appears to someone else. Nussbaum argues that Smith's suggestion of the judicious or impartial spectator would serve as a good example of empathy used by judges in criminal procedures.[44] The judicious spectator is an artificially constructed person that serves as a role model of public rationality, and he uses the example of reading literature or watching a theatre play to illustrate how one puts oneself in someone else's position but with a certain distance. When reading literature, one is intensely involved and engaged

Reentry Courts and Rehabilitation: Mister Jourdain of Desistance (Paris, Editions L'Harmattan, 2014), Bergman Blix and Wettergren, *Professional Emotions in Court. A Sociological Perspective.*

[40] S. Bergman Blix, 'Professional Emotion Management as a Rehearsal Process', *Professions and Professionalism,* 5 (2015), 1–15.

[41] W. J. Brennan Jr, 'Reason, Passion, and the Progress of the Law', *Cardozo Law Review,* 10 (1988), 3–23, Nussbaum, 'Emotions in the Language of Judging', S. Bandes, 'Empathetic Judging and the Rule of Law', *Cardoso Law Review De Novo,* (2009), 133–148, K. Abrams, 'Empathy and Experience in the Sotomayor Hearings', *Ohio North University Law Review,* 36 (2010), 263–286, T. B. Colby, 'In Defence of Judicial Empathy', *Minnesota Law Review,* 96 (2012), 1945–2015, Mikael Mellqvist, 'Om empatisk rättstillämpning' *Svensk Juristtidning,* (2013), 494–501, Bergman Blix and Wettergren 'A Sociological Perspective on Emotions on the Judiciary', and Bergman Blix and Wettergren, *Professional Emotions in Court. A Sociological Perspective* have explored the role of empathy in legal decision-making thoroughly whereas S. Roach Anleu and K. Mack, 'Judicial Authority and Emotion Work', *Judicial Review: Selected Conference Papers: Journal of the Judicial Commission of New South Wales,* 11 (2013), 329–347, L. Flower, *Loyalty Work: Emotional interactions of defence lawyers in Swedish courtrooms,* (Lund, Faculty of Social Sciences, Lund University, 2018) and Bergman Blix and Wettergren, *Professional Emotions in Court. A Sociological Perspective,* have examined the role of empathy in relation to the parties in criminal trials.

[42] Bandes, 'Empathetic Judging and the Rule of Law', p. 133. See also M. F. Basch, 'Empathic Understanding: A Review of the Concept and Some Theoretical Considerations', *Journal of American Psychoanalytic Association,* 31 (1983), p. 101.

[43] Bergman Blix and Wettergren, *Professional Emotions in Court. A Sociological Perspective,* p. 11.

[44] Nussbaum, 'Emotions in the Language of Judging' and Adam Smith, 'The theory of moral sentiments', in D. D. Raphael and A.L. Macfie, (eds.) (Oxford University Press, 1976).

in the participants' situations while at the same time aware that it is not one's own situation. Nussbaum argues that Smith in this way shows that 'empathetic identification accompanied with a kind of critical external assessment are crucial in determining the degree of emotion that it is rational for the participants in the case to have.'[45]

In judging, empathy might be used as a tool to understand parties and witnesses, to assess someone's credibility or the defendant's criminal intent. Apart from that, empathy might also serve as a means and approach to legitimate the procedure by treating the victims, witnesses and other persons involved in an empathetic way during the trial.[46] Empathy thus has two crucial functions in a legal decision-making perspective: the first in the knowledge-seeking process, and the second in the process of legitimation of the judiciary.

Elitism

One of the contemporary challenges that independent judiciary is facing all over Europe is the populist and nationalist narrative depicting judges as elitist and even as 'enemies of the people'.[47] One way to address the threat of lost legitimacy on these grounds is to explore how judges use and might use emotions in a cognisant and reflexive way to gain the trust of the public. Safeguards should come both from the outside, as formal responses (*de jure* protections) but also from within the judiciary. This response to the threat is thus part of an answer to the question of how to secure judicial independence in practice. It is also part of what the editors call the 'hidden aspects' of judicial independence.[48] Judges are not dispassionate nor are their actions devoid of emotions. On the contrary, emotions play an important role in legal decision-making. By using empathy and emotion management, judges can display fairness in a sense of being empathetic to resist the public's image of distanced and elitist judges. This line of argument is closely linked to procedural

---

[45] Nussbaum, 'Emotions in the Language of Judging', p. 27. Bergman Blix argues that the analogue to reading fiction misses the fact that in contrast to a reader, the judge do have something at stake, the power to decide. A predicament that indeed can influence their empathic capacity. S. Bergman Blix, 'Different Roads to Empathy: Stage Actors and Judges as Polar Cases'. *Emotions & Society*, 1 (2019), 163–180.

[46] L. Henderson, 'Legality and Empathy', *Michigan Law Review*, 85 (1987), 1574–1655, T. Booth, '"Cooling Out" Victims of Crime: Managing Victim Participation in the Sentencing Process in a Superior Sentencing Court', *Australian and New Zeeland Journal of Criminology*, 45 (2012), 214–230, M. L. Schuster and A. Propen, 'Degrees of Emotion: Judicial Responses to Victim Impact Statements' *Law, Culture and Humanities*, 6 (2010), 75–104, Bergman Blix and Wettergren, *Professional Emotions in Court. A Sociological Perspective*, and Bandes, 'Empathetic Judging and the Rule of Law'.

[47] See for example N. Friedman, *The Impact of Populism on Courts: Institutional Legitimacy and the Popular Will* (The Foundation for Law, Justice and Society, 2019) and N. Lacey, 'Populism and the Rule of Law' *Annual Review of Law and Social Science*, 15 (2019), 79–96.

[48] Introduction, in this volume.

justice and it will be argued that the role of emotions is an important tool in the enforcement of the procedural justice principles.[49] The following sections will show examples of how emotion management and empathy can serve or fail the purpose of gaining the trust of the public by legitimising the judiciary.

Procedural justice and its fundamental concepts

In accordance with procedural justice theory, the trust and legitimacy of the judiciary is highly strengthened by procedural justice principles.[50] People's sense of procedural justice depends on four grounds: voice, meaning that the participants experience that they are allowed to make their voice heard; respect, pointing out the importance of treating the participants with dignity and respecting their rights; trustworthiness, where judges appear sincere and caring; and neutrality, i.e., the court is applying rules in an impartial and transparent way. These grounds, as identified by Tyler, will be used in this section to show the effect of using emotions in court.[51]

Voice

The experience of being heard and taken seriously is a fundamental aspect of procedural justice; this can be accomplished by the use of empathy and emotion management.[52] One important aspect of how to use empathy in an emotion management perspective is how judges treat the laypeople who are present in the court as parties or witnesses. By treating these people in a human and polite way, the judge both prepares for a good hearing and gains legitimacy by decreasing the gap between her and the person entering the court. As a result, the individual experiences respect from the judge and is more willing to cooperate with the court. Second, the judge gains trust and legitimacy by enabling laypeople to experience being seen, listened to and treated with respect. Research shows that the experience of fairness in a trial is decided by the impression of the procedure rather than the outcome of the case.[53] The aspect of voice is closely linked to the aspect of respect.

---

[49] S. Leben, 'Exploring the Overlap Between Procedural-Justice Principles and Emotion Regulation in the Courtroom', *Oñati Socio-legal Series*, 9 (5) (2019), 852–864.
[50] T. R. Tyler, *Why People Obey the Law* (New Haven, Yale University Press, 1990) and J. Thibaut and L. Walker, *Procedural justice: A Psychological Analysis* (Hillsdale, Lawrence Erlbaum, 1975).
[51] T. R. Tyler, 'Procedural Justice and the Courts', *Court Review*, 44 (2008), 26–31. And put in an emotional theory context by Leben, 'Exploring the Overlap Between Procedural-Justice Principles and Emotion Regulation in the Courtroom'.
[52] Leben, 'Exploring the Overlap Between Procedural-Justice Principles and Emotion Regulation in the Courtroom'.
[53] S. Bennett, L. Hine and Lo. Mazerolle, *Procedural justice* (Oxford Bibliographies, 2018).

Respect

Cases played out in the courtroom may often be highly emotional, involving parties that burst into anger or tears. In another context, the expected way to handle these emotional persons that share traumatic events in their lives would be to try to console them and express one's compassion and sympathy. But in court, there are other emotional regimes deciding the appropriate way for a judge to meet an emotional party or witness. The emotional regime of objectivity and dispassion is most often met by the display of the 'stone face'.[54] The professional way to show impartiality and objectivity is thus to be non-emotional, to *not* display any emotions. But, due to the emotional intensity of a horrifying case, this might, by the public, be experienced as both condescending and rude.[55] If these emotions were seen as not being allowed, this might risk that the public, already caught up in the 'elite judges' narrative, would get grist to their mill. The ability to address and respond to emotions displayed by the parties and witnesses is essential for trust in the procedure.[56] Research on the experiences and expectations of laypeople shows that to place an expectation on them to leave their emotions out will lead to confusion and a reduced experience of procedural justice while creating the risk of these participants omitting legally relevant material when submitting evidence.[57]

Trustworthiness

Another component of procedural justice is that of trustworthiness, in the sense that the judge appears sincere and caring.[58] If a witness cries when telling her story in court, the judge might not leave her place to give the witness a hug but can offer her a glass of water or a break, in order to, in a subtle but respectful way, show the witness that she understands that this is a hard time. The judge can keep his or her distance, his or her 'stone face' will still be on, but 'the embodiment of power as a personal responsibility [i]s geared towards empathy'.[59] This illustrates how delicately a judge must balance the display of his or her emotions in a particular situation not to appear as elitist and as someone who rules by fear.

---

[54] Bergman Blix and Wettergren, *Professional Emotions in Court. A Sociological Perspective*.
[55] Bergman Blix and Wettergren, *Professional Emotions in Court. A Sociological Perspective*.
[56] Tyler, 'Procedural Justice and the Courts'.
[57] B. Toy-Cronin, 'Leaving emotion out: litigants in person and emotion in New Zeeland Civil Courts', *Oñati Socio-legal Series,* 9(5) (2019), 684–701.
[58] Tyler, 'Procedural Justice and the Courts'.
[59] Bergman Blix and Wettergreen, *Professional Emotions in Court. A Sociological Perspective*, p. 119. The reports from the Texas 204th District Court in the US after the conviction of the former police officer who shot her neighbour to death shows the judge hugging first the victim's family members and then the offender is an example of an emotional expression that would be a rare sight, at least in a Swedish context.

Neutrality

Neutrality in the context of procedural justice is primarily explored from a formal perspective; legal rules must be applied in a transparent and impartial way. The idea of neutrality can also be interpreted as requiring that the appearance of the judge be experienced as neutral. This might be done in a stone-faced way or in such a way that the emotional expressions that the judge displays are balanced. So, judges can use emotional expressions actively to display impartiality. In a study concerning Swedish courts, judges described how, if in a court case they got irritated and angry with one of the legal actors (for example, the defence counsel) and failed to hide it, they could manage the situation by compensating this outburst; they would find a moment to display the same anger towards the prosecutor to re-establish the balance between the parties.[60] This particular strategy is not necessarily a good one, but to think of impartiality/neutrality as a balancing act rather than as a stone face act, can promote an experience of neutrality for those engaged in court proceedings.

Procedural justice is integral to gaining public trust and legitimacy. Its components are strengthened by the active work of emotions. By using emotions in a conscious way, the gap between the judges and the public will diminish, the view of judges as elitist will be refuted and the fundamental elements of procedural justice will be strengthened.

Artificial intelligence in judging

The field of artificial intelligence (AI) in legal decision-making has been discussed for more than 30 years and has developed into a research field of its own.[61] The epistemology is inspired by mathematics, and a crucial aim is to find and develop methods and arguments that reach the 'best' or most true result[62] by building on rational arguments and excluding irrelevant facts.[63] AI, it is argued, can be seen as a way to secure legitimate and objective legal decisions by leaving out a decision-making subject as well as subjective components in the decision-making process.

---

[60] The situation is recapitulated from a trial observation in the research project Emotions in judicial decision-making.

[61] R. E. Susskind, 'Expert systems in law: a jurisprudential approach to artificial intelligence and legal reasoning', *Modern Law Review*, 49 (1986), 168–194, F. J. Bex et al., 'A hybrid formal theory of arguments, stories and criminal evidence', *Artificial Intelligence and Law*, 18 (2010), 123–152.

[62] K. Mancuhan and C. Clifton, 'Combating discrimination using Bayesian networks', *Artificial intelligence and Law*, 22 (2014), 211–238, C. Dahlman, 'Oacceptabla generaliseringar i bevisvärdering', *Tidsskrift for Rettsvitenskap*, 5 (2015).

[63] Dahlman et al. 'Är det sant att lekmannadomare påverkas av juridiskt irrelevanta omständigheter, men inte juristdomare?', *Juridisk tidskrift vid Stockholms universitet*, 2 (2017–18), J.-C. Pomerol, 'Artificial intelligence and human decision making' *European Journal of Operational Research*, 99 (1997), 3–25.

In this way, AI research equates judicial decision-making with logical deduction, making emotional dimensions of any kind superfluous.[64]

AI has no set definition and can include many types of techniques, such as different forms of machine learning and robotics. In a legal framework, AI mostly refers to different kinds of algorithmic decision-making using 'big data' from previous cases or to logical deduction from new information. By focusing on argumentation strategies and often on Bayesian methodology working on conditional probabilities and correlations, the aim is to find methods to make visible and handle bias.[65] Some forms of AI are already being tested or implemented in real legal practice. Two encompassing examples refer to the standardisation of sentencing in China and the US.[66] In the Hainan province in China, courts employ machine learning to identify relevant facts from different types of evidence and ultimately suggest a written judgment.[67] Both examples build on analyses of big data from previous cases. Within the European Union, ANTAI[68] in France is an automated system that processes traffic offences,[69] and in Poland, the courts use an algorithm to allocate cases to judges across the country. The last example is motivated by referring specifically to its avoidance of the biasing effects of emotion: 'the selection will be made solely by a machine, a computer system that is blind like Themis, and chooses without emotions, without views or biases, and in a manner fully free from possible accusations of corruption'.[70] Clearly, the use of AI in legal decision-making raises many different issues; here, the focus will be on this last point, the assumption that emotions only have a biasing or disrupting effect in decision-making. This assumption is founded on an understanding of the human decision-maker as biased by default.

This section will take as its vantage point two dimensions of emotions that were introduced above: foreground emotions and background/epistemic emotions.

---

[64] See for example Bex et al., 'A hybrid formal theory of arguments, stories and criminal evidence'; T. Bench-Capon et al., 'A history of AI and Law in 50 papers: 25 years of the international conference on AI and Law', *Artificial intelligence and Law,* 20 (2012), 215–319, B. Verheij, 'Proof with and without Probabilities', *Artificial Intelligence and Law,* 25 (2017), p. 127.

[65] Bex et al., 'A hybrid formal theory of arguments, stories and criminal evidence'.

[66] COMPAS (Correctional Offender Management Profiling for Alternative Sanctions) is a machine-learning algorithm software developed by Equivant, which is used in US courts to assess recidivism. The algorithm has been criticised of augmenting racial bias in sentencing by overrating black defendants risk of recidivism while underrating white defendants recidivism risk (see: J. Larson et al., 'How We Analyzed the COMPAS Recidivism Algorithm', *ProPublica,* 23 May 2016, online at: https://www.propublica.org/article/how-we-analyzed-the-compas-recidivism-algorithm).

[67] Yuan S., 'AI-assisted sentencing speeds up cases in judicial system', *China Daily,* 18 April 2019, online at: http://www.chinadaily.com.cn/cndy/2019-04/18/content_37459601.htm (last accessed 26 January 2022).

[68] National Agency for the Automated Processing of Offences.

[69] Agence nationale de traitement automatisé des infractions, online at: https://www.antai.gouv.fr/?lang=en (last accessed 26 January 2022).

[70] M. Spielkamp (ed.), *Automating Society – Taking Stock of Automated Decision-Making in the EU,* Report, (Berlin, AlgorithmWatch, 2019) p. 107; Shenggao, 'AI-assisted sentencing speeds up cases in judicial system'.

As shall be shown, these dimensions serve important functions in judicial decision-making, thus illustrating how the positivist prerequisite of AI and the practical implication thereof is incapable of questioning law when necessary, disregards the context-bound element of 'chance' in decision-making and does not make allowance for the interactive unfolding of decisions in a bounded process.

Foreground emotions as a backstop

As described above, judicial decision-making commonly utilises subtle emotions working with cognition in the weighing of alternatives. However, the most apparent reason for letting a human have the final say in decisions is her ability for strong foreground emotions that alerts the subject if something might be wrong. Even in matters where a computer can make better calibrated propositions than humans, when they are wrong, they are usually very wrong. This can partly be explained by the fact that things that are evident to a human being, such as the ability to distinguish a human from a bicycle, requires vast amount of analysis for a computer, and because a computer lacks the ability to make (good) judgments.[71]

As argued by Rt Hon the Lord Thomas of Cwmgiedd, in times of crisis, when lawmakers are dismantling democratic laws and withdrawing human rights, there is an urgent need 'for constant vigilance'[72] among lawyers in general and judges in particular. Graver's work on judges' opposition towards the transformation into totalitarian states is a case in point.[73] Graver analysed German judges' resistance towards the Nazi regime and found that the judiciary's embeddedness in the tradition of autonomy to some extent secured deference from the totalitarian regime. He argues that although opposition often were isolated instances, they still serve an important source of knowledge to enhance the possibility of future opposition.[74] When democracy is under threat, the judiciary and the role of the (human) judge, by being able to act on foreground emotions and good judgment, can be seen as safeguards to the rule of law and human rights.[75]

---

[71] One example is the self-driving car that run over and killed a pedestrian in Arizona, USA in 2018: This example is interesting for two reasons: first, because the computer had troubles identifying the pedestrian ('it classified her first as an unknown object, then as a vehicle and finally as a bicycle, each of which had a different predicted path according to the autonomy logic'), something that would have been obvious to a human driver; and second, because the human safety driver sitting in the car apparently trusted the car to be in control and failed to pay attention to the upcoming situation – she relaxed her decision-making ability. Wikipedia, *Death of Elaine Herzberg*, online at: https://en.wikipedia.org/wiki/Death_of_Elaine_Herzberg (last accessed 26 January 2022).

[72] As reflected in the remarks of the Right Hon the Lord Thomas of Cwmgiedd, 'Epilogue: Judicial Independence: The Need for Constant Vigilance', in this volume.

[73] H. P. Graver, 'Why Adolf Hitler Spared the Judges: Judicial Opposition Against the Nazi State', *German Law Review*, 19 (2018), 845–877.

[74] Graver, 'Why Adolf Hitler Spared the Judges', p. 849.

[75] See also J. Eekelaar, 'Judges and Citizens: Two Conceptions of Law', *Oxford Journal of Legal Studies*, 22 (2002), 497–516, A. W. B. Simpson (ed.) *Oxford Essays on Jurisprudence* (Oxford, Oxford

Foreground emotions can also safeguard decisions in less dramatic situations. A judge in Sweden refused to dispense the public case act containing all the evidence in a criminal case of child pornography.[76] This was before the law was changed to make these types of documents confidential, so the judge broke the law by acting on her (good) judgment. For a judge to make a decision that goes against the law (but in this case, arguably in line with its intentions since the possession of child pornography was illegal), bundles of motivating and directing emotions are necessary, such as fear and/or shame of the consequences if she were to dispense the acts; pride in maintaining the law's intentions; refuting or managing guilt of breaking the law and so forth. An AI system built on algorithms can determine whether a case file is public or confidential as such, but algorithms cannot make value judgments and therefore cannot 'decide' whether this particular file *should* be released or not.

Background/epistemic emotions in the process of decision-making

The importance of keeping a human judge in charge discussed above actualised the importance of (good) judgment in legal decision-making. In a previous study of Swedish judges we found that 'good judgement' was deemed an important feature by the judges themselves.[77] Good judgment is a rather vague term that can imply many things, but focusing on decision-making the importance of judgment highlights the fact that decision-making by necessity includes some level of chance.[78] The proposition 1+2=2 does not demand a decision, the answer falls out by calculus: '[s]omething that has already been determined in all respects cannot be decided'.[79] This means that something more than logic is needed to make decisions. Flexibility, creativity, intuition and persuasion are often mentioned here,[80] features that are embodied, context-bound and demand emotional sensitivity, emotion

---

University Press, 1973), in line with the remarks of Right Hon the Lord Thomas of Cwmgiedd, vigilance, that is being alert to the need to make decisions, is vital in these situations.

[76] Decision taken on 16 April 1993 by Stockholm District Court in the case B 5946–92. In Sweden, when a case has been prosecuted, all the case files – including all evidence, e.g., transcriptions of oral interrogations, photographs of injuries, etc., are public and anyone can access them from the court. The Swedish Public Access to Information and Secrecy Act states that as a general rule, all documents held by a public authority are official.

[77] Bergman Blix and Wettergren, *Professional Emotions in Court: A Sociological Perspective*, p. 164.

[78] Polanyi famously wrote on expert knowledge: 'We know more than we can tell.': M. Polanyi, *The Tacit Dimension* (Gloucester, Peter Smith Publications, 1983). In AI research, this is expressed as the 'qualification problem': in the messy reality of the real world, we can never fully list all potential conditions necessary for an action or event to have a specific outcome. L. Pettersen, 'Why Artificial Intelligence Will Not Outsmart Complex Knowledge Work', *Work, Employment and Society* (2018).

[79] N. Luhmann, 'The Pardodox of Decision Making' in D. Baecker (ed.), *Organization and Decision* (Cambridge, Cambridge University Press, 2018).

[80] D. H. Autor, 'Why are there still so many jobs? The history and future of workplace automation' *Journal of Economic Perspectives,* 29(3) (2015), 3–30, p. 6, Pettersen, 'Why Artificial Intelligence Will Not Outsmart Complex Knowledge Work', J. Wajcman, 'Automation: is it really different this time?', *The British journal of sociology,* 68 (2017), 119–127.

management and empathy. We will use two examples that highlight the importance of these features for judicial decision-making: the non-quantifiable core of some of the judicial concepts and legal facts; and the importance of understanding decision-making as an interactive process consisting of many small decisions in a bounded sequence.

First, instead of treating the application of law as something fixed that can be applied onto reality, a context-bound perspective understands law as being made or given meaning every time it is applied.[81] Even though examples can be provided to delineate concepts such as intent, carelessness, concerted action, self-defence or credibility, there are no fixed or measurable definitions of these legal concepts, and they need context-bound interpretation in every instance.[82] To decide whether a defendant has acted in self-defence, the judge needs to listen attentively to the narratives of the event (epistemic emotion of interest), situate herself in the defendant's, as well as in the plaintiff's, shoes (empathy), and perhaps signal to the lawyer that the court has understood the argument (background irritation when an efficient process is at risk while managing emotional display to keep up an impartial demeanour). So far, these intricate emotive-cognitive adaptions and evaluations are fundamentally human.

The second example concerns the gradual unfolding of decision-making in an interactive case-bound process. Alluding to collaboration might seem odd in relation to the fundamentally autonomous judiciary. However, as argued by Dreyfus, collaboration is essential for learning.[83] In relation to judicial decision-making, this learning can be illustrated by the way the decision-making process is organised through a multitude of small decisions unfolding during the move of a case through the system. In our ongoing research, following cases from decisions to prosecute to judgments in lower and appeal courts, we have found that the process where a decision by one practitioner (e.g., prosecutor) is checked by another (e.g., judge) who confirms or rejects that the practitioner is on the right track can be understood as an emotive-cognitive process. For example, if the prosecutor's request for detaining a suspect is granted by the court, it raises his confidence in the prosecution: 'if he is detained I don't have to be ashamed to prosecute' since the court has agreed on reasonable grounds for detention.[84] These pieces of emotional-cognitive information spur engagement, give rise to pride when succeeding and potential shame or anxiety when being overruled (for example, a lower court judge who sees several verdicts reversed in a higher instance), and thus test the case throughout its journey through the system and secure objective decisions in many small steps.

[81] Bladini, *I objektivitetens sken.*

[82] The leeway for interpretations within an objective paradigm can be seen in the generally accepted notion that two 'rational' decision-makers confronting the same situation may make two different decisions: Pomerol, 'Artificial intelligence and human decision making'. This is also generally accepted and built into the judiciary through the system of the court hierarchy where a court decision from a district court may be tried in a court of appeal.

[83] H. L. Dreyfus, *What computers still can't do: A critique of artificial reason* (Cambridge, MA, MIT Press, 1992).

[84] Prosecutor Linus, 40+ years, referring to one of the defendants in a large fraud case.

Conclusion: Protecting an independent judiciary by abandoning the myth of dispassion

Two narratives that challenge an independent judiciary have been focused on in this chapter. The first is populist movements' portrayal of judges as elite decision-makers, far away from the reality they are obliged to deal with. The second is the appeal of automation through various forms of artificial intelligence in the judiciary. These narratives build upon the traditional idea of rationality and emotion as being separate. The authors have shown how these threats can be met by a more profound understanding of emotions in judicial decision-making. By the use of emotions in a cognisant and reflective way, judges can gain the trust of the public and diminish the risk of losing legitimacy. The role of emotions contributes to the understanding of judging as something particularly human.

Although the courts are full of emotions, in the sense that the most dramatic life events are dealt with, emotions are traditionally seen as something primarily *not* relevant in legal decision-making. The prevailing objectivity ideal builds on the idea of the separation of rationality and emotion. But the ideal of the dispassionate judge has been questioned from several perspectives, and studies within law and emotions show that emotions play an important role in the process of objective decision-making. The ability to handle others' and one's own emotions in a professional way and the use of empathy is fundamental in the work of a judge.

One aspect of the populist agenda is to point out the people in power as elitist, arbitrary and high-handed, coming from a different societal class, and hence completely negligent and uninformed about people's real lives. That procedural justice can play an important role in diminishing the gap between the people and the judiciary is a well-known fact. What is not as acknowledged is that empathy, as well as emotion management, play an important role in the quest for procedural justice. This is a 'hidden' aspect of the task of refuting the challenges of the independent judiciary. To make visible the emotional aspects of legal procedure is a way to legitimate and secure the independence of the judiciary.

Research on artificial intelligence in judicial decision-making builds upon a traditional view of knowledge where reason, as separated from emotion, has universal qualities. Algorithmic logic quantifies the evaluation of facts as well as the reasons to be used on the assumption that the context, as well as the intuitive processes that build on previous experiences, can be 'put aside'. This line of research disregards the fact that a case, whether criminal or civil, as well as its evaluation, indeed take place within a context. The law builds on the very idea that each case should be evaluated individually and the judge thus needs to understand the specificities of each individual case, including contextual and relational aspects. In sum, this chapter elucidates some crucial human aspects of legal decision-making and argues that emotions drive the objective process towards professionalism, strengthening the experience of procedural justice and operating as an emergency brake when laws are invaded by undemocratic forces.

13

Epilogue: Judicial Independence: The Need for Constant Vigilance

THE RIGHT HON THE LORD THOMAS OF CWMGIEDD

The background

THE BACKGROUND TO the need for constant vigilance to safeguard the independence of the judiciary can be briefly summarised.

The change in the position of the judiciary within the state

First, there has been a change in the position of the judiciary within the state. The use of the notorious phrase 'enemies of the people', applied to two senior colleagues and myself in *Miller*, together with other abuse, brought this change home to many in the UK. This is not simply a UK phenomenon. Similar attacks have been made in the United States. Far worse has happened in other states, such as Poland and Turkey. Why? The rule of law is an almost universally accepted concept. Charters and constitutional provisions securing fundamental rights have been enthusiastically adopted. Judicial review is seen as an effective course of action. The judiciary's role in respect of each has undoubtedly been effective and beneficial. However, at the same time, some have questioned this change because it is thought the judges have acquired an unacceptable degree of influence; they have criticised the judiciary for going beyond its constitutional role. More significantly, others have seen the changed position of the judiciary as a threat to popularly elected governments. They have reacted with abuse or worse.

The change in the functions of the judiciary

Second, but less perceptibly, has been the assumption of wider functions by the judiciary. Its primary role has always been to ensure that disputes are expeditiously

Proceedings of the British Academy, **250**, 241–247, © The British Academy 2022.

managed in a manner consistent with fairness and at reasonable cost, determined at trial and a reasoned judgment given. It is clear that the judiciary now has a wider role. This varies from state to state. In many, the judiciary is seen as acting to enhance, rather than merely to protect, access to justice, to improve procedure, particularly if the state will not provide adequate legal advice and assistance; to require explanatory accountability of the prosecution service or the police, for failing to prosecute or provide proper disclosure to the defence; and to ensure that the Intelligence and Security Services discharge all their functions in accordance with the law – something that would have been regarded as unreal some years ago.

How should constant vigilance be exercised?

Although the judiciary enjoy, in most states, a very high degree of public trust – what can be viewed as a very large credit balance – which the judiciary must be careful not to dissipate, there is much that could be done. I will highlight 10 actions.

What the judges do must be done effectively and efficiently by them

First, the foremost safeguard to judicial independence is the effective and efficient discharge of the judiciary's functions – whether the functions be broad or narrow or somewhere in between. For example, to take the universal function of the judge – bringing cases to trial, the trial and providing a reasoned judgment – judges must do their work efficiently on the resources provided. Nothing undermines the position of the judiciary more swiftly than delay in getting cases to trial, for trials to take an inordinate amount of time and for reasoning in judgments to be poor. Poland provides an excellent example of the way a public perception of poor performance has been used to undermine the independence of the judiciary.

It is essential that the judiciary has the capability to ensure the efficient conduct of the business of the courts within the resources provided, but also to make clear its position if the resources provided to it by a legislature or an executive are inadequate. The same will apply to other functions entrusted to the judiciary.

There must be a proper scheme of the governance of the judiciary

Second, the judiciary cannot discharge its functions efficiently without an effective scheme for the governance. Although Councils for the Judiciary have been the subject of some attention, particularly from the Consultative Council of European Judges (CCJE),[1] this is an issue that has not been sufficiently studied. My

---

[1] *Opinion no.10(2007) of the Consultative Council of European Judges (CCJE) for the attention of the Committee of Ministers of the Council of Europe on the Council for the Judiciary at the service*

view[2] is that each judiciary should have a structure suited to its role. In some states, the legislature or the constitution will set this. In others, such as England and Wales, the judiciary has been able to develop its own structure of governance. It is important that in the structure there is a balance between the hierarchy of the judiciary and participation by the entire judiciary in its governance; without such a balance, there can be considerable tensions. A clear leadership structure enables decisive action to be taken in a way that takes into account the position and views of the judiciary as a whole. In larger states, a degree of local governance is necessary, if everything is directed from the centre, the judiciary's independence and sense of purpose can be lost. Outside members bring an external and independent perspective, as is the position in many Councils for the judiciary on the European continent.

There must be absolute protection for the individual independence of each judge – a point sometimes overlooked. The way in which a judge decides a case must be for the judge, subject to open systems of appeals. Each judge must be protected against the dangers of a judicial hierarchy seeking to exert influence over the decision.

With such a governance structure, a judiciary is able, in relation to the basic common function of the judge, to set standards for the efficient delivery of justice and ethical standards, including the assignment of cases and deployment; to provide adequate training; to provide proper arrangements for health and welfare; and to deal with any judge, if necessary through discipline, who fails to live up to those standards. Other functions will include public accountability, communications with the media, relations with the public and communities, and relations with the executive and legislature.

Reform, where needed, must be carried out

Third, reform and modernisation must be effectuated so that the judiciary maintains in an up-to-date state the effectiveness, efficiency and cost of those areas for which it is responsible. This is particularly important in the fourth industrial or the digital revolution. Even if the functions allocated to the judiciary are narrow and do not include court administration, the judiciary must nonetheless ensure that it can decide cases in the fairest and most effective way through the use of technology.

A real threat to judicial independence is the failure to modernise and reform the judiciary whenever this is necessary. As is rightly said, if you do not reform yourselves, someone else will gladly reform the system in a way you may certainly not like as much as if you had done it yourself.

---

of society, Strasbourg, 23 November 2007, online at: https://rm.coe.int/168074779b (last accessed 26 January 2022).
[2] In the Lionel Cohen lecture at the Hebrew University of Jerusalem on 15 May 2017, I set out what I thought was necessary: https://www.judiciary.uk/wp-content/uploads/2017/05/lcj-lionel-cohen-lecture-20170515.pdf

Court administration

Fourth, the judiciary must have control over or a decisive influence in court administration, as good court administration working closely with judges is essential to the effective delivery of justice and to the morale of the judiciary.

Historically, England and Wales enjoyed a variety of systems where there was much local control, often exercised by the judiciary. Under the circuit system, High Court Judges still, in the second half of the 20th century, visited the towns of each county on the basis they had done in England since the 12th century and in Wales since 1830. Although many judges had wanted to reform the system by changing the sitting pattern so they sat where the business was in the 20th century, they had not been able to bring about such reform. Reform of the towns visited was therefore made for them by Lord Beeching's Commission in 1969. It concluded that the system was not run effectively; he recommended the creation of administrators who, although supposed to work with the judges, were to a considerable extent independent of the judges. While the Lord Chancellor remained Head of the Judiciary and the minister to whom the administrators were accountable, there was by and large no problem. However, when the Lord Chancellor ceased to occupy this dual position, the obvious tensions in the system came to the fore. The result was a compromise under which the administration became jointly accountable to the judiciary and to the minister.

The relationship between the judiciary and the court administration differs considerably from state to state. In some, it is entirely accountable to the body that governs the judiciary, often a Council for the Judiciary. In others, it is largely the responsibility of the Minister of Justice. Although this is a complex subject in its own right, I must draw attention to it as one of the areas where vigilance is necessary to maintain the independence of the judiciary. For example, where court administration is the responsibility of the judiciary, it is imperative that it is carried out effectively and a constant watch is kept on it.

Appointments, etc.

Fifth is the need to ensure that there is a coherent system for recruitment, appointment, career development, succession planning and promotion. There should be clarity as to matters such as the role (if any) for politicians, the extent to which a judiciary should be reflective of society and the use of quotas. If politicians have a role and consider that judges are making decisions they do not like, experience shows they will seek to exercise considerable influence over appointments. The judiciary should therefore do what they can to establish an independent and open process for appointments that, as an integral part of the process, keeps political considerations out of the appointments to the judiciary to the greatest extent possible. Just as a judiciary can be successfully attacked for delivering an ineffective, unfair and inefficient system of justice, so too it can be attacked if the judiciary's composition at all levels has not been the subject of clear thought.

Public accountability

Sixth, it is almost universally accepted that an institution exercising power must be accountable for the exercise of that power. Judges have always been accountable for decisions made where cases are heard in public, reasoned judgments given and appeals can be made; this is a classic form of explanatory accountability.

Where judges have assumed other functions, judges have to devise a form of accountability for the exercise of those functions. This was not a subject that was much discussed in the United Kingdom prior to the early 2000s; elsewhere, it was a surprise that this was an issue. However, within the past decade, there has been a growing acceptance that judges have a duty of explanatory accountability for all the other functions they perform. Provision of a report and a willingness to answer questions guards the judiciary against attack as an 'unaccountable judiciary'.

Communications with the media

Seventh is the need for good communications. The judiciary has had to decide in the past 20 or so years how it communicates through the media. In the UK, there were very strict rules[3] against judges speaking extrajudicially. With the abolition of the rules came the public expectation, encouraged by the media, that public institutions ought to communicate directly what they do. The early lead was taken by Lord Bingham of Cornhill in developing relations with the media and communicating effectively.

The judiciary now accepts that it is necessary to provide a readable summary of important judgments so they can be readily understood. The televising of the appeal to the Supreme Court in *Miller* was successful in enabling many to understand the judicial process; it removed any doubts about the televising or audio transmission of appeals.[4] It is now also accepted that there is a need to examine what parts of the trial process should be open either for television or audio transmission. Although in trials where witnesses are involved no additional pressure should be placed through television or audio transmission of a witness' evidence, there is much else that should be televised. Those who are less enthusiastic tend to overlook the public expectation of being able to see important issues being debated; or when important decisions are being announced, the decision-maker makes the announcement.

---

[3] The Kilmuir Rules.
[4] It was unfortunate that legislation prevented this being done in the Divisional Court, though an immediate transcript of the hearing was provided.

We should not forget that there has been a progressive decline in the number of court reporters. I would not be surprised if, in the relatively near future, the only way in which court reporting will continue to be sustainable is if those that provide the reporting can utilise live or recorded material for public viewing or listening.

Relations with the public and communities

Eighth, the judiciary should engage directly with the public in other ways, not only to help the public understand the importance of justice, but to keep judges 'in touch'. Visits to schools and court open days are important. Over 100 Diversity and Community Relations Judges play an important role in promoting a greater understanding of justice by communities and a better judicial understanding of diversity issues. Engagement with scientists and forensic scientists has provided the judiciary with a better understanding of contemporary scientific advances; one result has been the production of 'primers', which provide accurate summaries of areas such as DNA and statistics. Engagement with the business community through, for example, the seminars provided by the Financial Markets Law Committee, keeps the judiciary abreast with the rapid pace of change in the markets.

Whatever is done must be done openly, as open justice is fundamental to confidence. The judiciary cannot afford to be thought of as receiving private briefings, as otherwise such engagement could be used as a means of attack on the judiciary. Nor can they afford not to keep abreast, as the danger of being seen as 'out of touch' is all too useful a weapon.

Relationships with the other judiciaries

Ninth is the importance of maintaining direct relationships between judiciaries of different states. The problems judiciaries face are generally similar. There is much that can be learnt from other judiciaries; England and Wales developed its system of media relations in part through learning useful lessons from the Dutch judiciary. Supporting other judiciaries when they come under attack is essential, as was demonstrated in relation to Poland and Kenya. However, caution is always needed, as a judiciary that is not independent but that has the façade of independence will seek to strengthen that façade by establishing good relations with truly independent judiciaries.

An independent but interdependent relationship with the other powers of the state

Tenth, and last, the judiciary has to be sure of its own relationship with the other branches of the state and make sure that the other branches understand that relationship. A good relationship will have two aspects: independence and interdependence. Although independence is well understood, that is not the case in respect of interdependence.[5] Interdependence[6] comprises three elements: a clear understanding by each branch of the state of the constitutional functions and responsibilities of the other branches of the state; mutual support by each branch of the other branches when carrying out the functions and responsibilities which the constitution has assigned to the other branches; and non-interference in the proper working of the functions and responsibilities that the constitution has assigned to another branch by showing a proper and mutual respect for the role of the other branches.[7]

At the heart of interdependence is a clear common understanding of the proper constitutional functions of the different branches of the state.

Although judges must act independently when deciding cases, a broader understanding of their independence enables judges to use their independence and expertise constructively in improving the good governance of the state. The judiciary can provide technical advice to the other branches of the state, as it did in relation to the reform of sentencing in 2012, where it assisted in delineating the available options with the advantages and disadvantages of each, leaving the decision to the legislature and the executive. Similarly, in relation to the replacement of the Brussels regulations on jurisdiction and the enforcement of judgments in the event of Brexit, Hamblen LJ chaired a Committee that provided options to the legislature and the executive on what was needed.

A proper understanding enables judicial engagement with the legislature. This is important when there are very few practising lawyers who are familiar with the contemporary operation of the courts and tribunals, and judges have little experience of the realities of legislative business. It also enables judicial engagement with ministers and the civil service. Ministers can obtain a better understanding of the way the judiciary works; when they lose a case, they should not abuse the judge but simply appeal. The judiciary can better understand the role government legal advisers can and do play. There is a real mutual benefit.

Conclusion

There are other steps than those I have highlighted. What matters is the judiciary should be proactively vigilant, particularly when times are good. There is no room for complacency or a lack of vigilance.

---

[5] A term used by Jackson J. in the US Supreme Court in *Youngtown Co v Sawyer* 343 US 579 (1952) at 635: 'While the Constitution diffuses power the better to secure liberty, it also contemplates that practice will integrate the dispersed powers into a workable government. It enjoins upon its branches separateness but interdependence, autonomy but reciprocity.'

[6] I set this out in more detail in the Ryle Memorial Lecture given in June 2017 at the Houses of Parliament: *The judiciary within the State – the relationship between the three branches of the State*, online at: https://www.judiciary.gov.uk/wp-content/uploads/2017/06/lcj-michael-ryle-memorial-lect ure-20170616.pdf (last accessed 26 January 2022).

[7] See, for example, *Axa General Insurance Ltd v Lord Advocate* [2011] UKSC 46; [2012] 1 AC 868 at [148].

14

Conclusion: On 'Crisis' and Threats to Judicial Independence As Constant Features in the Landscape of Judicial Activity

YVONNE MCDERMOTT AND DIMITRIOS GIANNOULOPOULOS

THE IDEA FOR this book, and the British Academy conference that preceded it, stemmed from a conversation between the editors in 2017. The *Daily Mail* had recently published its 'Enemies of the People' front page in response to the ruling of the High Court of England and Wales in the case of *R (Miller) v Secretary of State for Exiting the European Union*.[1] On the other side of the Atlantic, President Trump had attacked judges who had stayed his travel ban and even the notion of an 'independent judiciary',[2] while judges in Poland, Italy, Guatemala, Turkey and the Maldives, among others, had been removed from office, publicly denounced, arrested and/or imprisoned.[3] It struck us that these attacks on the judiciary were of serious concern and that their scale was, to some extent, unprecedented. But did they represent a crisis?

The term 'crisis' stems from the Greek word *krisis* (decision), which in turn derives from the verb *krinō* (meaning 'to "separate" (part, divorce), to "choose", to "judge", to "decide"').[4] From its juridical meaning in Ancient Greece,[5] the term

---

[1] *Miller & Anor, R (On the Application Of) v The Secretary of State for Exiting the European Union (Rev 1)* [2016] EWHC 2768 (Admin).

[2] Garrett Epps, 'Trump is at War With the Whole Idea of an Independent Judiciary', *The Atlantic*, 4 March 2020, online at: https://www.theatlantic.com/ideas/archive/2020/03/trump-independent-judici ary/607375/ (last accessed 26 January 2022).

[3] Report of the Special Rapporteur on the independence of judges and lawyers, D. García-Sayán, UN Doc. A/75/172, 17 July 2020, paras. 73–81; Mandates of the Special Rapporteur on the independence of judges and lawyers and the Working Group on Arbitrary Detention, AL MDV 2/2018, 9 February 2018; Mandate of the Special Rapporteur on the independence of judges and lawyers, AL TUR 2/2019, 30 January 2019; Council of Europe, *The independence of judges and the judiciary under threat*, Strasbourg, 3 September 2019.

[4] R. Koselleck (trans. M. W. Richter), 'Crisis', (2006) 67 *Journal of the History of Ideas* 357–400.

[5] Koselleck, 'Crisis', p. 359, citing Aristotle, *Politics*, 1289b, 12.

Proceedings of the British Academy, **250**, 248–252, © The British Academy 2022.

entered the English language in the early 16th century in a medical context, where 'crisis' denoted a crucial point of a disease when it would be determined whether the patient would live or die.[6] An early adaptation of the term into political discourse can be observed by the words of Sir Benjamin Rudyerd over a century later in the context of Charles I's power struggles with Parliament: 'This is the crisis of Parliaments: we shall know by this if parliaments live or die.'[7]

By today, 'crisis' is perhaps an overused term[8] and one that departs quite significantly from the concept's original meaning of a situation giving rise to unavoidable, existential dilemmas. The Google search engine reveals over 700 million results for the word online, with almost daily news stories on the climate crisis, the Covid-19 crisis and numerous others. In his inauguration speech of January 2021, President Biden noted, 'We will be judged... for how we resolve the cascading crises of our era',[9] before outlining four crises: the coronavirus pandemic, climate, economy and racial injustice. Politicians tend to frame issues as new and exceptional crises, whereas Koskenniemi, reflecting on his former role as legal adviser with the Finnish foreign ministry, noted:

> For the politicians, every situation was new, exceptional, crisis. The lawyer's task was to link it to what had happened previously, a case, a precedent, tell it as part of a history. The point of the law was to detach the particular from its particularity by linking it with narratives in which it received a generalizable meaning, and the politician could see what to do with it.[10]

In this vein, and recognising that a framing of threats to judicial independence as standalone crises may be conceptually unhelpful,[11] many contributors to this volume push back against the notion of 'crisis'. Notably, the late Lord Kerr recalls the words often misattributed to former Prime Minister James Callaghan – 'Crisis? What crisis?'. For Lord Kerr, crisis is not defined by external factors but by our reactions to them.[12]

---

[6] Koselleck, 'Crisis', p. 360.

[7] R. Cust, 'Charles I, the Privy Council and the Parliament of 1628', *Transactions of the Royal Historical Society* 2 (1992) 25–50.

[8] I. Scobbie, 'Crisis? What damned crisis', forthcoming in M. Mbengue and J. d'Aspremont (eds.), *Crisis Narratives in International Law* (Brill, 2021) (on file with authors).

[9] *Inaugural Address by President Joseph R. Biden Jr.*, January 2021, online at: https://www.whiteho use.gov/briefing-room/speeches-remarks/2021/01/20/inaugural-address-by-president-joseph-r-biden-jr/ (last accessed 26 January 2022).

[10] M. Koskenniemi, 'International Law in Europe: Between Tradition and Renewal', *European Journal of International Law* 16 (2005) 113–124, p. 120.

[11] Similarly, see H. Charlesworth, 'International Law: A Discipline of Crisis', *Modern Law Review* 65 (2002) 377–392.

[12] In a similar vein, in a speech in 1959, President John F. Kennedy noted, 'The Chinese use two brush strokes to write the word 'crisis.' One brush stroke stands for danger; the other for opportunity.' This misinterpretation has entered popular culture, despite having been shown to be categorically incorrect: Victor H. Mair, 'Danger + Opportunity ≠ Crisis. How a misunderstanding about Chinese characters has led many astray', online at: http://www.pinyin.info/chinese/crisis.html (last accessed 26 January 2022).

Other authors express similar doubt about the notion of judicial independence being in a state of crisis. For Aguirre, judicial independence in Myanmar cannot be said to be in crisis because 'the judiciary *is functioning precisely as intended*: it enforces law and order on the public and legally discriminates against minorities without holding authorities accountable.' Grieve notes that, far from being cowed by public denunciations, judges have demonstrated 'robust willingness to interpret our written and unwritten constitutional rules and conventions in a manner that suggests that threats to judicial independence are having little practical impact'. Skinner warns against drawing parallels with fascism in the first half of the 20th century, a comparison that he sees as unhelpful and inappropriate.

Nevertheless, it would be a 'misguided reflex'[13] to assume that our democratic heritage will protect us from such threats. This sentiment is echoed in Lord Thomas' warnings on the 'need for constant vigilance' and Jolly's argument that the rule of law must be taught to a much broader constituency than just lawyers to protect it into the future. It is also reflected in Sklansky's call to consider the two competing visions of democracy, that is, populism vs. pluralism, and the place of judicial independence in both, a position echoed by Müller, who argues that attacks on the judiciary are part of the fabric of populist movements.

Rather than framing our current era as a time of crisis, therefore, it is perhaps more fitting to consider the threats to judicial independence discussed in this volume – be they trends towards the populist vision of democracy,[14] tensions between the executive and judicial branches,[15] a perceived need to impose severe restrictions in the face of terrorist threats[16] or moral panics against a criminal justice system deemed to be too lenient to violent offenders[17] – as constant features in the landscape of judicial activity. Constitutional, political and economic 'crises' may come and go, but these features are likely to be omnipresent, if only in the background of seemingly more urgent situations.

Judicial independence: From theory to practice

As several authors note, the idea of an independent judiciary is a notion that almost no one would contest. Where the tension arises is in making that abstract concept of independence a reality. Several incidents detailed in this volume illustrate how quickly the deference between the distinct branches of government, a fundamental facet of the rule of law, can erode when judicial decisions are perceived to step into the boundaries of law-making, overriding the sovereign will of Parliament

---

[13] T. Snyder, *On Tyranny: Twenty Lessons from the Twentieth Century* (London, Penguin Random House, 2017), p. 63.
[14] As described in the chapters by Müller and Sklansky.
[15] As highlighted, among others, in the chapters by Jolly and Grieve.
[16] As evidenced in the chapters by Parizot and Jackson.
[17] As analysed by Feilzer and Roberts in their chapters.

and/or running contrary to 'the will of the people'.[18] On the other hand, several contributions illustrate how a façade of legality or constitutionalism can be utilised to facilitate the arbitrary abuse of power.[19]

While concern has been raised about expressions of 'anti-juridical sentiment'[20] in the press, authors are keen to emphasise that judicial independence should not be equated with judicial supremacy, where judges are shielded from scrutiny of their decisions.[21] Lord Thomas, for example, emphasises the role of outreach and the importance of external communication of judicial activity, while Müller argues that 'there is plenty of space for reasonable disagreement, and outright political conflict, about what "independence" should mean in practice.' To this end, Bladini and Bergman Blix convincingly make the case for moving away from a conceptualisation of judicial objectivity as requiring dispassion on the part of judges. Situated in a rich and developing interdisciplinary literature on 'law and emotions', their chapter argues that the role of emotions in judging deserves particular attention in an era where it has been suggested that autonomous artificial intelligence systems could be fairer or more efficient than human judges in resolving legal disputes. Feilzer, in analysing public opinion on judicial activity through a lens of theories of legitimacy, argues that such surveys distract from more fundamental structural issues around judicial independence, including the chronic underfunding of the criminal justice system (as also emphasised by Grieve), an erosion of judicial discretion (a point also discussed by Roberts) and a lack of representativeness in the judiciary.

Several contributions to this volume discuss the national, regional and international mechanisms for the protection of judicial independence. These include governance structures for the setting and upholding of standards of judicial conduct; national legislation, and regional and international bodies tasked with protecting human rights, including the European Court of Human Rights and UN human rights mandate-holders. They also include 'softer' mechanisms of protection, including trial-monitoring activities, international cooperation and learning from the experiences of other judiciaries, and judges themselves simply discharging their functions in an efficient and effective manner. Jackson, drawing on historical experiences from Northern Ireland and contemporary counter-terrorism measures, notes that judicial independence remains unscathed but emphasises the importance of transparency and the principle of open justice to ward off concerns that judges are influenced by the executive in terror trials.

On a less hopeful note, Parizot observes the declining judicial role in decisions over the deprivation of liberty in France, a development that appears at odds with the European Court of Human Rights' jurisprudence, while Roberts charts the development of the Parole Board into an independent judicial body but underscores

---

[18] See, *inter alia*, the chapters by Petley; Grieve; Jolly; Feilzer; and Roberts.
[19] See, *inter alia*, the chapters by Müller and Aguirre in this regard.
[20] A term used by Petley in his chapter.
[21] Jackson emphasises the importance of public trials and judgments, which allow the public to scrutinise the operation of the criminal justice system.

how ministerial interference in the wake of the John Worboys case undermined that independence. Similarly, Aguirre pointedly remarks on the inadequacies of the international legal framework in the specific context of Myanmar, while Müller notes that protests in defence of the rule of law had borne little discernible impact by the time of writing.

By the time we came to complete this manuscript in 2021, the world had been gripped by cataclysmic events, when the Covid-19 pandemic shaped almost every aspect of human life in every region of the world in ways that would have been previously unimaginable. In some countries, the pandemic was used as a pretext to stifle free speech and exercise disproportionate executive power.[22] For many of these states, a strengthening of the authoritarian grip took place in the context of rising populism, where leaders sought to foster mistrust in democratic institutions. The economic shockwaves of the pandemic caused cuts to be made to the already-straitened justice system budgets of many states. Meanwhile, the murder of George Floyd by a white police officer renewed a wave of activism highlighting the racial disparities and injustices in policing and criminal law around the world. Any one of these events taken alone might be deemed a 'crisis', but in many ways, they shone a light on existing injustices and challenges to human rights and the rule of law that have come to define the modern era. This collection of essays brought together insights from comparative, historical, political, philosophical and legal perspectives to examine the core shared values of our legal and political systems that judicial independence seeks to protect, and how the judiciary can be insulated from threats to that independence, in times of crisis or otherwise.

---

[22] Report of the Special Rapporteur on the promotion and protection of the right to freedom of opinion and expression, D. A. Kaye, Disease pandemics and the freedom of opinion and expression, UN Doc. A/HRC/44/49, 23 April 2020, [4].

Index

Page numbers in **bold** refer to tables.